New German Dance Studies

New German Dance Studies

Edited by
SUSAN MANNING AND
LUCIA RUPRECHT

University of Illinois Press
URBANA, CHICAGO, AND SPRINGFIELD

© 2012 by the Board of Trustees
of the University of Illinois
All rights reserved
Manufactured in the United States of America
1 2 3 4 5 C P 5 4 3 2 1
♾ This book is printed on acid-free paper.

Library of Congress Cataloging-in-Publication Data
New German dance studies / edited by Susan Manning
and Lucia Ruprecht.
    p.   cm.
Includes index.
ISBN 978-0-252-03676-7 (hardcover : alk. paper)
ISBN 978-0-252-07843-9 (pbk. : alk. paper)
1. Dance—Germany. 2. Dance—Study and teaching—Germany.
3. Dance—Social aspects—Germany.
I. Manning, Susan. II. Ruprecht, Lucia, 1972–
GV1651.N48   2012
793.31943—dc23   2011035701

Contents

Editors' Acknowledgments   vii

Contributors' Acknowledgments   ix

Introduction: New Dance Studies/
New German Cultural Studies   1
Susan Manning and Lucia Ruprecht

1. Affect, Discourse, and Dance before 1900   17
   Christina Thurner

2. Lola Montez and Spanish Dance in the 19th Century   31
   Claudia Jeschke

3. Picturing Palucca at the Bauhaus   45
   Susan Funkenstein

4. Rudolf Laban's Dance Film Projects   63
   Susanne Franco

5. Hanya Holm and an American *Tanzgemeinschaft*   79
   Tresa Randall

6. Lotte Goslar's Clowns   99
   Karen Mozingo

7. Back Again? Valeska Gert's Exiles   113
   Kate Elswit

8. *Was bleibt?* The Politics of East German Dance   130
   Marion Kant

9. Warfare over Realism: *Tanztheater*
   in East Germany, 1966–1989   147
   Franz Anton Cramer

10. Moving against Disappearance: East German Bodies
    in Contemporary Choreography   165
    Jens Richard Giersdorf

11. Pina Bausch, Mary Wigman, and the Aesthetic
    of "Being Moved"   182
    Sabine Huschka

12. Negotiating Choreography, Letter, and Law
    in William Forsythe   200
    Gerald Siegmund

13. Engagements with the Past in Contemporary Dance   217
    Yvonne Hardt

14. Lecture Performance as Contemporary Dance   232
    Maaike Bleeker

15. Toward a Theory of Cultural Translation in Dance   247
    Gabriele Klein

    Contributors   259

    Index   265

Editors' Acknowledgments

SUSAN MANNING AND LUCIA RUPRECHT

We first must thank all our authors, who responded excitedly to our initial queries four years ago and who have responded to all our subsequent queries with equal enthusiasm. No edited volume can encompass all the first-rate scholarship in a field, and we are well aware of how many other authors might have added their voices to this collection. Indeed, this anthology emerged from our sense that the last decade has witnessed such a rich outpouring of scholarship on dance in German-speaking Europe that a collection was warranted. So in the broadest sense, we are indebted to all the authors who have contributed to the field, whether they are represented in this volume or not. We have attempted to survey the broader field through our introductory essay, yet we fear that we undoubtedly have included only the proverbial tip of the iceberg.

Our home institutions contributed financial support that enabled us to engage graduate students as our able assistants. At Cambridge University Charlotte Lee, Christopher Geissler, and Max Haberich translated essays written in German into (British) English. At Northwestern University Tara Rodman served as our (American English) copy editor and our project organizer, tracking all the myriad details necessary for collaboration across two continents. For granting us permission to reprint illustrations, we thank the Bauhaus Archive in Berlin, the Bildarchiv Preußischer Kulturbesitz/Art Resources, the Derra de Moroda Dance Archive, Galerie Baudoin Lebon, the German Dance Archive in Cologne, the Harvard Theatre Collection, Museum of Fine Arts in Boston, the New York Public Library for the Performing Arts, the Staatliche Kunstsammlungen in Dresden, Stiftung Archiv der deutschen Frauenbewegung, and the Transit-Film-Gesellschaft.

After years of conversations at theater and dance conferences, Susan finally sent a book proposal to Joan Catapano, associate director and editor in chief at the University of Illinois Press, and Joan proved as wonderful an editor as Susan had always suspected she would be. But, alas, Susan had waited too long and Joan retired just after the manuscript was accepted. For more than two decades, Joan had published dance scholarship, first at Indiana University Press and then at Illinois. On behalf of the field as a whole, we extend our thanks to Joan for her many years of editorial support.

Luckily, Joan passed the job of seeing the manuscript through publication to her able associate, Danny Nasset, and we thank Danny and the remainder of the team at Illinois—Nancy Albright, Jennifer Clark, Roberta J. Sparenberg—for their professionalism. As readers for the press, Susan Foster and Helga Kraft helped us balance our address to scholars in German studies and in dance studies and we appreciate their divergent perspectives.

Lucia has spent much of her career at precisely this intersection between German cultural studies and dance studies. Working with Susan and with all the contributors to this volume has encouraged her interest in bringing the two fields together, an interest not least fueled by the increasing number of students of German who turn to her with much enthusiasm about dance and little guidance about how to find out more. It is to these students that she would like to dedicate her work on *New German Dance Studies*.

Susan first met Lucia in Paris at the joint conference hosted by the Society of Dance History Scholars and the Congress on Research in Dance at the Centre national de la danse. In that Paris summer, Susan reconnected with the family that had first welcomed her to Germany nearly forty years before, and she would like to dedicate her work on this volume to her adopted family—with deep affection for Tina and Konny and in loving memory of Hans, Traud, and Frank.

Contributors' Acknowledgments

All translations from German by the authors unless otherwise noted.

Chapter 1—Christina Thurner
  Translated by Charlotte Lee.

Chapter 2—Claudia Jeschke
  Translated by Lisa Jeschke.

Chapter 3—Susan Funkenstein
  Portions of this essay were previously published in my article "Engendering Abstraction: Wassily Kandinsky, Gret Palucca, and 'Dance Curves,'" *Modernism/Modernity* 14:3 (September 2007), 389–406. I am grateful to the editors of *Modernism/Modernity* for their permission to republish here. I am also thankful to the editors of *New German Dance Studies*, Susan Manning and Lucia Ruprecht, for their insights and encouragement with this essay. Earlier versions were presented at the 2006 Society of Dance History Scholars Conference and at a 2009 colloquium in the Department of History of Art and Architecture, University of Pittsburgh, and I would like to thank the attendees for their feedback, especially Susan Cook, Drew Armstrong, and Terry Smith.

Chapter 4—Susanne Franco
  The research work for this essay has been carried out in the frame of the international project: *Coreografiar la historia europea: cuerpo, política, identidad y género en la danza de la edad moderna y contemporánea*, financed by the Ministerio español de Ciencia e Innovación (MICINN HAR2008-03307/ARTE).

Chapter 9—Franz Anton Cramer
Translated by Christopher Geissler.
I would like to thank Dr. Thomas Kemper for his valuable assistance in finding some of the quoted source material in Leipzig, Frankfurt, and Berlin libraries.

Chapter 10—Jens Richard Giersdorf
A different version of this essay appeared as "Border Crossings and Intra-National Trespasses: East German Bodies in Sasha Waltz's and Jo Fabian's Choreographies." *Theatre Journal* 55:3 (2003), 413–432. © 2003 The Johns Hopkins University Press. I would like to thank the John Hopkins University Press for permission to republish here.

Chapter 11—Sabine Huschka
Translated by Charlotte Lee.

Chapter 15—Gabriele Klein
Translated by Max Haberich.

New German Dance Studies

Introduction
New Dance Studies/
New German Cultural Studies

SUSAN MANNING AND LUCIA RUPRECHT

New German Dance Studies offers fresh histories and theoretical inquiries that will resonate not only for scholars working in the field of dance, but also for scholars working on literature, film, visual culture, theater, and performance. The volume brings together essays by scholars working inside and outside Germany, by established leaders in the field as well as new voices. Topics range from eighteenth- and nineteenth-century theater dance to popular social dances in global circulation, although emphasis falls on twentieth- and twenty-first–century modern and contemporary dance. Three research clusters emerge: Weimar culture and its afterlife, a focus that is still particularly strong in German studies outside Germany; the GDR (German Democratic Republic), where our contributions work toward filling a persistent gap in East German cultural history; and conceptual trends in recent theater dance that are only slowly finding an audience outside continental Europe.

This introductory chapter sketches the intellectual and artistic trends over the last thirty years that have shaped the scholarship featured in *New German Dance Studies*. This overview follows the broadly chronological organization of the volume as a whole: opening essays on theater dance before 1900; then research clusters on Weimar dance, dance in the GDR, and conceptual dance; and a closing reflection on the circulation of dance in an era of globalization. Throughout we emphasize the complex interplay between dance-making and dance writing, as well as interrelations between dance practice and research and artistic and intellectual trends in German culture at large. Although we cannot detail all these interconnections, we remain aware that the essays collected in *New German Dance Studies* participate in broader cultural transformations even while documenting and narrating how these transformations have impacted dance research.

From *Germanistik* to *Kulturwissenschaft*

Over the past decades, the emergence of a new type of German cultural studies (*Kulturwissenschaft*) has replaced more traditional separations between disciplines. *Kulturwissenschaft* has opened the academic field of German literature (*Germanistik*) to transdisciplinary inquiries on a broad range of research topics, demonstrating a new awareness of historical contexts and theoretical questions without necessarily abolishing a strong philological grounding. Mindful of the analytical demands posed by social and political structures, practitioners of German cultural studies acknowledge their British and American predecessors while maintaining strong interests in specific areas such as historical discourse analysis, the formation of knowledge, and theories of performance—all interests represented in this volume. *Kulturwissenschaft* does not constitute yet another trend within the methodological and theoretical debates of the late twentieth century but shows how current research operates both informed by and "after" theory.

Cultures of the body have contributed to this new kind of research, both as textlike objects for study and as alternative models to the textual paradigm. Dance studies can have a prime impact here, and it is this volume's aim to encourage and further the inclusion of dance scholarship in the broadened spectrum of research enabled by the turn of *Germanistik* toward *Kulturwissenschaft*. As Gabriele Brandstetter suggests: "It is one of dance studies' tasks to provide historical research and theoretical positions for choreographers and dancers, but also for cultural studies at large."[1]

Christina Thurner's essay, "Affect, Discourse, and Dance before 1900," demonstrates what can be gained from a transdisciplinary approach. Her analysis of aesthetic treatises historicizes claims that see dance as an art of expression that projects emotions in an immediate fashion. As she notes, such a mythical understanding often prevails up to today. Thurner emphasizes that important aspects of a major event in the history of dance—ballet reform in the eighteenth century—were actually prescribed in aesthetic discourse before their implementation on stage. Her essay also provides crucial historical background to the renewed interest in expression in dance after 1900.

Claudia Jeschke's essay, "Lola Montez and Spanish Dance in the 19th Century," narrates the career of a performer who trafficked in staging the Spanish dancer as a figure of otherness on the stages of nineteenth-century Europe. Jeschke addresses both performative qualities and written discourse, in particular Montez's own writings, as strategies for self-fashioning. Here, discourse itself gains a performative potential, pronouncing into being a successful persona that relied on a variety of marketing tactics. Jeschke casts new light on dance history by exploring how a dilettante female performer used constructions of gender and alterity to forge a star identity for herself.

In their engagement with relatively unknown autobiographical writings and dance treatises not usually considered by anyone but specialists, both Jeschke's and Thurner's contributions exemplify the debt of *Kulturwissenschaft* to New Historicism. Both also point up the relevance today of historical stagings and discussions of alterity and affect. Above all, their essays demonstrate pre–twentieth-century dance's inextricable embeddedness within cultural discourse and practice.

The two opening essays continue a body of work situated within one of the most prolific fields of interaction between dance studies and German cultural studies to date, which can be broadly subsumed under the heading of discourse analysis. This approach highlights the discursive framing of dance, and investigations span the seventeenth to the twenty-first century. Authors writing in this area often have a background in literary studies. They explore the ways in which aesthetic, literary, and journalistic writings speak about dance and how this discourse illuminates dance history as well as the history of literature and aesthetics.[2] Studies on dance and discourse explore the descriptive and prescriptive potential of language that relates to the physical art, but also the ways in which language may define a type of movement as dance in the first place, whether in an aesthetic, social, or political framework.

One of the most potent topoi in the history of dance writing is the assumption of the body's pre-discursive status. This assumption is implied in dance's association with the unspeakable in the sense of that which must not be expressed—the socially or politically censored—and that which cannot be expressed—the ineffable. Mobilizing literary studies to explicate dance studies, Brandstetter has identified key moments for these two types of unspeakability in the history of German literature: Goethe's *Werther*, which establishes the dancing body in the eighteenth century as a prime figure for new forms of sensitive subjectivity, but also for gendered identity and the code of intimacy that results from social censorship; and Hugo von Hofmannsthal's turn-of-the-century writings that celebrate dance together with the other silent arts as alternative sign systems at a time of fundamental revisions in the order of representation.[3] Here and elsewhere, Brandstetter's investigations demonstrate how dance and writing reinforce, but also challenge, the assumption of the body before or beyond language.

Whatever the stated topic, many of this volume's contributions necessarily deal with dance and discourse. Dance studies demands a certain amount of dance writing, the description of what happens on stage or, in the case of Jens Richard Giersdorf's article, while walking on the street. Description thus retrospectively reanimates bodily movement while also enacting interpretive approaches to the physical event. Because of dance's unstable ontological status as a corporeal art of movement, much literary writing has revealed a melancholic awareness of the impermanence of the dancing body. More recently, the renewed interest in phenomenological approaches has superseded this stance and its underlying dualism of body and mind, stage and page. Scholars now engage with the modes in which movement is thought and experienced by performers and viewers and how this kinesthetic imaginary affects our language.[4]

Ideas of the thinking body that have arisen from such engagements often retain as much of a mythical aura as those of the unthinking body. Yet they also open up distinctive modes of research and practice where authors and artists do not dwell on the referential gap but analyze, deconstruct, or shift its implications, treating it as a fact that enables instead of disables insight. New scholarship inquires into the ideological contexts that insist on dance as fleeting, indescribable movement or, in Thurner's account, as immediate emotional expressiveness. This approach characterizes not only current directions in dance studies but also conceptual dance as a mode of creative research and critical theory. In other words, topical questions in dance research cannot be separated from the emergence of conceptual dance, and conceptual dance in turn cannot be separated from the accompanying shift from broadly sociohistorical to broadly philosophical approaches to dance history.

Similarly, the broadly sociohistorical histories of Weimar dance, dance in exile, and dance in the GDR cannot be separated from the emergence of *Tanztheater* in both East and West Germany, as artists and intellectuals in the 1960s and 1970s took critical stances to the founding ideologies of both German states. Nor can the turn from *Tanztheater* to conceptual dance be disentangled from the reconfiguration of German artistic and intellectual life after the fall of the Berlin Wall and national reunification.

From *Ausdruckstanz* to Weimar Dance

In the late 1970s and 1980s, German critics and historians engaged by the rise of *Tanztheater* began to investigate German modern dance between the two world wars, or *Ausdruckstanz* (dance of expression) as the practice was known. As Johann Kresnik, Pina Bausch, Susanne Linke, Gerhard Bohner, and others created socially critical and vividly theatrical alternatives to the postwar ballet boom in West Germany, Tom Schilling, Arila Siegert, and others sought to reform and revitalize the East German dance stage. Although dance training in both German states during the postwar years emphasized ballet, many of the artists who created *Tanztheater* also had studied with survivors of *Ausdruckstanz*. While Schilling had studied with Mary Wigman and Dore Hoyer, Siegert had studied with Gret Palucca in Dresden. Linke and Bohner also had studied with Wigman, while Bausch had studied with Kurt Jooss in Essen. As critics and scholars often noted, these artists' early exposure to

Ausdruckstanz informed their later rejection of the ballet boom in its varied forms in East and West Germany.

As *Tanztheater* became an emergent and then dominant form in the 1980s and 1990s, research into the lives and careers of individual dancers in the 1920s and 1930s revealed the breadth and depth of dance reform and experimental dance in Germany and in German-speaking Europe between the two world wars.[5] This research inevitably engaged the question of how practitioners of *Ausdruckstanz* had negotiated the radical break of 1933, when the Weimar Republic gave way to the National Socialist state. Biographers of individual artists handled this question in varying ways. Some studies, such as Hedwig Müller's biography of Mary Wigman, sought to understand the choreographer's involvement with the Nazi state from the artist's own perspective during the Third Reich, emphasizing her commitment to German culture as expressed through her letters and diaries of the time.[6] Other studies, such as Valerie Preston-Dunlop's biography of Rudolf Laban, sought to portray the artist's involvement with the Nazi state from the perspective of his 1938 exile, acknowledging his earlier employment by the Nazi cultural bureaucracy but emphasizing the hardships he endured after his employment contract had been terminated.[7]

It was not until studies were published that examined the broader role of *Ausdruckstanz* under National Socialism that questions of individual culpability could be seen in relation to larger institutional and ideological dynamics. In 1993 a major exhibition staged at the Academy of Arts in Berlin traced the history of *Ausdruckstanz* from 1900—when the movement emerged as part of the life reform movement—through the years of the Weimar Republic—when a broad range of expressive dance practices became an integral component of the era's artistic experimentation—and into the Nazi years—when the National Socialists embraced *Deutscher Tanz* ("German Dance," as *Ausdruckstanz* was now called) as part of a *Volksgemeinschaft* (literally "folk community") that divided "true Germans" from Communists, Jews, homosexuals, and other "outsiders." Titled after Laban's statement that "everyone is a dancer," the catalog accompanying the show printed primary documents from the three Dancers' Congresses in 1927, 1928, and 1930 organized by proponents of *Ausdruckstanz* and from the German Dance Festivals in 1934 and 1935 and the 1936 Olympic Festival organized by the National Socialists, as if to underscore how the *Ausdruckstanz* ideal of a *Tanzgemeinschaft* ("dance community") had given way to the *Volksgemeinschaft*.[8] Over the next decade, other scholars also published their primary research into the broader question of the alliance of *Ausdruckstanz* and National Socialism, and varied perspectives on the troubling alliance became subject to debate.[9]

Further research also made clear that the methods associated with Mary Wigman, Rudolf Laban, and their disciples—the social and artistic formation known as *Ausdruckstanz*—comprised only part of the flourishing dance scene of the interwar years. Valeska Gert and other cabaret dancers, the Tiller Girls and other groups of precision dancers on the revue stage, Oskar Schlemmer at the Bauhaus, the craze for jazz dance documented in silent films of the era—all these movement forms were equally significant, as were the varied systems of "aesthetic gymnastics" (*Tanzgymnastik*) that were central to physical culture of the Weimar years. In a review of the literature published in 2007, Susanne Franco suggested that dance historians follow the lead of film scholars and adopt the term *Weimar Dance* to encompass the broader range of dance and movement forms.[10] Younger scholars immediately saw the need to do so.

Once the major contours of Weimar dance became visible, scholars could look more closely at interrelations between Weimar dance and other artistic and social practices of the time. While some scholars have considered the overlap and interplay between Weimar dance and physical culture, others have examined the overlap and interplay between Weimar dance, theater, film, and visual culture.[11] At its best, such cross-disciplinary research challenges standard disciplinary narratives. In this volume, Susan Funkenstein's essay, "Picturing Palucca at the Bauhaus," examines the visual images of Palucca created by students and teachers at the Bauhaus. In so doing, Funkenstein challenges the standard literature that associates Bauhaus dance exclusively with Oskar Schlemmer. Susanne Franco's essay, "Rudolf Laban's Dance Film Projects," considers how film offered Laban yet another arena within which to promote his distinctive vision of dance. Yet Franco also wonders aloud whether Laban's apparent turn away from film in the mid-1930s reflected his engagement with the National Socialist cultural bureaucracy and the opportunities it offered for his vision of mass dance.

A generation ago, the most explosive scholarship on Weimar dance focused on its entanglement with the Nazi state. More recently, scholars have examined the interplay of dance and cultural politics in Weimar dance in exile and in dance in the GDR. Such inquiries contribute to what Jürgen Habermas famously discussed as Germany's preoccupation with a "double past," the demand to "work off the past" of the Nazi state and the GDR without equating their status and impact.[12]

Beginning in the 1920s and accelerating through the 1930s, German dancers emigrated to a variety of locations, and students trained in Germany broadly circulated what they had learned across Europe, the Americas, and Asia.[13] In this volume, three authors probe the complexities of German émigré experience in the United States. Tresa Randall's essay, "Hanya Holm and an American *Tanzgemeinschaft*," counters the standard narrative of Holm's assimilation and Americanization. Focusing on Holm's writings during her early years in the United States, Randall demonstrates how she saw her New World milieu through an Old World lens, conceptualizing the United States as a fragmented society (*Gesellschaft*) in need of a community that integrated its members and that dance could provide (*Tanzgemeinschaft*). Karen Mozingo's essay, "Lotte Goslar's Clowns," examines the performance of clowning in Goslar's works, an artistic strategy that marginalized the choreographer in histories of modern dance on both sides of the Atlantic. Writing Goslar back into both histories, Mozingo articulates a richly alternative vision of how dance engages its historical time and place. And Kate Elswit's essay, "Back Again? Valeska Gert's Exiles," questions what exile means for an artist whose performances relied on a strategy of estrangement. In so doing, Elswit follows Gert through her American exile and back to Germany, exploring the shifting dynamics of her reception abroad and upon her return to a very changed homeland.

After World War II, exiled dancers returned to a homeland divided first between the Soviet and Allied sectors and, from 1949 to 1990, into the Federal Republic of Germany and the GDR. During those forty years, theatrical dance took distinctive forms and developed distinctive structures for patronage in the two Germanys. Thus two interrelated histories ran parallel.[14] In the years immediately following reunification, as West Germany absorbed the infrastructure erected in the East, histories of Germany tended to bracket East Germany as "the failed socialist experiment"—as one chapter was titled in a 1995 introduction to German cultural studies.[15] Yet with more time and distance came more interest in probing the forty years of art and cultural politics in the GDR.

In this volume, three essays make a provocative and multifaceted contribution to the existing literature on dance in the GDR. In "*Was bleibt?* The Politics of East German Dance," Marion Kant, who established her career as a critical intellectual within the GDR, looks back at how dancers during the years immediately following World War II negotiated the terrain of divided Germany: while Mary Wigman and Marianne Vogelsang ended "in the West," Gret Palucca and Jean Weidt found themselves "in the East." In Kant's polemical essay, their choices are subject to intense scrutiny. In "Warfare over Realism: *Tanztheater* in East Germany, 1966–1989," Franz Anton Cramer, a former managing director of the dance archive in Leipzig, intentionally takes a more distanced approach. Rereading the debate over socialist realism and revisiting the *Tanztheater* created by Tom Schilling at the Komische Oper in East Berlin, he invites us to set aside the earlier dismissal of Schilling's *Tanztheater* by West-oriented critics and to explore the intersection of aesthetics and politics in East German dance theory and practice. In "Moving against Disappearance: East German Bodies in Contemporary Choreography," Jens Richard Giersdorf probes the representation of East Germany by choreographers who grew up on opposite sides of the wall, Sasha Waltz and Jo Fabian. Like Fabian, Giersdorf came of age in East Germany in the 1980s, and his perspective reflects the thrill of that first walk across Berlin and his dismay at the erasure of his experience. Despite their very different perspectives, all three authors call for a more nuanced view of East German dance and cultural history.

Strikingly, all but one of the authors in this volume writing on Weimar dance, dance in exile, and dance in the GDR are based wholly or partly outside Germany. Marion Kant divides her time between Cambridge (U.K.) and Philadelphia, while Franz Anton Cramer divides his time between Paris and Berlin. Susanne Franco teaches in Venice and in Salerno. Jens Richard Giersdorf, Karen Mozingo, Tresa Randall, Susan Funkenstein, and Kate Elswit are affiliated with colleges and universities in the United States. Many of these authors build on the significant body of work produced in Germany by Hedwig Müller, Patricia Stöckemann, Franz-Manuel Peter, among others—the generation inspired and provoked by the emergence of *Tanztheater* in the 1980s to excavate and fathom the history and politics of Weimar dance.

The one exception is Sabine Huschka, whose essay "Pina Bausch, Mary Wigman, and the Aesthetic of 'Being Moved'" rethinks the relationship between Wigman and Bausch from a viewpoint informed by recent philosophical approaches to dance history. Challenging often-stated continuities between the two choreographers based on genealogies of pedagogical transmission, Huschka's aesthetic analysis of major choreographic concepts in Wigman and Bausch reflects back on the different politics of the body and the different social and cultural concerns that the two artists espoused. But her inquiry into the charged emotionality of *Ausdruckstanz* and *Tanztheater* also complements Thurner's investigation of dance's history as an expression of affect.

From *Tanztheater* to *Konzepttanz*

As Huschka's essay exemplifies, a significant intellectual development within Germany is the shift from the generation that focused on the politics of Weimar dance in the wake of *Tanztheater* in the 1980s to the generation that focuses on the philosophy of contemporary and historical dance in the wake of the emergence of conceptual dance (*Konzepttanz*) over the last two decades. *Konzepttanz* is the controversial label for works since the 1990s by choreographers such as Xavier Le Roy, Meg Stuart, Jochen Roller, Martin Nachbar, Katrin Deuffert and Thomas Plischke, Thomas Lehmen, and Eszter Salamon—to mention only some of those based in Berlin, which is a center for this type of performance.[16] Although sometimes used in a pejorative sense, as criticizing a form of contemporary dance that is lacking in movement interest, the notion of *Konzepttanz* represents, in fact, a very heterogeneous body of experimental pieces that share a certain theoretical attitude: they all think about dance within the frame of dance; to do so, they often (but not always) include language. "If the use of the notion of *Konzepttanz* is to have any meaning at all," Gerald Siegmund claims, "it must refer to the questioning of dominant techniques of movement and the bodily norms that these techniques generate, as well as to the rethinking of their status and reception in society."[17]

As *Konzepttanz* both generates its own theory and lends itself to the theoretical gaze of the viewer, one of the most prominent current research interests concerns the relationship between dance and knowledge.[18] If dance constitutes a culture of knowledge, in which ways does its dynamic, sensuous, and corporeal practice affect our general understanding of knowledge in diverse realms of the humanities, social sciences, and natural sciences? One of the premises of *Kulturwissenschaft* is the assumption that any type of cultural enunciation can be approached like a (polysemous) text. Current German dance studies largely subscribes to this hypothesis, while offering at the same time a particularly acute understanding of aspects that involve going beyond textuality, such as physical presence and performative enactment.

In this volume, Yvonne Hardt's essay, "Engagements with the Past in Contemporary Dance," looks at the performative reconstruction of past knowledge in new stagings of historical choreographies. She addresses practices between theoretical inquiry and performance and shows how these practices revise traditional forms of knowledge preservation such as the archive. The works addressed by Hardt are part of a combined effort of dance practice and theory to rethink history—and historiography—from the perspective of performance.[19] Dance's engagement with its status as an art based on physical memory thus feeds into a research focus on cultural memory within the humanities and humanistic social sciences. Whereas memory is often primarily considered as "static, architectonic, quantitative and encyclopedic," dance's negotiation of cultural heritage as something that is passed on from body to body draws attention to "the performance aspect, the movement inherent in any active recollection [. . .]."[20]

The "lecture performance" is a key genre in the field of *Konzepttanz*.[21] Maaike Bleeker's essay, "Lecture Performance as Contemporary Dance," situates this trend within a genealogy of bodily knowledge and its academic dissemination that had reached its first high point in the dance conventions during the Weimar years. By analyzing particular examples of lecture performances, Bleeker demonstrates in detail the self-reflexive structures that emerge between scientific paper and corporeal act. And she explains in which ways lecture performances redefine what it means to be a dancer, seeing it as an attitude rather than a profession.

While both Hardt's and Bleeker's essays give evidence of new theoretical investments arising from *Konzepttanz*, Gerald Siegmund's essay, "Negotiating Choreography, Letter, and Law in William Forsythe," considers an artist whose intellectual choreographies form a unique—and uniquely successful—part of Germany's dance culture.[22] Reflecting on the aesthetic experience of Forsythe's productions, Siegmund explores how they provoke a theoretical rethinking of the notion of choreography. Whereas Bleeker focuses on the potential of *Konzepttanz* to draw attention to the fact that dance is always already exceeding physical movement, making visible the discourses, practices, norms, and regulations that influence formations of subjectivity, Siegmund engages with the ways in which Forsythe's choreographic methods allow for such formations to emerge. At once aesthetic and political, choreography is presented as a fundamentally social practice, molding subjects and enabling them to interact. Hardt's, Bleeker's, and Siegmund's articles demonstrate the insights made possible by an investment in dance literacy for contemporary cultural theory, and vice versa.

The shift in interest from the politics of Weimar dance to the philosophy of early twenty-first–century dance accompanied a changing infrastructure for dance studies: before the Fall of the Wall, dance history (*Tanzgeschichte*) was written mostly by journalists and published mostly in dance magazines, yearbooks, and encyclopedias. After the Fall of the Wall, as the formerly West German system absorbed East German institutions, the production of *Tanzwissenschaft* ("dance science" or "dance studies") entered the German university system—ironically, a move anticipated by the founding of a dance studies program in Leipzig in 1986.[23]

After reunification, the Free University in Berlin became the center for *Tanzwissenschaft*, as Gabriele Brandstetter led the move to distinguish *Tanzwissenschaft* within *Theaterwissenschaft* ("theater science" or "theater studies"). Brandstetter's pathbreaking transdisciplinary approach has raised awareness of dance's importance within the wider field of cultural studies.[24] In fact, the researchers and writers associated with this approach have become known informally as the "Berlin School." In addition, the Hochschulübergreifendes Zentrum Tanz Berlin (Inter-University Center for Dance) was founded in 2006. It is based organizationally at the two Berlin art academies, the Universität der Künste (University of the Arts) and the Hochschule für Schauspielkunst 'Ernst Busch' (University of Drama). Complementing the Free University's teaching of theoretical and historical aspects of dance, the Inter-University Center emphasizes practical guidance for aspiring contemporary dancers and choreographers.

Beyond Berlin

Within the German-speaking countries today, significant alternatives to the "Berlin School" are the dance programs at the Institute for Applied Theater

Studies in Giessen and at the Institute for Theater Studies in Berne. There are dance studies pathways within the departments of theater studies in Leipzig and Munich, and at the University of Music and Dance in Cologne. Together with Claudia Jeschke's Department of Dance Studies in Salzburg, the Austrian center for contemporary dance and theory "Tanzquartier" in Vienna, and the Institute for Performance Studies established at the University of Hamburg by Gabriele Klein, they represent a thriving research culture.[25] Whereas in Berlin and elsewhere, the focus is on "high art" and theatrical dance, Klein works from the premises of sociology, and she has written widely on popular dance and cultural theory.[26] Her concluding essay to *New German Dance Studies*, "Toward a Theory of Cultural Translation in Dance," uses a case study of tango to point toward a broad range of research topics made possible through ethnographic approaches and theories of globalization.

Klein's essay takes on a special relevance when contrasted with Claudia Jeschke's essay on Montez. As a pioneer of dance studies, Jeschke started her career when an academic position in the field was barely conceivable in German-speaking Europe, and she has subsequently helped establish academic programs in Cologne, Leipzig, and Salzburg, where she is now head of the Department of Dance Studies and director of the Derra de Moroda Dance Archives. Her publications have laid substantial methodological foundations for the study of dance, ranging from reconstructions and systematic movement analysis to new forms of historiography.[27] Klein too is a pioneer; she started her career at a time when "performance studies" was not a viable practice in German-speaking Europe, and she has broadened the field of dance studies beyond the theatrical stage. The distance from Jeschke's account of an exoticized Spanish dancer on the nineteenth-century stage to Klein's account of tango's global circulation frames the last three decades of scholarship on German dance.

It is our hope that the essays in *New German Dance Studies* will enrich both dance studies and German cultural studies. Indeed, we believe that dance studies can profit from cultural studies approaches, and cultural studies can profit from the inclusion of dance. At the intersection between fields, dancing bodies articulate forms of knowledge and practice as they negotiate psychosocial potentials and prohibitions, intellectual innovations and traditions, cultural imagination and physical reality.

Notes

1. Gabriele Brandstetter, "Intensive Suche nach einem neuen Denken: Ein Manifest für den Tanz," *Theater der Zeit* 12 (2004): 22–25, here 25 (translated by Lucia Ruprecht). It has been argued before that cultural studies can profit from specialist research on embodied forms of representation and interaction; however, the discussion within dance studies tends to focus more on the benefits and problems of its own theoretical turn

toward cultural studies approaches; see programmatic publications such as Ellen W. Goellner and Jacqueline Shea Murphy, eds., *Bodies of the Text: Dance as Theory, Literature as Dance* (New Brunswick, N.J.: Rutgers University Press, 1995); Gay Morris, ed., *Moving Words, Rewriting Dance* (New York: Routledge, 1996); Jane Desmond, ed., *Meaning in Motion: New Cultural Studies of Dance* (Durham, N.C.: Duke University Press, 1997); *Dance Research Journal* 41:1 (2009), Special Issue on Dance, the Disciplines, and Interdisciplinarity; *Forum for Modern Language Studies* 46:4 (2010), Special Issue on Evaluating Dance: Discursive Parameters.

2. See Gabriele Brandstetter, *Tanz-Lektüren: Körperbilder und Raumfiguren der Avantgarde* (Frankfurt: Fischer Taschenbuch, 1995); Gregor Gumpert, *Die Rede vom Tanz: Körperästhetik in der Literatur der Jahrhundertwende* (Munich: Fink, 1994); Nicole Haitzinger, *Vergessene Traktate—Archive der Erinnerung: Zu Wirkungskonzepten im Tanz von der Renaissance bis zum Ende des 18. Jahrhunderts* (Munich: epodium, 2009); Alexandra Kolb, *Performing Femininity: Dance and Literature in German Modernism* (Oxford: Lang, 2009); Roger Müller-Farguell, *Tanz-Figuren: Zur metaphorischen Konstitution von Bewegung in Texten* (Munich: Fink, 1995); Lucia Ruprecht, *Dances of the Self in Heinrich von Kleist, E.T.A. Hoffmann and Heinrich Heine* (Aldershot, England: Ashgate, 2006); Stefanie Schroedter, *Vom "Affect" zur "Action": Quellenstudien zur Poetik der Tanzkunst vom späten Ballet de Cour bis zum frühen Ballet en Action* (Würzburg: Königshausen und Neumann, 2004); Christina Thurner, *Beredte Körper—bewegte Seelen: Zum Diskurs der doppelten Bewegung in Tanztexten* (Bielefeld: transcript, 2009).

3. Gabriele Brandstetter, "Tanz und Literatur: Anstöße zu kulturwissenschaftlicher Forschung," *Die Neue Gesellschaft/Frankfurter Hefte* 11 (1997): 1011–1014, here 1011f.

4. See Isa Wortelkamp, *Schreiben mit dem Stift in der Hand: Die Aufführung im Schriftzug der Aufzeichnung* (Freiburg: Rombach, 2006); Gabriele Wittmann, "Dancing Is Not Writing: Ein poetisches Projekt über die Schnittstelle von Sprache und Tanz," in *Tanz Theorie Text*, eds. Gabriele Klein and Christa Zipprich (Münster: LIT, 2002), 585–596.

5. See Gabriele Brandstetter and Gunhild Oberzaucher-Schüller, eds., *Mundart der Wiener Moderne: Der Tanz der Grete Wiesenthal* (Munich: K. Kieser, 2009); Evelyn Dörr, *Rudolf Laban: The Dancer of the Crystal* (Lanham, Md.: Scarecrow Press, 2007); Katja Erdmann-Rajski, *Gret Palucca* (Hildesheim: Georg Olms, 2000); Leonard Fiedler and Martin Lang, *Grete Wiesenthal: Die Schönheit der Sprache des Körpers im Tanz* (Salzburg: Residenz, 1985); Susanne Foellmer, *Valeska Gert: Fragmente einer Avantgardistin in Tanz und Schauspiel der 1920er Jahre* (Bielefeld: transcript, 2006); Yvonne Hardt, *Politische Körper: Ausdruckstanz, Choreographien des Protests und die Arbeiterkulturbewegung* (Münster: LIT, 2004); Yvonne Hardt, "*Ausdruckstanz* on the Left and the Work of Jean Weidt," in *Dance Discourses: Keywords in Dance Research*, eds. Susanne Franco and Marina Nordera (London: Routledge, 2007), 61–79; Yvonne Hardt, "*Ausdruckstanz*, Workers' Culture, and Masculinity in Germany in the 1920s and 1930s," in *When Men Dance*, eds. Jennifer Fisher and Anthony Shay (New York: Oxford University Press, 2009), 258–275; Isabelle Launay, *A la recherché d'une danse moderne, Rudolf Laban–Mary Wigman* (Paris: Librairie de la Danse, 1996); Susan Manning, *Ecstasy and the Demon: The Dances of Mary Wigman* (Berkeley: University of California Press, 1993; 2nd ed. Minneapolis: University of Minnesota Press, 2006); Anna and Hermann Markard, eds., *Jooss* (Cologne: Ballett-Bühnen-Verlag, 1985); Hedwig Müller, *Mary Wigman: Leben und Werk der grossen Tänzerin* (Weinheim: Quadriga, 1986); Hedwig Müller et. al., *Dore Hoyer-Tänzerin* (Berlin: Edition Hentrich,

1992); Gunhild Oberzaucher-Schüller and Ingrid Giel, *Rosalia Chladek: Klassikerin des bewegten Ausdrucks* (Munich: K. Kieser, 2002); Frank-Manuel Peter, *Valeska Gert: Tänzerin, Schauspielerin, Kabarettistin* (Berlin: Frölich and Kaufmann, 1985); Frank-Manuel Peter, ed., *Der Tänzer Harald Kreutzberg* (Berlin: Edition Hentrich, 1997); Frank-Manuel Peter and Rainer Stamm, eds., *Die Sacharoffs: Zwei Tänzer aus dem Umkreis des Blauen Reiters* (Cologne: Wienand, 2002); Valerie Preston-Dunlop, *Rudolf Laban: An Extraordinary Life* (London: Dance Books, 1998); Dirk Scheper, *Oskar Schlemmer: Das Triadische Ballett und die Bauhausbühne* (Berlin: Akademie der Künste, 1988); Ralf Stabel, *Tanz, Palucca!* (Berlin: Henschel, 2001); Patricia Stöckemann, *Etwas ganz neues muss nun entstehen: Kurt Jooss und das Tanztheater* (Munich: K. Kieser, 2001); Patrizia Verioli, *Milloss: Un maestro della coreografia tra espressionismo e classicità* (Lucca, Italy: LIM, 1996); Brigitta Weber, ed., *Die Tänzerin und Choreographin Yvonne Georgi (1903–1975): Eine Recherche* (Hannover: Niedersächsische Staatstheater, 2009); Giorgio Wolfensberger, ed., *Suzanne Perrottet: ein bewegtes Leben* (Bern: Benteli, n.d.). An edited anthology by Gunhild Oberzaucher-Schüller, *Ausdruckstanz: eine mitteleuropäische Bewegung der ersten Hälfte des 20. Jahrhunderts* (Wilhelmshaven: Florian Noetzel, 1992; 2nd ed. 2004) brings together a wide range of biographical and thematic essays.

6. Müller, *Mary Wigman*, 214–268. For an English-language account, see Hedwig Müller, "Wigman and National Socialism," *Ballet Review* 15:1 (Spring 1987): 65–73.

7. Preston-Dunlop, *Rudolf Laban*, 172–203.

8. Hedwig Müller and Patricia Stöckemann, eds., " . . . *jeder Mensch ist ein Tänzer": Ausdruckstanz in Deutschland zwischen 1900 und 1945* (Giessen: Anabas, 1993). The exhibition, which was shown in Dresden as well as Berlin, was titled "Weltenfriede-Jugendglück: Vom Ausdruckstanz zum Olympischen Spiel."

9. See Inge Baxmann, *Mythos: Gemeinschaft. Körper- und Tanzkulturen in der Moderne* (Munich: Wilhelm Fink, 2000); Terri J. Gordon, "Fascism and the Female Form: Performance Art in the Third Reich," *Journal of the History of Sexuality* 11:1:2 (2002): 164–200; Laure Guilbert, *Danser avec le IIIe Reich: Les danseurs modernes sous le nazisme* (Brussels: Éditions Complexe, 2000); Laure Guilbert, "Fritz Böhme (1881–1952): Archaeology of an Ideologue," in *Dance Discourses: Keywords in Dance Research*, eds. Susanne Franco and Marina Nordera (London: Routledge, 2007), 29–45; Yvonne Hardt, "Ausdruckstanz und Bewegungschor im Nationalsozialismus: Zur politischen Dimension des Körperlichen und Räumlichen im modernen Tanz," in *Körper im Nationalsozialismus: Bilder und Praxen*, ed. Paula Diehl (Munich: Wilhelm Fink, 2006), 173–190; Lilian Karina and Marion Kant, *Tanz unterm Hakenkreuz* (Berlin: Henschel, 1996; 2nd ed. 1999); English translation of Karina and Kant by Jonathan Steinberg, *Hitler's Dancers: German Modern Dance and the Third Reich* (New York: Berghahn Books, 2003); Marion Kant, "Practical Imperative: German Dance, Dancers, and Nazi Politics," in *Dance, Human Rights, and Social Justice*, eds. Naomi Jackson and Toni Shapiro-Phim (Lanham, Md.: Scarecrow Press, 2008), 5–19; Susan Manning, "Modern Dance in the Third Reich: Six Positions and a Coda," in *Choreographing History*, ed. Susan Foster (Bloomington: Indiana University Press, 1995), 165–176; Gunhild Oberzaucher-Schüller, "Dramaturgy and Form of the 'German Ballet': Examination of a National Socialist Genre," in *Dance and Politics*, ed. Alexandra Kolb (Oxford: Peter Lang, 2010), 145–165.

10. Susanne Franco, "*Ausdruckstanz*: Traditions, Translations, Transmissions," in *Dance Discourses: Keywords in Dance Research*, eds. Susanne Franco and Marina Nordera (Lon-

don: Routledge, 2007), 80–98. This volume was first published in Italian as *I discorsi della danza: Parole chiave per una metodologia della ricerca* (Torino: UTET Libreria, 2005).

11. See Gabriele Brandstetter, "Unter-Brechung: Inter-Medialität und Disjunktion in Bewegungskonzepten von Tanz und Theater der Avantgarde," in *Bild-Sprung: TanzTheaterBewegung im Wechsel der Medien* (Berlin: Theater der Zeit, 2005), 160–181; Michael Cowan, *Cult of the Will: Nervousness and German Modernity* (University Park: The Pennsylvania State University Press, 2008); Michael Cowan and Kai Marcel Sicks, eds., *Leibhaftige Moderne: Körper in Kunst und Massenmedien 1918 bis 1933* (Bielefeld: transcript, 2005); Michael Cowan and Barbara Hales, eds., Moving Bodies, Moving Pictures: Dance in Early German Cinema, special issue of *Seminar* 46:3 (2010); Andrew Hewitt, *Social Choreography: Ideology As Performance in Dance and Everyday Movement* (Durham, N.C.: Duke University Press, 2005); Juliet Koss, "Bauhaus Theater of Human Dolls," in *Modernism after Wagner* (Minneapolis: University of Minnesota Press, 2010), 207–243; Karl Toepfer, *Empire of Ecstasy: Nudity and Movement in German Body Culture 1910–1935* (Berkeley: University of California Press, 1997).

12. See Jürgen Habermas, *A Berlin Republic: Writings on Germany* (Lincoln: University of Nebraska Press, 1997).

13. Ramsay Burt, *Alien Bodies: Representations of Modernity, Race and Nation in Early Modern Dance* (London: Routlege, 1998); Delfin Colome, "East Dance–West Dance," *Asia Europe Journal* 2 (2005): 247–257; Jens Richard Giersdorf, "Von der Utopie zum Archiv: Patricio Bunster und die politische Funktion der Choreographie," *Forum Modernes Theater* 23:1 (2008): 29–36; Giora Manor, "Influenced and Influencing—Dancing in Foreign Lands: The Work of Choreographers/Dancers Persecuted by the Nazis in Emigration," in Gunhild Oberzaucher-Schüller, ed., *Ausdruckstanz: eine mitteleuropäische Bewegung der ersten Hälfte des 20. Jahrhunderts* (Wilhelmshaven: Florian Noetzel, 1992; 2nd ed. 2004): 471–485; Susan Manning, "Ausdruckstanz across the Atlantic," in *Dance Discourses: Keywords in Dance Research*, eds. Susanne Franco and Marina Nordera (London: Routledge, 2007): 46–79; Joellen Meglin, "Blurring the Boundaries of Genre, Gender, and Geopolitics: Ruth Page and Harald Kreutzberg's Transatlantic Collaboration in the 1930s," *Dance Research Journal* 41:2 (Winter 2009): 52–75; Shigeto Nuki, "Übersetzbarkeit von Tanz: Der Fall Butoh," in *Tanz anderswo: intra- und interkulturell* (Münster: LIT, 2004): 121–124; Isa Partsch-Bergsohn, *Modern Dance in Germany and the United States: Crosscurrents and Influences* (Chur, Switzerland: Harwood Academic Publishers, 1994); Valerie Preston-Dunlop, "Rudolf Laban and Kurt Jooss in Exile," in *Artists in Exile*, ed. Günter Berghaus (Bristol: Bristol University Press, 1990), 167–178; Nina Spiegel, "Cultural Formulation in Eretz Israel: The National Dance Competition of 1937," *Jewish Folklore and Ethnology Review* 20 (2000); Patricia Stöckemann, "Emigranten und ihre Zufluchtsorte," *Tanzdrama* 42 (1998): 19–27; Yukihiko Yoshida, "National Dance under the Rising Sun," *International Journal of Eastern Sports and Physical Education* 7:1 (October 2009): 88–103.

14. The parallel histories were visualized in an exhibit at the Academy of Arts in Berlin in 2003. See Hedwig Müller, Ralf Stabel, and Patricia Stöckemann, *Krokodil im Schwanensee: Tanz in Deutschland seit 1945* (Frankfurt: Anabas-Verlag, 2003).

15. Rob Burns, ed., *German Cultural Studies: An Introduction* (Oxford: Oxford University Press, 1995).

16. On *Konzepttanz*, see Gerald Siegmund, *Abwesenheit: Eine performative Ästhetik*

des Tanzes. William Forsythe, Jérôme Bel, Xavier Le Roy, Meg Stuart (Bielefeld: transcript, 2006); Susanne Foellmer, *Am Rand der Körper: Inventuren des Unabgeschlossenen im zeitgenössischen Tanz* (Bielefeld: transcript, 2009); Pirkko Husemann, *Choreographie als kritische Praxis: Arbeitsweisen bei Xavier Le Roy und Thomas Lehmen* (Bielefeld: transcript, 2009); André Lepecki, *Exhausting Dance: Performance and the Politics of Movement* (New York: Routledge, 2006); Helmut Ploebst, *no wind no word: Neue Choreographie in der Gesellschaft des Spektakels. 9 Portraits: Meg Stuart, Vera Mantero, Xavier Le Roy, Benoît Lachambre, Raimund Hoghe, Emio Greco/PC, João Fiadeiro, Boris Charmatz, Jérôme Bel* (München: Kieser, 2001); Annamira Jochim, *Meg Stuart: Bild in Bewegung und Choreographie* (Bielefeld: transcript, 2008); *tanzjournal* 2 (2004), Special Issue on *Konzepttanz*.

17. Gerald Siegmund, "Konzept ohne Tanz? Nachdenken über Choreographie und Körper," in *Zeitgenössischer Tanz: Körper—Konzepte—Kulturen. Eine Bestandsaufnahme*, eds. Reto Clavadetscher and Claudia Rosiny (Bielefeld: transcript, 2007), 44–59, here 48 (translated by Lucia Ruprecht).

18. See Inge Baxmann and Franz Anton Cramer, eds., *Deutungsräume: Bewegungswissen als kulturelles Archiv der Moderne* (Munich: Kieser, 2005); Inge Baxmann, ed., *Körperwissen als Kulturgeschichte: Die Archives Internationales de la Danse (1931–1952)* (Munich: Kieser, 2008); Gabriele Brandstetter, Sibylle Peters, and Kai van Eikels, eds., *Prognosen über Bewegungen* (Berlin: b_books, 2009); Sabine Gehm, Pirrko Husemann, and Katharina von Wilcke, eds., *Knowledge in Motion: Perspectives of Artistic and Scientific Research in Dance* (Bielefeld: transcript, 2007); Sabine Huschka, ed., *Wissenskultur Tanz: Historische und Zeitgenössische Vermittlungsakte zwischen Praktiken und Diskursen* (Bielefeld: transcript, 2009).

19. See Janine Schulze, ed., *Are 100 Objects Enough to Represent the Dance? Zur Archivierbarkeit von Tanz* (Munich: epodium, 2010); Christina Thurner and Julia Wehren, eds., *Original und Revival: Geschichts-Schreibung im Tanz* (Zürich: Chronos, 2010); and the series *Tanz and Archiv: Forschungsreisen* (Munich: epodium).

20. Gabriele Brandstetter, "Dance as Culture of Knowledge: Body Memory and the Challenge of Theoretical Knowledge," in Gehm, Husemann, von Wilcke, eds., *Knowledge in Motion*, 37–48, here 39.

21. See Gabriele Brandstetter, "Tanzen Zeigen: Lecture-Performance im Tanz seit den 1990er Jahren," in *Konzepte der Tanzkultur: Wissen und Wege der Tanzforschung*, eds. Margrit Bischof and Claudia Rosiny (Bielefeld: transcript, 2010), 45–62; Sibylle Peters and Martin Jörg Schäfer, eds., *"Intellektuelle Anschauung:" Figurationen von Evidenz zwischen Kunst und Wissen* (Bielefeld: transcript, 2006); Lucia Ruprecht, Martin Nachbar, Jochen Roller, "On the Road with *Mnemonic Nonstop*," in *Memory Culture and the Contemporary City: Building Sites*, ed. Uta Staiger et. al. (Basingstoke, England: Palgrave Macmillan, 2009), 223–233; http://www.unfriendly-takeover.de.

22. See Christiane Berger, *Körper denken in Bewegung: Zur Wahrnehmung tänzerischen Sinns bei William Forsythe und Saburo Teshigawara* (Bielefeld: transcript, 2006); Senta Driver, ed., *William Forsythe: Choreography and Dance* (London and New York: Routledge, 2000); Wibke Hartewig, *Kinästhetische Konfrontation: Lesarten der Bewegungstexte William Forsythes* (Munich: epodium, 2007); Hartmut Regitz and Arnd Wesemann, eds., *Forsythe: Bill's Universe. Yearbook Ballettanz 2004* (Berlin: Friedrich, 2004); Gerald Siegmund, ed., *William Forsythe: Denken in Bewegung* (Berlin: Henschel, 2004); Steven Spier, ed., *William*

Forsythe and the Practice of Choreography: It Starts from Any Point (New York: Routledge, 2011); Gaby von Rauner, ed., *William Forsythe: Tanz und Sprache* (Frankfurt am Main: Brandes und Apsel, 1993).

23. See Jens Richard Giersdorf, "Dance Studies in the International Academy: Genealogy of a Disciplinary Formation," *Dance Research Journal* 41:1 (Summer 2009): 23–44; tanz.de: Zeitgenössischer Tanz in Deutschland—Strukturen im Wandel—eine neue Wissenschaft, Special issue of *Theater der Zeit*, 2005.

24. See Gabriele Brandstetter and Hortensia Völckers, eds., *ReMembering the Body* (Ostfildern-Ruit: Hatje Cantz, 2000).

25. The founding of dance programs has led to a number of programmatic methodological or introductory publications. See Margrit Bischof and Claudia Rosiny, eds., *Konzepte der Tanzkultur: Wissen und Wege der Tanzforschung* (Bielefeld: transcript, 2010); Gabriele Brandstetter and Gabriele Klein, eds., *Methoden der Tanzwissenschaft: Modellanalysen zu Pina Bauschs "Le Sacre Du Printemps"* (Bielefeld: transcript, 2007); Gabriele Klein and Christa Zipprich, "Tanz Theorie Text: Zur Einführung," in *Tanz Theorie Text* (Münster: LIT, 2002), 1–14; Katja Schneider and Frieder Reininghaus, eds., *Experimentelles Musik- und Tanztheater* (Regensburg: Laaber, 2004); Gerald Siegmund, "Zur Theatralität des Tanzes," in Claudia Fleischle-Braun and Ralf Stabel, eds., *Tanzforschung and Tanzausbildung* (Berlin: Henschel, 2008), 28–44.

26. See Gabriele Klein, *Electronic Vibration: Pop Kultur Theorie* (Hamburg: Rogner and Bernhard, 2004); Gabriele Klein, ed., *Bewegung: Sozial- und kulturwissenschaftliche Konzepte* (Bielefeld: transcript, 2004); Gabriele Klein, ed., *Tango in Translation: Tanz zwischen Medien, Kulturen, Kunst und Politik* (Bielefeld: transcript, 2009). Gabriele Klein and Malte Friedrich, *Is This Real? Die Kultur des HipHop* (Frankfurt: Suhrkamp, 2003).

27. See Claudia Jeschke, *Tanz als BewegungsText. Analysen zum Verhältnis von Tanztheater und Gesellschaftstanz* (Tübingen: Niemeyer, 2000); with Ann Hutchinson-Guest, *Nijinsky's Faune Restored* (London: Gordon and Breach, 1991); with Nicole Haitzinger and Gabi Vettermann, *Les Choses Espagnoles: Research into the Hispanomania of 19th Century Dance* (Munich: epodium, 2009); with Hans-Peter Bayerdörfer, ed., *Bewegung im Blick: Beiträge zu einer theaterwissenschaftlichen Bewegungsforschung* (Berlin: Vorwerk 8, 2000).

1. Affect, Discourse, and Dance before 1900

CHRISTINA THURNER

"The most secret movements of the soul," writes Friedrich Schiller in 1780, "are revealed on the exterior of the body"; each emotion has its own specific means of expression or, more precisely, "its peculiar dialect, by which one knows it."[1] Accordingly, the "language" of the emotions is—in the opinion of Schiller and his contemporaries—a physical one. It follows that the dancer, whose means of expression is the body, has a virtually unparalleled command of this language. The philosopher Johann Georg Sulzer likewise observes in 1774 in his *Allgemeine Theorie der schönen Künste* (General Theory of the Fine Arts) that "there is no state or character of the soul, no passion, which cannot be portrayed in the most vivid way through dance,"[2] from which he concludes that "no art form can exceed the dance in terms of its aesthetic power."[3]

Such outspoken admiration for dance was new for the time: even though dance served major politically representative functions in the shape of the court ballet, from an aesthetic point of view it had been perceived until then as a subordinated medium that functioned solely to complement a good education, for social enjoyment or as a passing decoration in the production of other art forms. Contemporary dance theorists now joined the exponents of philosophy and general aesthetics in this new stream of praise with their emphasis on the advantages of dance over other forms of expression, especially over language. For example, the French dance theorist Jean Georges Noverre, to this day the most famous of the eighteenth century, who was active as a dancer and choreographer in, among other places, Berlin, Stuttgart, and Vienna, commented in his *Letters on Dancing and Ballets*: "If one be deprived of the sight of the facial expression of the orator, it requires a little time to fathom his meaning. It requires no time for the face to express its meaning forcibly; a flash of lightning comes from the heart, shines in the eyes and, illuminating every feature, heralds the conflict of passions and reveals, so to speak, the naked soul."[4]

This quote is paradigmatic of the ways in which dance and its effect on the audience were being discussed in the eighteenth century. But it also represents trivial preconceptions about dance that are valid to this day. At least in nonspecialist circles, dance is still seen as an art that is emotional rather than intellectual, even though contemporary productions continue to refute this claim. I would like to argue that such an understanding goes back to the eighteenth-century redefinition of ballet that aimed at bestowing a new kind of autonomy to the dancing body and sought to enhance its status in comparison to the other arts. The eighteenth-century aesthetic discourse on dance is therefore of historical importance to our current perspective on dance.[5]

But let us return to the quote itself. The stirring of souls and the conquering of hearts by emotion signal a conception of art in general, and of dance in particular, which no longer strove toward mimesis, an aesthetics of representation, but initiated instead a sensualist aesthetics of effect. Noverre for his part attributes to the nonverbal gestures of dance a distinct effect, which emerges in tandem with these new theories of reception; this effect moves the viewer immediately, happening as if it were unmediated. Indeed, the movement on stage should transfer suddenly, inevitably to the audience. The metaphorical language used here connotes sudden, intense events: a flash of lightning, a bang, a spark. Thus the heart, emblem of the emotions, becomes the symbolic center of an exchange, in motion and emotionally charged, between stage performers and their audience—an exchange for which the art of dance was to emerge in a new, dramatic form in the eighteenth century. Now expression and effect would be determined at the moment of being affected or moved, which always involves being in motion and being moved emotionally.[6]

There is even talk in contemporary sources of spectators bursting into tears or fainting at dramatic performances of dance; with regard to Noverre's ballet *Medea and Jason* in particular, which was first staged in Stuttgart in 1763, Monika Woitas writes that the choreographer "pulled out all the technical and mechanical stops, and this, combined with an ardent and vividly expressive style of performance, could not fail to have the desired impact."[7] Scene 1 (Figure 1.1) and especially scene 9 of this ballet seem to have been particularly moving: In the latter, Medea murders their children in front of her husband Jason. He then grabs the dagger and uses it to kill himself, breaking down in the arms of his lover Creusa. The sky darkens, the palace collapses and Medea escapes by being lifted up and vanishing into the scenery of destruction. The dancers performed this spectacle according to the demands of the new style to great dramatic effect.[8] Noverre had originally created the ballet-pantomime in two acts, set to music by Johann Joseph Rudolph, as a self-contained *divertisse-*

Figure 1.1. Scene from Noverre's *Medée et Jason* (staged by Gaetano Vestris). Engraving, attributed to Francesco Bartolozzi, London 1781/82.

ment forming part of the birthday celebrations for the Duke of Württemberg, in whose service Noverre worked from 1760 until 1767. The piece was clearly a great success, and was not only revised several times and put on again by Noverre himself—in Vienna in 1767, in Paris in 1775 and 1780, and in London in 1782—but was also staged in an expanded version by, among others, Vestris, the lead in the original production.[9]

The mythical theme of the jealous betrayed woman, whose despair finally reaches its climax in a murderous act of madness and infanticide, created an opportunity for the choreographer to portray passion of the highest drama. This matched Noverre's demand for expression in mime and for the creation in and through dance of profound empathy.

The dictum that dance in particular speaks directly from "heart to heart," overcoming linguistic barriers in the process, thereafter became a trope which to this day continues to find validation. The notion of dance as a universal emotional force, however, makes dance into something of a myth. By returning to the eighteenth century, we can establish how the culturally and historically transcendent conception of dance as an affective correspondence between stage and audience took root.

This "new" dance was understood as a moving corporeal language, which, by means of "natural" indicators of emotions and passions, could express itself in such a way that it could unleash interior stirrings of feeling in the spectator. The concept of an emotional art in motion was the result of what is known as ballet reform. This is dated retrospectively to the middle of the eighteenth century and, with the exception of a few anticipatory contributions from, for example, John Weaver, Marie Sallé, and Franz Anton Christoph von Hilverding, first took shape in essays by a select few ballet masters who were engaged mostly at German and Austrian courts. In contrast to the mainly representative function of French ballet, which was at the time still embedded within the grand, centralized, and highly formal culture of the court, German ballet was protected by much more compartmentalized and regionally splintered courtly structures. They enabled the burgeoning bourgeoisie to intervene in the traditional aesthetic demands of the art by developing new forms of expression.[10] Ballet reform should not, however, be seen as a sudden act that brought about an abrupt swing in attitudes; rather, it was at once a complex development in the field and the result of more general aesthetic and anthropological paradigm shifts. The discourse on the relationship between body and soul in Friedrich Schiller, for instance, is an example of the shifting conceptions of man, of his newly valued faculties of expression, and consequently of the arts. Schiller seeks in his early writings to ground in discourse the substance of body and soul. His reflections on psychophysical matters should, moreover, be considered in close relation to reforms in the performing arts, or at least to the related theories that revolved around the emotions and all associated external and internal movements.[11] It can be assumed that Schiller not only knew Noverre's works, but that his early dramas were heavily influenced by the latter's dramatic theory of dance.[12]

Even if Noverre was not—as is often claimed[13]—the founder of ballet reform, it is nonetheless worth noting that his contemporaries took considerable interest in his writings;[14] furthermore, from today's perspective, their theoretical worth consists in a remarkably wide-ranging redefinition of ballet, which breaks firmly with accepted practices of dance of that era and which resonates with aesthetic theories current in our own. The chief purpose of his ballet reform was "to liberate dance from the ossified, hollow relics of the baroque court ballet."[15] In opposition to court ballets, which were designed to represent the feudal order, Noverre demanded that the body speak through mime, that the principle of imitation take precedence.[16] An aesthetics of representation in dance was superseded by one of expression and effect.

However, the principles that we find in the historical sources on ballet reform were only much later realized on stage. I would like, therefore, to focus in this piece on the *discourse* of dance, because the way in which dance was, indeed is, spoken and written about has a major bearing on how it is perceived and brought to the stage. It is particularly important to ask how the concept of interaction between dancers and the audience is treated in historical texts, how it perpetuates itself, and finally how it affects the general perception of dance. I shall look in particular detail at the eighteenth century: it is precisely in the German-speaking world of that period, and in the context of developments in aesthetics in relation to other art forms, that important hypotheses about dance took root. Many of these continue to shape our understanding of the form, even if stage practices have radically changed.

The eighteenth-century reformers demanded that the "new" dance replace virtuosic technique with the expressive signs of sensibility; it should, according to contemporary descriptions, seduce the eyes, not merely dazzle them, it should capture the heart and rouse it to vivid emotions. Thus the art of dance became stylized as the aesthetic expression of the new directions taken in German anthropology, which established a fresh understanding of the human being around that time. Man was no longer seen as part of a rigid social order, but as a sensitive individual with unique feelings. A human needed to be defined not by belonging to a larger whole but by embodying the newly acclaimed values of subjectivity. In this context, discussion of emotions or passions tended to center on the notion of the soul set in motion.[17] Both aesthetic theorists and men of letters participated actively in the anthropological debate that was awakening.[18] But thinkers such as Gotthold Ephraim Lessing, Friedrich Nicolai, Moses Mendelssohn, or Friedrich Schiller were not only interested in the question of reception; rather, they became increasingly concerned with psychophysical interaction, that is, the influence of the moving body on the soul and vice versa.[19] In his *Hamburg Dramaturgy*, Lessing writes: "the modifications of the soul which bring forth certain changes in the body are also caused by those same bodily changes."[20] Frequent attention is given in these descriptions to the notion of symbiosis in movement: the idea, that is, that those who are moving (dancing) also move the hearts and minds of those watching. The discourse of this reciprocal, double movement—as I have called it—movement in the physical and the emotional sense, peaked for the first time in the late eighteenth century.[21] The reciprocal relationship of body and soul was the topic of increasing research; now the object was a "*commercium mentis et corporis*," and the metaphysical dualism propounded by René Descartes was treated with distance.[22]

This new focus on reciprocity should be considered in the context of the wider-reaching paradigm shift mentioned above, which also transformed the conception of body language and its meaning. The courtly art of disguise was superseded by antirhetorical concepts of the "natural." The focus shifted in the process to nonverbal systems of signification such as the languages of gesture and mime.[23] These were considered to be more "natural" and "instinctive" means of bodily expression, which would have a direct effect on the feelings of the recipient. If the courtly arts, the *ballet de cour* among them, served to reinforce the distribution of power within the absolutist system, then the aspiring bourgeoisie sought to define itself through individualized behavior and through new words such as "interiority," "humanity," and "sympathy," qualities that were given expression in the *ballet d'action* in particular and in the mimetic performing arts in general. Figure 1.2 illustrates the new style called for by performers. In this pas de deux of the ballet *Sylvie*, Marie Allard as a nymph follows Diana and is followed herself by Jean Dauberval.

As briefly discussed above, in the eighteenth century, people began, whether they were on the stage or in the audience, to perceive themselves as individu-

Figure 1.2. Marie Allard and Jean Dauberval in a pas de deux from the ballet *Sylvie* by H. M. Le Breton and A. Trial. Colored engraving after L. C. de Carmontelle, Paris 1766. Museum of Fine Arts Boston.

als, as human beings capable of causing and experiencing stirred emotions, of moving to tears and being moved to tears.[24] According to the dance theorists, this privileging of the emotions should function in its related art form by means of a system of codes, which, however, was no longer to be recognizable as such: that system, after all, was no longer based on external rules of representation, as in court ballet, but on the notion of an understanding that was "interior" and sensual. Thus the demand for the performative signs of this understanding was that they be of a universal character, relevant to all mankind. This expectation is at once constituted by and reflected in contemporary texts about dance.[25]

Noverre emphasizes the difference between the language of words and that of gestures accordingly, arguing that the latter is shorter and more succinct than verbal discourse,[26] and he uses the aforementioned image of lightning, which makes visual the suddenness and intensity of nonverbal communication. The power of a language consisting solely of gestures and mime lies, following Noverre's line of argument, in the specific effect, one that is moving emotionally and is supposed to grip the soul of the audience without first passing via the intellect.

The dramatic theorist Johann Jakob Engel, on the other hand, uses the metaphor of melting to describe this process; he presents the communication between stage performer and spectator as a merging, a coming together of signs in their production and reception. Engel's description suggests on the symbolic level an act of fertilization between stage and audience, between action and perception; "in the soul, the image of the object and that of the emotion, which the object arouses, are quite unsevered, are profoundly mingled one with the other, indeed are one."[27] He calls for unity in signification, claiming that the human being should know "straight away, even through the terminology used, that the two images are intimately linked . . . and precisely connected."[28] The same phenomenon is suggested in Engel's description, in his *Ideen zu einer Mimik* (Ideas on Mime), of a mingling of signs as in Noverre's account of the speed and forcefulness of nonverbal expression. Interestingly, though, Engel clearly attached importance to an awareness that syntax—that is, the arrangement of signs in verbal language—is replaced in nonverbal forms of expression by a system that is no longer regulated chronologically. Instead, the organic exchange of signs constitutes a spatial presence that is experienced as a unity.[29]

Engel himself mentions in this context "the great speed in the succession of feelings, and the fine nature of their admixture."[30] Although he is still working here with the notion of a succession of events, he claims that this becomes imperceptible because of its speed and is replaced for those experiencing it by the sense of a complex mixture. This cannot be conceived of in one-dimensional terms, chronologically or syntagmatically. Rather, on the basis of these claims, we can speak of the introduction of a spatial dimension in the model of nonverbal communication. Expressive body language is thus understood as a dynamic system of signs, which—released from a syntagmatic structure, of ordering in chronological time, and from the arbitrariness of language—should enable "natural," direct communication in theatrical space.[31]

This new vision for the communication of feelings via movement is accompanied in each case by the intention to produce a particular effect. For this reason, the reformers postulated the study not only of sequences of steps and gestures, but above all of emotions and passions, of feeling itself.[32] A dancer should not, therefore, simply practice and memorize a particular routine, but rather should know the spectrum of emotions so well within his own body that he would be able to externalize interior movements convincingly.

Thus the stage performer is stylized through the discourse on dance into a human of self-conscious emotions: it is now a given that feelings are eminently determinable, can be communicated in a three-dimensional fashion, and can literally be shared. The consensus formed in the corresponding aesthetic theories of the eighteenth century that communication between performers and the audience is founded on knowledge of the emotions, represented a new, all-encompassing emphasis. The claim was made, moreover, that feelings are based on, and can be conveyed through, physical movement.[33]

It is no coincidence that at precisely this time, when dance was endeavoring to establish itself as an autonomous art form on the stage, there was an abundance of texts concerned with how dance should look and what the effects of certain performances would be. Books on gesture showed and described poses and moves, and attributed to each a particular emotion. These served on the one hand to provide dancers with a model for "correct" expression, and on the other were intended to instruct spectators on the "right" way of reading or interpreting the gestures—consciously, but above all unconsciously. Dance as a performing art is thus based, like every utterance, on a specific mode of discourse and is the product of a particular historical and cultural order. But in the particular case of dance, the label of "naturalness" conceals the fact of the discourse itself.

In the writings of the ballet reformers, more weight is given to the allegedly indescribable, involuntary movement that exerts a total hold over the audience than to rational reflection. The reception of a dance performance is thus stylized into an event that cannot be understood by the intellect alone, however enlightened it might be. (It is interesting, however, that this stylization is achieved by means of language, which clearly doubts its own ability to perceive and describe dance.)

If the writings of this time are to be believed, the audience's experience of a consummate piece of dramatic dance evades—as indeed does dance itself—all definite or definitive description.[34] And yet it is precisely this looser discourse, one which excluded all binding tests and exact definitions, which enabled the figure of the spectator to establish itself as a being of individualized experiences, and which thereby shaped the general understanding of the meaning and purpose of dance.[35] "If the audience does not wish to deprive itself of the most beautiful aspects of our art," writes Gasparo Angiolini, a contemporary of Noverre working in Vienna, then "it must of its own accord become accustomed to being moved, and to weeping."[36] The ballet reformers postulated that dance on the stage should "share with the best plays the merit of affecting and moving, and of making tears flow. . . ."[37] Thus it was established that the emotions of the dancers on the stage should correspond with those of the spectators in the audience.

The assumption that dance should literally make an impression finds expression in various metaphors for the performer-spectator relationship. As far back as the ancient world, Lucian described the reception of dramatic dance as a reflection in the sense of mirroring: he contends that the spectator "sees in the dancer as in a mirror his very self."[38] Noverre and his contemporaries replaced the image of the mirror with metaphors of three-dimensional, dynamic movement and modified the individual point of view to encompass not only the emotional identification of the spectator with the performer, but also the transfer of feeling from the actor on stage to the audience, or of a profound emotional impression on the spectator.[39] Noverre, for example, writes that the observer should be so taken in that he should feel "transported in a moment to the spot where the action has taken place";[40] elsewhere, indeed, he describes the effect as a physical one: "[the] pathos [of Mr. Garrick, the English actor] was touching; in tragedy he terrified with the successive movements with which he represented the most violent passions. And, if I may so express myself, he lacerated the spectator's feelings, tore his heart, pierced his soul, and made him shed tears of blood."[41] The reciprocal relation of stage and audience should move the individual to his core.

On this subject, Noverre writes that ballet "will always have a lively interest for every spectator possessed of a feeling heart and an all-seeing eye," but, he concedes, "provided that the executants have a soul and a feeling for lively expression."[42] Nothing less than life itself, then, unites performer and spectator. One portrays or displays life, the other is moved as a living being. One of the most significant paradoxes of the discourse on dance at that time becomes clear, however, with regard to the emotional involvement of the audience: although the concept of a language of movement that is universally accessible and comprehensible because of its nearness to life is established, there are nonetheless limitations where the reception of dance is concerned. For it is not life itself (or not solely), which is present on the stage; rather, life is mediated through signs and gestures. Here again, a discrepancy arises between supposedly "natural" and "immediate" expression and the indirect nature of representation. This contradiction is present in notable texts on dance.

Noverre, for example, contends on the one hand that "[t]he arts are of all countries, let them assume a voice suitable to them; they have no need of interpretation, and will affect equally both the connoisseur and the ignoramus."[43] On the other hand, he concedes that the passions that guide the artist differ "in proportion to their sensibilities. . . ."[44] In this context he mentions cultural differences between peoples and formulates consequences for the arts: "Every nation has its own laws, customs, manners, fashions and ceremonies, which are entirely different from those of another. Each nation differs in its tastes, architecture and mode of cultivating the arts. A skillful painter then should be able to seize on the different characteristics and depict them with a faithful brush. If he be not a cosmopolitan he cannot be true and he is no longer in a position to please."[45]

Thus Noverre's conception of an effective artist must not only reflect and portray experiences common to all mankind, but must also give the audience an active sense of cultural difference.[46] With the metaphor of being at home, Noverre draws the boundary between what is one's "own," which he equates with what is "true," and that which is "foreign." This applies both to the producer of art, who should be "truthful," and to the recipient, who can clearly find pleasure only in what is "true," that is to say, in what he knows. Writing about art in general, Noverre stands here in contradiction to the concept of a universal aesthetic, itself by no means undisputed in the general discourse on aesthetics of the period.[47] However, a new power is ascribed precisely to dance, which is held to be capable of disguising the fact both of its mediation and of its determination by historical and cultural factors. Noverre and those who think as he does thus layer the practice of dance and its corresponding language over one another in such a way that the boundaries between them become blurred, indeed, that the two can no longer be treated separately. The discourse of movement meets, is even directed toward, solid, physical movement, and vice versa.

This essay shows that, from the eighteenth century into our own time, the discourse of dance for the most part ignores the parameters that allow us to perceive the interaction between dancers and audience as immediate, as the double movement of an emotional relationship in motion. This made perfect sense in the context of ballet reform, and the associated paradigm shift toward a sensualist aesthetic, but it has only limited application to later developments in the art of dance. It is, therefore, astonishing that even in our own time, the universal effect of the "language" of dance is talked about again and again—and, for example, in so prominent a context as the message on International Dance Day. A yearly event since 1982, this takes place on April 29th, Noverre's birthday, and exponents of dance give statements "to celebrate Dance, to revel in the universality of this art form, to cross all political, cultural and ethnic barriers and bring people together with a common language—Dance."[48] The German choreographer Sasha Waltz exclaimed in her message on International Dance Day in 2007 that "dance is a universal language: emissary for a peaceful world, for equality, tolerance and compassion. Dance teaches us sensibility."[49] Auspicious though this utopian thought may seem, it is doubtful, especially with regard to dance on the stage today. We must question whether a world-encompassing language of dance, together with the corresponding emotions, really exists,[50] as well as, whether, given modernist and postmodernist developments in the art form, it is desirable or in the spirit of our time to promote such a language. Yet the fact that such an overtly idealistic notion continues to be invoked shows all the more clearly how profoundly and how permanently the *discourse* of the ballet reformers (more so than their works for the stage) has shaped our conception of the art of dance.

Notes

1. Friedrich Schiller, "On the Connection between the Animal and the Spiritual Nature in Man," in *Aesthetical and Philosophical Essays*, vol. 2, ed. Nathan Haskell Dole (Boston: Francis A. Niccolls and Co., 1902), 131–172, here 164.

2. Johann Georg Sulzer, *Allgemeine Theorie der Schönen Künste* (General Theory of the Fine Arts), vol. 4 (Leipzig, 1787), 419.

3. Ibid., 423.

4. Jean Georges Noverre, *Letters on Dancing and Ballets*, trans. Cyril W. Beaumont (Alton: Dance Books, 2004; facsimile edition of the original 1930 translation), Letter IX, p. 78; See also Letter X, p. 107: "the life-blood of the fine arts is, if I may so express myself, like an electric spark. It is a fire which spreads rapidly, and in a moment captivates the imagination of the spectator, stirring his soul and rendering his heart susceptible to every emotion."

5. Editors' Note: For a discussion of affect in twentieth-century theater dance, see the essay by Sabine Huschka in this volume.

6. See Johann Christoph Adelung, *Grammatisch-kritisches Wörterbuch der Hochdeutschen Mundart, mit beständiger Vergleichung der übrigen Mundarten, besonders aber der Oberdeutschen*, second extended and improved edition, 4 vols., reprint of the Leipzig edition 1793–1801 (Hildesheim: Georg Olms, 1990), 1206.

7. Monika Woitas, *Im Zeichen des Tanzes: Zum ästhetischen Diskurs der darstellenden Künste zwischen 1760 und 1830* (Herbolzheim: Centaurus, 2004), 120; see also Sibylle Dahms, "Jean Georges Noverre," in *Pipers Enzyklopädie des Musiktheaters*, ed. Carl Dahlhaus, vol. 4 (Munich: Piper, 1997), 476–484, here 477.

8. Dahms, *Jean Georges Noverre*, 477.

9. Woitas, *Im Zeichen des Tanzes*, 120.

10. Stephanie Schroedter, "Pionierwerke deutscher Tanzliteratur—Tanzdiskussionen zwischen Rechtfertigung und Sittenlehre," in the appendix of Louis Bonin, *Die Neueste*

Art zur Galanten und Theatralischen Tantz=Kunst; Meletaon: Von der Nutzbarkeit des Tantzens, ed. Claudia Jeschke (Berlin: Edition Hentrich, 1996), 604–654.

11. See inter alia Gabriele Brandstetter, "'Die Bilderschrift der Empfindungen'—Jean-Georges Noverres *Lettres sur la Danse, et sur les Ballets* und Friedrich Schillers Abhandlung *Über Anmut und Würde*," in *Schiller und die höfische Welt*, eds. Achim Aurnhammer et al. (Tübingen: Max Niemeyer, 1990), 77–93.

12. See Peter Michelsen, *Der Bruch mit der Vater-Welt: Studien zu Schillers "Räubern"* (Heidelberg: Winter, 1979), 27–28; also Peter-André Alt, *Schiller: Leben—Werk—Zeit* (München: C. H. Beck, 2000), vol. 1, 48.

13. Even Noverre himself viewed his letters in retrospect as having instigated a revolution in dance comparable to that which Gluck brought about in opera; Jean Georges Noverre, *Lettres sur la danse, sur les ballets et les arts* (St. Petersburg: Schnoor, 1803), vol. 1, IIIf.: "If one reflects on what opera was in 1760, and what it is today, it is difficult not to recognize the effect which my letters have had. They have also been translated into Italian, into German and into English. The glory of my art and my time, as well my own numerous and brilliant achievements, give me leave to say that I have brought about in dance a revolution as striking and as lasting as that which Gluck effected in music." In 1760, however, almost forty years earlier, Noverre wrote that he did not want to achieve the "standing of a reformer," rather that he wanted to "avoid this at all costs." [Translator's note: the reference cited by author is *Briefe über die Tanzkunst und über die Ballette*, Letter I, p. 7, but no equivalent could be found in the published English translation; hence this is my own, from the German citation in the article.]

14. See inter alia Woitas, *Im Zeichen des Tanzes*, 257.

15. Brandstetter, "'Die Bilderschrift der Empfindungen,'" 79.

16. Ibid., 81.

17. See Ulrike Zeuch, "Der Affekt: Tyrann des Ichs oder Befreier zum wahren Selbst? Zur Affektenlehre im Drama und in der Dramentheorie nach 1750," in *Theater im Kulturwandel des 18. Jahrhunderts: Inszenierungen und Wahrnehmung von Körper—Musik—Sprache*, eds. Erika Fischer-Lichte and Jörg Schönert (Göttingen: Wallstein, 1999), 69–89, here 75; also Caroline Torra-Mattenklott, *Metaphorologie der Rührung: Ästhetische Theorie und Mechanik im 18. Jahrhundert* (München: Wilhelm Fink, 2002). On the "touching of the heart" [*Herzrührung*], see inter alia Ursula Geitner, *Die Sprache der Verstellung: Studien zum rhetorischen und anthropologischen Wissen im 17. und 18. Jahrhundert* (Tübingen: Max Niemeyer, 1992), 189; also Carsten Zelle, *Die doppelte Ästhetik der Moderne: Revisionen des Schönen von Boileau bis Nietzsche* (Stuttgart, Weimar: J. B. Metzler, 1995), 109, 118. See also more recent research on emotions in the arts, including Klaus Herding and Bernhard Stumpfhaus, eds., *Pathos, Affekt, Gefühl: Die Emotionen in den Künsten* (Berlin: Walter de Gruyter, 2004); Hermann Kappelhoff, *Matrix der Gefühle: Das Kino, das Melodrama und das Theater der Empfindsamkeit* (Berlin: Vorwerk 8, 2004); Doris Kolesch, *Theater der Emotionen: Ästhetik und Politik zur Zeit Ludwigs XIV* (Frankfurt: Campus, 2006); Burkhard Meyer-Sickendiek, *Affektpoetik: Eine Kulturgeschichte literarischer Emotionen* (Würzburg: Königshausen und Neumann, 2005).

18. See Albrecht Koschorke, *Körperströme und Schriftverkehr: Mediologie des 18. Jahrhunderts* (München: Wilhelm Fink, 1999), 9.

19. Alexander Košenina, *Anthropologie und Schauspielkunst: Studien zur "eloquentia corporis" im 18. Jahrhundert* (Tübingen: Max Niemeyer, 1995), 11; also Hans-Christian

von Herrmann and Bernhard Siegert, "Beseelte Statuen—zuckende Leichen: Medien der Verlebendigung vor und nach Guillaume-Benjamin Duchenne," in *Kaleidoskopien* 3 (2000): 66–105, here 70.

20. Gotthold Ephraim Lessing, *Hamburg Dramaturgy*, trans. Helen Zimmern (New York: Dover Publications, 1962), 13.

21. See Christina Thurner, *Beredte Körper—bewegte Seelen: Zum Diskurs der doppelten Bewegung in Tanztexten* (Bielefeld: transcript, 2009).

22. See Košenina, *Anthropologie und Schauspielkunst*, 11–12.

23. See Günther Heeg, *Das Phantasma der natürlichen Gestalt: Körper, Sprache und Bild im Theater des 18. Jahrhunderts* (Frankfurt: Stroemfeld/Nexus, 2000), esp. 125; also Košenina, *Anthropologie und Schauspielkunst*, 24, who notes that the language of gesture has been a theme since antiquity. He emphasizes, however, that "the interest stimulated by Sulzer in the 'recreation of the inner state of a person' is nonetheless wholly new."

24. See Koschorke, *Körperströme und Schriftverkehr*, 12.

25. The early dance masters such as Johann Pasch, Gottfried Taubert, or Samuel Rudolf Behr, as well as John Weaver in England, already confirm in their writings that they are fully aware that the universal character of their mimetic art reform is a construct.

26. Noverre, *Lettres sur la danse, sur les ballets et les arts*, vol. 2, 107.

27. Johann Jakob Engel, *Ideen zu einer Mimik: Zwei Teile*, reprint of the edition of 1785/86 (Darmstadt: Wissenschaftliche Buchgesellschaft, 1968), 59.

28. Ibid.

29. Ibid.

30. Ibid., 284.

31. See Geitner, *Die Sprache der Verstellung*, 5.

32. Noverre, *Letters on Dancing and Ballets*, Letter IV.

33. See Erika Fischer-Lichte, *Kurze Geschichte des deutschen Theaters* (Tübingen: Francke, 1993), 126–127, in which she speaks with reference to Lessing, among others, of gestural signs as "the result of a complex process of observation, registration, selection and synthesis."

34. See Brandstetter, "Die Bilderschrift der Empfindungen," 91.

35. See Claudia Jeschke, "Vom *Ballet de Cour* zum *Ballet d'Action*: Über den Wandel des Tanzverständnisses im ausgehenden 17. und beginnenden 18. Jahrhundert," in *Le Bourgeois gentilhomme: Problèmes de la comédie-ballet*, ed. Volker Kapp (Paris: Papers on French Seventeenth Century Literature, 1991), 185–223, here 190.

36. Gasparo Angiolini, "Das steinerne Gastmahl," reprint in *Christoph Willibald Gluck: Sämtliche Werke*, ed. Gerhard Croll, Abt. VII: Supplement vol. 1: Libretti: Die originalen Textbücher der bis 1990 in der Gluck-Gesamtausgabe erschienenen Bühnenwerke: Textbücher verschollener Werke, ed. Klaus Hortschansky (Kassel: Bärenreiter, 1995), 177–180, here 179.

37. Noverre, *Letters on Dancing and Ballets*, Letter II, 20.

38. Lucian of Samosata, "The Dance (Saltatio)," in *Lucian of Samosata* (Cambridge, Massachusetts: Harvard University Press; London: William Heinemann, 1960–68), vol. 5 (1962), 209–289, here 283. Of note is the fact that this text was widely read in the German-speaking lands and was translated by Christoph Martin Wieland. It provided a reference for many dance historians, although its status between a fictional, literary text and a serious aesthetic treatise was not always investigated in great detail.

39. Woitas, *Im Zeichen des Tanzes*, 66.
40. Noverre, *Letters on Dancing and Ballets*, Letter II, 16.
41. Ibid., Letter IX, 82.
42. Ibid., Letter VIII, 72.
43. Ibid., Letter X, 103.
44. Ibid., Letter I, 13.
45. Ibid., Letter VIII, 62.
46. As early as 1700, dance theorists had established that the impression that the dancer made on the audience was subject to certain cultural conventions, which were, however, obscured by the truthful-seeming nature of that impression. The Leipzig dance master Gottfried Taubert, for example, made clear in 1717 that the reality behind the fact that "ballets are now staged in all corners of the earth" was the role of artists as cultural translators, and it was this which allowed their work to spread from one people to another; Gottfried Taubert, *Rechtschaffener Tantzmeister oder gründliche Erklärung der Frantzösischen Tantz=Kunst*, reprint of the Leipzig edition 1717, ed. Kurt Petermann (Leipzig: Zentralantiquariat der DDR, 1976), 934.
47. Cf. Jean-Jacques Rousseau, *The Collected Writings of Rousseau*, vol. 10, eds. Alan Bloom et al. (Hanover: The University Press of New England, 2004), 253–352.
48. International Dance Committee, http://iti-worldwide.org/danceday.html, 12.6.2009.
49. Waltz in: Unesco, http://portal.unesco.org/culture/en/files/33748/11769011899International_Dance_Day_Message.pdf/International%2BDance%2BDay%2BMessage.pdf, 12.6.2009. Editors' Note: For another view of Sasha Waltz, see the essay by Jens Richard Giersdorf in this volume. For another view on cultural translation in dance, see the essay by Gabriele Klein in this volume.
50. See Sabine Huschka, *Moderner Tanz: Konzepte—Stile—Utopien* (Reinbek: Rowohlt, 2002), 21.

2. Lola Montez and Spanish Dance in the 19th Century

CLAUDIA JESCHKE

The concept of alterity has often been applied in studies on the discourse about women in nineteenth-century dance.[1] These studies focus predominantly on male fantasies of otherness, and their projection onto the female body through strategies of containment and control. Yet as the example of the self-declared Spanish dancer Lola Montez (c. 1820–1861) demonstrates, otherness can also provide particular insights into a woman's own discourse. Apart from her specific style of dance, Montez also produced a number of successful writings, among them her *Memoirs* (1851), *Lectures of Lola Montez, (Countess of Landsfeld) Including Her Autobiography* (1858), and *The Arts of Beauty; or, Secrets of a Lady's Toilet. With Hints to Gentlemen on the Art of Fascinating* (1858).[2] While Montez established dilettantism as a transgressive quality in dance, her texts display her potential to self-fashion through stylized femininity, professional marketing of her public persona, and provocation of social morals. In contrast to the above-mentioned male discourse, the female performer deployed alterity as a mode of emancipation.

The sociologist Alois Hahn defines alterity as a social "ascription," as the definition of a "relation."[3] For Hahn, being "other" involves two dimensions: the dimension of "being different" and the dimension of "not knowing."[4] Hence Hahn widens the focus of the definition of the other from ethnic difference to diversity even within an ethnic group; he sees alterity as something opaque that cannot be fully analyzed. As encounters with the unknown, experiences of otherness are generally of ambivalent quality. In a positive sense, this can be understood as a chance for a repositioning. Conversely, it can also be experienced as a threat to the (individual and collective) self. The oscillation between these two perceptions leads to either revulsion or the strengthening of one's identity.[5]

The construction of alterity is a historically specific cultural practice. It is therefore necessary to (re-)construct the social, aesthetic, political, and historical systems within which the other is defined. Indeed, alterity must be understood as a dual process of production and reception. The goals of producing otherness, the commercial forms this production takes, and the location of its reception within the cultural field must all be considered.

Lola Montez provides an apposite example for studying the construction of alterity, as a brief biography of the dancer reveals: Eliza Gilbert staged herself as the "Spanish dancer" Lola Montez—whose name and (supposedly Spanish) origin and profession are invented, fictitious. Without being a trained dancer, Lola Montez traveled to European and non-European countries. As the mistress of the Bavarian King Ludwig I, she became a dubious celebrity in Bavaria—in the course of the political upheavals around 1848, his love for her cost him his throne.[6]

Her traveling is similar to that of other famous ballerinas of her time; but in contrast to them, she insisted on a transnational biography. In her memoirs, Montez presents herself as a "global player": "Irish through my father, Spanish through my mother, English through my education, French by inclination and cosmopolitan through the circumstances, I can say of myself that I belong to all nations or none."[7]

As a survival strategy and through a mixture of cold reasoning, playfulness, and narcissism, she appropriated (contemporarily innovative) strategies of consuming and producing alterity in a web of newly developed media and forms of presentation. The illustrated press provided a perfect second "stage" for Montez's spectacles; her scandalous performances fueled critical comments by the (primarily male) reviewers and caricatures by the (primarily male) caricaturists, which gratified the (also male?!) readers lusting for sensation.[8] Later in her life—no longer just as a dancer, but as a writer—she also endeavored to elicit positive reactions from female audiences. The fact that Lola Montez was known over a period of twenty years—throughout Europe and in the British "colonies," United States, and Australia—was also due to these forms of reception. As a protagonist of alterity and a privileged visual object, Montez became a target of public discussion, a media star, a cult star.

Even when Lola Montez presented herself as Spanish, she represented multiple identities and attracted her contemporaries precisely through the embodiment of various different facets of otherness. Lola Montez—such is my thesis—administrated various possible forms of alterity in the mid–nineteenth century; she drew on the categories of Spanishness as a form of exoticism, dance, and the feminine, with the Spanish functioning as a focus or catalyst of this heterogeneity.[9] Employing Hahn's terminology, one can say that Lola Montez established a dynamic relationality of alterity by appropriating different identities—through consumption, production, marketing, and the resulting reception of this undertaking. Lola Montez is a suitable object for study in this volume because she was uniquely aware of the discourses surrounding the profession of dance in the nineteenth century, and manipulated them to her own advantage.

Identity I: The Spanish Dancer

On June 3, 1843, a poster for Her Majesty's Theatre in London announced Lola Montez's debut as a Spanish dancer: "between the acts of opera, DONNA LOLA MONTEZ, of the Teatro Real, Sevilla, will have the honor to make her first appearance in England in the Original Spanish dance *El Oleano*."[10] When it became known after the first performances that Lola was neither Spanish nor had been employed by the Teatro Real, the interest in her performances became even greater (Figure 2.1). With her "authentic" Spanish dance, she hit a nerve of popular culture: contemporary hispanomania in theatrical and ballroom dance. In the 1830s and 1840s, Spanish dance circulated widely and Fanny Elssler and Marie Taglioni were acknowledged as famous performers of the *escuela bolera*.[11] While these two dancers—as well as many others—integrated national dances into their stage repertoire, Lola Montez, as mentioned above, did not have significant dance training. Probably in 1842, only a year before her debut, she began familiarizing herself with the techniques of Spanish dance with the help of a ballet master from the Opéra. By her own account, she also spent substantial periods of time in Spain for in-depth study; although this claim, like many others, cannot be verified, it shows that she wanted to give the appearance of originality and authenticity to her dancing.

Despite significant differences among contemporaneous dance theories, reviews, and iconographic sources, all the documents emphasize three characteristics attributed to Southern European (including Spanish) dances. The special, "other" corporeality of the dancers, particularly with reference to female beauty, was foregrounded through the heightened visibility of body parts such as the eyes (and sometimes eyebrows), the lips (and teeth), and skin color. Further, while the work of the legs was less virtuosic than in traditional ballet, arms and hands showed a considerable range of movement and expressivity. With great precision, the sources describe the emotional interaction between the dancer(s) and the spectators—the dance has a dramatic, mimetic component as it mediates a story. And the documents accentuate the rhythmic component, which is produced or supported by the dancers themselves through the use of instruments such as castanets and the tambourine. The specific corporeality, audience interaction, and rhythm were essential factors in the staging practices of Southern European dances; they allowed for the development of a body-oriented and dynamic repertoire of movement different from traditional

Figure 2.1. Maria Countess of Landsfeld (Lola Montez). Steel engraving by Joseph Karl Stieler, 1847. Sheet 16 of King Ludwig I of Bavaria's Gallery of Beauties. Derra de Moroda Dance Archive.

stage dance. The classically trained dancers, Fanny Elssler, Marie Taglioni, and Fanny Cerito, all incorporated these qualities into their performances as a way of transgressing traditional dance models.

At her debut in London, Montez received particular praise for her *El Oleano*, a hybrid dance that resembled an Italian tarantella in Hispanic guise. Despite the choreographed nature of this presentation, a review mentions the national authenticity of the dancing, distinguishing it from the Spanish dances by performers such as Elssler and Taglioni: "El Olano [sic] is, like the Cachuca [sic]—not the Cachuca of Duvernay, Elssler, or Cerito—an intensely national dance, and will be as new to the generality of English eyes as we believe it to be beautiful."[12] The critic refers to the visual effect of her dancing when he continues with the description of the characteristics of the Italian Tarantella, a dance that was often fashioned to embody the frenzy induced by a tarantula's bite: "The head lifted and thrown back, the flashing eye, the fierce and protruded foot which crushed the insect, make a subject for the painter which would scarcely be easy to forget."[13] In London, *El Oleano* was staged in a moorish room in the Alhambra; a Spanish wall was positioned in front of the exit in the center of the back part of the stage; moreover, Benjamin Lumley, the artistic director of Her Majesty's Theatre had placed ballet girls on stage. Lumley himself thought of Montez's style as new, surprising and provocative, emphasizing that " . . . she was but the veriest novice in her art, which she had never studied, *as an art*, at all."[14] Lumley was one of many to observe the obvious discrepancy between Lola Montez's beauty, which did in fact seem "Spanish," and the quality of her artistic performance.[15]

In her first period as a dancer between 1843 and 1846, Lola Montez's repertoire was exclusively made up of dances with Spanish names, including *La Sevilliana, Los Boleros de Cádiz, La Saragossa, Cachucha,* and the already mentioned *El Oleano*. After a pause of almost five years triggered by her liaison with Ludwig I in Munich, she took up her career as a dancer again in 1851 and expanded her repertoire by including other national dances, albeit using them in a similarly unspecific—i.e., historically or locally indefinable—way, just as she had with the Spanish tarantella *El Oleano*: "The Countess put herself under the artistic guidance of Monsieur Mabille, the proprietor of the famous Jardin Mabille, an open-air dance hall in the Champs Elysées far more renowned among admirers of beautiful women than among connoisseurs of dance. Mabille choreographed several dances for the countess, among them a tarantella (probably related to the 'Oleano' of her London debut), a Bavarian dance, a Hungarian dance, and a Tyrolean dance."[16]

At the beginning of Lola Montez's career in the 1840s, ballroom dance as well as stage dance were similarly characterized by the inclusion of national dances in their respective repertoires. This meant that in the understanding of theory, pedagogy, and choreography, ballroom and stage dance were treated as equals. Around 1850, however, dance teachers began to distinguish the two fields. The national dances were no longer simply additions to the stage dance repertoire, but they also revolutionized ballroom dance in unprecedented ways through the introduction of new interactive styles. Even though Lola Montez's artistic abilities had only partly satisfied the professional and aesthetic expectations of audiences and reviewers during the first stage of her career, her comparatively greater authenticity—which had after all been registered positively—contributed to the emancipation of national dances from the stage and paved the way for their amateurization and commercialization. What is more, the fact that the little-trained Montez had promoted highly effective forms of dilettantism in dance made the cultural translation of stage dances into ballroom dances even more attractive. Montez, in turn, reacted to the increased popularity of social dancing and presented a more varied repertoire, which she developed with Monsieur Mabille. To an even greater degree than in her earlier performances, Montez employed instinct and taste, rather than skill and knowledge, to construct the second successful stage of her career.

In her memoirs, Montez claims that she executed "the expressive dances of [her] country *instinctively*, . . . in the way [she] might have danced them on the lap of [her] mother in Sevilla"[17] and that she was simultaneously "dancer" and "woman" and knew that she "was beautiful and . . . had to please in the *wild fervor* [of the] movements."[18] Thus, Montez emphasizes her femininity, passionate display, and freedom of movement, depicting these characteristics as typically Spanish, in order to commercialize herself as a "native" Spanish dancer in non-Spanish societies. In this effort, we see that Montez instinctively directed her repertoire of signifying gestures and movements to inscribe her elected national identity.

Lola Montez made use of Western notions of Spanishness in order to market the product Donna Montez. Her passionate, rhythmic movement suggested to critics an "inner involvement," which they associated with Montez's (fictitious) national, ethnic "instinct." The classification of her dance as visually appealing (through her feminine, Spanish persona) and as not distanced (through her seemingly spontaneous and direct way of performing) appears to be an essential reason why it was perceived as more authentic and Spanish than the shows of other (professional) dancers. Lola Montez did not conceive of her movements as artifacts but as the expression of her Spanish character—and thus contributed to their authentification.[19]

In 1851, the influential critic Théophile Gautier praised the skill of Lola Montez in her second debut at the Opéra which he traced back to her lessons with Mabille. Before that, however, he had manifested an ambivalent relation to her performances: he appreciated Montez's dancing in the Théâtre de Porte Saint-Martin in 1845 after having written a negative review of the evening at the Opéra a year earlier.[20] Gautier's 1851 reaction might suggest the new stance toward dance taken by critics and spectators during this period—a stance that points to the diminishing importance of traditional aesthetic skill and the increasing degree of stimulating performative qualities, which are notable in Lola Montez's performances.

Incidentally the critics—usually men—give only meager bits of information concerning the actual performative elements of Lola's shows[21] and, as was common during this period, concentrate instead on their visual impressions of Montez's bodily merits.[22] Nor do the contemporary illustrations show a dance-specific engagement with her productions; they are mainly portraits or, remarkably, caricatures. Thus, they depict Montez's artistic achievements in a comic, distorted, exaggerated way and recurrently focus on the representation of a single pose.

Figure 2.2 shows Montez, not particularly Spanish, in a so-called arabesque: a very unstable position, she stands on the tip of her toe on one leg while the other one is stretched to the back; both arms point downward. Images of Elssler or Taglioni are more neutral and descriptive; even if they include idealizing characteristics, they usually display a signature pose from the respective national dance. Often, they focus on the dancer alone. In the case of Montez iconography, however, the caricaturists, without exception, add a satirically interpretive level by including the exaggerated reactions of audience members in their depictions.[23] Hence, Montez's visual representation was continually

Figure 2.2. Caricature of Lola Montez, artist and original publication unknown. Derra de Moroda Dance Archive.

subject to commentary, just as her real appearances always triggered a chain of critical appraisals.

The cartoonists don't always localize Lola Montez's performances on a theater stage; rather, they portray her various social surroundings. The liaison with the Bavarian King Ludwig I is probably the best known and most closely documented entanglement of two of Lola Montez's identities: one as a dancer and another as a socialite who presented herself at several important royal houses and courts. It is in this liaison that Montez excelled in the staging of the different levels of alterity—Spanishness, dance, and the feminine. Hence, on the one hand, she was antibourgeois and anarchistic and embodied an early form of the femme fatale; but as lover and wife, on the other hand, she exhibited bourgeois, traditionally feminine traits.

Montez's ability to switch back and forth between different social realms becomes visible in her many journeys and was emphasized in contemporaneous depictions of her as a "romantic character," transgressing the limits of "ordinary Philistine life."[24] When her biographer Paul Erdmann makes this observation, he gives her an unsteady, gypsylike allure that was perceived as fascinating but was also associated with feigning, cheating. This ambivalence followed a broader cultural perception of those who appeared to be Spanish, gypsylike, and bohemian: in 1841, the art critic Charles Roehn pointed out that Spanishness was considered an antibourgeois pose sanctioned by the bourgeoisie that thus contained reactionary potential.[25]

Identity II: Author of an Autobiography

With the publication of her autobiography in 1858, Lola Montez created another forum for self-dramatization and marketing. With this product, she attached herself to the group of writing women—not only authors proper but also suffragettes and actresses—a development that literary scholar Mary Jean Corbett has examined for Victorian England.[26] Corbett claims that in the nineteenth century, the actress was seen as the prototype of the unconventional woman who could embody all roles—an observation that can easily be applied to Lola Montez. As Corbett further points out, women in the public sphere turned into divided subjects; their participation in public life excluded the communication of aspects of their private preoccupations. Thus, when an actress wrote an autobiography, it rarely contained any information on her private life, but rather concentrated on factual reports as if the public role absorbed her personal identity. Lola Montez breached this pattern. Her autobiography oscillates between the public and the private, blurring this boundary. The appropriation and marketing of a Spanish identity, understood as a sensual-aggressive product of an extraordinary feminine beauty, further determines the form and publication of her memoirs.[27] Beginning in February 1858, she read selections from her memoirs to rather closed, small audiences "in persona" and also planned the serial publication of her "autobiography" in the magazines *Le Figaro* and *Le Pays*. Ultimately, both declined the contract.[28] Nevertheless, this represents another marketing strategy that took advantage of the burgeoning nineteenth century practice of commercializing mass literature by publishing the serialized novel in illustrated newspapers. For authors, this process guaranteed a swift distribution of their product while the editors made use of this format to increase their sales.

This edition of her autobiography appeared in 1858 in London under the title *Lectures of Lola Montez, (Countess of Landsfeld) Including Her Autobiography*. In the *Lectures*, she argues from a populist feminist viewpoint, which also dominates the content of her book *The Arts of Beauty; or, Secrets of a Lady's Toilet. With Hints to Gentlemen on the Art of Fascinating*, published in the same year.[29] As is so frequently the case in her biography, here, too, her approach is simultaneously pragmatic and progressive: on the one hand, she represents bourgeois norms concerning, for instance, her wish for social status or the theme of feminine beauty; on the other hand, she deviates from such norms by rejecting marriage or by conceiving of beauty as something produced by women themselves. In both cases, she directly addresses women as consumers of her book; she makes use of her own market value, and similarly recognizes that of her female readers. Montez writes:

> If, however, a lady wishes to use such helps to beauty, I must advise her, by all means, to become her own manufacturer—not only as a matter of economy, but of safety—as many of the patent cosmetics have ruined the finest complexions, and induced diseases of the skin and the nervous system.[30]

And further:

> All women know that it is *beauty*, rather than *genius*, which all generations of men have worshipped in our sex.... When men speak of the *intellect* of women, they speak critically, tamely, coldly; but when they come to speak of the *charms of a beautiful woman*, both their language and their eyes kindle with the glow of an enthusiasm, which shows them to be profoundly, if not, indeed, ridiculously in earnest. It is a part of our natural sagacity to perceive all this, and we should be enemies to ourselves if we did not employ every allowable art to become the goddesses of that adoration. Preach to the contrary as you may, there still stands the eternal fact, that the world has yet allowed no higher "mission" to woman, than to be beautiful.[31]

All the chapters in *The Arts of Beauty* emphasize that a "natural" approach to beauty also strengthens the independent disposition of a woman. They show a development in Montez's biography in which the idea of beauty, derived from the image of the Spanish and the foreign, had detached itself from the dancing body and became a product of its own. Beauty is no longer foreign or Spanish but can be produced through cosmetic measures as well as through recourse to the individuality of a woman.[32] The self-marketing found in the autobiography and the beauty advice toward the end of Montez's career, thus largely exclude dance and the figure of the Spanish other from the essential facets of her identity and concentrate instead on the ethnically unmarked feminine.

Identity III: The Critic of the Critics

As we have seen, the years of greater activity as a dancer show a much more complex connection between private and public person. They also document yet another variation of how Eliza Gilbert attempted to control her product, Lola Montez, when dealing with the media.

Before her 1843 debut in London, the powerful artistic director Benjamin Lumley arranged a meeting with a journalist who was supposed to predispose critics positively. (I have already mentioned Lumley's interest in Lola Montez's unusualness as well as his clear assessment that she couldn't dance.) Even though it is impossible to construct an immediate connection between the conversation with the press and the reaction to the debut, the success of the performances manifests itself in the reviews. From then on, Lola Montez sought out the press, always in a symbiosis of private person and dancer—for example, as lover, as hostess, or as star in interviews.[33] Especially when the media discussed her private sphere, her Spanish origin or her daily examples of inappropriate, i.e., nonbourgeois behavior, Lola Montez would react through letters to the editor, counterstatements, with personal visits of protest directed at the respective press representatives. "The lady perched herself in our office on Tuesday, for the space of four hours, with the view of impressing upon us the identity of her person—she presented herself subsequently at our private residence, and in the evening we saw her at the Opera . . ."[34] an anonymous journalist of *Age* writes, slightly annoyed. It is questionable whether Montez really felt hurt by the journalists' representations of her and needed to defend herself or whether she simply wanted to remain in the media and might even have invented reasons, insults, attacks against her person to reply to them in order to increase publicity. The relatively accurate article on her origin that appeared in the *Pictorial Times* in 1847, for example, could in fact have threatened her relationship with Ludwig I. Hence it is understandable (if not particularly feminine) that Montez immediately took action and sent letters to all the leading newspapers in Paris, London, and Germany defending her Spanish origin.[35] Later on, she used the same strategy for her evening talks as for her dance productions. It is interesting that Lola Montez used the press in relation to dance or her lectures only when this created publicity; all the same she turned violent when the public challenged the "taboo" of the supposed integrity of her bourgeois and/or dance-related Spanish identities.

With her theatrical—and some would say, hysterical[36]—ways of behaving, Lola Montez shifted the center of attention from the (artistic) stage into the (social) foyer. She understood her professional activity mainly as the audience-oriented marketing of her person, a self-managed product. While accepting the reactions of spectators as well as critics in the field of her identity as a dancer, she refuted them in other areas in order to improve the market value of her performances. In the field of her Spanish and feminine identities, she actively intervened in the opinion-making processes of the press. Lola Montez turned into an aggressive critic of the media when they refused to accept the Spanish illusion of her personality; hence, just like the press, the foyer became a second stage for her.[37]

Although Taglioni and Elssler—as well as other dancers who were raised within the institution of the theater—were primarily discovered by men, usually from their own nuclear or extended family, Montez came from a bourgeois family and did not stand in any a priori relation to the theater or media world. In this sense, she can be seen as the creator of herself, acting as her own promoter, demanding letters of recommendation from powerful men, including noblemen, bankers, publishers, and industrialists. She never exclusively functioned within the institution stage. Rather, the "other" aspects of her dancing, the Spanish and the feminine, interacted dynamically with each other while also being controlled by Montez.

The example of Lola Montez is representative of a more general trend in the dance world around 1850, where dance technique or the analysis of movement was no longer the primary criterion for defining alterity in dance; rather, the construction of originality, authenticity, origin, and race filled this role. Moreover, other important aspects for the marketing of dancers—particularly those characterized as other—were their beauty and dubious morals, as defined by bourgeois society. In no way did this harm their market value; on the contrary, beauty and moral laxity contributed to the expectation of their availability. Thus, "other" morals, deviating positively or negatively from one's own, were an additional point of attraction in iconography, literature, and dance. Lola Montez marketed both her theatrical otherness as well as her private otherness so that they worked together in a mutual symbiosis. Issues of credibility, whether of her dancing skills or her national identity, only enhanced her notoriety, and thus her public presence.

In the case of Lola Montez, exhibition and marketing, staging and consuming condition each other and constantly create new transitions between her three essential identities sketched here. As a beautiful Spanish dancer, she embodies the other; as author, she introduces readers to the unknown and makes possible their acquaintance with certain constructions of identity. Further, by publishing the "secrets" of her beauty, she also unveils secrets of femininity and corporeality; and as a critic of critics, she exhibits unusual behavior that oscillates between the usual habits of bourgeois and professional women. Through Montez's efforts, dance in particular became linked to the processes of self-invention, to the multiple identities of Eliza Gilbert alias Lola Montez alias Countess Landsfeld. Montez's specific physical, as well as discursive, conditioning was embedded in a more general preoccupation with (Hispanic) otherness in the dance world of the mid–nineteenth century. But it was her idiosyncratic, provocative behavior, above all, that turned otherness into a strategy for female self-fashioning and emancipation.

Notes

1. See Lynn Garafola, ed., *Rethinking the Sylph: New Perspectives on the Romantic Ballet* (Hanover: Wesleyan University Press, 1997) and Felicia McCarren, *Dance Pathologies: Performance, Poetics, Medicine* (Stanford: Stanford University Press, 1998).

2. Lola Montez (Gräfin von Landsfeld), *Memoiren 1851*, ed. Kerstin Wilhelms (Frankfurt: Zweitausendeins, 1986); Lola Montez, *Lectures of Lola Montez, (Countess of Landsfeld) Including Her Autobiography* (London: Gilbert, 1858); Lola Montez, *The Arts of Beauty; or, Secrets of a Lady's Toilet. With Hints to Gentlemen on the Art of Fascinating* (New York: Dick and Fitzgerald, 1858).

3. Alois Hahn, *Konstruktionen des Selbst, der Welt und der Geschichte* (Frankfurt: Suhrkamp, 2000), 31.

4. Ibid., 33.

5. Ibid., 151.

6. When Ludwig I naturalized his beloved Lola Montez and made her the Countess Landsfeld, the aristocratic government resigned and there were demonstrations against the persona non grata. Lola Montez left the country. When rumors suggested that Lola Montez had returned to Munich, she was not only—and again—the target of the conservative aristocrats who wanted her out of the country (and distant from the king), she also became the model for the free-minded citizens for whom she demonstrated sympathy. In response to the revolts, Ludwig had to agree to having the government withdraw Lola Montez's citizenship; he resigned. Cf. Michael Ruhland, "Ach Lolitta. 1848 begehren die deutschen Bürger auf—in München freilich gegen die Mätresse des Königs," *Süddeutsche Zeitung*, January 19/20, 2008, 46.

7. Montez, *Memoiren*, 25. Lola Montez was born as Eliza Gilbert in Ireland, and in 1823 the family moved to India; when her father died and her mother remarried, she was sent back to Europe in 1826 and raised in an English boarding school. She married at age seventeen and returned to India with her husband, but she left him after a few years and arrived in Southampton as Lola Montez in 1841. [Editors' Note: For a contemporary approach to transnationalism in dance, see Gabriele Klein's essay in this volume.]

8. For the discourse on dancers in the press, see John V. Chapman, "Jules Janin: Ro-

mantic Critic," in Garafola, *Rethinking the Sylph*, 197–244; Lucia Ruprecht, "'Elle danse, tout est dit'—die Metapher des Poetischen in der Kritik des romantischen Balletts," in *Souvenirs de Taglioni*, ed. Gunhild Oberzaucher-Schüller, vol. 2 (Munich: Kieser, 2007), 333–344; Christina Thurner, "In eine andere Welt gehoben: Théophile Gautiers Diskurs der Emphase," ibid., 345–356.

9. Editors' Note: For a detailed discussion of dance and exoticism in the nineteenth century, see Claudia Jeschke, Gabi Vettermann, and Nicole Haitzinger, *Interaktion und Rhythmus: Zur Modellierung von Fremdheit im Tanztheater des 19. Jahrhunderts* (Munich: epodium, 2010).

10. Poster in the Derra de Moroda Dance Archives, Salzburg.

11. Nancy Lee Chalfa Ruyter, "La Escuela Bolera," *Dance Chronicle* 16:2 (1993): 249–257; Javier Suárez-Pajares and Xoán M. Carreira, eds., "The Origins of the Bolero School," *Studies in Dance History* IV:1 (Spring 1993); Claudia Jeschke, Gabi Vettermann, and Nicole Haitzinger, *Les Choses espagnoles. Research into the Hispanomania of 19th Century Dance* (München: epodium, 2009).

12. *Morning Post* (London), June 3, 1843, quoted from Bruce Seymour, *Lola Montez. A Life* (New Haven: Yale University Press, 1996), 34.

13. Ibid., 34.

14. Concerning Lumley's view of Lola Montez, see Benjamin Lumley, *Reminiscences of the Opera* (London: Hurst and Blackett, 1864), 77.

15. *London Illustrated Life*, July 16, 1843, 229: "Nature has done much—art but little—for this daughter of Spain. We duly appreciate the beauties of her person, but are compelled . . . [to observe that the] admiration excited by the graceful management of arm and pliancy of waist exhibited in the Cachucha-like movements of *El Oleano* suffered much diminution by the want of firmness and precision in those, to a dancer, all-important members, the legs and feet." Similarly: *Gautier on Dance*, ed. and trans. Ivor Guest (London: Dance Books, 1986), 130, 159.

16. Seymour; *Lola Montez*, 277. Mabille Père (Lahire Mabille), who earned a fortune through the organization of the famous public balls in the Jardin Mabille, was the father of Charles Mabille, the preferred dance partner of Augusta Maywood (also temporarily her husband and the father of her child). See Maureen Needham Costonis, "'The Wild Doe': Augusta Maywood in Philadelphia and Paris, 1837–1840," *Dance Chronicle* 2 (1994): 141.

17. Montez, *Memoiren*, 69.

18. Ibid., 471f.

19. See Dean McCannel's term of "staged authenticity" in "Staged Authenticity. Arrangements of Social Space in Tourist Settings," *Journal of American Sociology* 79 (1973): 589–603.

20. One explanation of this change of mind would be that Gautier was house critic of *La Presse*, owned by (among others) Alexandre Henri Dujarier, Lola's lover in 1845.

21. Lola Montez primarily performed as a soloist; the first London performance, however, also already points to other forms of performance, featuring her within a decorative group as well as in duos either with a woman or a man. Seymour, *Lola Montez*, 51. In general, Montez followed the strategy of scheduling her guest performances only for short periods of time in order not to invite weariness concerning her small repertoire and her limited abilities; she mainly focused on the alluring effect of her performances.

22. The observations made by Luise von Kobell, a contemporary from Munich, are not essentially different from the descriptions of her male colleagues. See Reinhold Rauh and Bruce Seymour, *Ludwig I. und Lola Montez. Der Briefwechsel*, (New York: Prestel, 1995), 11.

23. For a typical image see ibid., 32, fig. 15.

24. Paul Erdmann, *Lola Montez und die Jesuiten. Eine Darstellung der jüngsten Ereignisse in München* (Hamburg: Hoffmann und Campe, 1847), 14.

25. "One must pay his tribute to fortune, must buy his reputation, so to speak. . . . We have said, that there exists a fashion in pictures. In order to be in fashion, in other words, to be in vogue, you have to be known. If you don't have real merit, but are convincing, you can manage to extort a momentary vogue; you will be flattered by a coterie of journalists, or you will have the talent to insinuate yourself into the good graces of some high and powerful amateur whose protection will have influence on your reputation as an eminent man." In *Physiology of the Art Market*, 1841, quoted from Marilyn R. Brown, *Gypsies and Other Bohemians. The Myth of the Artist in Nineteenth-Century France* (Ann Arbor: University of Michigan Research Press, 1985), 10.

26. Mary Jane Corbett, *Representing Femininity. Middle-Class Subjectivity in Victorian and Edwardian Women's Autobiographies* (New York: Oxford University Press, 1992).

27. "[P]ractically the whole of the Autobiography of Lola Montez was written for her (on a profit-sharing agreement) by a clerical collaborator, the Rev. Chauncey Burr," claims Horace Wyndham, *The Magnificent Montez from Courtesan to Convert* (London: Hutchinson, 1935), 230.

28. Ibid., 231.

29. The 50(!) instructions for gentlemen on how they can have a fascinating effect on women are as amusing as ironic.

30. Montez, *The Arts of Beauty*, xii.

31. Ibid., xv.

32. To the extent that being a woman was linked with physical beauty, beautiful women were increasingly used for marketing beauty products for the upper class; working-class women could neither afford the glossy magazines in which the advertisements appeared nor the promoted products, nor did they have the time to apply them. Lola Montez makes use of this marketing strategy but also subverts it by promoting natural beauty, beauty that can be achieved with simple cheap household remedies.

33. Seymour, *Lola Montez*, 74, 278, 332.

34. Ibid., 40.

35. Ibid., 149.

36. E.g., Reinhold Rauh, "Von Lola Montez bis Madonna," in *Lola Montez oder eine Revolution in München*, ed. Thomas Weidner (München: Stadtmuseum/Edition Minerva, 1998), 115.

37. Corbett, *Representing Femininity*, 20. In general, the ability of marketing, as Corbett claims, presented an essential condition of professionalism. As she further explains, the ideology of being professional mystifies the relation between producer and consumer through the specification of knowledge rather than through the specification of the product; it is mainly a function of how the product can be exchanged on the market. This function can be created only through a professional corpus, regardless of whether it is one of an individual practitioner like Lola Montez or one of a corporation. In this sense, Montez established her professional status outside of these institutions.

3. Picturing Palucca at the Bauhaus

SUSAN FUNKENSTEIN

Gret Palucca quickly ascended to dance stardom in the 1920s. Born in 1902, Palucca received her dance training at Mary Wigman's pioneering Dresden studio in the early 1920s and was among the first generation of Wigman students, including Vera Skoronel and Hanya Holm, to go on to innovate in the world of dance.[1] Prominent dance critics recognized Palucca's talent while she was still a student, and in 1925 Palucca left Wigman and opened her own Dresden-based dance studio, rivaling her former mentor for students and fame. Known for her careerist drive, Palucca toured extensively and became one of the most recognized dancers of the mid- and late 1920s. With signature movements of airborne springs, dramatic lunges, and high leg extensions, her rhythmic, geometric, and optimistic dancing style was noted by some critics as a balance of contrasts: strength and softness, pushing out and pulling in, light innocence and seriousness. Youthfully pretty, and regularly featured in books, dance reviews, and women's magazines, the much-celebrated Palucca was portrayed—and portrayed herself—as an avant-garde performer and a mass-media star.

During her career ascent, Palucca positioned herself in close proximity to visual artists, and she especially touted her relationship with artists at the Bauhaus, the innovative school for art and design in Weimar Germany.[2] During her visits to the Bauhaus, which began with her first performance there on March 18, 1925, Palucca performed in formal and informal venues, posed for photographs, and socialized with the faculty, such as Wassily Kandinsky, Paul Klee, and László Moholy-Nagy. Equally noteworthy, she partied with the students. Between visits, Palucca corresponded with artists about art acquisitions and assigned her dance pupils to write essays about modern art; in turn, Bauhaus artists visited her in Dresden, met with her after her performances, and wrote statements about her dancing that were published in her promotional materials. And, they created works of art inspired by those experiences.

This Palucca-Bauhaus interdisciplinary engagement was due to Palucca's strong efforts, but she also chose to interact with an institution that strove to bring the arts together. At its founding, the Bauhaus was modeled after the ideal of the Gothic cathedral, in which artists and craftspeople collaborated to build soaring structures of spiritual and civic pride. Pedagogically, all Bauhaus students took the Preliminary Course and introductory courses in form and color, taught by Josef Albers, Johannes Itten, Kandinsky, Klee, and Moholy-Nagy, and these theoretical and aesthetic principles served as shared foundations for later work in media-specific workshops.

The Bauhaus ideal of unity, however, frequently did not correspond to its more fractured reality. Concerned that female students would dominate the institution, Bauhaus masters accepted limited numbers of women into the school and curtailed women's artistic and design training to those media deemed "decorative," namely the weaving workshop.[3] Officially, the Bauhaus assumed a new aesthetic identity in 1923, in which the emotionalism and trembling lines of expressionism gave way to the hard-edged constructivism captured by the slogan "Art and Technology, a New Unity," but ongoing infighting regarding this aesthetic shift continued for years. Moreover, the Bauhaus's already turbulent town-gown relationship and financial state reached a crisis during the mid-1920s, as pressures on both fronts in 1925 forced the closure of the Weimar campus and the institution's relocation to the city of Dessau. Palucca's March 1925 premiere in Weimar happened to coincide with this particularly stressful moment. In this context, it is understandable why Klee wrote wistfully of Palucca's 1925 dance concert that her efforts "brought her that otherwise infrequent unanimous praise from our former Weimar community."[4]

How did Palucca manage to receive that elusive "unanimous praise"? And if women were envisioned as a threat to the institution, why was Palucca so popular with both masters and students, male and female alike? Palucca succeeded, I would argue, because of her ability to fulfill a wide range of artistic and personal needs and priorities. Savvy regarding her relationships with these celebrated, promising, and well-connected artists, she presented a clear dancing style, yet did so in a manner that served as conduits and triggers for the Bauhaus artists' own aesthetic issues, gender concerns, and relationships with modernity. The complexity of her performance of gender, which intersected with the Bauhaus's contradictory attitudes and policies about women, contributed to interpretations of Palucca as both—and simultaneously—androgynous and girlish, athletic and diminutive, career-driven and flirtatious. Although not limited to a single style or medium, artistic depictions of Palucca were all decidedly modern, as if the clean lines, geometric precision, or tilted angles of Bauhaus work correlated to the perceived innovations of her dancing style and New Woman image.

So, why is my focus on dance at the Bauhaus on Palucca and not Oskar Schlemmer, the dance choreographer and master of the Theater Workshop? After all, the Bauhaus promoted Schlemmer as the leader of performance at the institution, and the 1925 publication *Die Bühne im Bauhaus* (The Theater of the Bauhaus) positioned him philosophically and pedagogically at the center of Bauhaus stagings of the body.[5] Postwar publications solidified his reputation as the preeminent voice of Bauhaus dance, and even though published student reminiscences extolled the excitement for performance at the Bauhaus, few sources mentioned Palucca.[6] Moreover, Schlemmer's costumes and choreographies complement the aesthetic of the Bauhaus. The abstraction of the body through the geometric marionette-inspired costumes, the corporeal movement along the spatial axes of the stage, and the use of metallic materials and effects all reflected Bauhaus priorities of abstraction, grids, and technology.

In contrast, Palucca was largely written out of much postwar scholarship on Weimar dance. Writers on Weimar dance focused on choreographers in West Germany or English-speaking countries, but Palucca's decision to remain in East Germany after World War II marginalized her from this network.[7] It is ironic because she was among the most famous German dancers of the 1920s in large part because of her approachability. Unlike Schlemmer, Palucca revealed her body, performing bare-legged and without masks. She played with gender, but unlike her mentor Wigman, Palucca did not challenge traditional structures of viewing, thereby facilitating a spectator's visual pleasure and desire for the dancer.[8] But like many dancers of the 1920s, she shared with Schlemmer a concern for the configuration of the body in space, and in this way both dancers embodied Bauhaus principles. To focus on Palucca's performance style coupled with the images of her from Bauhaus artists thus affords us a view of the art school that is distinct from the standard narrative of Bauhaus dance.

Unlike most other German-language studies of Palucca's relationship with the visual arts that focus on senior artists, I emphasize here her relationship with Bauhaus students and junior faculty.[9] This illuminates the broader interest in Palucca at the Bauhaus and the collaborative interactions she had with people closer to her own age. Running against a master narrative approach, in which singular works by well-known senior (and male) artists are emphasized, my approach also recuperates a history of dance at the Bauhaus in which dance functioned as a part of everyday life and as a site for women's creative expression. Methodologically, I am working within the interdiscipline of German studies, at the intersections of dance history, art history, and gender studies. As such, my essay reveals the variety of modernisms that thrived in the 1920s through their exchanges with dance and illuminates visual artists' respect for the impressive physical and creative feats of the female dancing body.

* * *

Palucca's status as a prominent Bauhaus guest and an art world darling were due in part to her impeccable connections. In January 1924 Palucca married Friedrich "Fritz" Bienert, and from the beginnings of their marriage until their divorce in 1930, Bienert played a strong role in steering Palucca's career. His efforts also undermined Palucca's projected image of an independent woman in charge of her own career, which she touted later in life.[10] Much of his clout derived from his family. His sister Ise (née Ilse) studied at the Bauhaus and provided her close friend Palucca with a distinct understanding of and relationship to the institution, its people, and its aesthetics. Fritz and Ise's mother Ida, widely recognized for her illustrious modern art collection, cultivated relationships with artists, including many Bauhaus faculty; by 1933, for example, her collection comprised thirty-eight works by Klee, ten by Kandinsky, and numerous others by masters Lyonel Feininger, Moholy-Nagy, and Schlemmer, not to mention works by Ernst Ludwig Kirchner and Pablo Picasso.[11]

Maximizing the Bienert family connections was one way in which Palucca and Fritz Bienert promoted her dance career; likewise, the couple paid great attention to her public reception, including the staging and circulation of her images, her reviews in the press, and the desires of her audience. Among her biggest promoters were women's magazines, which were often read by women in their twenties—the age of a Bauhaus student. Palucca's big break, a November 1923 article in the popular bourgeois women's magazine *Die Dame* (The Lady), was published while she was still a student. *Die Dame* critic Pawel Barchan termed her a "Hochtänzerin" (high dancer) given her frequent leaps and springs, in contrast to Wigman's more earthbound "Tieftänzerin" (low dancer) movements.[12] But more frequently, Barchan and other critics described Palucca's dancing as a feeling or personality: optimistic, instinctive, and projecting an almost naive purity not laden with symbolism or intellectualism. And equally, she was a model of the New Woman, the career-minded individualist with the athletic androgynous body and ubiquitous *Bubikopf*, the bob hairstyle widely recognized as the iconic style of the youthful, cosmopolitan, emancipated woman. The critic for the *Jenaische Zeitung*, the local Weimar paper that reviewed Palucca's 1925 performance for the Bauhaus community, focused on these same issues: "Wasn't it rhythmic gymnastics that the young, pretty artist with the fabulously trained body and bob hairstyle presented on stage?"[13]

It was along these lines that the Bauhaus community might have appreciated Palucca's performance. When the *Jenaische Zeitung* review associated Palucca's precision leaping style with rhythmic gymnastics, not to mention her physical appearance as a New Woman, its critic aligned the young dancer with popular trends in German culture that the Bauhaus students also espoused. And yet, Palucca performed primarily to classical music accompaniment and within traditional structures of gendered spectatorship; this may have framed her innovative movements in a way that would have been easier for many members of the Bauhaus faculty to digest.[14] Modern, innovative, and technically impressive, Palucca's emancipation would have made her an ideal role model for the Bauhaus students. And yet, Palucca's choreographic style could frame her as an attractive young woman who was not a threat to male hegemony. In these ways, Palucca's representation of female liberation coincided perfectly with the Bauhaus's own insistence on gender-defined cultural parameters.

As with the gender dynamics within the press and her performances, Palucca's own self-proclamations as an emancipated woman, true as they were in some regards, were undercut by the behind-the-scenes machinations of her husband. Following the Weimar premiere, for example, Bienert strategized how Bauhaus masters could lend their voices to the dancer's promotional materials. Active in steering her career, he expanded the Palucca dance-school brochure for 1926, *Palucca Tanz* (Palucca Dance), to include photographs of Palucca springing in soft-lit studio settings, quotations from glowing press reviews, and statements by prominent intellectuals and artists. These statements were initiated by Palucca's circle, as Bienert's own secretary, masquerading as the not-yet-opened Palucca School secretary, sent letters requesting comments to artists including Kandinsky, Klee, and Moholy-Nagy.[15] The initial impetus was to boost Palucca's avant-garde credentials by enlisting the artists to generate positive press, but it likewise appears that the artists reciprocated amicably and favorably.

In an elaborate example, Kandinsky's essay for *Palucca Tanz*, "Tanzkurven" (Dance Curves), originated as a response to a form letter from the secretary, but Bienert quickly took the reins. Bienert encouraged the artist to turn his statement into a multipage essay and loaned Kandinsky four images by dance photographer Charlotte Rudolph, upon which he based his four drawings. Kandinsky's completed version of "Tanzkurven" was enclosed in a letter sent directly to Bienert and published verbatim in *Das Kunstblatt*, one of the most illustrious cultural journals of the Weimar era, six months later.[16] Kandinsky also included Palucca in his Bauhaus theoretical treatise, *Punkt und Linie zu Fläche* (Point and Line to Plane), completing the manuscript within weeks of submitting "Tanzkurven."[17] His final four images exhibit an economy of visual language, in which Palucca's dancing form is reduced to a series of geometrically simplified arcs, straight lines, and acute angles. For Kandinsky, Palucca's performances embodied his own expounded theories of composition, such as a balance of warm and cool and light and heavy; not surprisingly, these qualities paralleled the contrasts critics described in Palucca's choreography.[18]

Whereas Palucca's interactions with the Bauhaus masters tended to be dominated by written correspondence and social visits, her relationships with Bauhaus students and junior faculty seemed more informal and collaborative. Several youthful Bauhaus recollections of Palucca align her with the fun experienced by students outside of the classroom. Clearly the students and young faculty were impressed: Marianne Brandt, student and later acting master in the metal workshop, reminisced, "Palucca enchanted us when she presented her newest dance."[19] Felix Klee, a Bauhaus student in the theater workshop and Paul Klee's son, recalled the students' "unique" feelings toward Palucca, one of their favorite choreographers. For Felix Klee, Palucca's dancing and costuming expressed the simplicity and beauty of the human body, issues important for the Bauhaus at the time, and he noted her well-trained body's capability to perform her legendary springs. Palucca fostered a warm atmosphere at the school on her visits, and the students were especially enthusiastic about her dance style. Klee also remembered their nickname for Palucca: Puck.[20] A character in William Shakespeare's *A Midsummer Night's Dream*, Puck is a happy, troublemaking elf—and male. An elf's small size implies a youthful figure, even an androgynous or feminized male, a characterization that captured how Bauhaus students understood Palucca in gendered terms.

Ise Gropius, the young wife of Bauhaus director Walter Gropius, often socialized with the students and wrote in her diary of the parties, guests, and personal dynamics at the school. Reminiscing about Palucca's 1927 Bauhaus visit, Ise Gropius wrote that the dancer charmed the students after her sold-out performance in the Bauhaus theater by taking over the neighboring cafeteria and amusing them with her rendition of the Charleston.[21] Her performance suggests a mingling of modernism and popular culture in which the singular theatrical performance was quickly followed by a rendition of popular social dancing. This breakdown of hierarchies was not fully accomplished, however. Palucca's formal dance concert of her choreographies for the Bauhaus community, including the masters, took place on the theatrical stage, but her more spontaneous Charleston, for students, exhibited more give-and-take between the audience and performer and occurred in the more informal campus space of the cafeteria. Only a temporary folding wall separated these two spaces at the compact Dessau Bauhaus, but that barrier also reinforced two very different Bauhaus experiences.

These different sites for performance created and reinforced contrasting spectatorial experiences of Palucca, the results of which are evident in the Bauhaus imagery of the dancer. The student works tend toward informality and collaboration, in which they interpret the dancer through their own priorities of mass media, technology, and Bauhaus daily life. More than anything, they fully recognize Palucca's star power. Seen in the collage by student Erich Comeriner, Palucca's name is surrounded by newspaper pages and words in Bauhaus lettering (Figure 3.1). The collage references a "tanzabend" (evening dance performance) and features Palucca's name, venues where she performed such as Odeon, as well as "kantine," the German word for cafeteria, likely an allusion to Palucca's 1927 Bauhaus performance. In addition, "hühner," which translates as "chickens," might suggest that Comeriner envisioned (or joked about) Palucca as petite or birdlike; it may also be a cropped and misspelled version of Blüthner-Saal, a prominent Weimar Berlin dance venue where Palucca performed.

Created for a typography class taught by Joost Schmidt, Comeriner's collage juxtaposes the traditional and spiky Fraktur typeface of pages from the *Anhalter Anzeiger* (Anhalt Gazette), the local newspaper of the Bauhaus's hometown of Dessau, with the Bauhaus's innovative experimentation with modern typefaces.[22] In German grammar, first letters of all nouns are capitalized, but Bauhaus typography challenges those fundamental rules, such that words are either all lowercase or entirely capitalized; the lower case *p* in *palucca*, *t* in *tanzabend*, and capitalized ODEON exemplify this. As with the universal

Figure 3.1. Erich Comeriner, *Collage "palucca"* (Collage "palucca"), 1927. Collection Bauhaus-Archiv Berlin. Photo: Bauhaus-Archiv Berlin. © Erich Comeriner Archiv/Galerie David, Bielefeld.

alphabet designed by Bauhaus typographer Herbert Bayer, the components of Comeriner's individual letters are comprised of standardized and interchangeable parts, with similar curves and straight lines repeated across the alphabet. The *u*, *h*, and *n* letters in *hühner* are based on the same components; the *N* in *ODEON* is so simple that it is read correctly both right-side up and upside down. Requiring few strokes to print, Comeriner's lettering is clear and efficient.

Comeriner's experimentation suggests to me how typeface can be used to express a notion of Palucca as a modern New Woman. In a clean, straightforward style that could be read quickly, Bauhaus letterings were to be readable on a train, equating a modern experience of reading with the rapid pace of cosmopolitan life.[23] This ideal of the modern typeface parallels the discourse on the Weimar woman. An integral participant in fast-paced urban centers, the modern Weimar woman wore straight-cut unfrilly dresses, and her frankness and directness paralleled the coolness of attitude that critics aligned with New Objectivity and industry. In Comeriner's collage, Palucca's name is written in this new lettering in red. A bold standout against the ways of old—the Fraktur typeface—the modern typographical form suggests that Palucca herself is a new type of dancer and woman. Comeriner expresses Palucca as pure precision in lettering as if evoking the pure precision of a dance curve. Through these choices, Comeriner describes Palucca as new, modern, and innovative, qualities also ascribed to the Bauhaus itself.

A 1929 photomontage by Marianne Brandt, *Palucca tanzt* (Palucca dances), portrays the artist's identification with the dancer as a New Woman (Figure 3.2). A student at the Bauhaus from 1924 to 1928, Brandt was the only woman to graduate from the male-dominated metal workshop. Championed by her mentor Moholy-Nagy as well as director Walter Gropius, Brandt had the greatest number of industrial contracts in that workshop, bringing in much-needed money for the institution, and served as acting director of the metal workshop upon Moholy-Nagy's departure in 1928. In July 1929 Brandt departed from the Bauhaus, and in August started a position designing furniture at Gropius's Berlin architectural studio. Throughout this time Brandt worked actively in photomontage as a private art for her personal enjoyment.[24]

In contrast to Comeriner's emphasis on pure text, Brandt's photomontage features a widely circulated Charlotte Rudolph photograph of Palucca performing one of her signature springs. Exemplifying Palucca's popularity in both avant-garde and popular contexts, this photograph was published in Moholy-Nagy's 1925 Bauhaus treatise *Malerei Fotografie Film* (Painting Photography Film), as well as in the February 1926 *Uhu* (The Owl) essay "Der fliegende Mensch" (The Flying Human). Brandt likely knew of both sources, the former because of Moholy's mentorship and the latter because Brandt saved clippings from the mainstream press for later photomontages. It is thus likely that *Uhu*

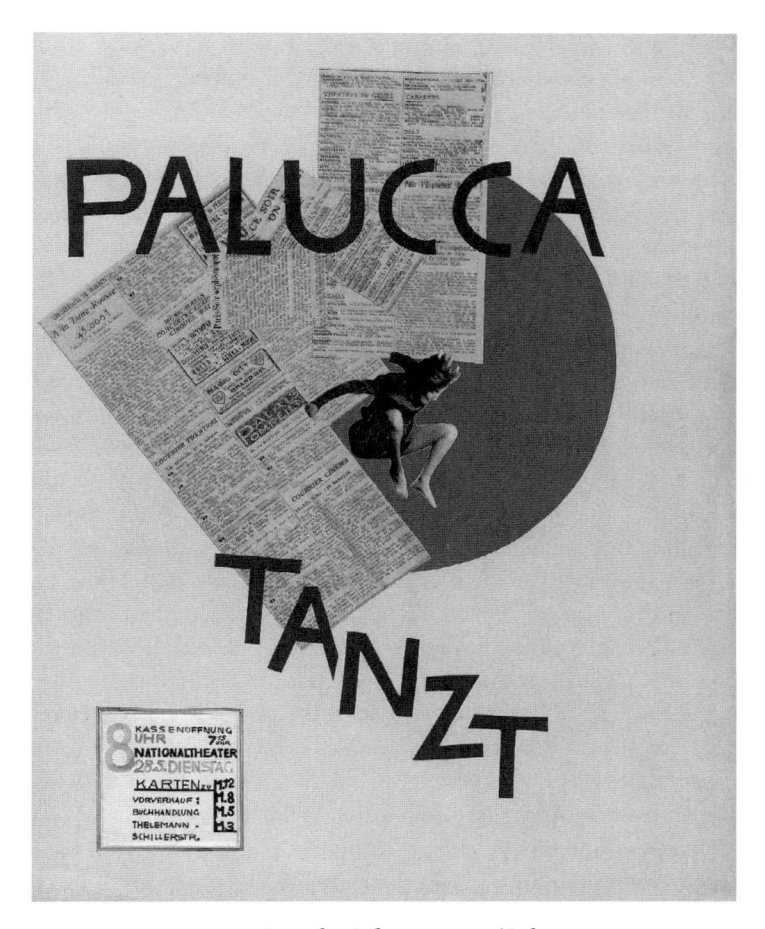

Figure 3.2. Marianne Brandt, *Palucca tanzt* (Palucca dances), 1929. Collection Kupferstichkabinett, Staatliche Kunstsammlungen, Dresden, Germany. Photo: Bildarchiv Preußischer Kulturbesitz/Art Resource, N.Y. © 2010 Artists Rights Society (ARS), New York/VG Bild-Kunst, Bonn.

was her source here.[25] These multiple sources for influence and imagery further speak to Tag Gronberg's assertion that women's modern artistic culture frequently bridged the avant-garde with mass culture.[26]

Whereas Comeriner's text prioritizes Palucca's dance venues, Brandt's text and image highlight the act of dancing. The centrality of the Palucca spring coupled with the words "Palucca tanzt" showcases her impressive corporeal feats, and Brandt's modifications to the original photograph further emphasize the dance. For example, Rudolph photographed Palucca in a spring staged for an optimal image. Dancing in a studio setting, with a plain floor and background, a spotlight creates a dramatic shadow of Palucca's body on the back wall. This shadow alludes to expressionism, evoking an instinctive, emotional aspect to her dance. (This parallels Kandinsky and Klee's Bauhaus explorations, which carried expressionist undercurrents despite their conversions to a constructivist aesthetic.) For her photomontage, however, Brandt cuts Palucca's springing figure out of the photograph, separating the dancer from her studio context and expressionist shadow, a change that enables Brandt to portray Palucca's work in the service of her own constructivist vision.

At the same time, Brandt's photomontage highlights Palucca's career success. In a poster format, Brandt's work promotes a Palucca dance concert. A box in the lower-left corner details ticket information, and clippings from French newspapers of various dance reviews, announcements, and advertisements jut diagonally across the picture plane. Suggestive of Palucca's extensive European touring calendar, the French clippings evince the cosmopolitanism of dancer and artist alike. Brandt likely cut the clippings from French newspapers during her nine-month stay in Paris from 1926 to 1927 and kept them for several years before using them here.[27] Palucca's springing form is placed off-center in a large red circle, highlighting her performance of pure dance within a space of pure geometry. Yet, this photomontage was not intended to promote Palucca; Brandt created her montages as a private art and did not expect to exhibit them publicly. Pencil marks on the page to indicate text placement further demonstrate that this photomontage was neither a finished product nor a final version of a poster set for mass production. What we see, then, is Brandt's vision of Palucca's dancing and career fashioned in an innovative Bauhaus style after posters that would have lined urban streets. The image promotes the New Woman, and along those lines, Brandt's photomontage echoes modes of female spectatorship in the 1920s, in which the flâneuse, strolling in a city like Berlin or Paris, would have related to her surroundings through her own visual pleasure of its surfaces: posters, store windows, and cinema screens.[28] Highlighting consumerism rather than sexual consumption, *Palucca tanzt* suggests how the modern woman in the metropolis might experience Palucca as a star.

Comeriner and Brandt were not alone among the younger Bauhaus generation in their enthusiasm for Palucca; the students seemed to have identified with her, admiring her as a model and relating to her as a peer. Close in age, the students welcomed her into their Bauhaus daily lives, which included taking photographs of each other. In these Bauhaus daily life settings, the process was collaborative, a give-and-take between the dancer and the *Bauhäusler*. For a savvy self-promoter such as Palucca, these instances allowed her to socialize with and learn from the students and permitted opportunities for her to shape how she would be portrayed. As an example, an unknown photographer—but quite possibly student T. Lux Feininger—photographs his brother, Andreas (sons of Bauhaus master Lyonel Feininger), taking a picture of Palucca as she climbs and springs on the rooftops of one of Gropius's master's houses[29] (Figures 3.3, 3.4). She appears stylishly modern in her street clothes, with her skirt length fashionably above the knees, and she smiles as she plays on the roof. Here, her choreographed springs are replaced by a lively climb and a jump in an informal setting, for her climbing reveals her knees and toned legs, evoking the similar youthful femininity remarked upon during her 1925 performance for the Bauhaus community. She conveys a happy, even flirtatious personality. Andreas Feininger's positioning plays into this flirtatiousness; with his long phallic camera lens pointed directly at Palucca, the photographer seems to gaze up her skirt as she leaps toward him.

These informal moments between the star guest and students also reveal their shared engagements with Bauhaus modernism. Andreas Feininger situ-

Figure 3.3. *László Moholy-Nagy fotografiert Gret Palucca vor einem Meisterhaus in Dessau* (László Moholy-Nagy photographing the dancer Gret Palucca in front of a Master House at the Bauhaus in Dessau), 1927–1928. The represented photographer might be Andreas Feininger. Photo: Unknown, possibly T. Lux Feininger. Collection Kupferstichkabinett, Staatliche Kunstsammlungen, Dresden, Germany. Photo credit: Bildarchiv Preußischer Kulturbesitz/ Art Resource, N.Y.

Figure 3.4. *László Moholy-Nagy fotografiert die springende Gret Palucca auf dem Dach eines Meisterhauses* (László Moholy-Nagy photographing the dancer Gret Palucca while jumping on the roof of a Master House at the Bauhaus in Dessau), 1927–1928. The represented photographer might be Andreas Feininger. Photo: Unknown, possibly T. Lux Feininger. Collection Kupferstichkabinett, Staatliche Kunstsammlungen, Dresden, Germany. Photo credit: Bildarchiv Preußischer Kulturbesitz/Art Resource, N.Y.

ates himself to photograph Palucca's movements from a skewed angle; this maximizes the defamiliarizing perspective common in Bauhaus photographic experimentation. The photographs overtly reference the process of taking a photograph, reinforcing modernism's priority on materiality and the technological emphasis of the later Bauhaus years. Moreover, the modernist architectural setting is integral to the photographic setting. The juxtaposition between the Gropius-designed architecture and dancer suggests a culture/nature divide of rigid modernist angles versus the curves of the body, and yet the shifting geometric configurations of her dancing form coupled with the straight silhouette of her clothing complement the structure of the building and highlight the shared attributes of both the architecture and her practice. T. Lux Feininger's own work in performance and photography—as a student in Schlemmer's Theater Workshop (1927–1929), a member of the Bauhaus jazz band (after 1928), and outside of the Bauhaus as a photographer for the Agency Dephot in Berlin (1927–1931)—bridged multiple media and gave him a distinct advantage to understand how to picture Palucca.[30] As with Kandinsky's experience of Palucca, the Feininger brothers' relationship with Palucca-as-dancer was mediated by photography. But, whereas "Tanzkurven" was based upon photographs chosen for him, T. Lux and Andreas Feininger experienced a more extended, temporally bound collaboration between themselves and Palucca. The Feininger photographs are blurry precisely because they demonstrate the impromptu, informal moments and the ever-changing spatial, personal, and spectatorial relationships between the dancer and her two photographers.

Palucca's popularity among Bauhaus women was because her New Woman performer persona meshed with women's own notions of themselves as both within and outside of the avant-garde. Despite numerous institutional biases against them, many Bauhaus women forged their own relationships with cultural production as an intersection of modernism, mass culture, and physical culture. One of the key ways was through gymnastics, and in particular through the person of Karla Grosch, the women's gymnastics instructor and a former student of Palucca's. Grosch's profile complemented the Bauhaus vision: while a dance student, she wrote essays for Palucca on modern art and on geometry that evoke Paul Klee's theories of form.[31] At the Bauhaus, she was a good friend of Felix Klee's and performed in Schlemmer's choreographies and toured with his Bauhaus dancers to Switzerland.[32] Featured in a 1930 article about Bauhaus women published in *Die Woche* (The Week), titled "Mädchen wollen etwas lernen" (Girls want to learn something), Grosch appears youthful, optimistic, and determined—the very qualities ascribed to Palucca. Among the activities of Bauhaus women featured in the article were Grosch's gymnastics classes, including a photograph of women throwing medicine balls.[33]

It was through their own bodies that many Bauhaus women expressed this connection with Palucca's principles. The movements Grosch taught combined athleticism with the arrangement of human form based in geometry. Taken by T. Lux Feininger, photographs of the gymnastics classes capture the precision of movement and the geometry of the body, not dissimilar from Kandinsky's own abstractions of Palucca. Weather permitting, the lessons took place on the roof of one of the Bauhaus buildings, combining the restorative power of fresh air with the modernist aesthetic of Gropius's architecture. Several photographs depict gymnastics students performing yoga inversions. In one example (Figure 3.5), Grosch supervises her students as they create triangular shapes from their bodies; two women form an isosceles triangle, posing in a shoulder stand and leaning their feet toward one another, using each others' arms and legs for support and resistance. These geometries are accentuated by Grosch's wide-legged stance that repeats her students' triangular form and by Feininger's choice of perspective, for which he positioned himself on the roof at their level. Taking lessons from Palucca's dance as geometry, Kandin-

Figure 3.5. *Sport am Bauhaus: Boden-Gymnastik der Frauen auf dem Dach des Bauhauses, mit Gymnastiklehrerin Karla Grosch* (Sport at the Bauhaus: Women's Floor Gymnastics on the Bauhaus Roof with Gymnastics Instructor Karla Grosch), 1930. Photo: T. Lux Feininger. Collection Bauhaus-Archiv Berlin. Photo credit: Bauhaus-Archiv Berlin.

sky's "Tanzkurven," Bauhaus student work, and the women students' daily lives, Grosch's teachings of gymnastics fused geometric abstraction with New Woman personal expression.

* * *

Whereas the Bauhaus masters addressed women's liberation abstractly and obliquely, the students and junior faculty more readily and directly incorporated its themes, materials, and attitudes in a celebratory way. With the students, the flow between modernism, mass culture, and the body was exceptionally fluid; diverse as their responses to Palucca were, each expressed their admiration for her through visual forms as well as through their own bodies. As we have seen, they tended to highlight moments of movement: climbing on master's house roofs, enjoying the Charleston in the cafeteria, or participating in a gymnastics class. Even examples that might seem static, such as Comeriner's typography experiment and Brandt's photomontage, are filled with lines, words, and geometric shapes on diagonals—a direction that visually implies movement. In all these examples, Bauhaus artists imaged Palucca because they envisaged something of themselves in her; Palucca's career savvy allowed her to maximize this potential. I would argue that this relationship worked because the pursuit of modernism and the expression of the body, on stage and as an everyday dynamic, were seen by the younger Bauhaus generation as one and the same. Indeed, Palucca's example demonstrates the centrality of the body in discourses on modernism.

Notes

1. Editors' Note: For Mary Wigman, see the essay by Sabine Huschka in this volume. For Hanya Holm, see the essay by Tresa Randall in this volume.

2. On Palucca's relationship with artists, see Staatliche Kunstsammlungen Dresden, Kupferstich-Kabinett, *Künstler um Palucca: Austellung zu Ehren des 85. Geburtstages* (Dresden: Die Kunstsammlungen, 1987); Ralf Stabel, *Tanz, Palucca! Die Verkörperung einer Leidenschaft* (Berlin: Henschel, 2001), 47–54.

3. Anja Baumhoff, *The Gendered World of the Bauhaus. The Politics of Power at the Weimar Republic's Premier Art Institute, 1919–1932* (New York: Peter Lang, 2001).

4. ". . . Gerade der Umstand, daß alles Allzuindividuelle, Zufällige überwunden und ins Typische gesteigert war, brachte ihr das sonst nicht immer einstimmige Lob unserer damaligen Weimarer Gemeinschaft," *Palucca Tanz* Prospekt III (1925/6), 4. Collection Stiftung Archiv der Akademie der Künste, Berlin, Gret Palucca Archiv no. 1034 (hereafter referred to as SAdK, GPA).

5. Oskar Schlemmer, László Moholy-Nagy, and Farkas Molnár, *Die Bühne im Bauhaus* (Munich: Albert Langen, 1925); Walter Gropius, ed., *The Theater of the Bauhaus*, trans. Arthur S. Wensinger (Middletown, Conn.: Wesleyan University Press, 1961).

6. Kunstsammlung Nordrhein-Westfalen, K. W., Sprengel Museum Hannover, Bühnen Archiv Oskar Schlemmer, eds. *Oskar Schlemmer: Tanz Theater Bühne* (Stuttgart: Gerd Hatje, 1994); Dirk Scheper, *Oskar Schlemmer: Das Triadische Ballett und die Bauhausbühne*

(Berlin: Akademie der Künste [West], 1988); Tut Schlemmer, ed., *Oskar Schlemmer: Briefe und Tagebücher* (Munich: Albert Langen-Georg Müller, 1958), later translated as *The Letters and Diaries of Oskar Schlemmer* (Middletown, Conn., Wesleyan University Press, 1972); Karin von Maur, *Oskar Schlemmer*, 2 volumes (Munich: Prestel, 1979). For student responses, see Felix Klee, "My Memories of the Weimar Bauhaus," and Xanti Schawinsky, "bauhaus metamorphosis," in *Bauhaus and Bauhaus People*, ed. Eckhard Neumann, trans. Eva Richter and Alba Lorman (New York: Van Nostrand Reinhold, 1993), 39–45, 155–162.

7. Neither a defector nor consistently adored by the East German government, Palucca faced numerous contradictory challenges in the postwar era. She allowed her school to be nationalized, but the cultural ministry stripped her of her school's directorship; she fled to the West only to return, likely to rejoin her partner, Dr. Marianne Zwingenberger; she was a founding member of the East German Academy of Arts but under surveillance for decades. Ralf Stabel, *IM "Tänzer": Der Tanz und die Staatssicherheit* (Mainz: Schott, 2008), 164–183; Stabel, *Tanz, Palucca!*, 128–237. [Editors' Note: See also Marion Kant's essay in this volume.]

8. On Wigman and structures of gendered spectatorship, see Susan Manning, *Ecstasy and the Demon: The Dances of Mary Wigman*, 2nd ed. (Minneapolis: University of Minnesota Press, 2006), 41.

9. Publications on Palucca from the German Democratic Republic in the 1970s and 1980s highlighted her Weimar life and work as modernist dancer and muse to visual artists (and, perhaps not uncoincidentally, passed over her involvement in the Third Reich and the problems she encountered with the German Democratic Republic government). See Akademie der Künste der DDR, *Palucca. Zum Fünfundachtzigsten. Glückwünsche, Selbstzeugnisse, Äußerungen* (Berlin: Akademie der Künste der DDR, 1987); Kupferstich-Kabinett, *Künstler um Palucca*; Gerhard Schumann, ed. *Palucca: Porträt einer Tänzerin* (Berlin: Henschel, 1972); Stabel, *Tanz, Palucca!*, 230–237.

10. Kupferstich-Kabinett, *Künstler um Palucca*, 4–30.

11. Will Grohmann, *Die Sammlung Ida Bienert, Dresden* (Potsdam: Müller and I. Kiepenheuer, 1933).

12. Pawel Barchan, "Palucca," *Die Dame* 51:3 (Nov. 1923): 7.

13. "War es nicht rhythmische Gymnastik, was die junge, hübsche Künstlerin mit dem fabelhaft trainierten Körper und dem Bubikopf auf der Bühne ausführte?" M.R., "Gastspiel von Gret Palucca im Nationaltheater in Weimar," *Jenaische Zeitung*, Jena (March 21, 1925). Collection SAdK, GPA, nos. 263–280.

14. Program, Weimar Nationaltheater, March 18, 1925. Collection SAdK, GPA, no. 265. See also Akademie der Künste der DDR, *Palucca. Zum Fünfundachtzigsten*, 118.

15. On this correspondence see Stabel, *Tanz, Palucca!*, 47–54, and Susan Laikin Funkenstein, "Engendering Abstraction: Wassily Kandinsky, Gret Palucca, and 'Dance Curves'" *Modernism/modernity* 14.3 (2007): 392–394.

16. Wassily Kandinsky, "Tanzkurven: Zu den Tänzen der Palucca," in *Kunstblatt* (March 1926), translated as "Dance Curves: The Dances of Palucca," in *Kandinsky: Complete Writings on Art*, vol. 2 (1922–1943), eds. Kenneth C. Lindsay and Peter Vergo (Boston: G. K. Hall, 1982), 519–523.

17. Letter to Will Grohmann, Nov. 3, 1925, cited in *Kandinsky: Complete Writings on Art*, 524 and 904 n. 2.

18. I discuss the gendered implications of "Dance Curves" at greater length in my article "Engendering Abstraction": 389–406. The Rudolph photographs and Kandinsky drawings are also illustrated there.

19. Marianne Brandt, "Letter to the younger generation," in Neumann, *Bauhaus and Bauhaus People*, 100.

20. Felix Klee, quoted in Akademie der Künste der DDR, *Palucca. Zum Fünfundachtzigsten*, 30.

21. "tanzabend palucca. *volkommen schön!* es gibt nichts mehr hinzuzusetzen und das schönste an dieser vollkommenheit ist, dass sie nicht einen gipfel bedeutet, der nun nicht mehr überboten werden kann, sondern dass die entwicklungsmöglichkeit unbegrenzt ist! nach dem eigentlichen abend tanzte sie in der kantine einen einen [sic] charleston, der wirklich für alle ein erlebnis war, die es gesehen haben." Ise Gropius, *Tagebuch, 1924–1928*, April 29, 1927, 177. Unpublished diary collection Bauhaus-Archiv, Berlin.

22. Ute Brüning, *Das A und O des Bauhauses. Bauhauswerbung: Schriftbilder, Drucksachen, Ausstellungsdesign* (Berlin: Bauhaus-Archiv and Edition Leipzig, 1995), 195.

23. Frederic J. Schwartz, "Utopia for Sale: The Bauhaus and Weimar Germany's Consumer Culture," in *Bauhaus Culture: From Weimar to the Cold War*, ed. Kathleen James-Chakraborty (Minneapolis: University of Minnesota Press, 2006), 119–125.

24. On Marianne Brandt's life and work in photomontage, see Elizabeth Otto, *Tempo, Tempo! The Bauhaus Photomontages of Marianne Brandt* (Berlin: Jovis, 2006) and Elizabeth Otto, "A 'Schooling of the Senses': Post-Dada Visual Experiments in the Bauhaus Photomontages of László Moholy-Nagy and Marianne Brandt," *New German Critique* 36:2 (Summer 2009): 89–131.

25. Otto, *Tempo, Tempo!*, 106 and 162 n. 3.

26. Tag Gronberg, "Sonia Delaunay's Simultaneous Fashions and the Modern Woman," *The Modern Woman Revisited: Paris between the Wars*, eds. Whitney Chadwick and Tirza True Latimer (New Brunswick, N.J.: Rutgers University Press, 2003), 109–123.

27. Otto, *Tempo! Tempo!*, 137.

28. See Mila Ganeva, *Women in Weimar Fashion; Discourses and Displays in German Culture, 1918–1933* (Rochester, N.Y.: Camden House, 2008); Janet Ward, *Weimar Surfaces: Urban Visual Culture in 1920s Germany* (Berkeley: University of California Press, 2001).

29. Scholars do not agree upon either the identity of the photographer or the depicted photographer in the two photographs. Although the Kupferstichkabinett in Dresden, which owns the originals, and the Bauhaus-Archiv Berlin both believe the photographer is unknown, I would make a case that T. Lux Feininger could be the photographer of these images. He was the dominant chronicler of Bauhaus everyday life, and the fact that his own brother is depicted in the scenes increases the likelihood that it was T. Lux Feininger. Moreover, in written correspondence with the author, T. Lux Feininger noted the photographs' date as 1931. If this information is correct, it suggests to me that T. Lux Feininger is the photographer of these two images, or at the very least that he had a close understanding of the photographs' creation. In any event, the informal style indicates to me that a student was the photographer. In terms of the depicted photographer, the Kupferstichkabinett believes him to be Moholy-Nagy, but the Bauhaus-Archiv Berlin identifies him as Andreas Feininger. The two men do look somewhat alike, but the photographer appears to be student-aged and with Feininger's thinner face. Furthermore, in written

correspondence with the author, T. Lux Feininger identified the depicted photographer as his brother Andreas. T. Lux Feininger, correspondence with the author, postmarked August 7, 2010.

30. Neumann, *Bauhaus and Bauhaus People*, 172.

31. Karla Grosch, "Über den Kreis" and "Meine Einstellung zur modernen, bildenden Kunst." SAdK, GPA, no. 1514 and 116.

32. During Schlemmer's 1929 tour Grosch performed his choreography *Metal Dance*, a photograph of which appears in RoseLee Goldberg, *Performance Art: From Futurism to the Present* (New York: Thames and Hudson, 2001), 119.

33. No author, "Mädchen wollen etwas lernen," *Die Woche* (Apr. 4, 1930): 30–33. The Bauhaus-Archiv, Berlin, attributes the photograph of Grosch to T. Lux Feininger.

4. Rudolf Laban's Dance Film Projects
SUSANNE FRANCO

Rudolf Laban was one of the leaders of *Ausdruckstanz*, and he has been studied as a thoughtful writer and theoretician, a talented choreographer, an inspired teacher, and a tireless organizer of schools, associations, and festivals. Less known are his mostly unrealized film projects, conceptualized for different purposes on different occasions. Our only access to these today is through their scenarios, written between the 1910s and early 1930s, because it seems that no footage has survived. Analysis of this limited material, however, can reveal important aspects of Laban's visions of a new dance and open up new perspectives in our knowledge of his way of thinking about movement. How do Laban's film scenarios relate to his larger artistic production and educational activities? To what extent can we study Laban's film projects as a springboard for, or as a consequence of, his theories about dance? Can his film projects shed light on the ideological and aesthetic trends within Weimar cinema?

Laban was interested in using cinema as a tool to disseminate his ideas and to expand the potential audience for modern dance, ensuring its position as a respectable social practice, as a form of high art, and as a professional field. He also understood the great economic potential that cinema, as a popular medium, could give to dance in supporting his enterprises.

The first trace of his interest in cinema dates back to World War I, during his residence in Zurich, where he established a *Labanschule* (Laban school). Here, beside the courses in music, eurhythmics, acting, declamation, costume, and stage design, Laban introduced a class in *Filmdarstellung* (film acting)[1] as part of *Bewegungskunst* (art of movement), which also included dance and pantomime. This class is mentioned in only one of the many versions of the school brochures, which he changed quite frequently as he did his ideas and ideals about the "perfect" dance education. The "Filmpantomime," whose incomplete scenario has been called after the main character, "Gualdi Fragment,"[2] was probably written as a pedagogical tool for this class. The subject, a short tale about a vampire, was useful for building up a series of scenes about hypnotization, magic rites, and dreamlike atmospheres. These themes were familiar from his theater productions of the time and similar to trends in early German film.[3]

The lack of other documents induces us to believe that Laban wrote most of his film projects toward the end of the 1920s. After leaving Zurich, he became one of the most well-known artists and dance advocates in Germany, with an impressive ability to constantly initiate new projects and new relationships. He moved in and out of several German towns, attempting to create art that would appeal to his society. Laban's career in public institutions reached a peak first in 1930, when he was appointed as ballet director at the Berlin State Opera Unter der Linden, and then in 1934, after the Nazis took power, when he was nominated director of the *Deutsche Tanzbühne* (German Dance Stage). As director he became responsible for the arrangement of the entire German dance scene. Over the last few decades, scholars have debated whether Laban's involvement with the Third Reich resulted from his commitment to the regime or from his dedication to keep working without fully agreeing with the regime's political agenda.[4] What is certain is that his involvement lasted for about four years, a period that provided him with remarkable professional opportunities and allowed him to play a crucial role in the transformation of German dance and body culture into a powerful tool for the diffusion of Nazi ideology.

The materials related to Laban's dance film projects consist mostly of incomplete files (scenarios, letters, reviews, and notes) in German and/or English and are housed in different archives and countries.[5] The incompleteness of these files, as with other documentation of his activities, is partly due to his working habits. Laban was more an inspired and enthusiastic pathfinder than a rigorous scholar, and he often didn't elaborate his seminal ideas but simply gave the initial impetus to his pupils and collaborators, who developed them further. In addition, the incompleteness of the documentation of his film projects, as well as his oeuvre overall, reflects the complicated legacies of his personal belongings after his definitive departure from Germany in 1937. Political tensions and sudden changes in personnel inside the major cultural institutions of the Reich pushed him to leave the country in a rush, so he left most of his important documents in Germany.[6] Moreover, many films preserved in other German archives were damaged or lost during the war, including at least a couple in which Laban was involved.[7] Despite the fact that Laban's film projects represent an interesting and sometimes surprising facet of his ideas on dance and dancing, they have received little attention from dance historians, probably since most of them were unrealized. There also seems to be a discrepancy between

Laban's evident interest in film and the fact that discussions of film aesthetics rarely appear in his writings. Is this theoretical silence a sign of frustration at his failure to transform these projects into real films?

Laban classified his film projects after the most popular genres of the time, like *Kulturfilme* (cultural films) and *Filmreportagen* (film reportages) or invented new definitions by adapting them to dance, such as *Tanz-Lehrfilme* (dance educational films) and *Tanzspielfilm* (dance feature films). *Kulturfilm* was a typical German genre that became known during the Weimar years and is hardly comparable to the more international tradition of documentary. Under this definition, which in its broad sense includes also several subgenres like *Lehrfilme*, a great number of films were produced and distributed, with the double mission of addressing a popular audience and of serving as an educational tool for students or, alternately, as a refined product for more restricted scholarly communities. In the first case, they were distributed as supplements to the main films scheduled on regular cinema programs; in the second, they were promoted mainly in the national educational system. In both cases, these films were produced in strict collaboration with scholars and scientists, and film industries organized screenings for professors and school teachers, who weren't always eager to use them.[8]

Cultural films were one of the largest and most important products of the nascent film industry, and the Universum-Film Aktiengesellschaft (UFA), founded in 1917, quickly became the largest film company in Germany and the leader in producing this genre. It was a Prussian right-wing, ultraconservative, and reactionary company, but it became famous for its revolutionary techniques, special effects, and camera movements. The department devoted to the production of cultural films, the UFA-Kulturabteilung, was considered the Weimar cinema outpost in experimenting with new technologies.[9] Technological innovations represented only one aspect of this genre, however, because culture films served a longstanding aesthetic, social, and educational program deeply rooted in German culture. As a result of its broad spectrum of purposes, the *Kulturfilm* was perceived as a "super genre" that included many different ways of documenting life, habits, trends, and so on.

As a teacher and school manager, Laban had a very open attitude toward the opportunity offered by the cultural films, and he had a clear understanding of their great potential for modern dance, at least his own vision of it. His vision, much like Weimar cinema, was the result of a peculiar mix of tradition and innovation. Most of his film projects aimed to insert his theory and practice in a scientific and historical frame in order to legitimate his way of seeing this art, its history, its aesthetic, and its social function, as well as to demonstrate his own dance pieces and training method.[10] In a few cases he also used filmed images for his lectures on dance.[11]

Laban's film projects are part of the golden age of world cinema, the German cinema of the twenties and early thirties, which is often identified with expressionism. Following the publication of Lotte Eisner's *The Haunted Screen*,[12] the term *expressionist* became synonymous with German film, but for film historians today it represents a problematic definition because it risks shadowing the ideological and aesthetic ambiguity of a much more complex phenomenon. As suggested by Thomas Elsaesser, a more useful definition for German cinema of the 1920s and 1930s, both in political and aesthetic terms, is "Weimar cinema." It enables us to distinguish the period style of expressionism from the extensive analysis of the cultural politics of the Weimar Republic and to highlight the diversity and variety of film productions of the period.[13] The same misunderstanding occurred with German modern dance of the period, which was named *Ausdruckstanz* by scholars after World War II. This definition similarly transmits a falsely monolithic aesthetic and an ideologically homogeneous image of this tradition, which wasn't entirely progressive, revolutionary, and antibourgeois.[14]

Weimar cinema was first and foremost a genre driven by commercial concerns, and Laban's aims were not an exception in this regard. Nonetheless, for him, a dance film was a way to construct a visualization of his theories about movement through performative actions and pictorial images. Cinema became the site where all his major interests could merge: painting, architecture, and dance. He also clearly mastered many aspects of the new media, such as production, distribution, and reception. As much as the Weimar cinema was "hyperconscious of how social life and individual subjectivity respond to specular embodiments and visual seductions,"[15] Laban aimed to establish a new understanding of culture, based on a less rational and more empathic communication through (dance) movement, and in so doing to develop a new and openly anti-intellectual culture for the masses. From his perspective, dance could activate spectators' senses and help them to experience the modern world, and he probably saw cinema as one of the tools to achieve these goals.

Laban's projects were part of a broader visual culture in a specific historical time, and they testify also to his awareness of the relationship between vision, knowledge, and power. In the frame of this precise scopic regime, Laban tried to structure his new adventures in motion pictures with original combinations of imagery, visual devices, and the gaze of potential spectators. He aimed to find ways of pairing the dancing body and camera without reducing the former to a mere object of the latter. Laban considered dance as a mass culture product, but one that could reveal hidden or secret dimensions of reality. Cinema's ability to organize nonlinear sequences of time and virtual spaces, and to address a large audience, made it the most powerful medium to express both these features.

In many of his film projects he presented a vision in motion of his complex *Choreosophie* (choreosophy), including movement analysis and dance notation, because he felt that the core of these different dimensions was a single element, rhythm. And from his point of view, rhythm was also the most important thing that dance and cinema had in common, as he wrote in his short article "Tanz im Film":

> It is not an obvious matter to bring to the screen dances conceived for the stage; choreographed movement has to be transformed in such a way that it responds to the expressive character of film. There is artistic potential not only in the revision of dance and dance pieces according to the demands of film, but also in the impact of dancerly movement on the kind of acting that is practiced in common dramatic genres of film. In film, in fact, the power of image is always a second-degree expression, while the central element lies in rhythm, which is also what dance and film have in common.[16]

Ways of Showing and Seeing Dance

Laban officially submitted his first complete project to UFA in 1920. This untitled *Tanzfilm*, which was not accepted, consists of a series of scenes, each dedicated to a different kind of rhythm, from waltzes to the minuet, and genres of dance, from exotic to circular.[17] It is worth mentioning that in 1920 the publication of Laban's *Die Welt des Tänzers* (The Dancer's World),[18] marked a turning point in his career, and it likely added to his credentials in the new market of cinema.

Despite this first unsuccessful approach to UFA, the firm offered Laban an important occasion to show a few sequences about his choreographic works to a large audience by including several scenes about his school and his performances in *Wege zu Kraft und Schönheit* (Paths to Strength and Beauty, 1925 and 1926).[19] This *Kulturfilm*, whose subheading was *Ein Film über moderne Körperkultur* (A Film on Modern Physical Culture), directed by Wilhelm Prager and written by Prager and Nicholas Kaufmann, was one of the most popular of the period, thanks to its domestic and international success. As a *Kulturfilm* it was both typical in regard to its structure and style, and atypical for its feature-film length. It was composed of six independent parts, each devoted to a precise historical moment of physical education, free body culture, life reform movement, sport, leisure, and dance. Its general intent was to actualize the ideal of classic antiquity and the harmony between body and spirit through a comparison of reenactments of Greco-Roman sports and leisure with modern training methods. The film followed the major cultural (and ideological) trends of the time, such as *Freikörperkultur* (movement for a free body culture) and *Lebensreformbewegung* (life reform movement), which aimed at counteracting industrialization and the degeneration caused by modern lifestyles by reappraising physical education and encouraging a closer connection to nature. Today *Wege zu Kraft und Schönheit* represents an interesting document about many aspects of the *völkisch* tradition that nourished National Socialism's ideology and its political goals.[20]

Laban and his students (among them Kurt Jooss) appear in several sequences. In the third section, they are shown in a significant transition from hygienic to rhythmic gymnastics articulated by the inter-title: "Rudolf Laban de Varalja ennobles gymnastics exercises to the dignity of a rhythmic dance." The fourth part, whose general title is "Dance," presents two sequences: one from the final scene of the dance-drama *Das Idol* (The Living Idol) choreographed by Laban and performed by himself and the dancers from one of his companies, the Kammertanzbühne Laban, and probably extracted from a group dance titled *Schwingende Gewalten* (Swinging Powers, 1923)[21]; and one from the solo *Orchidée* (Orchid, 1922) by and with Dussia Bereska, member of the Hamburg-based Laban School. The presence of his followers in both parts of the film was strategic at a delicate moment for Laban's achievement in different fields of *Körperkulturbewegung*. In 1925, and for a short time thereafter, he became one of the leaders of the Deutscher Gymnastik Bund (German Gymnastic League) and, in 1926, he published two volumes on this very topic, *Des Kindes Gymnastik* (Gymnastics for Children) and *Gymnastik und Tanz* (Gymnastics and Dance). The separation between these two fields and perspectives in physical training soon became a controversial issue for its ideological implications, and Laban changed his position in a radical defense of the artistic value of modern dance. It is in this sense that we must understand one of the slogans of the association of Laban schools, "Tanz ist die beste Gymnastik" (dance is the best gymnastics).[22]

Laban's experience with Prager's film must have been encouraging, because a couple of years later the two collaborated again on a scenario for a sound-film, codirecting the recording of the dance piece *Drachentöterei* (Dragon Slaying), choreographed by Bereska and part of the repertory of the Kammertanzbühne Laban since 1923. The film was successfully screened at the *Dresdner Jahresschau* (annual showing in Dresden), but unfortunately it has not been preserved, with the exception of few pictures printed in *Die Schönheit*[23] (Figure 4.1). Another occasion to showcase his dancers—in this case, celebrities of the Berlin Opera, like Regine Gallo, Golli Caspar, and Robert Robst—occurred when Laban participated, as ballet master, in an unsuccessful production by Kosmosfilm (Hamburg), *Spuk im Spielklub* (Ghost in the Casino), also known as *Ein Spiel Karten* (A Game of Cards, 1934).[24] Victor Schamoni directed the film, whose dance sequences were considered unequal to the script.[25]

Laban built up a complex dance theory drawing from a wide range of sources, from natural philosophy to psychology, from sciences to religion, from art to

Prinz Drachentöter, der Drache und die Mädchen (Laban — Drachentöter)   Lignose-Hörfilm

Figure 4.1. Footage from *Drachentöterei* (Dragon Slaying), sound film by Rudolf Laban and Wilhelm Prager, 1927.

occult Masonic thought.[26] He shared with many contemporary artists and thinkers, who inherited the German tradition of romantic *Naturphilosophie*, the need to understand the role of man in the universe. The central ideas of this vision were that all creatures were organized according to a common plan, and that they followed identical and eternal principles of movement. Laban was particularly influenced by the German Darwinist Ernst Haeckel, who established a strong link between science and religion, the material and the spiritual, the rational and the emotional. The most powerful translation of these scientific theories into aesthetic terms appeared in *Abstraktion und Einfühlung* (Abstraction and Empathy, 1908) by Wilhelm Worringer, a treatise considered a pillar of expressionism. Laban's intellectual investigations shared Worringer's imaginary and found an appropriate iconographical representation of it in the crystal,[27] which in his practice took the form of the icosahedron, a Platonic solid made up of twenty equilateral triangles arranged around a single point, with twelve vertices, thirty edges, and twenty faces. Laban was convinced that the dancer could recognize the rhythm of nature and transform it into an artistic practice by moving inside this imagined solid with sequences of movements (movement scales), which connect different parts of the body with different directions and levels in space. Crystalline formations were also perceived as symbols of the perfection of the cosmos, and of the sense of unity suited for the ideal community.[28]

Another important idea that Laban introduced was that every human being had to be a dancer to be alive, and that dance is everywhere, or, in his words, that "dance is life." *Tanz ist Leben* (Dance Is Life) was also the title chosen by Laban and Prager for the film project that they submitted to UFA, although it was never realized. Conceived as an "overview of the history and the essence of dance in different artistic cultural contexts," it aimed to follow the great success of *Wege zu Kraft und Schönheit*.[29] Laban and Prager divided the scenario into six independent sections plus an introduction, ready to be sold as short *Kulturfilme*. Even shorter material could have been drawn for the *Wochenschau* (The Newsreel).[30] The music was reported as a "maestoso"[31] (performed in a majestic mood or speed), and the layout and photography were supposed to be assigned respectively to Willi Geiger and to the famous Ateliers D'Ora of Paris. The total cost of this adventure was expected to be about 200,000 DM and the net proceeds about 135,000 DM, an amount that they planned to invest in future projects. The short extracts would have been even easier to sell because, thanks to their supposed "timeless" and international topics (national dance, choreography, the beauty of movement, physical education through dance, children's dance, exotic and religious dance), the extracts didn't need to be advertised only as news. The expected international success was also carefully planned in advance: the proposal included a long list of countries where the film would be sold, from Sweden to China, from Brazil to Australia, thanks to the already existing network created by Prager for *Wege zu Kraft und Schönheit*. More specifically, Laban and Prager wanted to address a very broad audience by adapting the short films to the needs of each country. For this reason, they would have special shootings of different traditional dances and some comic scenes of dancing animals, such as dogs, monkeys and horses.

Tanz ist Leben was conceptualized as a documentary with high aesthetic qualities, thanks to the use of several cinematic techniques, such as overlapping, cutting, close-ups, light effects, and, above all, fading in and out. The latter suited the key concept of the content very well: a progressive and evolutionary transition from the most insignificant growth in nature—the flourishing of flowers, the rhythmical moves of the waves, and the formation of snow crystals—to more organized bodily movement in different cultures. Laban visualized dance history from his point of view, as a central European male dancer not systematically trained in ballet. His exposure to dance practices was mostly informed by his travels (in Europe, in the Balkans, and in the United States), his historical-anthropological knowledge about the origin and the purpose of dance, and the orientalist and primitivist trends of the time.

Shaped around these geographical and historical axes, the representation of dance in *Tanz ist Leben* is predictable: after a short introduction organized as "a dance of nature through the seasons of the year," the natural laws of dance movements are shown in the crystalline structure of the icosahedron. The subsequent parts are dedicated to the neglected figure of the male dancer in dance throughout history, with a focus on war dances of different times and places, from ancient Greek to the "negro" dances, from traditional country to refined Baroque dances. In the next sections dance is analyzed in its artistic dimension using "rhythm" as a key word to investigate different cultural interpretations (from African dances to Tango and Charleston), interpretations that express cultural meanings, national identities, or spiritual freedom both in Western and Eastern countries. For Western cultures, the central image is that of workers dancing on the roof of a factory; for Eastern cultures, a series of cultic dances. The birth of ballet (French, Russian, and Italian) and of theatrical dance is simply a way to introduce modern dance and its German representatives—Laban, Mary Wigman, Oskar Schlemmer—whose performances are mixed with other major figures in Western ballet tradition, like Anna Pavlova and Tamara Karsavina, in addition to the iconic black dancer Josephine Baker. The latter embodied simultaneously the image of the sexualized savage and a symbol of freedom and experimentation for the artistic avant-garde; in other words, she perfectly expressed the way exotic imagery was perceived as part of modernity's doubled mystique in which primitivism was also a subversive sign of liberation. Modern dance is here juxtaposed to "other" forms of spiritual dance, such as Javanese temple dances, which are considered extremely refined and hence legitimately part of the narrative of dance history of that time. The beauty of body in dance and gymnastics is the topic of the closing session, which, once again, limits its scope to Germany.

The project was never realized. Were its structure, style and technique too similar to *Wege zu Kraft und Schönheit*? Did UFA fear the possibility of replicating a successful film without attaining the same impact? In a letter addressed in 1929 to the cultural section of Tobis-Industriegesellschaft (Berlin), Laban briefly refers to a film project whose title was *Tanz und Gesellschaft* (Dance and Society)[32]: was this a second attempt to sell the same unrealized project to another producer? Prager isn't mentioned: was their professional relationship over? Was Laban too busy with his career? How can we explain the fact that, despite the collaborative proposal that Laban and Prager submitted to UFA in

1929, the famous director realized his last experiment with dance, *Rhythmus und Tanz* (1932), with Jutta Klamt?[33] As a matter of fact, Jutta, together with her husband Gustav, took over Laban's leading role in German body culture after his definitive departure and maintained it until the end of the Nazi era.

The emphasis on modern dance as a logical consequence of natural phenomena of all kinds and a similar trajectory in dance history can be found in two other unrealized film projects—*Die Befreiung des Körpers: Filmreportage über den Tanz* (The Liberation of the Body: Dance Reportage, 1930)[34] and *Tanz der Menschheit* (Dance of Humanity, undated).[35] The former takes an explicitly mystic approach to recurrent topics in Laban's thought: the body as medium of spiritual and emotional qualities, and its liberation as a crucial part of his idea of *Festkultur* (festive culture). Dance is presented here as the perfect medium through which the body can be educated for very different purposes (war as much as sensuality) and the dancer as a person who should know the styles of different populations and "races." The characters correspond to the key figures of the cultural contexts in which Laban found most of his disciples and a large part of his audience: a follower of Nietzsche's philosophy, a dancer of the Duncan tradition, representatives of the middle and upper-middle class, members of a movement choir, a professor of anatomy, and a military gymnast.

The second film is an adaptation of the central piece of Hungarian theater's repertory, *Die Tragödie des Menschen* (Tragedy of Man, 1861) by Imre Madách, divided into a series of eight parts, or *Reigen* (round dances). Despite the fact that this was a sound film and had a much stronger dramaturgical intent, this *Tanzfilm-Reportage* was ultimately less sophisticated than Laban's other projects. The main characters are Adam, Eve, and Lucifer, who travel from the Garden of Eden to visit different turning points in human history, assume many different roles, and by way of this journey trace the "canonical" history of dance from ancient Egypt to Greece, from the Renaissance to the French Revolution. The vision of the future points toward a general deterioration of life conditions and social patterns, such as the emergence of *Radiotötung* (radioactive killing), the rise of what Laban defines briefly as *"schlechte Rasse"* (bad race), and the presence of workers moving like automata. This vision seems to have been influenced by one of the most famous films of the Weimar cinema, *Metropolis* (1927) by Fritz Lang. On the other hand, Laban indirectly provided a choreographic pattern for Lang's film: the erotic dance performed by the false and near-topless Maria (the robot) at the Yoshiwara club, makes a clear reference to *Orchidée* when she kneels on the floor and rotates her torso while wearing a headdress (Figure 4.2). *Orchidée* was part of the repertoire of Laban's company until 1928 and audiences of the time were probably able to easily recognize it. As suggested by Allison Whitney, it was chosen by Lang as an example of modern body culture portraying a "natural" body but framed in a narrative context where it acquired a different cultural meaning.

Figure 4.2. Dussia Bereska in *Orchidée*, footage from *Wege zu Kraft und Schönheit*, directed by Wilhelm Prager, 1925. Transit-Film-Gesellschaft.

In *Metropolis* the dance became a symbol of a "sexual aberration designed to support technological supremacy"[36] and challenged the ambitions of German dance culture to restore the body to a "natural" state, particularly in the face of the dangerous technologies represented in *Metropolis*. This is an example of how the study of the migration of images from dance to film, a topic that remains largely unexplored for Weimar cinema, could help in understanding the controversial aspects of this dance tradition and its reception both in Germany and abroad.

Written Images and Notated Movements for Visual Pleasures

Cinema was for Laban also an occasion to investigate his artistic perspective on movement, and to transform his choreographic skills into visual products. As much as in his choreographic works, Laban wanted to achieve an artistic effect "through moving lines and forms, groups and masses."[37] In *Film über die Harmonische Bewegung des Menschlichen Körpers* (Film about the Harmonious Movement of the Human Body, undated)[38] he seems to mix his ability to design spaces and organize time, thanks to refined use of the camera. Here, contrasts, counterpoint, rhythmic unison, and opposition effects have the potential of creating tactile surfaces on the screen, where appearing and disappearing figures replace more traditional characters. Visual and sound effects were planned to be interwoven throughout the film. The initial dark background is transformed into the interior of a crystalline cavity, as the movements adapt to this new setting. Stylized bodies in motion leave traces that are transformed into lines suggesting rays or shining circles, which create different spatial structures. These shapes were superimposed onto clouds, trees, waves, and so on, or to airplanes, turbines, and other technical-mechanical devices of the modern world, transmitting the many tensions and contradictions of (dance) modernism. In this dreamlike succession of structures and shapes as "spatial waves," living dancers alternating with inanimate silhouettes eventually lead the audience into a series of different genres of dances, from social to cultic pantomimes, and of different subjects, children, adults, and also animals. Clearly nourished by Laban's education in architecture and by his practice as a painter and designer, the scenario presents an aesthetic quality close to surrealist and Dada experiments with cinema, like those made by Hans Richter, whom Laban had met in Zurich during World War I. At the same time, this abstract film vision (and partially that of *Tanz ist Leben*) seems to anticipate the development of a new genre, *ciné-dance*, during the early 1940s.

This ability to visualize abstract lines and shapes and to transmit a sense of movement was also the result of Laban's long training in imagining a new way to record movements into written signs. Begun at the same time as his more practical and theoretical explorations of dance, this was an activity that he never interrupted over the years. In 1926, Laban inaugurated the Choreographic Institute, a school intended for future professional dancers and choreographers, which was established in Würzburg and later moved to Berlin. Here the students learned how to create dances through an intensive teaching program grounded in movement analysis and dance notation. Two years after establishing the Institute, Laban founded the German Society for Dance Notation and published the volume that was supposed to be the summa of his system.[39]

Laban believed also that his *Kinetographie* would facilitate the making of dance films because of the possibility of translating the dancing parts into a written score, thereby preparing a helpful sort of parallel script.[40] As much as Étienne Marey's film experiments gave to the movement a spatial and temporal coherence, Laban's analytical observations intended to confer upon movement a form of rationality, by way of a decomposition and reunification process, and a form of legibility, by way of a complex representational practice. His notation system, known as *Kinetographie* or *Schrifttanz* (written dance), was a direct consequence of his movement analysis and transformed isolated movements into readable sequences where the notion of time is combined with the representation of the direction of movement. The dancers were educated to think in movement concepts, and the bodily structure was the measure of the written dance, whose iconography corresponded to architectonically constructed spatial images.

Deeply convinced that "Every art ha(d) to have its written form,"[41] Laban was also aware of the enormous potential that a notation system had in controlling the dissemination of his choreographic patterns into large movement choirs, in disciplining the bodies of the dancers, and in spreading his dance concepts throughout German society. Indeed, Laban used *Tanz ist Leben* to express the merit of his notation system for pedagogy and choreography. After a brief focus on some footprints in the snow, which signifies the origin of all kinds of dance writings, Laban inscribes his *Kinetographie* in a prestigious historical line starting with Egyptian hieroglyphics and ending with Feuillet's notation system. By presenting it in this way, *Kinetographie* gains its status as a "natural" and necessary reinvention of a tradition and as a revolutionary way of thinking about dance in modern times. Aiming to become universal, Laban's notation system was indeed very difficult, and to master it students needed to train for a long time. How to capture their attention for this field, which was also a potential new profession in dance? An example of Laban's ability to communicate the idea of the easiness and the amusing aspects of *Kinetographie* can be found in a sequence of *Tanz ist Leben*, very much influenced by the futuristic aesthetic, which shows the transition from a large group of dancing couples to a series of sixty-four isolated legs that, thanks to a special effect, suddenly disappear, leaving the shoes dancing alone on a Charleston rhythm over abstract white lines, i.e., the empty notation score.

In a scenario for a *Tanz-Lehrfilm* written the same year, *Das lebende Bild* (The Living Picture, 1929),[42] and based on the fundamental elements of Laban's movement notation and theory of harmony, his intentions were explicitly announced: it should be primarily an educational tool. For this purpose it was supposed to be addressed mainly to students and dancers who wanted to learn more about his dance theory, either in class or using it in addition to the traditional textbooks for their autodidactic practice. Like other multicombinatory projects, the film could have been easily reworked as a *Kulturfilm* as well, adding some scenes to contextualize this dance education in the larger frame of social dance, sports, and gymnastics, and thanks to translations in many languages, it could have been exported abroad. The living models—only "good looking girls" and some men and groups as he indicates in a draft of the project—were the necessary corollary to the explications of each of the hundred basic scenes about movement concepts and notation signs.

In an article about dance audiences, Laban affirms how important he considered the question of the reception of modern dance. Here he clarifies what he meant to be a relevant difference between visual and performing arts: whereas the visual arts are perceived from the audience as a total experience, and only later as a complex of single pieces that are part of a unity, the performing arts are revealed only gradually. In other words, modern dance—particularly his *Tanzdrama* (dance-drama)—required close attention in order for the spectator to retain a comprehensive memory of dance movement sequences.[43]

With his film projects, Laban searched how to make more appealing the philosophic and aesthetic values of his vision of dance. The difficulties in ordering these mostly undated scenarios alongside his other artistic productions limit our understanding of his creative process; nevertheless, it is clear that these varied dimensions of his career were in a close and dynamic relationship to each other. As much as his drawings and paintings, another parallel activity during his entire career, these scenarios seem to have been the site where he could fully express his amazing ability to visualize (dance) movements.

Thanks to his interest in the film industry, Laban seems also to have fully grasped what Jonathan Crary identifies as a specifically modern issue, the "suspension of perception,"[44] or in other words, its fragmentation and dispersal. Cinema was the most powerful and popular invention of the nineteenth century that transformed vision into something more subjective, in which the body became the "active producer of the optical experience."[45] In the transition from the cultural-historical trope of *Gemeinschaft* (community) to the emergence of mass culture—a development crucial to Nazi ideology—Laban's film projects explored new solutions for a totalizing experience of the world through dance. Dance in turn transformed single individuals within a large community. Why did Laban decide to no longer invest in cinema after the early 1930s? Was this only because of financial reasons? Was it because of the frustration due to his several unaccepted or unrealized projects? Or was it also because he had other, more appealing, possibilities to realize his ambition to catalyze large masses around his *Weltanschauung (worldview)* and his kinesthetic imaginaries?

Notes

1. Labanschule (brochure), Tanzarchiv Leipzig (TAL), Rep. 028 IV c. 2. 1.

2. Evelyn Dörr, *Rudolf Laban: Das choreographische Theater* (Norderstedt: Books on Demand, 2004), 124–125.

3. At least three short scenarios were probably written during the same years for what we can assume was supposed to be a *Filmpantomime*. They are titled *Die schöne Tamara* (The beautiful Tamara), *Die Orchideenbraut* (The Orchid Bride), and *Die Spieluhr* (The Music Box). See TAL, Rep. 028 III 1-a n. 1. See also Dörr, *Rudolf Laban*, 336–343.

4. See Marion Kant and Lilian Karina, *Hitler's Dancers: German Modern Dance and the Third Reich*, trans. J. Steinberg (New York: Berghahn Books, 2003) (original edition *Tanz*

unterm Hakenkreuz, Berlin: Henschel, 1996); and Laure Guilbert, *Danser avec le IIIème Reich. Les danseurs modernes sous le nazisme* (Brussels: Complexe, 2000).

5. The archives are: Tanzarchiv Leipzig (TAL); National Resource Center for Dance, University of Surrey (NRCD); John Hodgson Archive, Special Collections of the Brotherton Library, University of Leeds (JH Archive). For their help I'm grateful to the librarians Gabriele Ruiz, Chris Jones, Helen Thomas, and Oliver Pickering. Some of the scenarios have been transcribed by Vera Maletic in *Body, Space, Expression: The Development of Rudolf Laban's Movement and Dance Concepts* (New York: Walter De Gruyter, 1987), 144–147; and by Dörr, *Rudolf Laban*, 502–538.

6. See Guilbert, *Danser avec le IIIème Reich*, and Kant and Karina, *Hitler's Dancers*.

7. I'm grateful to Thomas Elsaesser and Jeanpaul Goergen for having updated my knowledge about this important issue.

8. Klaus Kreimeier, "Ein deutsches Paradigma. Die Kulturabteilung der Ufa," in *Geschichte des dokumentarischen Films in Deutschland*, eds. K. Kreimeier, A. Ehmann, and J. Goergen (Stuttgart: Ditzingen Reclam, 2005), vol. II, 67–86.

9. Ibid., 81.

10. To give an idea of his work with lay movement choirs (ensembles of amateur dancers improvising on the basis of Laban's movement analysis) he prepared a fragmentary scenario, *Gruppenform-Lehrfilm* (educational film about group forms). See Film zu Gruppenform-Lehrfilm, undated typescript by Laban, TAL, Rep. 028 III-3 n. 6. Performed initially by relatively small groups sharing a desire for communality, Laban's movement choirs under the Nazis became an important element of many theater productions and of mass parades organized to celebrate the *Volksgemeinschaft* (folk community).

11. For instance, the short documentary on the training offered at his Berlin school, *Tanz und Bewegungsübungen der Schule Rudolf v. Laban* (1928).

12. Lotte Eisner, *The Haunted Screen: Expressionism in the German Cinema and the Influence of Max Reinhardt*, trans. Roger Greaves (London: Thames and Hudson, 1969).

13. Thomas Elsaesser, *Weimar Cinema and After* (London: Routledge, 2000), 18–60. See also *The Many Faces of Weimar Cinema: Rediscovering Germany's Filmic Legacy*, ed. Christian Rogowski (Rochester, N.Y.: Camden House, 2010).

14. Susanne Franco, "Ausdruckstanz: Traditions, Translations, Transmissions," in *Dance Discourses: Key Words in Dance Research*, eds. Susanne Franco and Marina Nordera (London: Routledge, 2007), 80–81.

15. Elsaesser, *Weimar Cinema and After*, 150.

16. Rudolf Laban, "Tanz im Film," *Die Schönheit*, no. 24 (1928), 194–195.

17. Undated typescript by Laban, TAL, Rep. 028 II a. 2 n. 50a.

18. Rudolf Laban, *Die Welt des Tänzers. Fünf Gedankenreigen* (Stuttgart: W. Seifert, 1920).

19. A second version of the same film was made with 60 percent new material in 1926 by the same director.

20. Theodore F. Rippey, "The Body in Time: Wilhelm Prager's *Wege zu Kraft und Schönheit* (1925)," in *The Many Faces of Weimar Cinema*, ed. Rogowski, 182–197.

21. See Dörr, *Rudolf Laban*, 496.

22. Verband der Labanschulen e. V. (brochure), TAL, Rep. 028 VI c.

23. See *Die Schönheit*, 1928, no. 24, 192–195. A first silent version of it was shot in 1927. See TAL, Archiv Ilse Loesch, o.n. A. (Auszug).

24. Ein Spiel Karten, undated typescript by Laban TAL, Rep. 028 III 1. a n. 18; see also Dörr, *Rudolf Laban*, 534–538, and Archiv Böhme, TAL, Rep. 019 IV a L n. 7 (75).

25. "R. Laban, Spuk im Spielklub. Ein Tanzfilm?" "Feuilletton," undated, Archiv Böhme, TAL, Rep. 019 IV a L n. 7 (75).

26. Marion Kant, "Laban's Secret Religion," *Discourses in Dance* 1, no. 2 (2002): 43–62.

27. On crystalline formations, see Laban, *Die Welt*, 59.

28. Inge Baxmann, *Mythos: Gemeinschaft. Körper- und Tanzkulturen in der Moderne* (Munich: Wilhelm Fink, 2000), 151–160.

29. Tanz ist Leben! (kurzer Inhalt), undated typescript by Laban, TAL, Rep. 028 IV b. 1 n. 1; Tanz ist Leben, undated typescript by Laban, TAL, Rep. 028 III-3 n. 1 (incomplete document); a similar document is preserved at JH Archive 12/18, with an additional detailed subdivision in scenes; Kaufmännisches Exposé zur Herstellung eines Filmes über den Tanz. Tanz ist Leben. Ein Film von Wilhelm Prager und Rudolf von Laban, undated typescript by Laban, JH Archive 12/18 and TAL, Rep. 028 III-3 n. 5. For the transcription of the incomplete document see Dörr, *Rudolf Laban*, 510–519.

30. Letter by Laban, and Prager (UFA and Tanzfilm G.M.b.H) to an unidentified receiver, 7–9–1928. TAL, Rep. 028 II a. 2n. 95a.

31. JH Archive 12/18 p. 2.

32. TAL, Rep. 028 II b. 2 n. 250.

33. The film is not preserved at Bundesarchiv-Filmarchiv, but the censorship card is there. It is worth noting that this was one of the earliest cultural films shot in color.

34. Die Befreiung des Körpers. Filmreportage über den Tanz, undated manuscript by Laban, TAL, Rep. 028 III 1 a. n. 1, and the four drawings by Laban for the film, TAL, Rep. 028 II a. 2 n. 33. See also Dörr, *Rudolf Laban*, 520–527.

35. TAL, Rep. 028 III 1 a n. 1, undated manuscript by Laban. See also Dörr, *Rudolf Laban*, 528–533.

36. Allison Whitney, "Etched with the Emulsion: Weimar Dance and Body Culture in German Expressionist Cinema," in *Moving Bodies, Moving Pictures: Dance in Early German Cinema*, special issue of *Seminar: A Journal of Germanic Studies* XLVI, no. 3 (September, 2010): 242–256.

37. Laban, *Die Welt*, 183.

38. (German version), NRCD, E (L) 42, 33; (English version), NRCD, E (L) 42, 33. For the transcription of the English version see Maletic, *Body, Space, Expression*, 144–147.

39. Rudolf Laban, *Schrifttanz. Methodik und Orthographie* (Vienna: Universal, 1928).

40. "Tanz im Film."

41. Laban, *Die Welt*, 187.

42. Das lebende Bild, undated typescript by Laban, TAL, Rep. 028 III-3 n. 3. The scenario was written on a few papers bearing the logo of the Choreographic Institute to which was attached the visiting card of the Hamburg based Gupas-Film Filmfabrikation/Photoindustrie.

43. "Tanz und Zuschauer," undated printed article by Laban, TAL, Rep. 028 IV b. 1 n. 27. For the typescript see TAL, Rep. 028 IV b.1 n. 25.

44. Jonathan Crary, *Suspensions of Perception: Attention, Spectacle, and Modern Culture* (Cambridge, Mass.: The MIT Press, 1999), 2.

45. Jonathan Crary, *Techniques of the Observer. On Vision and Modernity in the Nineteenth Century* (Cambridge, Mass.: The MIT Press, 2001), 69.

5. Hanya Holm and an American *Tanzgemeinschaft*

TRESA RANDALL

Hanya Holm arrived in the United States in September 1931 to open the New York Wigman School, created under the patronage of impresario Sol Hurok. On the heels of Mary Wigman's first, highly acclaimed U.S. tour from 1930 to 1931, interest in the Wigman method was high among American dancers, and a small staff from the Wigman Central Institute in Dresden, led by Holm, were sent to New York to capitalize on it. According to Wigman's biographer Hedwig Müller, Wigman was invigorated by the opportunity to conquer America.[1] Hanya Holm—her loyal follower, a true believer in the Wigman cause—was willing to take on the challenge of spreading the Wigman influence in the New World. Holm's initial voyage to the United States, then, was undertaken neither as an immigrant in search of a better life, nor as an artist in search of greater freedom. Rather, I contend, Holm traveled to the United States, in part, as a businesswoman but, more urgently, as a missionary.

In the American dance history literature, Holm is most often referred to as one of the "four pioneers" of American modern dance and as a brilliant choreographer of American musical theater. Her canonization as one of the four pioneers, though, has been a tenuous one; she does not fit well into nationalist narratives of American modern dance and has received less critical attention than her contemporaries Martha Graham and Doris Humphrey. For several decades, analysis of her role in American dance history emphasized her Americanization, or how she adapted her approach to dance to reflect the American temperament—a narrative first established by critic John Martin in the late 1930s and reinforced by Holm's biographer Walter Sorell, among others.[2] As Susan Manning has demonstrated, this narrative served to elide the German influence on American dance and thus bolster claims of its Americanness.[3] In the late 1930s, the Americanization narrative about Holm served specific political ends: it enabled Holm to survive the political controversy surrounding Wigman's collaboration with the Nazis, and it enabled the American modern dancers to claim modern dance as a native American art form during a time of rising nationalism.

Holm herself proposed that "the spirit of America" had become the inspiration for her work in the late 1930s, and she did certainly change her approach to dance after her emigration, in order to better reflect the American temperament, sense of space, tempo, and concept of modern dance. After all, she explained, "The dance, like any cultural expression, when brought from one country to another must undergo some changes."[4] However, I argue that Holm had a rather different understanding of this adaptation process than dance history has most often described. As I will explain, it was not a repudiation of her German modern dance approach, but, in significant ways, its fulfillment. Her concept of dance mandated that she engage directly with "the people" to create a new community of dance (*Tanzgemeinschaft*) in the United States. In the late 1930s, Americans celebrated how Holm had captured the spirit of the American folk in her work;[5] they may not have realized that this was what her concept of dance required her to do (Figure 5.1).

Figure 5.1. Hanya Holm in *Sarabande*. Photo: Anonymous. Jerome Robbins Dance Division, The New York Public Library for the Performing Arts, Astor, Lenox and Tilden Foundations.

Nationalist accounts of American modern dance have largely set the terms by which we have been able to understand Hanya Holm's work. This essay offers a new way to conceptualize Holm's approach to dance and the trajectory of her American career by outlining the aspects of her philosophy and worldview that guided her responses to America and her cultural migration. Hanya Holm was a key figure in the transmission of modern dance across national borders in the 1930s, a history that has only begun to be written.[6]

The politics of this era of German-American interchange in dance are complex and highly fraught, and Hanya Holm's role in the deployment of national agendas is no exception. It is important to remember that even though her migration occurred just a few years prior to the wave of exiles from Nazi Germany, Holm herself was not an exile. She was not forced to leave Germany but left voluntarily as the employee of an international business venture. Further, and even more importantly, the mandate of her concept of dance prevented her from adopting a position of exile in her adopted home. According to her own accounts, she felt out of place, even unwelcome at first—she was a foreigner at a time of isolationism, anti-immigrant nativism, and anti-German sentiment. However, she also knew that she must overcome the liminality of exile—the condition Milan Kundera has called "the unbearable lightness of being"—and instead put down roots in this new place. Exile is alienation, but, as I describe below, German modern dance was intended to be a *solution* to the modern condition of alienation.

Dance as Life Reform

At the time of Holm's arrival in New York in 1931, Mary Wigman was at the height of her international renown and influence. Wigman was a towering figure on both sides of the Atlantic, acknowledged by many as a leader of modern dance and one of the most powerful performers on the concert stage. Throughout the 1920s and 1930s, she toured widely throughout Europe as a solo performer and with her group. She called her work "absolute dance," and she embodied Nietzschean confidence and willpower. Wigman was unrelenting in her vision of a new dance, which she hoped would take over the public theaters in Germany.[7] Thousands of young women, throughout the world, were inspired by her example. By the early 1930s, there were between 1,500 and 2,000 students in eleven Wigman Schools in Germany, many of them international students.[8] Her influence also extended to the schools run by her former students such as Gret Palucca and Berthe Trümpy. In fact her system of dance-gymnastics had a profound effect on amateur dance and body culture in Germany.[9] A journal devoted to her vision of dance, *Die Tanzgemeinschaft—Vierteljahresschrift für tänzerische Kultur* (Dance Community—Quarterly of

Dance Culture), was published from 1929 to 1931, edited by Felix Emmel, a teacher in the Wigman School.

Wigman exuded a mystical aura that pervaded both her stage persona and her pedagogical style, and she attracted fiercely loyal disciples, not least of them Hanya Holm. When Holm joined Wigman's first professional class in 1921 at the age of twenty-eight, she had recently divorced her husband, expressionist artist Reinhold Martin Kuntze. She later described her commitment to Wigman as "another kind of marriage for me, one to last forever."[10] As Hedwig Müller has noted, joining Wigman's mission was a life-altering decision for all her disciples.[11] A career as a dancer was not considered socially respectable, so they risked suffering the displeasure of their middle-class families, and they faced certain poverty and other sacrifices. But they devoted themselves to Wigman completely because they believed in her genius, the cause of free dance, and its revolutionary potential.

As a Wigman disciple, Holm was part of a cultish community that worked for Wigman's vision of dance. Wigman referred to her dance community as a form of *Gemeinschaft* (cultural community), a natural, communal form of togetherness, bound by shared beliefs. Inge Baxmann has illustrated the special role that dance played in the pervasive myth of *Gemeinschaft* in the early twentieth century, as it became associated with the desire to "re-ritualize" modern society and reinvigorate the national community.[12] Anthropologists such as Marcel Mauss and Karl Bücher and psychologists such as Wilhelm Wundt saw in dance a paradigm of sociality and the unity of rhythm, movement, work, and play that characterized "primitive" communities.[13] There was a pronounced faith that the generative strength of dance, rhythm, and movement could be made accessible by new rituals and practices and with it the "suffering German body" of the postwar period could be transformed and healed. These claims must be understood within the context of the bourgeois life reform and body culture movements, which began around the turn of the twentieth century and became part of popular culture after World War I. Modern dance was one practice among many with utopian aspirations to transform everyday life through self-discipline, to heal the modern human—body, mind, and spirit— and therefore heal the nation.[14] Wigman, for example, declared that her system of dance-gymnastics could be practiced by anyone, dancer or layperson alike, to overcome the physical, psychological, and spiritual ailments of modernity.

I argue that we must consider this cultural significance of German modern dance as life reform in order to understand Hanya Holm's initial mission in the United States. She expended considerable energy analyzing the American temperament, so that she could tailor her approach to neutralize the negative effects of modernity in American life. To her, America was the epitome of the frantic pace of modernity, so she emphasized "release" as the starting point for all classes at the New York Wigman School and continually stressed to her American students the need to slow down and allow movement to emerge naturally.[15] The physical practice of "release" created a responsive body, she explained, which was necessary for new, healthier movement patterns to emerge. "The effortless flow of natural movement that can take place only in an unresistive, responsive body is the secret of that vividness and vitality that lifts dancing from the category of exercise to its true place as an expression of life."[16]

Ultimately, this was always the goal—to lift dancing from mere exercise or fun to life consciously lived and vitally experienced. In lecture after lecture during her first few years in the United States, Holm asserted that modern dance was the "doorway to a more intense and fuller life," not only an elite artistic technique.[17] She wrote in 1932 that, "as the dancing body is freed from habitual restraints, and reaches out for new experiences in movement, the mind, too, will grow and encompass new ideas, new impressions, and new fantasies."[18]

Wigman's approach to dance promised to heal the body, mind, and spirit through the awakening of the body and its innate knowledge. Central to this project of awakening the body was the use of so-called "primitive sources" and natural movement patterns, which would bring the modern human back to a condition of unity. Holm explained: "when we speak of the 'primitive' dance we refer in this instance to a culture wherein dancing is not an art divorced from daily life. In the primitive dance then, there is no division between artist and layman, professional and audience."[19] For modern people, she argued, this approach to dance could serve as an "educational medium," a way to develop social consciousness, knowledge of the self, and "an awareness of a body sensitive, alive, and free for living."[20]

The School as Community

This emphasis on dance as life reform and health—and the central importance of amateurs (called "laymen") to the Wigman community—pervaded all the promotional literature produced during the New York Wigman School's first year. In the school prospectus, Wigman called to the school "those thousands, untutored in the rich speech of the body, who might gain in life through physical and emotional exercise."[21] The promotional literature also expressed the hope that the school would become a "cultural workshop where artists in other mediums will come for social and intellectual exchange, where American dancers will brilliantly mature, and where laymen will find satisfying recreation along high levels."[22] In other words, the school aspired to be an *Arbeitsgemeinschaft*, a working community devoted to shared experience, exchange, and transformation.[23] It was to be a central meeting place not only for its students, but also for other interested artists and laypeople.

As a form of *Gemeinschaft* the school was intended to be a cohesive community bound together by shared values. Wigman and her associates believed that working together fostered the ability to "swing together" on personal, emotional, social, and even spiritual levels. This made participants more wholly themselves at the same time that it bound them together. The school also served as a repository for the shared knowledge generated out of teachers' and students' communal explorations of dance. Wigman explained: "The school is the focal point for all those who wish to serve its basic ideas. The aim of each individual, his personal accomplishments as a dancer—these are binding and create a common spirit as to convictions and conceptions of life. . . . In its ultimate and purest sense, the school is the guardian of its products and performances, of the dance work growing in and through it."[24]

In Germany, the Wigman School administered a Central Institute in Dresden and a network of branch schools in Berlin, Chemnitz, Erfurt, Frankfurt, Freiburg, Hamburg, Leipzig, Magdeburg, Munich, and Riesa. The Central Institute served to establish the curriculum, train professionals and teachers in rigorous three-year certificate programs, and house Wigman's performing group. The branch schools taught the laymen's curriculum to amateurs of all ages, including children's classes and special classes for men. (Students were allowed to start the professional certification course at the branch schools, but they had to complete the certification course at the Central Institute in Dresden.) The New York Wigman School was the only branch school on foreign soil. But despite its distance across an ocean, the New York school was intended to serve the same goals as the other branch schools: to spread the gospel, to recruit new followers, and to support the Central Institute and Wigman's artistic work. A legal agreement between Wigman and Holm asserted that Holm was expected to "apply all her strength to the advancement of the New York Wigman School, to conduct the work according to Mary Wigman's ideas and those of the Central Institute in Dresden, and to see that the M. W. philosophy of dance is implemented faithfully within and outside the New York Wigman School in every possible way."[25] Holm was, in all respects, Wigman's representative in the New World.

The ideal of *Arbeitsgemeinschaft* was reflected in the curriculum of the New York Wigman School. While the school delineated professional and amateur courses of study, all students took classes in group dance, which were intended to develop social contact, responsiveness, spontaneity, sensation, and cooperation. Students in group dance classes were asked to work improvisationally to "get a feeling for the other person's rhythm," to solve movement problems as a group, or to explore themes such as "horizontal circles" or "feeling for distance in forms."[26] With its emphasis on social cooperation and interpersonal relations, group dance was essential to developing a community and brought professionals and amateurs together. When Wigman was in town, she also continued her practice from Dresden of choric dance evenings, during which she would lead the students improvisationally in a group dance event. To further develop the sense of community, the school staff organized special events such as teas, special lectures with accompanying receptions, and master classes. Educational philosopher John Dewey, dance critic John Martin, Wigman, Holm, teaching assistant Fé Alf, and Hanns Hasting, Wigman's musical director, all gave special lectures to the entire student body during the school's first year.

In her first few years in the United States, Holm gave countless lectures and lecture-demonstrations at colleges, dance symposia, and progressive education conferences and published several articles in dance and progressive education journals. Her outreach to progressive education advocates—and her association with John Dewey—indicate that she saw schools as a primary location to implement Wigman's approach to dance, and that she saw progressive educators as potential allies. It is beyond the scope of this essay to discuss this in depth, but I would like to propose that this was part of Holm's larger goal to foster a broad-based *Tanzgemeinschaft* in the United States, to extend the community of the Wigman School into a broader cultural context. Holm had taught Dalcroze Rhythmic Gymnastics to amateur women and children for several years prior to beginning her studies with Wigman, and it had a profound effect on her. She was a fervent believer in the need to create an amateur dance culture—for the health of individuals and the whole social body—and she placed strong emphasis on dance education for children. In the spirit of life reform, she insisted that dance for children should be concerned with the education of the human being, not preprofessional training.[27]

Assessing American Rhythms

If her mission were to foster a Wigman *Tanzgemeinschaft* in the United States, then Holm believed it would be imperative for her to determine the health of the sociological soil in which the Wigman seed would be planted. She took a distinct interest in learning about America and her American students and documented her impressions of America in private notes and in correspondence with her colleagues in Dresden. Among Holm's papers are a number of items specifically devoted to this project, including one entitled "Notes on the American Spirit," written in the early 1930s.

This impulse certainly reflects Holm's responsive pedagogical style; it was important to her to understand the American perspective so she could adapt her teaching strategies accordingly. She later wrote, "In undertaking the guidance of each new group there are numerous adjustments to be made by the truly sensitive teacher. How much greater must be the awareness and responsiveness of one who would bring her message . . . to a new country and new people."[28] However, I assert that Holm's language and conceptual constructs of the early 1930s indicate something more than responsive pedagogy. As I discussed above, modern dance was part of a larger cultural project that aimed to remedy the negative effects of modernity. So in order to know what her students needed to become more harmonious, healthy human beings, Holm had to diagnose them, as it were.

Further, Holm was bringing her approach to "a new country and a *new people*" (my emphasis). Her frequent use of the term "student-material" connected her to *Volkish* thought and the tendency to classify humans by race.[29] To her, America was not only a nation, it was a *Volk*, a people, and she believed that each *Volk* had certain innate physical, spiritual, and mental characteristics. Part of her task in the United States was to determine how to make the Wigman method—and its promise of health and community—applicable to the American people/nation/race.

Holm's view of America was rooted in the Weimar-era German discourse on *Amerikanismus* and a deep cultural pessimism, both of which colored her impressions. Soon after disembarking from the ocean liner *Aquitania*, she told an interviewer that she had come to teach Americans to "think with their bodies." The American students who had come to the Wigman School in Dresden, she claimed, approached the work intellectually, and she hoped to teach them "that one could know things just as well with the body, with the feelings."[30] She attributed Americans' rationality, in part, to the fast pace of life in the United States: "The girls who come to us from America work so feverishly trying to become dancers overnight as your great buildings are built overnight."[31] Along with other Germans of her generation, Holm considered America the epitome of modernity and its problems: industrial efficiency (also called *Fordism* or *rationalization*), a frantic pace, over-rationality, loss of authentic community, mass consumer culture, alienation from nature, and what was considered racial degradation.[32] The Weimar-era *Amerikanismus* discourse reflected one of the fundamental dilemmas of the period: how Germany should modernize, and what modernization would mean for German culture. America evoked both an admirable model for Germany to emulate, and a specter of decline—the loss of tradition, social distinctions, and culture.[33]

Much of the *Amerikanismus* discourse centered on the supposed Puritan influence on American culture; in a contorted way, some Germans theorized that Puritanism had paved the way for mass consumption by stressing conformity in belief and lifestyle and by condemning individuality as arrogance.[34] Holm echoed this theory repeatedly and attributed many characteristics of the American mentality to the influence of Puritanism. For example, in a report Holm and assistant teacher Fé Alf sent back to the Central Institute after the first term of the New York Wigman School, they proposed that the rationality of the American "life-attitude" was a result of a deep-rooted Puritanism that caused Americans to negate anything emotional.[35] Wigman's approach to dance was antirational, even irrational, guided by sensation, emotion, instinct, and physical exploration rather than rational thought, and they saw Americans' so-called rationality as a hindrance to artistic growth. This "student type," Holm and Alf asserted, "differs from the German substantially."[36] The Americans refused to take anything on faith, Holm complained: "The notion of belief is essentially alien to them . . . there is no bridge they are able to cross toward irrationality or mysticism. They are notorious doubters as long as they do not know, as long as they have not been completely convinced."[37] This was a major obstacle for teaching the Wigman method; the Wigman community was modeled on a religious community, with its priestesses and laymen. Holm struggled to instill in them the sort of faith that Wigman required of her community members.

Holm sought to counteract the briskness of the American tempo by encouraging her students to allow the primal impulses of rhythm and movement to speak to them. She emphasized the importance of studying percussion as a way to tap into those impulses. "Preaching patience belongs to my daily routine,"[38] she noted, because her American students did not take the time for self-exploration required by the Wigman method. She concluded that the pace of American life was frenzied because there was great desire for constant change, excitement, and physical gratification. "The greed for sensation is like a gaping mouth that is always wide open. New, new, and new again; racing forward: future and present are one. The will to live is splendid and young."[39] She admired this vitality but was concerned by its superficiality.

Since amateurs were such an important component to the Wigman *Tanzgemeinschaft*, Holm was particularly dismayed at the lack of "true amateurs" among her New York students: "They are dilettantes of life as well as art, very difficult to educate and teach. As far as I can say at the moment this type is a product of the city."[40] The American students in the laymen's classes were not as interested in dance as health, vitality, or a fuller experience of life as she hoped. "A tiny minority," Holm noted, "come to dance in order to relax, unwind, find balance, refresh themselves." The others, however, felt themselves to be dancers and lusted after the stage. Holm described them as "wandering meaningless like glow worms from school to school, racing through in search of the stone of wisdom."[41] This situation deeply concerned her because it threatened to undermine her mission in the United States. She was offering dance as a solution to the problems of modernity, but the students were not interested in dance for those reasons.

Holm also expressed dismay about the commodification of American culture and its lack of authenticity. Looking at America, she saw the effects of mass production everywhere. Even young American women seemed to be mass-produced: she later recalled that there was a "uniformity of a look, each one wanted to be a starlet and to be discovered [by Hollywood]."[42] After two years in New York, she concluded that some Americans felt frustrated by this uniform existence, but that they did not have the capacity to change: "One feels the superficiality, wishes to be different, talks about it and does not know which one of the cans of preserves might contain that herb of deepening. Among the supermarket articles one will search in vain."[43]

Holm's critique of mass production in American culture extended to American dance as well. She wrote in a notebook in 1932: "They teach dancing differently than we do. They invent a routine and then sell it. A routine is a movement sequence made up of ballet or tap steps or Greek-American sculptural movements. It has nothing to do with dance as the art of expression. Those applied sequences are finished with more or less technical bravura and one does not care one bit about individuality or experience."[44] In another document, Holm referred to this approach as "canned dances."[45] The process of inventing routines as products to be sold, or of learning a codified technique, stood in direct contrast to Wigman's improvisational, mystical approach, in which students were urged to unearth emotions, instincts, and primal movements through ecstatic group dance explorations. Wigman and Holm stressed that *experience* should guide artistic creation, and that dances should not be created from set formulae or predetermined movement vocabularies. Each dance, its movement vocabulary, and even its approach to movement should emerge organically, as a whole, not simply as recycled codified steps.

Holm declared American dance a product of the metropolis.[46] She proposed that the leading American modern dancers—particularly Martha Graham and Doris Humphrey—had created styles that were private, artificial, and mechanical.[47] This stood in stark contrast to German modern dance's search for communal, organic, authentic cultural forms. Holm asserted that the American dancers made dance "modern" by making gestures abstract and mechanized, and in doing so denied emotions and communal knowledge. She described Graham's work, for example, as "American in its impulsiveness, and peculiarly metropolitan in its lack of elasticity and its somewhat deadened intensity."[48] In Holm's view, Graham's approach to training dancers had serious consequences: "There evolves a method from her dance education, which rapes the living-material, the dancer-human."[49] She noted, "Martha Graham is a very strong person and has an opposing personality against the keep-smiling America. But opposition alone is not necessarily the birth of an art movement."[50] Humphrey's work, Holm felt, was too consciously aesthetic, intellectual, and separated from human experience.[51] Neither choreographer had achieved the "essential," and therefore they did not embody the ultimate goal of modern dance, "moving and reshaping humanity" (bewegte und geformte menschlichkeit).[52]

Political Tensions

From the time of her arrival in September 1931, Holm worked tirelessly to develop a Wigman *Tanzgemeinschaft* in the United States. She was convinced that America was desperately in need of the healing offered by the Wigman method. However, she encountered obstacles. In a 1933 report sent to the Central Institute in Dresden, she asserted: "It is very clear that we have here an open battle field and we have to fight for our place. As I said, the bastion is solid."[53] She was a warrior fighting for the Wigman cause in a foreign land, and she seems to have encountered more resistance than she had expected. Perhaps the large number of Americans who traveled to the Wigman School to study had given her false confidence about how willingly Americans would accept the New York Wigman School. The burgeoning energy of the American modern dance movement may have surprised her. As she reported to her colleagues, the Americans saw German modern dance as a competitor: "[W]e can state that the mere existence of the school has made America nervous, has made it feel unsettled. One knows that here there is something that they do not have themselves; one knows that here there is something that cannot be bought. One senses that here something is given that has to be experienced."[54] She noted that the Wigman method had made some inroads into the American educational system but that she and her colleagues were embattled on the professional dance front.

At the time she wrote this report, Holm did not seem to have realized that politics were about to radically alter the trajectory of her American career. The National Socialists had taken power in March 1933, and change was swift, including at the Wigman School: within one month, Wigman dismissed from the faculty Fred Coolemans, who was of Jewish, Dutch, and Javanese descent, and dismissed most of the Jewish students.[55] In July, Wigman held a conference for all the Wigman, Palucca, and Trümpy schools in Germany—a strategic meeting to discuss the place of the Wigman schools in the new Nazi bureaucracy. This is the meeting for which Holm had written her report, quoted above, about her progress with the New York branch. During the conference—which Holm's teaching schedule prevented her from attending in person—Wigman and her associates decided to join the National Socialist Teachers League and the Fighting League for German Culture. Letters sent to all Wigman graduates in Germany encouraged them to follow this example, and letters to the branch schools pointed out that they would have to agree to rigorously enforce the "personnel conditions for membership," which implied they would need to dismiss their Jewish teachers and pupils.[56] Werner Hoerisch, the new administrative director of the school, sent copies of these letters to Holm in New York. No mention of how the new Nazi regulations would affect the New York branch, particularly its high percentage of Jewish students, exists in the surviving correspondence, even though Holm and Wigman corresponded about the conference itself.[57]

Publicly, Holm maintained fastidious silence about the political changes in Germany and at the Wigman Schools. However, there are indications that privately this was a period of deep crisis for her. In contrast to her first two years in New York, she began corresponding infrequently with Wigman, who expressed concern over Holm's lack of communication.[58] Jane Dudley, who studied with Holm from 1931 to 1935, later observed that around 1934, "Hanya Holm lost faith in what she had brought with her and her work was greatly weakened."[59] In a sense, Holm was suddenly set adrift, without a mission or guiding principles. She could no longer operate the New York school as a true branch, since the Wigman School in Germany was changing in ways that could not apply to the United States. Privately, Holm worried about the fate of her teenage son Klaus, who remained in a German boarding school. Her longtime friend Gabi Poege advised her to bring him to the United States before he could be drafted into the Hitler Youth, but it took Holm more than two years to accomplish this in the face of financial, legal, and political battles. Her close associate and roommate Louise Kloepper later indicated that this was the source of Holm's anxiety during this period.[60]

At the same time, Holm was gaining recognition for her work from significant American individuals and institutions. In the summer of 1933, she taught at the Perry-Mansfield camp in Steamboat Springs, Colorado, an important venue for modern dance. The following summer, 1934, she was invited to teach both at Mills College in California and in the new Bennington College Summer School of the Dance in Vermont, along with Graham, Humphrey, Charles Weidman, John Martin, and Louis Horst. In each of these schools, she was lauded as a leading teacher of modern dance in the United States.

Holm's lectures and articles of this period, from 1933 to 1935, indicate that her concepts and vision had not changed. However, she was walking a fine line—she was receiving recognition as a teacher in American contexts but was still employed by a German institution. She had applied for an immigration visa in 1932 and had committed to staying in the United States. Wigman's response to this is telling; she wrote, "I was very happy to read in your letter that you are so sincerely and wholly ready for the work in New York."[61] Immigration was confirmation that Holm would carry on the Wigman work in a foreign land; it was not a betrayal of her loyalty to Wigman.

Despite her unflagging loyalty to her mentor and her mission, Holm did begin to make specific accommodations to American modern dance, adapting her activities to reflect its two central concerns, composition and technique. She began to choreograph dances for the group of advanced dancers who performed in her famous lecture-demonstrations. By 1935, Hanya Holm and the Mary Wigman Dancers had generated a full concert, with compositions by Holm and by her dancers Jane Dudley, Nancy McKnight, Lucretia Barzun, and Miriam Blecher; they performed this concert in educational settings throughout the Northeast states. Sometimes these choreographies were presented along with their Demonstration Program, a lecture-demonstration of the Wigman concepts that Holm had been honing since 1932. The content of the Demonstration Program gradually shifted over the 1930s, becoming less about mysticism and more about concrete movement concepts. "Circles," for example, had originally been a way for dancers to practice attending to their own sensations until they "became" a circle, until the dancer became the embodiment of circling space, a mystical form. By the late 1930s, Holm's approach to circles emphasized very specific technical skills, such as the placement of the feet, the amount of rotation of the hips, and the tilt of the spine toward or away from the center of the circle. However, her Demonstration Program remained true to the fundamental movement concepts of the Wigman method, including tension-release, swing, rhythm, elasticity, and space.

In the face of demands by her American students for a codified technique, Holm reluctantly introduced specific warm-up exercises into her classes, although she refused to codify a technique or completely abandon improvisation as a teaching method. Holm's student Franziska Boas noted that in the early 1930s American dancers found the improvisational Wigman approach too chaotic, which "created an impasse" for Holm. By 1933, Boas argued, Holm's "attempts at developing sensitivity, feeling and the individuality of the student" were "forced into the background."[62] Holm made these changes very reluctantly.

In trying to determine what forced Holm to adapt her approach, it is impossible to disentangle cultural differences from the political tensions of this time. The partisan and nationalist tone of American modern dance increased in 1934, when Louis Horst founded *Dance Observer*, a periodical devoted expressly to the development of American modern dance. Blanche Evan, who had just completed a summer course at the New York Wigman School, wrote an essay for the leftist journal *New Theatre*, charging that American modern dance had entered a dangerous period of chauvinism, evidenced by prejudice directed at German dance and German dancers.[63] Holm also noted an increase in hostilities against the school in 1934, oriented against the "national origin of the school."[64]

At the same time, some of Holm's own dancers, involved in leftist dance, created works protesting Nazi policies and actions. Miriam Blecher, a member of Holm's performance group, created *Van der Lubbe's Head* in 1934 to criticize Hitler's regime; the dance portrayed the false accusation and beheading of Marinus Van der Lubbe, who had been blamed for the Reichstag fire in 1933. *Van der Lubbe's Head* won first prize in the Second Annual Spartakiade of the Workers Dance Festival and became one of the seminal works of leftist dance.

It is beyond the scope of this essay to detail Holm's complex relationship with leftist dance, but I would like to note that when she first arrived in New York, the politically radical young dancers involved in leftist dance were among the most enthusiastic students at the New York Wigman School. They were invigorated by Wigman's emphasis on dance for laymen and its revolutionary potential for transforming everyday life. Most importantly, though, they saw in her improvisatory approach to choric dance a model for mass dance, a promising tool for leftist propaganda. Nevertheless, Holm's uneasy relationship with leftist dance went into crisis after 1933. It was the leftist dancers who led the charge against Wigman in the mid-1930s, when news of her Nazi accommodation was made public.

By 1935, Holm was besieged by public condemnations of Wigman's collaboration with the Nazi regime. Susan Manning, Ellen Graff, Claudia Gitelman, and others have already written this history, so I will not give the details here.[65] Many people—privately and publicly—implored Holm to sever her ties to Wigman. When she repeatedly refused, students boycotted the New York school. Finally, in October 1936, Holm broke her official ties to the Wigman School, renaming the New York branch the Hanya Holm Studio. At this time, she made a public statement: "A racial question or a political question has never existed and shall never exist in my school. In my own opinion there is no room for politics in art. I most emphatically refuse to identify myself with any political creed which strangles the free development of art, regardless of whether these political straight jackets are imported from Europe or manufactured here."[66]

As Manning has pointed out, Holm's affirmation of the independence of art and politics aligned her with the "humanist" wing of American modern dance, enabling her to survive the controversy.[67] In many ways, this statement also affirmed continuity with Wigman's most sacred principles. For Wigman and Holm, the German dance revolt had always been about *Kultur* and *Gemeinschaft*, not politics. They sought to combat moral decay and modern alienation by forging a new kind of community through dance, and they were absolute artists who did not need to deal in the shady world of politics.[68] Holm was exasperated; she felt that she had already made accommodations to American dance, but now leftist dance wanted her to denounce Wigman. This she refused to do. She changed the name of the school as a political concession, but she did not go so far as to denounce her mentor, and her statement did not invalidate her mission.

American Migration

The following month, November 1936, Holm debuted her dance company in Denver, Colorado, declaring in a radio interview that "the spirit of America" had become the inspiration for her works.[69] How are we to understand this declaration? Certainly the political situation, and the fear it engendered, encouraged her decisions. But there is more to the story. German modern dance was a search for primal rhythms, nature, and a unified, emotional cultural community. It was intended to "awaken the body," not only of the individual person but of the society as a whole. What had changed by 1936 was not this mission, but rather the community with which Holm was concerned: now she was concerned with redeeming the American rather than German people. In this way, I see the year 1936 as the moment of Holm's true migration from Germany to the United States.

The first appearance in Denver represented Holm's debut into American dance as well as the debut of her performing group. In actuality, her performing group, under the name "Hanya Holm and Group of the New York Wigman School of the Dance" had performed this same concert of Holm's work, including *In Quiet Space*, *Drive*, *City Nocturne*, and *Primitive Rhythm*, at Bennington College in August. However, Holm declared the Denver concert the true debut of her independent group, the Hanya Holm Company. This concert symbolized not only her break from the Wigman School but also her shift from Germany to America: here was a company of young American women—most from the West and Midwest—performing in Colorado, with its evocations of the American frontier and the stunning landscape of the Rocky Mountains. Publicity in Denver emphasized their Americanness as well as their modernity, comparing them with the modern trains they had taken across the country from New York.

Holm's performing group, and its repertory, represented an American *Tanzgemeinschaft*. By 1936, she seems to have largely abandoned the hope of fostering a widespread amateur dance culture in America and therefore turned her attention more toward professional dance. She continued to hope for America's redemption through dance and community, but, following the model of American modern dance, her mission was transferred onto choreographic themes. Her critiques of the metropolis, for example, became pieces such as *Drive* (1935) and *City Nocturne* (1936); *Dance in Two Parts* (1936) and *Trend* (1937) dramatized a narrative from alienation to community; and *Primitive Rhythm* (1935), *Festive Rhythm* (1936), and *Dance of Work and Play* (1938) celebrated "primitive" and folk forms of togetherness.

With her company, Hanya Holm sought to demonstrate how a genuine American dance could emerge out of what she called the "American spirit." As discussed earlier, she believed that the "metropolitan" American modern dance approaches of Graham, Humphrey, and others did not represent the true American spirit. An American dance, she proposed, must emerge out of native rhythms and a transcendental American essence. She believed that the American spirit was vital and energetic, and she had absolute faith that Wigman's approach, by accessing the "eternal source of dancing," could unearth a more genuine American dance:

> These principles which are incorporated in the educational method of Mary Wigman have, I believe, much that will be worthwhile to the American dancer. Through her the existence and importance of the eternal source of dancing—sensed by many others at this time—is made articulate. Realizing the error and futility of teaching dance forms in themselves, her credo leaves open all question of personal or national systems and results, and is content to point out the underground springs that wait to be tapped by the individual artist. In America, more perhaps than anywhere else in the world today, there waits fresh and vigorous material for the dance. In its environment and in the temperament and vitality of its people the future American dance has an enviable heritage.[70]

After the political controversies of the mid-1930s, this became Holm's reoriented mission: to tap "the underground springs" of the American spirit in order to develop the "future American dance." Dance critic George W. Beiswanger declared Holm's success in this project in 1939 when he wrote, "Hanya Holm has caught the American folk in its moments of pure excitement, exuberance and animal joy."[71] Later in her career, when she enjoyed great success as a choreographer of Broadway musicals, commentators often remarked on her ability to work in distinctly American idioms.

Following Holm's own statements after 1936, dance historians repeatedly have proclaimed Hanya Holm's Americanization both as a way to declare the "American-ness" of modern dance and to acknowledge how Holm changed her approach to dance to accommodate American temperaments. Yet, as I have argued here, Holm's statements must not be seen as a rejection of her initial mission to foster a Wigman-style *Tanzgemeinschaft* in the United States. On the contrary, the Americanization of her approach can be seen as Holm's attempt to fulfill the mandate of Wigman's system of dance-gymnastics: to tap into folk and so-called primitive sources to unleash the natural forces of dance and thereby bring about personal and cultural healing. Holm made accommodations to the American modern dance model—which emphasized performance and composition rather than life reform, education, or the development of cultural community—while remaining true to her fundamental values and beliefs. Like other migrants, she negotiated a plurality of competing visions and survived through creative adaptations. Colorado, with its rugged mountain setting and evocations of the frontier, came to symbolize Holm's true American home; she founded a summer program there in 1941, which she maintained for over forty years. It was there—far from the dangerous metropolis and its alienating experiences—that she could find the American *Gemeinschaft* she sought.

Notes

1. Hedwig Müller, *Mary Wigman: Leben und Werk der grossen Tänzerin* (Weinheim: Quadriga, 1986), 154. [Editors' Note: On Wigman, see also Sabine Huschka's and Marion Kant's essays in this volume.]

2. John Martin, *America Dancing* (New York: Dodge Publishing, 1936); John Martin, *Introduction to the Dance* (1939, reprint New York: Dance Horizons, 1965); Walter Sorell, *Hanya Holm: The Biography of an Artist* (Middletown, Conn.: Wesleyan University Press, 1969).

3. Susan Manning, *Ecstasy and the Demon; The Dances of Mary Wigman*, 2nd ed., with a new introduction (Minneapolis: University of Minnesota Press, 2006).

4. Hanya Holm, in *The Modern Dance*, ed. Virginia Stewart (1935; reprint New York: Dance Horizons, 1970), 80.

5. George W. Beiswanger, "The New Theatre Dance," *Theatre Arts Monthly* 23:1 (January 1939): 50–51.

6. Manning, "Introduction to the New Edition," *Ecstasy and the Demon*, xxiv.

7. Mary Wigman, "Der neue Künstlerische Tanz und das Theater," in *". . . jeder Mensch ist ein Tänzer": Ausdruckstanz in Deutschland zwischen 1900 und 1945*, eds. Hedwig Müller and Patricia Stöckemann (Gießen: Anabas, 1993), 77–82.

8. Jeschke and Vettermann report that in 1926, there were 360 students at the Central Institute and another 1,200 in the branch schools. Horst Koegler estimates that there were almost 2,000 students in the Wigman Schools in the early 1930s. Claudia Jeschke and Gabi Vettermann, "Germany; Between Institutions and Aesthetics: Choreographing Germanness?" in *Europe Dancing: Perspectives on Theatre Dance and Cultural Identity*, eds. Andrée Grau and Stephanie Jordan (London: Routledge, 2000), 59. Horst Koegler, *The Concise Oxford Dictionary of Ballet*, 2nd ed. (London: Oxford University Press, 1982), 449.

9. "New York Wigman School of the Dance," School prospectus, c. 1931. Jerome Robbins Dance Division, New York Public Library for the Performing Arts (hereafter JRDD, NYPL-PA).

10. Hanya Holm quoted by Walter Sorell, *Hanya Holm: The Biography of an Artist* (Middletown, Conn.: Wesleyan University Press, 1969), 14.

11. Hedwig Müller, "Introduction: A Matter of Loyalty—Hanya Holm and Mary Wigman," in *Liebe Hanya: Mary Wigman's Letters to Hanya Holm*, ed. Claudia Gitelman, trans. Shelley Frisch (Madison: University of Wisconsin Press, 2003), xxii.

12. Inge Baxmann, *Mythos: Gemeinschaft. Körper- und Tanzkulturen in der Moderne* (München: Wilhelm Fink, 2000), 9.

13. Baxmann, *Mythos: Gemeinschaft*, 9.

14. See Chad Ross, *Naked Germany: Health, Race and the Nation* (Oxford: Berg, 2005); Michael Hau, *The Cult of Health and Beauty in Germany: A Social History, 1890–1930* (Chicago: University of Chicago Press, 2003); Karl Toepfer, *Empire of Ecstasy: Nudity and Movement in German Body Culture, 1910–1935* (Berkeley: University of California Press, 1997); Michael Cowan, *Cult of the Will: Nervousness and German Modernity* (University Park: The Pennsylvania State University Press, 2008).

15. Hanya Holm and Fé Alf, "Schul-Bericht Wigman School New York," n.d., 2. Original in German. Hanya Holm Papers (S) *MGZMD 136/298, JRDD, NYPL-PA.

16. Hanya Holm, untitled lecture manuscript, January 1933, 4. Hanya Holm Papers (S) *MGZMD 136/590, JRDD, NYPL-PA.

17. Hanya Holm, "The Educational Principles of Mary Wigman; Their Application to the Role of the Dance in Modern Education," *Journal of Health and Physical Education* (June 1932), 7.

18. Hanya Holm, untitled lecture manuscript, May 13, 1932. Hanya Holm Papers (S) *MGZMD 136/592. JRDD, NYPL-PA.

19. Holm, "The Educational Principles of Mary Wigman," 7.

20. Hanya Holm, "The Aim of the Modern Dance," n.d., 1. Hanya Holm Papers (S) *MGZMD 136/593. JRDD, NYPL-PA.

21. "New York Wigman School of the Dance." JRDD, NYPL-PA.

22. "Announcing the Opening of the New York Wigman School of the Dance," brochure, n.d. JRDD, NYPL-PA.

23. Preface to "Richtlinien für die tänzerische Berufsausbildung," n.d., 2. Original in German. Hanya Holm Papers (S) *MGZMD 136, JRDD, NYPL-PA.

24. Mary Wigman, "Statements on the Dance: The School," in *The Mary Wigman Book: Her Writings*, ed. and trans. Walter Sorell (Middletown, Conn.: Wesleyan University Press, 1973), 129.

25. Gitelman, ed., *Liebe Hanya*, 18.

26. Margaret Gage, "Notes on Wigman Technique 1932–1933." Mary Wigman, Letters to Margaret Gage, 1947–1973 (S) *MGZMC-Res. 16, JRDD, NYPL-PA.

27. Hanya Holm, "The Dance, the Artist-Teacher, and the Child," *Progressive Education* (October 1935), 388.

28. Hanya Holm, in *The Modern Dance*, ed. Virginia Stewart (1935; reprint New York: Dance Horizons, 1970), 80.

29. Marion Kant brings attention to the disturbing significance of classifying humans as "material," something Wigman did often and which pervaded Nazi language. Marion Kant, "Mary Wigman and Hanya Holm: A Special Relationship," *Dance Chronicle* 28 (2005): 421.

30. Hanya Holm in Ruth Seinfel, "American Girls Reason Too Much, Says Dancer Who Teaches Them to Think with Their Bodies," *New York Evening Post*, September 26, 1931.

31. Holm in Seinfel, "American Girls Reason Too Much."

32. Mary Nolan, "Imagining America, Modernizing Germany," in *Dancing on the Volcano: Essays on the Culture of the Weimar Republic*, eds. Thomas W. Kniesche and Stephen Brockman (Columbia, S.C.: Camden House, 1994), 71–84.

33. Beeke Sell Tower, "'Ultramodern and Ultraprimitive': Shifting Meanings in the Imagery of Americanism in the Art of Weimar Germany," in *Dancing on the Volcano: Essays on the Culture of the Weimar Republic*, eds. Thomas W. Kniesche and Stephen Brockman (Columbia, S.C.: Camden House, 1994), 85.

34. Nolan, "Imagining America, Modernizing Germany," 79. See also Moritz J. Bonn, *Amerika und sein Problem* (Munich: Meyer and Jessen, 1925), 89; Lujo Brentano, "Amerika-Europa," *Die Gesellschaft* 9 (1926): 75–76; Heinz Mar, "Die Moral des 'Fordismus,'" *Ford und Wir*, ed. Soziales Museum Frankfurt a. M. (Berlin: Industrieverlag Spaeth and Linde, 1926), 75–76.

35. Holm and Alf, "Schul-Bericht Wigman School New York." Wigman's legal battle with New York's Sabbath Laws in 1931—when she went to court over her right to dance

on Sunday—must have confirmed Holm's belief about the Puritan foundation of American culture. "Sunday Dancing Legal; Mary Wigman, Summoned for Her Recital, Wins Dismissal," *New York Times*, December 22, 1931.

36. Holm and Alf, "Schul-Bericht Wigman School New York," 2.

37. Hanya Holm, untitled document (hereafter Document I), n.d., 7. Original in German; translated by Marion Kant. Based on the content, I believe it was written in June 1933. Hanya Holm Papers (S) *MGZMD 136, JRDD, NYPL-PA.

38. Holm, Document I, 8.

39. Ibid., 3.

40. Ibid., 8.

41. Ibid., 8.

42. Hanya Holm, "Experiencing and Experimenting in Three Generations of Dance," March 9, 1984. Sound Cassette. Learning from Performers Series, Harvard University.

43. Holm, Document I, 3.

44. Hanya Holm, "Bemerkungen," December 1932. Original in German; translated by Annette Steigerwald. Hanya Holm Papers (S) *MGZMD 136/598, JRDD, NYPL-PA.

45. Hanya Holm, "Eight-Day Holiday Course for Teachers and Dancers Offering a Quick Glimpse of the Scope and Aim of Wigman Training" (1931), Hanya Holm Papers (S) *MGZMD 136, JRDD, NYPL-PA.

46. In an earlier article, I argued that Holm constructed a binary opposition between German dance (Gemeinschaft, nature, authentic, organic) and American dance (Gesellschaft, metropolis, artificial, stylistic), which echoed concepts common in Weimar Germany. See Tresa Randall, "Dance and Locality: Hanya Holms Suche nach einem 'Amerikanischen Geist,'" in *Tanz Metropole Provinz*, eds. Yvonne Hardt and Kirsten Maar, *Jahrbuch Tanzforschung* 17 (Hamburg: Lit Verlag, 2007), 49–65.

47. Hanya Holm to Jarmila Kroeschlova (1962–1965). Hanya Holm Papers (S) *MGZMD 136/136, JRDD, NYPL-PA.

48. Hanya Holm, "Notes on the American Dance," trans. Marjorie Bahouth, n.d., 1. Hanya Holm Papers (S) *MGZMD 136/589, JRDD, NYPL-PA.

49. Hanya Holm, "Schulbericht Wigman School New York January–February 1932," 4. Original in German; trans. Annette Steigerwald. Hanya Holm Papers (S) *MGZMD 136/298, JRDD, NYPL-PA.

50. Holm, "Schulbericht Wigman School New York January–February 1932," 4.

51. Holm, "Notes on the American Dance," 1.

52. Holm, "Schulbericht Wigman School New York January–February 1932," 4.

53. Holm, Document I, 6.

54. Ibid., 9–10.

55. Lilian Karina and Marion Kant, *Hitler's Dancers: German Modern Dance and the Third Reich*, trans. Jonathan Steinberg (New York: Berghahn Books, 2003), 152.

56. This letter is reproduced in Karina and Kant, *Hitler's Dancers*, "Document 3," 195–197. A copy of this letter and the letter to the branch schools are in the Hanya Holm Papers (S) *MGZMD 136/625, JRDD, NYPL-PA.

57. In essence, the changes made by the Wigman Schools in Germany prevented Jewish American students from acquiring a professional Wigman certificate because they could not finish the third year of the program at Dresden, as required. Out of approximately ten third-year students in the professional course at the New York branch during the 1933–1934

school year, only two, Drucilla Schroeder and Lucretia Barzun, traveled to Dresden to complete their certificates.

58. Gitelman, ed., *Liebe Hanya*, 45.

59. Jane Dudley, "The Early Life of an American Dancer," *Dance Research* 10:1 (Spring 1992), 13.

60. Reminiscences of Louise Kloepper (1980), page 18, Columbia University Oral History Research Office Collection.

61. Gitelman, ed., *Liebe Hanya*, 44.

62. Franziska Boas, "Some Comments on Dance and Its Development and Some of Its Present Problems" (1948). Box 66, folder 13, Franziska Boas Collection, Music Division, Library of Congress, Washington, D.C.

63. Blanche Evan, "The Star Spangled Dance," *New Theatre* (October 1934), 24.

64. Hanya Holm, "New York Wigman School Jahres Bericht 1933–1934," 8. Hanya Holm Papers (S) *MGZMD 136/298, JRDD, NYPL-PA.

65. See Manning, *Ecstasy and the Demon*, 275–279; Claudia Gitelman, "Dance, Business, and Politics: Letters from Mary Wigman to Hanya Holm, 1930–1971," *Dance Chronicle* 20:1 (1997), 16–18; Ellen Graff, *Stepping Left: Dance and Politics in New York City, 1928–1942* (Durham: Duke University Press, 1997), 115–116.

66. There is a copy of this statement in the Hanya Holm Papers (S) *MGZMD 136, JRDD, NYPL-PA.

67. Manning, *Ecstasy and the Demon*, 271.

68. I am not proposing that Wigman did not *actually* deal with politics; rather, she thought that dance and her career should be valued enough that she should not *have to* barter with politicians. Holm, for her part, denied throughout her life that Wigman willingly accommodated the Nazi regime.

69. "Pro Musica—Miss Hanya Holm," radio transcript, November 16, 1936, 4. Hanya Holm Papers (S) *MGZMD 136, JRDD, NYPL-PA.

70. Holm in *The Modern Dance*, 86.

71. Beiswanger, "The New Theatre Dance," 51.

6. Lotte Goslar's Clowns

KAREN MOZINGO

Lotte Goslar's autobiography, *What's So Funny? Sketches from My Life*, begins with a series of self-portraits of Goslar as clown. The sketches are simply drawn, ink outlines, which mirror the spare quality of her solos. In the first, Goslar stands in a loose-fitting gown, with bulbous shoes protruding from under the hem. She holds a heart in her right hand, and another heart is safety-pinned to her left bosom. She leans backward, her left wrist flexed coquettishly. Her nose is long, reminiscent of Pinocchio, and she glances mischievously out of the corner of her eyes at the reader. Her raised eyebrows convey the notion that she is flirtatious and that things are not as straightforward as they seem.[1] In the series of portraits, Goslar shifts from standing to lying and sitting, then back to standing. The final sketch depicts Goslar standing grumpily on a pedestal, her back leg in attitude, and her right arm wielding an axe.

In contrast to this wry image stands the grandly heroic 1938 oil painting by Arthur Kaufmann, *Die geistige Emigration* (The Intellectual Emigration, 1938),[2] depicting thirty-eight German artists and intellectuals who had emigrated to the United States. That Goslar's memoirs juxtapose this grand painting with her simple sketches suggests that behind Goslar's comedic narrative lies a history of war and exile. As this painting evidences, most early exile research focused on male intellectual exiles, often dubbed the "illustrious immigrants," including Albert Einstein, Bertolt Brecht, Thomas Mann, Erwin Piscator, and George Grosz.[3] Goslar is one of only six women represented, whose positions on the outer edges of the triptych expose the complicated struggles of women to be visible in exile research.

The period from 1933 to 1945 forced modernist artists and women into a time of turbulent change. Goslar's opening with self-portraits suggest that, like the clown, Goslar represents herself as both inside and outside of her autobiographical narrative. Her clown sketch series and autobiographical vignettes slice through the historical narrative of intellectual emigration. Similarly, Goslar employed clowning and fairy tales throughout her choreographic career to create a feminist disruption of romanticism and tragedy in German and American dance representations of women. Goslar's departure from the tragic moods and narratives of *Ausdruckstanz* and her resistance to conventional representations of the intellectual emigration trouble the histories of dance and exile on both sides of the Atlantic.

Lotte Goslar (1908–1997) studied dance with German expressionist dancers Mary Wigman and Gret Palucca.[4] During the 1930s, she performed in Erika Mann's exiled Peppermill Theater in Zurich and the Liberated Theater in Prague. For political reasons, she chose not to return to Germany, and in 1937, she emigrated to the United States with the Peppermill Theater. Goslar's first full performance was part of a "4 star" series at Columbia University in 1937 with concerts by Martha Graham, Trudi Schoop, and Agna Enters. In the 1950s, Goslar began her company, Pantomime Circus, which integrated dance, clowning, mime, and theater.

In spite of her early success in modern dance venues and her commissioned work for companies such as the Hartford and Joffrey Ballets, critics publicized Goslar as a dance-mime or clown, which obscured her training in *Ausdruckstanz* and placed her in a realm outside of dance.[5] Because German and American modernist dance proponents strove to exclude narrative in favor of essential formal elements, dance scholarship also routinely overlooks comedic narrative forms in favor of choreographers such as Martha Graham and Doris Humphrey, who tackled serious and tragic themes.[6] In this regard, it is interesting to note that the work of Trudi Schoop, Agna Enters, and Lotte Goslar in the "4 star" series at Columbia integrated comedy and character-based styles. Both Schoop and Goslar were emigrants and former members of Erika Mann's political Peppermill Theater. By the early 1940s, however, American modern dance was centered around the "Bennington Four," while the "stars" of 1930s modern dance and *Ausdruckstanz* were marginalized.

Goslar's artistic strategies in exile situated her at a unique juncture between several dialectics within the American modern dance community: Germanness versus Americanness, national identity versus transnational identity, dance versus theater, content-based choreography versus design-based choreography, improvisational techniques versus codified techniques, and popular versus concert dance. Her works pushed the boundaries of performance disciplines and the nationalist tendencies of modern dance history, making Goslar fall on the "other" side of what counted as "serious" modern dance in the United States for various reasons: her integration of theater and pantomime, her use of parody, and her German identity. Similarly, Goslar's interdisciplinary artistic strategies seemed to hit the German side of the aesthetic divide when she had trouble booking international tours in the 1980s. For Goslar, returning to Germany on tour went well in the 1950s, but in the 1970s the dance scene had shifted to *Tanztheater*, which was more political and edgy, compared to her more tender, comedic, and entertaining work. Presenters and audiences often thought her company was a circus and did not want to book it or attend performances. Goslar's success in the United States was greater than that of her *Ausdruckstanz* predecessor and sister exile, Valeska Gert, perhaps because the childlike comedy of her work allowed it to be read on multiple levels, while Gert's political satires aroused criticisms of nostalgia for 1920s Berlin and excluded American audiences.[7]

Goslar's autobiographical writings dramatize the research on women in exile, which shows that the discontinuities of exile frequently spur them toward a new configuration of their self-identity and artistic work—a process often revealed in their memoirs. The rhetorical strategy of a woman narrating herself intersects with an interruption of the traditional representations of women that have circumscribed her experience. Sidonie Smith writes, "Autobiographical practices become occasions for restaging subjectivity, and autobiographical strategies become occasions for the staging of resistance."[8] This is certainly true of Goslar's work. From the beginning, her dances rebelled against expected female roles and behavior: "Girl dancers wanted to be beautiful and pretty but I wore a big nose and big eyebrows because I liked to. I just found it ridiculous, too much prettiness. I had a sense of satire about it."[9] In exile, Goslar's clowning in her dances and writing interrupted audience reception of modernism and linked to a resistant history of female fools in German fairy tales and dramatic narratives.

Although female clowns in theatrical history are rare, fairy tales often cast "fool" characters as female.[10] The wise fool commonly appears as a comedic, unassuming old crone, mother goose, or fairy godmother, who guides the protagonist and mediates between the tale and the reader. Through her antics, she exposes the deeper meanings of the fairy tale and points the way toward an alternate reality. As theatrical figures, clowns or fools appear at significant points in a play or performance, often poised between involvement in the narrative and "calculated distance."[11] The clown disrupts the narrative and expresses what the world of the play makes inexpressible. In *No Kidding*, Donald McManus writes that the modernist clown, in particular, also embodies the "contemporary tragic impulse," transcending both genre and theatrical convention.[12] Goslar used clown figures and fairy tales to create worlds of possibility for women in dance, as well as to expose the "fairy tale" entrapment of modernist dance narratives for women.

During the 1920s and 1930s, German women dancers found themselves at the junction of the New Woman, physical culture, and the blossoming of *Ausdruckstanz*. The popularity of dance as an avenue for women was not limited to Germany but extended throughout Europe and the United States. Many young women rebelled against the wishes of their parents and pursued the freedom of movement through training in *Ausdruckstanz*, eurythmics, or gymnastics. Images of Isadora Duncan, Rudolf Laban, and Jaques Dalcroze's students reflected the desires of women to cross into public space, gain athleticism, and find sensual freedom. Like other dancers, such as Mary Wigman and Valeska Gert, Goslar's world expanded when she began studying modern dance. Goslar auditioned privately for Gret Palucca, and Palucca invited her to join the school and dance with her company. Palucca's solo performances inspired Goslar: "Anyone who has never seen Palucca dance cannot even imagine her . . . it was the confirmation of everything I was striving for."[13] Soon Palucca invited Goslar to play percussion for her solos. Along with new attention, Goslar gained access to Palucca's circle of acquaintances. She accompanied Palucca to Bauhaus performances, where she met Paul Klee, Wassily Kandinsky, László Moholy-Nagy, Walter Gropius, and Marcel Breuer.

Even as Goslar was learning Palucca's dance style and accompanying her concerts, her own artistic voice was growing restless. Although her emerging style differed significantly from Palucca's, Palucca was a supportive mentor for her work: "I was amazed. What I loved about Palucca's art was the abstraction; what came out of me was foolishness, clownerie, theater."[14] Two of Goslar's early dances, *The Disgruntled* and *Waltzmania*, commented on the role of dancing in German culture by distancing the viewer through clown and fairy tale imagery. Modern dance connected Goslar's fairy tale imagination to her love for kinesthetic sensation, while her use of clowning and the unaware female fool from fairy tale narratives exposed the romantic utopianism that often lay underneath women's pursuit of freedom through dancing.

Lotte Goslar's first clown character appeared in her dance, *The Disgruntled* (1931). For the solo, Goslar sported a large nose, bags under her eyes, pointed eyebrows, and a large frown. The clown runs onto the stage in a spiral, step-hopping and galloping. He stops, grows taller, and then goose-steps from left to right and back. He abruptly dances a Charleston and then sits and stomps his feet. He rises, side-galloping and stomping from stage left to stage right and back and then moves in a circle to center stage. Planting his feet squarely, he stares at the audience.[15] In *The Disgruntled*, Goslar masks her gender with makeup and costume, subverting the male gaze and exposing the ugliness and anger rising in German culture. The goose-step clearly references the Nazi marching style, while also portraying it as silly childish stomping. She breaks the marching with a Charleston excerpt—an ironic choice given that Nazi regulations later forbade popular social dances and jazz. The baggy gown and clown face recall the mask and gown of Mary Wigman's *Witch Dance* (1926), suggesting a deeper discourse with the modernism of German expressionist dance. The clown's seated stomping resembles Wigman's similar movement, creating a parody of the earnestness and anger of Wigman's solo.

In *Witch Dance*, Mary Wigman sought to embody the *Gestalt* of "witchness." Her costume consisted of a brocade cape with an Asian pattern and a mask depicting a distorted version of her face with elongated eyes. In the clip of the solo that survives on video, she sits on the floor in a cross-legged position, clasping her knees with her elbows and shoulders lifted.[16] She sways and claws with her twisted hands. At times she stomps her feet, rotating her body in a circle on her sitz bones, then draws her knees together, sends her elbows akimbo, and snaps her head with a percussive clap of the accompaniment. Rudolf Bach's description of the solo envisions Wigman as demon: "Like a giant, the red and gold, phantomlike figure rears up in the space. Now it leaps around in a circle. . . . It is as if something invisible were being severed with eerie industry, again and again."[17] At the end of the dance, she falls back to the ground, then rears her head again to stare into the audience.

As Susan Manning writes in *Ecstasy and the Demon*, Wigman's mask and cape, her demonic sense of "otherness," and her direct gaze at the audience freed her from the male gaze in theatrical dance and resisted the beauty and verticality found in ballet. Yet, the visual qualities of her mask and cape also suggest that her expression of feminine "witchiness" as otherness is orientalized, a frightening vision considering the role her dance would come to play in the development of a German dance aesthetic and its involvement with the rise of a Nazi cultural agenda. Lotte Goslar's *The Disgruntled* also challenged ballet's representation of femininity, while accomplishing something that Wigman's dance could not—the pointed criticism of fascist arrogance and anger.

As Goslar critiqued the images of the *Ausdruckstanz* aesthetic and the National Socialist movement, her works also explored the ways women were caught between romantic utopianism, National Socialism, dance, and fairy tales. In *Waltzmania* (1939), Goslar parodied German fairy tales such as the Brothers Grimm's *The Worn-Out Dancing Shoes* and the popular waltz dances of Austrian modern dance pioneer, Grete Wiesenthal. The solo was a parody of dancers carried away by the strains of a Strauss waltz, particularly the *Blue Danube*. Suddenly "the romantic one-two-three of the waltz tempo turns into the young woman's nightmare, as the power of the dance overtakes her and she cannot stop dancing. The music ends and the lights fade as the young woman frantically tries to stop her anguished dance."[18] In his 1948 study of the waltz, Mosco Carner writes, "with the reaction in the first three decades of our century against romanticism, the waltz was considered outmoded and has often been made the subject of musical parody."[19] Goslar accomplishes a double parody with *Waltzmania* by exposing the reliance of the waltz and Austrian modern dance on romantic nationalism.

Goslar's *Waltzmania* also included a feminist critique in its reference to the narrative of *The Worn-Out Dancing Shoes*. In the Grimm's fairy tale, a king promises the hand of one of his twelve daughters to the first man who can determine how they wear out their dancing shoes each night. A poor soldier, returned from the war, pretends to fall asleep and discovers that the twelve princesses escape their room each night to a magical realm below the castle, where they dance and drink wine with many suitors until their shoes are full of holes. The soldier betrays the princesses by disclosing their revels to the king, who then gives the eldest daughter to the soldier as his prize.[20]

A similar dancing trap occurs in Hans Christian Andersen's tale, *The Red Shoes*, in which a young girl, Karen, becomes enamored with her red dancing shoes and wears them everywhere, ignoring piety and proper decorum. While in church, the lure of the red shoes overcomes her thoughts. She wears them to a dancing ball, but once she begins dancing, the shoes take over and she is unable to stop. Condemned by the villagers and her family, she dances through day and night. Maria Tatar writes, "The moment of Karen's deepest personal degradation and social disgrace comes when she is in perpetual motion, a socially disruptive nomadic figure unable to remove the shoes that signal her pride."[21] Exhausted but unable to stop dancing, Karen asks the village executioner to sever her feet. He makes wooden feet for her, and she retreats to her room to sit and pray for penance. In her stillness, she merges with a brilliant angel who visits her room, and her soul flies to heaven.[22] In *Waltzmania*, Goslar uses images from the waltz and both fairy tales to link the ecstasy and perceived women's freedom of expressive dancing to the ecstatic dancing and mesmerism of the fairy tale, suggesting that what appears as freedom quickly becomes a narrative trap of heterosexual marriage or death.

For modernist dancers, like Isadora Duncan, whose artistic achievements of kinesthetic freedom created positive steps for women, the historical narratives of their lives and careers often served to support the myth of the tragic woman artist. Duncan's unconventional life and death often overshadowed her artistic accomplishments. Likewise, for Wigman and her contemporaries, the downfall of *Ausdruckstanz* after 1936 mythologized the pioneer dancers who stayed in Germany during the war and created a tragic narrative based on their errors in judging the consequences of Nazism. Like Karen and the twelve dancing princesses, the *Ausdruckstanz* pioneers found in dance both their freedom and their narrative end.

In the decades following World War II, the writings of Wigman and Laban perpetuated the historical narrative that the Nazi regime halted *Ausdruckstanz* because its philosophy and expression conflicted with Nazi cultural policies.[23] Not until the leading dancers had died did Susan Manning, Marion Kant, and their generation of dance historians reveal the many dancers whose careers continued after Hitler's rise to power—including Mary Wigman, Rudolf Laban, and Harald Kreutzberg. As the comparison between Goslar's *The Disgruntled* and Wigman's *Hexentanz* reveals, the expressionist modernism of *Ausdruckstanz* served to support National Socialist ideals through its romanticized German origins, abstracted physicality, and orientalized images. In *Women, Modernism, and Performance*, Penny Farfan questions the use of women as tragic subjects, since usually the: "nature of the tragic misstep or error in judgment—the hamartia—that leads to their reversal of fortune may be said to be gender-inflected, relating to their incursions into the male-dominated realm of public life."[24] Farfan's discussion of the role of tragedy in curbing women's resistance suggests that the narrated death of *Ausdruckstanz* served to shield female modern dance pioneers—who made up the majority of the dance field—from criticism, while simultaneously reversing their transgression of the conventional, male-dominated, modernist movement.

Goslar's *Valse Very Triste* (Very Sad Waltz, 1959) (Figure 6.1), choreographed during exile, captures her departure from formalist modernism and explores comedy as an alternative path for resistance. Critic Polaczek describes how Goslar's dance exposed the paradox of *Ausdruckstanz*: "In the fluttering black symbolic figure is easily seen the character of Harald Kreutzberg. . . . The fatal mixing of irrationality and suggestion, claim of artistic autonomy and still astoundingly plain need for representation adjusted to national socialist stylization, as Kreutzberg wrought perhaps in *Waffentanz* to music from Werner Egk for the Olympic Games 1936, is simply overcome—through ridicule."[25] The dance begins with melancholy music as a male dancer enters in a black unitard and cape. He shrugs, shakes his head, and walks dejectedly. The dancers enter, dressed in black and writhing under a black shroud. Goslar, dressed in white, frees the dancers and attempts in vain to raise their spirits. The dancers resist her and continue their angular, weighted movements, percussive contractions, and flexed foot gestures, while Goslar points repeatedly toward the sky. The dancers counter her with downward gestures, pathos, and shrugs of despair. The male dancer collapses in depression and tries to pull Goslar down with him. Although the black cloth eventually buries Goslar, on the last trill of the music, she frees her hand and points it triumphantly toward the sky.[26]

A German critic compared the "sad dancers" of *Valse Very Triste* to Martha Graham's dancers, asserting that Goslar "illumines the fear and aggression-dimmed modern dance atmosphere of a Martha Graham."[27] Despite the fact that these are two different critics writing in two different decades, the comparison to Graham, alongside the comparison to *Ausdruckstanz* and National Socialism, underscores the similarity in the aesthetic vision and appearance of German and American modern dance, as well as the service of the dance forms to a nationalist agenda. American modern dancers opposed the rise of

Figure 6.1. Lotte Goslar, *Valse Very Triste*. Photo: John Lindquist. © Harvard Theatre Collection, Houghton Library, Harvard University. Jerome Robbins Dance Division, The New York Public Library for the Performing Arts, Astor, Lenox and Tilden Foundations. Dancers: Joseph Scoglio, Ron Platts, Lance Westergard, Kathleen Carlin, Lotte Goslar, Paul Magloff, Linda Talbert (Tawney); Jacob's Pillow, 1968.

fascism and criticized the compliance of German dancers like Wigman, yet they simultaneously advocated for dances based on a romanticized American past and frontier spirit as the basis for an indigenous modern dance. In addition to her defiance against nationalist narratives of German and American dance, Goslar's finger also points to her struggle against the closed narratives for women in the modernist representations and tragic genres of female theater and dance artists.

Goslar's resistance to tragedy, as well as formalist and expressionist modernism, forms a bridge between her German cultural past and her American present while opening the way for an alternative modernist discourse. As Farfan writes, "... feminist artists in the late-nineteenth and early-twentieth centuries engaged with the texts of the culture at large through their relationships to the texts of the theatre, so that their responses to dramatic literature and theatrical practice in effect constituted feminist critical discourse both through theatre and about theatre itself. Such feminist discourse was a defining feature of modernism."[28]

Goslar's repeated themes of banishment and clever escape also create an alternative discourse within exile studies. Since the mid-1990s feminist researchers have considered exile not only as a time of isolation and hardship, but also as a time of profound growth and creativity. German Studies scholar Renate Posthofen writes that, for women artists, the creative work of their professional lives often provided a sense of continuity between their German past and exile present: "The [artistic] reality becomes the author's imagined homeland, she herself in turn becomes a symbol of her homeland in exile."[29] Living in a state of displacement allowed Goslar to create alternative discourses to the narratives of German and American dance modernism and to imagine potential escapes from tragic patriarchal narratives, both historical and artistic.

Like the clown exposing the tragic ironies of formalist and expressionist modernism, Goslar's fairy godmothers challenge the closed narratives of history and women's representation. Goslar's later dances choreographed in the United States incorporate fairy godmother characters, reminiscent of significant characters from her German childhood: "The midwife for my mother had become a friend and we would visit her in her tiny place. She was crippled by that time and obviously she was poor.... There was always some gentle laughter and there were cookies in a big blue jar and her brown eyes were dancing with some sort of mischief. Her name was Mrs. Fuhr and I have always through my life looked for the Mrs. Fuhrs of our time."[30] In fairy tales, the fairy godmother was often a figure derived from the spirit of an animal helper, who represented an absent or dead mother. The good fairy godmother watched over and provided moments of wish fulfillment for the young female child. Many narratives represented fairy godmothers as old crones or hags who toyed with the young girl and her romantic interest: "Godmothers acted as co-maters: they stood *in loco parentis*.... All these older malevolent women stand in some degree of parental or guardian relation to the young on whom they prey."[31] The fairy godmother often interferes in the girl's romantic relationship with the young prince. For Goslar's work, fairy godmothers serve as a modernist critique of the nineteenth century ballet representations of women.

La Donna della Dondolo (1979) (Figure 6.2) is a parody of fairy tale ballets, in which Goslar is the fairy godmother, who repeatedly clobbers the prince and his bride over the head with her magic wand. Goslar divides the dance into three sections, which parody the ballets *Sleeping Beauty*, *La Sylphide*, and *Swan Lake*, through narrative structure and visual imagery. In each section, the godmother interferes in the development of the young couple's relationship, and black shrouds, fainting spells, or death remove the princess from the ballet. In the first section, a nun *bourreés* onstage and finds a baby girl hidden in leaves. A fairy godmother, danced by Goslar in a white tunic and blue cone-shaped hat, blesses the baby and then whacks it with her wand.

There is a break, and fifteen years later a young man enters carrying a stuffed lamb. The nun enters with the baby, now a young lady, and presents her to the man. They dance a romantic, swinging duet with lifts but are interrupted by three dancers, who cover the young woman in a black shroud. Once again, the fairy godmother enters and whacks the princess with her wand, which breaks over the young woman's head. The young woman collapses, and Goslar exits with her dangling wand. The young man continues to dance with the young woman, but she collapses repeatedly. He catches her after every turn sequence, as she falls under the fairy godmother's spell. Another dancer covers the young woman with a black cape.

Figure 6.2. Lotte Goslar, *La Donna Della Dondolo*. Photo: John Lindquist. © Harvard Theatre Collection, Houghton Library, Harvard University. Jerome Robbins Dance Division, The New York Public Library for the Performing Arts, Astor, Lenox and Tilden Foundations. Dancer: Lotte Goslar; 1979.

In the third section, two women stomp grapes in a tavern, where the young man is drinking and pining for the princess he loves. Suddenly a mystical veiled woman appears on his shoulder and then disappears. The young man is imprisoned, and the princess appears to beg for his release. "Mercury" enters and delivers a message to the jailor, who releases the prince and reunites him with the princess. At midnight, the fairy godmother appears again and whacks the man over the head with her wand, causing him to collapse. All of the dancers point offstage, gesturing for Goslar to leave, but she "looks around, then defiantly points to the right—exactly the opposite direction—and exits, triumphantly the mistress of her own destiny."[32] As she heads offstage right, Mercury tries to stop her, but she whacks him over the head, as well.[33]

In each of the sections of *La Donna della Dondolo*, Goslar's fairy godmother interrupts the narrative before it closes around the princess, exposing the inevitable fate for women in ballet. Marina Warner writes that there is an "affinity between the teller who knows from the beginning the heroine's hidden virtue and the fairy godmother, who brings about her happy recognition."[34] Banished from the stage by her fellow performers, Goslar chooses her own exit, suggesting the necessity of finding one's own way out of the tales' expectations and exposing the banishment of women who defy patriarchal conventions within the ballets' restricted narratives.

Goslar created her most famous fairy godmother–like solo *Grandma Always Danced* in 1953 and performed it for the next thirty-eight years. The dance recuperates the image of the old crone by portraying her life from infant to angel. Goslar kneels center stage in a large bonnet and bounces like a jolly infant to a German folk song. She grows quickly into a stretching toddler and then skips and dances as a young, coquettish girl. She becomes a young lady, faints, and then cradles two babies, one on each elbow. Soon she is herding the children and then stretching and rubbing her aching back. She becomes an old matron and shrivels, and then she grows feisty. Her dance begins in her hips, moves to her shoulders, and grows larger as she dances and skips, shaking her finger. She exits except for her right hand, which remains visible and points resolutely toward the sky. She returns as an angel with her silver halo, looks around below her, flaps her wings, and waves to people still on earth. God tells her to stop dancing. She shrugs, flutters her hands defiantly, and lifts them upward with the last trill of the piano.[35]

As if commenting on a lifetime of discourse with women's roles in dance, Goslar regularly ended a performance with *Grandma Always Danced*, or she included it as the last number before the finale. Her raised finger of protest against a God who would forbid her dancing recalls her reemergence from the shrouded grand narrative of modernist dance and her consistent "yes" uttered against the "no" of Nazi oppression. By integrating comedy, clowning, fairy tales, and dance, Goslar broadened the boundaries of American and German definitions of modernism and subverted the representations of gender that were integral to both dance traditions. Her work disrupts the current narratives of German and American dance history by showing alternative modernist performance traits and strategies. As clown and fairy godmother, Goslar splits open the patriarchal narratives of cultural history and aesthetic representation, reminding us of what is possible in the midst of unimaginable loss.

Notes

1. Lotte Goslar, *What's So Funny? Sketches of My Life* (Amsterdam: Harwood Academic Publishers, 1998).

2. Arthur Kaufmann, *Die geistige Emigration* (Sammlung Kunstmuseum Mülheim). The painting is a triptych, with the crowd of emigrants spanning the three panels and standing as if for a group portrait. A swastika hangs over the upper-left corner of the left panel, while the center panel shows a ship sailing over the emigrants' heads. The third panel, in which Goslar is depicted, shows the buildings of New York City, the Statue of Liberty, and the American flag in the upper-right corner. As a group portrait, the emigrants project an identity that spans the depths of the Atlantic Ocean, stretching between Germany and the United States as a tunnel of exiles.

3. Sibylle Quack, "Introduction," *Between Sorrow and Strength: Women Refugees and the Nazi Period*, ed. Sibylle Quack (Cambridge: Press Syndicate of the University of Cambridge, 1995); see Claus-Dieter Krohn, *Intellectuals in Exile: Refugee Scholars and the New School for Social Research*, trans. Rita and Robert Kimber (Amherst: The University of Massachusetts Press, 1993) and Anthony Heilbut, *Exiled in Paradise: German Refugee Artists and Intellectuals in America from the 1930s to the Present* (Boston: Beacon Press, 1984).

4. Editors' Note: On Mary Wigman, see the essays by Sabine Huschka and Marion Kant in this volume. On Gret Palucca, see the essays by Susan Funkenstein and Marion Kant in this volume.

5. Goslar's autobiography is catalogued in the pantomime section of libraries, meaning that dancers browsing the dance shelves would not encounter her.

6. In her dissertation, "'Grandma Always Danced': The Mime Theatre of Lotte Goslar" (PhD diss., University of Colorado, 2002), Annette Thornton divides Goslar's dances into two categories—dances employing a comedic approach and dances focusing on choreographic craft. Within these two larger categories, Thornton identifies four subcategories of Goslar's work: "pieces where narrative is primary, those that explore a certain theme or emotion, those from a distinctive female point of view, and dances that are for the pure love and joy of movement"(194). Although Thornton's categories are helpful, I feel that they simplify Goslar's work and reify the separation of craft or abstraction from content and dance from theater. Other published studies of Goslar are mostly biographical and partial in their examination of Goslar's life and work. Beate Schmeichel-Falkenberg's article, "Aufforderung zum Überleben: Lotte Goslar und das Exil," in *Frauen und Exil: Exilforschung*. (Band 11, 1993), 216–228, is a biographical account of Goslar's career during her exile. In spite of Goslar's mixed German, gypsy, and Jewish heritage and leftist

political leanings, Schmeichel-Falkenberg includes Goslar among those exiles who left Germany by choice. Katrin Sieg's *Exiles, Eccentrics, and Activists* (1994) acknowledges the danger faced by Erika Mann's Peppermill Theatre and leans toward an interpretation of Goslar's exile as forced, though perhaps not in the beginning. Her study focuses solely on Goslar's performances with the Peppermill Theatre and her identity as a cabaret and grotesque dance artist. Marianna Vogt's master's thesis, *Lotte Goslar: A Clown between Borders* (University of Missouri-Kansas City, 2007), questions Goslar's exile identity, asserting that because Goslar remained employed throughout her seventy-year career and was never homeless, she never experienced the effects of exile. All of the studies about Goslar miss what was significant about Goslar's clowning—her use of the clown figure to disrupt and call into question the representations of women across the performance genres of dance, cabaret, and theater.

7. Editors' Note: On Valeska Gert's exile, see Kate Elswit's essay in this volume.

8. Sidonie Smith, *Subjectivity, Identity, and the Body: Women's Autobiographical Practices in the Twentieth Century* (Bloomington: Indiana University Press, 1993), 156.

9. Quoted in C. W. Vrtacek, "Life's Light Side Motivates West Cornwall Performer," *Litchfield County Times* (September 1, 198?): n.p.

10. In *Fools and Jesters in Literature, Art and History* (1998), Vicki Janik writes that the "most significant fool [precursor to the clown] in Western culture, Erasmus's Stultitia (Folly) in *The Praise of Folly*, is female; but in most cases the fool is male, with a masculine pronoun referent" (Janik, xiv). She adds that it is common for the dress and behavior of both male and female fools to signify sexual ambiguity.

11. Bente A. Videbaek, *The Stage Clown in Shakespeare's Theatre* (Westport, Conn.: Greenwood Press, 1996), 2.

12. Examples of clowns in modernist theater include the clown roles in Vsevolod Meyerhold's *The Fairground Booth* and *Columbine's Scarf*; Bertolt Brecht's *Mann ist Mann*; and Samuel Beckett's *Waiting for Godot*, *Endgame*, and *Act without Words*. Clown figures in dance were also found in the works commissioned by Sergei Diaghilev and created by Michel Fokine and Jean Cocteau. See Donald McManus, *No Kidding! Clown As Protagonist in Twentieth-Century Theater* (Newark: University of Delaware Press, 2003), 11.

13. Goslar, *What's So Funny?*, 14–15.

14. Ibid., 15.

15. *Lotte Goslar's Pantomime Circus: Children's Show*, DVD, camera: Peter Kluge (Fourth Internationales Tanzfestival Nordrhein-Westfalen, 1990).

16. Allegra Fuller Snyder, *Mary Wigman, 1886–1973: When the Fire Dances between the Two Poles* (Berkeley, Calif.: University of California Extension Media Center, 1982).

17. Susan Manning, *Ecstasy and the Demon. The Dances of Mary Wigman*, 2nd ed. (Minneapolis: University of Minnesota Press, 2006). Translated from Rudolf Bach, *Das Mary Wigman Werk* (Dresden: Carl Reissner, 1933), 29–30.

18. Thornton, "'Grandma Always Danced,'" 84.

19. Mosco Carner, *The Waltz* (New York: Chanticleer Press, 1948), 69.

20. Valerie Paradiž, *Clever Maids: The Secret History of the Grimm Fairy Tales* (New York: Basic Books, 2005), 146–149.

21. Maria Tatar, ed., *The Classic Fairy Tales: Texts, Criticism* (New York: Norton and Company, 1999), 213.

22. Hans Christian Andersen, trans. R. P. Keigwin, *Eighty Fairy Tales* (Skandinavisk Bogforlag, Flensteds Forlag, 1976). Reprinted in Maria Tatar, ed., *The Classic Fairy Tales: Texts, Criticism* (New York: W. W. Norton and Company, 1999), 241–245.

23. Vera Maletić, *Body, Space, Expression: The Development of Rudolf Laban's Movement and Dance Concepts* (Berlin: Mouton de Gruyter, 1987), 23–34; Manning, *Ecstasy and the Demon*, 222.

24. Penny Farfan, *Women, Modernism, and Performance* (Cambridge: Cambridge University Press, 2004), 103.

25. Harald Kreutzberg (1902–1968) was a German modern dancer and choreographer, who trained with Rudolf Laban and Mary Wigman. He became a major figure in *Ausdruckstanz* and toured internationally with his dance partner Yvonne Georgi. Review of performance in Frankfurt Theater, Frankfurt, Germany, *Frankfurter Allgemeine Zeitung* (March 19, 1981), n.p.

26. *Choreography by Lotte Goslar*, Videocassette (WGBH and Florida State University, 1976 and 1980). *Lotte Goslar's Pantomime Circus*, DVD, prod. Maria F. Loffredo (Joyce Theatre, N.Y., 1984). *Lotte Goslar's Pantomime Circus*, Videocassette (Sharon Playhouse, Sharon, CT, 1989).

27. Hartmut Regitz, "Im Liebestraum vom Stuhl gesunken," *Rheinische Post* (February 27, 1997).

28. Farfan, *Women*, 2.

29. Renate S. Posthofen, "Claire Goll (1891–1977): Visionary Power and Creative Symbiosis-Fictionalized Identity as Survival Strategy," *Transforming the Center, Eroding the Margins: Essays on Cultural Boundaries in German Speaking Countries*, eds. Dagmar Lorenz and Renate S. Posthofen (Columbia, S.C.: Camden House, 1998), 93.

30. Lotte Goslar, "Reflections," *Mime, Mask and Marionette* (1979–1980), 23.

31. Marina Warner, *From the Beast to the Blonde: On Fairy Tales and Their Tellers* (New York: The Noonday Press, 1996), 204.

32. Thornton, "'Grandma Always Danced,'" 213.

33. *Lotte Goslar's Pantomime Circus*, 1989.

34. Warner, *From the Beast to the Blonde*, 216.

35. *Choreography by Lotte Goslar*, Videocassette (WGBH and Florida State University, 1976 and 1980). *Lotte Goslar's Pantomime Circus*, 1984.

7. Back Again? Valeska Gert's Exiles

KATE ELSWIT

Valeska Gert (1892–1978) claimed she once asked Bertolt Brecht to define epic theater, to which he replied: "What you do."[1] While this apocryphal anecdote is often taken as shorthand for Gert's artistic oeuvre, it risks flattening the multiple kinds of otherness that delineated her career. As Svetlana Boym points out, the actual experience of exile may sometimes function not as an extension, but rather as the ultimate test, of artistic metaphors and theories of estrangement.[2] Through Gert's exile and her return to a homeland that had changed in the intervening years, her performance practices, which were based in a certain presumed outsiderness, were transformed under new conditions and audiences. Her story materializes the complicated entanglement between the modernist preoccupation with alienation and political exile itself.

To offer a brief chronological overview: Gert came into the public eye as a soloist in the late teens, touring mostly through Germany but also abroad during the Weimar Republic, including to the Soviet Union where Sergei Eisenstein wrote that she was "only barely social satire. But she is one hundred percent pure nitric acid for bourgeois ideology."[3] Because the National Socialist rise to power had less aesthetic impact on dance than on other arts, dancers tended to leave Germany for political and "racial" reasons.[4] However, after 1933, Gert had few options, given that she was Jewish, her work was politically left-oriented, and her artistic modes of experimentation tended toward avant-garde forms that did not easily assimilate into the new aesthetic strategies of the Nazi state. Her 1932 cabaret venture, Kohlkopp (Cabbage Head), closed. She was no longer permitted to perform in Germany except within the *Jüdischer Kulturbund* (Jewish Cultural Union), and that was curtailed after an incident in 1934 when she explained to a British newspaper that her husband would be unable to see her upcoming dance performance because "the Ghetto with all its ancient restrictions has been revived in Germany.... No Christian in any capacity is allowed to enter a Jewish theater."[5]

From 1933 to 1938, Gert appeared in European cities, including London, Paris, Budapest, Krakow, and Prague, as well as in New York. She acquired British citizenship through a convenient second marriage in 1936, and in 1939 Gert emigrated to the United States, where she was primarily based in New York City with short stints in Hollywood and Provincetown. She ran one of the more successful exile cabarets in New York from 1941 to 1945, named the Beggar Bar because, as she explained to a reporter, she had to beg together the money and fittings to open it.[6] After the Beggar Bar closed for licensing problems, she briefly tried another cabaret venture in Provincetown, but decided to return to Germany following Brecht's advice to go via Switzerland. Gert performed in Zurich, opening Café Valeska und ihr Küchenpersonal (Café Valeska and Her Kitchen Staff) in 1948, before relocating again in 1949 to what became West Berlin. After a series of guest performances on a temporary visa, she settled to open Bei Valeska (Valeska's Place) in 1949, which quickly closed, and then Hexenküche (Witches' Kitchen) in 1950, which closed in 1956. Finally, she retreated to the cabaret Ziegenstall (Goat Shed) that she had opened in 1951 on Kampen auf Sylt and remained there until her death in 1978. She was rediscovered by German avant garde filmmakers in the 1960s and later seen as a stylistic progenitor of the *Tanztheater* of the 1970s.[7] She has increasingly been the object of dance scholarship over the last few decades, and the Free University in Berlin established a guest professorship in her honor in 2006.[8]

The persistent image of Gert's Brechtian alienation fulfills Ian Buruma's observation that the idea of exile has been "in fashion," at times exhausted by the fragmentation of the postmodern condition or by the way many intellectuals and artists consider themselves to be "a romantic outsider living on the edge of the bourgeois world."[9] However, to separate Gert's often-discussed techniques of artistic alienation from her physical displacement requires particularizing at least three periods of exile, each of which operated differently. In the first instance, Gert was acclaimed by the Weimar arts community for dance performances that capitalized on the romantic and modernist image of artists as exiles in the sense of being positioned as outsiders who pushed the boundaries of aesthetically and socially acceptable practices. (Witness the subtitle to Peter Gay's famous 1968 study of Weimar culture: *The Outsider as Insider.*) In the second instance, Gert's forced migration caused her work to embody the foreignness she had previously claimed; however, to survive she developed a performance space where she reperformed her situation in a manner that domesticated her otherness into something commercially viable. In the final instance, Gert's remigration to Germany reversed her geographic exile, yet manifested another form of estrangement because her work had continued to develop in other geographic places, thus displacing her from the social position reserved for a returning Weimar Jewish artist.

The histories of German exiles and emigrés like Gert and Brecht tend to be haunted by assimilations of foreignness, as found for example in the presentation of exiles as keepers of the "other Germany," which accentuated the Germanness and German-oriented activities of the emigrants.[10] Such nationalist claims resist acknowledging German dance's mutation during and as a result of World War II. Yet, although exile tends to be understood as a way dance resisted co-option by Nazi ideology, what if exile not only acted as a mechanism of preservation but also facilitated more hybrid encounters that were then carried back through remigration?

I am interested in the historical particularities of Gert's work in these three specific times and places, at the same time as I take her experience to be not entirely unique. Gert was not the first German dancer to leave because of the Nazi regime, nor, upon returning, was she alone in feeling displaced from a cultural legacy.[11] However, Gert's particular brand of audience encounter lends itself to thinking about the reception, development, and alteration of her work in relation to foreign audiences. It also highlights how that changed work enacted another encounter on her return to Germany, beyond the confrontation of Weimar nostalgia with the post-Hitler situation. Gert's returning performances came not only from another time but also from another place.

Exile Number One

Gert made her name in 1910s and 1920s Germany with aggressively grotesque and decisively physical performances that confronted audiences with brief sketches materializing carefully observed elements of the social, cultural, and artistic moment. As one well-known dance writer explained, Gert "marks problems of the present without solving them."[12] She was described as dancing "the world of the bar, of the dancing cafes, of the circus, and of the operetta; in short, of all the amusements of civilization, behind the shine of whose arc-lamps the chaotic darkness of the bad districts of the city threatens . . . transmitted with diabolical joy."[13] Her open thematic engagement with low culture corresponded with her stated intention to portray simple, human topics that could be understood by all and with her claim to dislike the intellectualism of the average German who favored art that "he does not understand and that bores him."[14] However, Gert's dances were particularly acclaimed by the educated middle class, a group often disillusioned with both the social and artistic status quo. One reviewer unflatteringly described her relationship to this particular set of spectators, saying that she "has the courage for vulgarity, which her community of metropolitan intellectuals prize as artistic truthfulness."[15]

In the midst of the Weimar Republic, Gert's popularity was explicitly tied to this "truthfulness," which emerged in relation to her artistic strategy of operating (or seeming to operate) on the margins of the socially and aesthetically acceptable. This strategy resembled the attitudes of many artists and writers for whom, as Edward Said puts it, exile was a metaphor for "life led outside the habitual order," the otherness of which allowed the self-identified exile to "cross borders, break barriers of thought and experience."[16] Gert likewise described identification with marginal figures of society, specifically dancing "those the bourgeois citizen despised: prostitutes, madams, the ones who slip away and who deviate."[17] This liminal practice was commended by reviewers who described her work in terms of a social topography, suggesting that she shifted the borders between darkness and illumination. According to one: "This woman places absolutely no value on niceness but rather pursues truth until reaching its blatant ugliness. Yes. She has a particular brilliance in revealing those night-sides of our world that have been hypocritically hidden, in unmasking the deceitful disguise."[18] Another suggested that audiences were drawn to Gert for her provocative portrayals of life from its shadowy corners, explaining that those audience members "who cannot bear the truth, unadorned and pitiless, should not go to her. . . . Those who however know that darkness gives light its brightness, who know that life is first the unification of good and evil, they must see Valeska Gert and her art."[19]

Although Gert's Weimar performances employed a metaphorical exile of sorts in her constant push to "exceed all bounds," as she later put it,[20] they were nonetheless fixed to a certain receptive community. As Koser's 1926 cartoon suggests (Figure 7.1), the idea that performance is constituted by its reception can be particularized through Gert, who claimed that she was no solo dancer, but rather that the audience was her partner.[21] She expected that her performances, despite or perhaps because of their confrontational manner, would be received with a certain reciprocity, by which the audience responses she elicited altered her performance. Her infamous 1919 prostitute piece *Canaille* (Riffraff) was possibly most emblematic of this relationship she maintained with her audience, recalling the prostitute's role as the social figure whose body served as a site of public interaction. Though Gert called *Canaille* her first socially critical dance pantomime, the dance was not simply a parody, nor even an indictment, of a society that facilitated prostitution. By allowing herself to publicly experience the full trajectory of the event, from solicitation through coitus and aftermath, Gert might have been studying what it meant to actually sell one's body, a practice heightened by the presence of an audience that had indeed paid to watch her body undergo the process.[22]

The effect of such process-based events is particularly evident in one review of an unsuccessful performance, which observed how "the tepidness of the Dusseldorf audience crippled her productive powers; since she did not dance

Figure 7.1. Tanzabend Valeska Gert. Photo: Koser. Printed in *ULK: Wochenschrift des Berliner Tageblatts* (Nr. 45, 44. Jg; 12 Nov 1926). Courtesy Deutsches Tanzarchiv Köln.

a routine, but rather art, she consequently failed."[23] Because Gert's work was highly reactive to audience encounters, it offers a potent case study for exile's effects. Later in her career, Gert was not permitted the privilege that she had in the Weimar Republic—of being an insider who deployed a sense of marginality as an aesthetic strategy. Instead, the borders that she crossed through actual exile and remigration pushed her into new audience encounters in which being an outsider was no longer a way in. Otherness thus became a much riskier position, shifting Gert from inclusion to exclusion.

Exile Number Two

Outside of Germany, when Gert was given a chance to test her theories of estrangement as performance technique, her foreignness was ultimately assimilated by being very much for sale, an export from the doomed Weimar Republic, which was transformed into a more pan-European product. After Gert's first 1934 performance in London, where she was billed as a "famous continental grotesque," one reviewer complained that her appeal did not rely on her work at all, but rather the chance to experience foreignness that was sold along with her performances: "I am not usually successful at games of chance, but I am willing to bet any of the bogus Bohemians in the audience two vermillion jumpers and a beard (part-worn) to a pint of English ale out of an English flagon that, had the lady's name been Edna Smith, she would not have been allowed to appear."[24]

To take one New York reviewer's derogatory comment—that Gert's performances indicated "a spectator's rather than a dancer's knowledge"[25]—literally, Gert's relationship to different receptive communities caused her to cultivate multiple exile identities in a manner that altered her performances. Arriving relatively unknown to the United States, Gert was alternately described as German and European. By the time of America's entry into World War II in 1941, even the German-Jewish newspaper *Aufbau* suggested that the Beggar Bar served a metonymic function, allowing audiences to draw their conclusions about Europe in general from its particular nature.[26] Another article in *Aufbau* described audiences as thinking "they have found what they have been searching for all their lives—a corner of genuine Europeana, Paris, if you wish, or Vienna, Budapest." Nonimmigrant newspaper treatments did everything from using the French signifier *Mlle.* for Gert to comparing Greenwich Village, where the bar was located, to the Left Bank.[27] Even Gert's advertisements suggested that the entertainment would be offered in English, French, Italian, Russian, and occasionally "Viennese," although, to the best of my knowledge, the largest portion of the Beggar Bar's entertainment was conducted in German and English.

During her first U.S. years, Gert occasionally came under scrutiny for being too foreign, presenting work that was "suffused with the overhanging morbid quality of doom which is peculiar in the European personality."[28] But by late 1940, she began to introduce new work in a "partly-English program" that recognized her new location with such titles as *World's Fair, Radio Speaker, Parodie auf Bonnie Baker,* and *Wie man in den verschiedenen Ländern lebt* (How People Live in Various Countries). National stereotypes had always been one of Gert's performance schema, and she continued to develop more such pieces in exile. However, the direct transfer of Gert's parodic treatment of national identities did not always work from an actual exile position, to judge by a letter she received from the editorial staff at *Aufbau* soon after opening the Beggar Bar, citing her parody of "American Daughter of Revolution in Coney Island" as an example of her bad taste. Gert was told that she was tactless and that "You mock this country's institutions, criticize its concept of freedom, and indulge in countless allusions, which you may not as an immigrant make under any circumstances."[29] The editorial staff felt that her performances had the potential to harm the position of the immigrant community at large in New York, and threatened to attack her in print. Sydney Jane Norton points out that this letter was written three weeks after the United States entered the war, which increased the jeopardy of a refugee presenting such performances that satirized American patriotism and challenged mainstream American cultural values.[30]

However, the Beggar Bar had only just opened, and in fact, the German emigré dance writer Artur Michel had published a glowing report about the nightclub in *Aufbau* three days before the editorial letter, thrilled that "now Greenwich Village has what it was missing: the Beggar Bar of our Valeska Gert."[31] The venue continued to operate without any more such interventions by *Aufbau*—on the contrary, it was represented by regular articles and listings in the newspaper—because Gert adapted it into a space that capitalized on her own position and thus reconstituted it, taming her foreignness into something available for purchase, and therefore not so threatening after all.

Aufbau articles reported that Gert had made her tavern into both an international hub and a landmark of Greenwich Village, with "foreigners" arriving in ever thicker flocks.[32] In this fascinating rhetorical twist, "foreigners" were defined by contrast to the "initiated" regulars who frequented the exile performer's establishment, many of whom might have been seen as foreigners elsewhere in New York. If Gert's Weimar tactics had involved using techniques of estrangement to draw attention to social issues that had become too familiar, then the Beggar Bar's situation in Greenwich village inverted this by localizing the foreign.

Among her large ensemble of regulars and special guests, Gert employed exile artists such as Kadidja Wedekind together with more local names. Her hybrid establishment became popular beyond the exile community by allowing American audiences to see not only the performers but also themselves as exotic through their encounter.[33] One of the regularly repeated promises in advertisements and listings was that, in addition to regularly scheduled performances, local artists and personalities might spontaneously perform. A cultural exchange was offered—"Two continents meet in the Beggar Bar. America and Europe have themselves a rendezvous. You can come too!"—which was not incongruous with the ad that claimed "A true Greenwich

Village atmosphere awaits you" when considered in light of another: "Here a new atmosphere is created for America."

In a certain sense, Gert learned how to capitalize on the foreignness of her exile by creating and inhabiting a fusion performance space, similar to late 1930s attempts at American versions of European cabaret, including Café Society where jazz was combined with political satire.[34] Her story contrasts with the many European political satiric cabarets that failed in America, among others a venture begun by Friedrich Hollaender, whose cabarets were among those that defined Weimar Berlin, and even Erika Mann's Die Pfeffermühle (The Pepper Mill), which Katrin Sieg posits as "an interesting exception to the equation of exile with disempowerment" during its three-year European tour prior to disbanding in New York.[35] Although it was not the sort of success Gert had hoped for, she kept the Beggar Bar open for four years. She thus found a way to continue to perform in the American climate that was often derided in émigré accounts as pandering to audiences and forcing artists to develop commercially viable work.[36] Rather than being associated with the antifascist cabaret of many German exiles in the United States, the Beggar Bar is seen as "indeed an interesting experiment, but even more as the attempt of a courageous artist to survive."[37] Gert embodied this survival strategy through the labor of maintaining the bar itself; she assumed many roles from dishwasher to accountant, physically carried the two ventilators required by New York licensing law on her back, and even went so far as to deconstruct her old dance costumes into decorations.[38]

Whereas Gert's earlier art as a metaphorical exile had been based on provocation, such a privileged aesthetic strategy of exile failed under conditions of forced migration. Negotiating her presence in the United States, Gert was no longer capable of achieving the necessary distance from her own foreignness to maintain estrangement as an artistic choice. Or, perhaps, it is more precise to say that her starting point was too foreign to do anything but reperform her own situation and thus commodify her physical displacement into an otherness that was still exciting and acceptable.[39] Gert did not necessarily let go entirely of her provocative tendencies, developing such pieces as *Interview mit einer 90 jährigen über Hitler* (Interview with a 90-year-old on Hitler). However, she also offered lighter, if still satiric, entertainment, as evident in an account where one of Gert's regular singers switched from a French ballad to a sea chantey at the request of a drunken sailor to "Give us an American song."[40]

Exile Number Three

The newspapers that lauded Gert's return to Berlin in 1949 first negated her foreignness with a rhetoric of artistic and social belonging. As in New York, her earlier exile aesthetics were disrupted, in this instance by a sense of something not geographically foreign in origin but nonetheless palpably remote. As one of the 4–5 percent of Jewish emigrés who returned, she both belonged to a certain legacy and yet was out of place. Otto Polemann described the scene before Gert's first Berlin appearance in the Renaissance Theatre as "prickling with the tension-laden feeling of a premiere," with the audience constituted by a mixture of two groups: "a faithful carcass-congregation who was spared by war, concentration camps, and gas chambers, together with the younger people, who are no less curious."[41] Reviews articulated various hopes that Gert might bring with her the feel of the Weimar era and become the ignition for a new Berlin cabaret. But one also pointed out how Gert's position had radically changed, saying that "She is today no longer the corrosive terror of the bourgeois, although she is still far from being a meek performer."[42] She now enriched Berlin, as Polemann put it, "by a distinctive artistic luxury-nuance, by nothing more, by nothing less."[43]

Not unintentionally, many reviews of Gert's initial postwar appearances referenced earlier figures of German arts and culture. Such articulation of Germanness was particularly loaded on Gert's return, since much of the ideology of the previous decades had depended on an opposition between German and not-German. (For example, a 1932 article had referred to Gert as "perhaps the most hideous woman who has sung and danced anytime and anywhere and spewed out her Galician hatred against everything German."[44]) However, the association of dance with geopolitical nation falters with regard to Gert's temporary encounter with America and her return to postwar Germany, because the imaginary community of the nation altered so radically in her absence. Although the small group that Polemann had called the "carcass-congregation" still remained, postwar Germany was attempting to renegotiate its identity and rebuild a future, among other things, through a model of victimization that did not always allow for those who returned.[45] If she had been *from another place* in New York City, Gert was *out of place* in postwar Germany. By 1957, a reviewer described her as a kind of disjointed time capsule emitting "the atmosphere of an exciting epoch of style, which signifies today for us realists of the economic miracle something like what the Romantic was for Herr Biedermeier."[46]

Here, Gert's earlier artistic exile, made concrete through actual exile, exposed her to a third exile through remigration. As much as German audiences themselves had changed, Gert was already exploring other performance techniques by the time she returned. Those foreign elements, which were remote from audiences' nostalgic memories of her, thus produced a doubled exile, by both coming from another geographical place and also locating her outside of the social place that had been reserved for a returning Weimar Jewish artist. She later addressed this displacement in an overtly critical piece called *Der*

Remigrant (The Remigrant), the text of which described the experience of returning from America to a warm welcome that turned cold.[47]

When Herbert Pfeiffer asked Gert in 1949 whether she had developed further from her Weimar grotesques, she responded "I see only . . . that life is grotesque in every minute, even today, and because of that I can portray it in no other way."[48] Nevertheless, Pfeiffer perceptively commented that Gert was too much of an artist not to have grown in the time she had been gone. A journalist summarized the shift in Gert's performance methods succinctly, saying that in the Weimar Republic, "she was a dance pantomime who had a few *diseuse* numbers in her program; in the following years she shifted the stress gradually until she became a pantomimic *diseuse*."[49] Another suggested that her return performance in Berlin's Renaissance Theatre was not a danced evening at all but rather a "danced cabaret": "The dancer has become a cabarettist, who uses the dance—admittedly certainly never incidental—more as a corollary instrument."[50]

Perhaps this was partially a function of the aging body of the solo choreographer-performer. Given that Gert was forty-nine when she left Germany and fifty-seven when she first returned, some of the strenuous movement of her earlier work might have been too difficult. However, her performances had been evolving for some time; in 1926, reviewers already noted that Gert's dance had outgrown the concert hall and now belonged in a cabaret or revue, and by 1929 Gert had become interested in shifting away from the physicality commonly associated with dance toward the potential dance of vocal performance.[51] What seemed to postwar audience members to be on stage in Gert's increasingly text-based performances was her whole charismatic persona and range of expressive abilities (Figure 7.2). A reviewer wrote that Gert had been an idiosyncratic grotesque dancer thirty-five years before, "But because she is a Berliner, she cannot hold her tongue, thus emerged this mix of dancer, singer, monologuist, brat, nerd, and lady; in short something particular that can only be labeled with the washed-out term 'Kabaret.'"[52]

It may be in part due to this change in medium that the language of reviews altered, although it was certainly also a function of the cultural climate and changing critical conventions. Prewar reviews had tended toward thick descriptions that tried to make sense of Gert's physicality, with the reviewers themselves often arriving at discussions of meaning through a visceral involvement in their own responses to her performances. By contrast, postwar reviews tended toward encapsulating the stories Gert staged, citing narratives that made her more easily apprehended through cognitive engagement. In writing primarily about the text that was spoken, rather than the event that occurred, the reviewers could engage with the elements that could be grasped and assimilated into the present, the era of the "economic miracle," without risking themselves becoming implicated in the out-of-placeness that was also part of her performances.

Figure 7.2. Celebrities, Valeska Gert. Photo: Lisette Model, Courtesy Galerie Baudoin Lebon. (ca. 1940s).

Many reviews of this period acknowledge other transformations in Gert as well, commenting with surprise on how her grotesque dance practices had softened. She began her first 1949 performance in Berlin by chatting with her audience about her experiences in America and her return. A reviewer suggested that those who went to see Gert "to catch up on something of the past, to experience the radical artistic originality of a women who had the effect of an enfant terrible twenty years ago, might perhaps be disappointed by her comeback," since Gert had "become more amicable and lost the aggressiveness of her youth."[53] She was described as having more tact than before, her biting nature had become milder, even kinder, and more forgiving.[54] As one critic noted: "She no longer lives in the no-man's-land of feeling and her blows do not hurt so much."[55]

Another reviewer observed that certain pieces succeeded, but that in others "it appeared that her long stay in America has not remained without influence. Probably . . . *die seltsame Reise des Professors Blitz* has more effect on American feelings than on us."[56] Although *The Strange Journey of Professor Blitz* may well have its origins in Gert's Weimar years, she certainly performed the piece in America. In the postwar years, *Professor Blitz* became one of her most often-discussed pieces, perhaps because the work was seen as not necessarily returning comfortably from exile. In short, Professor Blitz is an aerospace researcher who is so dazzled by the moon that he falls out of his rocket ship. His wife joins him and they rotate together in the moon's orbit on a couch, until they catch onto a meteor, which is so heavy that they drop through the earth's crust into the horrors of hell, to ultimately be kept alive in the hearts of the friends who remember them.[57] *Professor Blitz* combined physical mime work with the oral recounting of a complicated story that appeared fantastical on the outside, but which materialized one of the fundamental political components of exile modernism: the focus on human suffering as a means to understand catastrophe so that the process of escape and survival is not rendered meaningless.[58]

Gert's performance in *Professor Blitz* was described as "humorous at the beginning, then tangled up in itself," and her listeners were "bewildered."[59] A reviewer said it manifested a "phantom realm of an ageless daydreaming child's fantasy," calling it an "incomparable piece . . . Genius in text and execution."[60] In retelling the story, many reviews touched upon the strong allegorical resonances that underlay the dreamy fairy tale of *Professor Blitz*: the distraction that began the catastrophic fall, the devoted wife who followed him even into extraterrestrial displacement, and the couple's ultimate survival by means of remembrance. As one reviewer explained the mechanism and effect of such a piece: "something has remained with her: a bizarre imagination that springs from ideas with which she animates the artistic in-between realms, where she has settled, into shreds of song, of words, and of movement. We saw and heard scenic sketches from her, in which she amusingly caricatures uncomplicated things and figures and displaces the irony in some few moments toward the boundary of shock."[61]

Professor Blitz was one of Gert's many pieces that returned to Germany with a similar framework, seemingly distant from reality, perhaps even absurd, but also packing a certain punch. Whereas Gert's earlier pieces had tended to deal more directly with vignettes of day-to-day life in the Weimar Republic, her later performances displaced those issues. For example, while Gert's *Der Tod* (Death) from 1922 played with the theatrical conventions of how close a performer could come to truly dying onstage,[62] her later death pieces, though numerous, seemed to negotiate that material in more distant scenarios. Aside from Professor Blitz's and his wife's descent into hell, there was a piece about murder on the autobahn, a dead actress making another career in film, and another of the more frequently discussed: the scene in the Japanese theater in which an unrequited lover killed himself by committing harakiri. The dance of death in which a Prussian aristocrat attempted to use the smell of moth powder in order to clean out her memories of an evening at a ball[63] also picked up on another repeated theme of Gert's later work: the passage of time and memory. Such pieces included an American nightclub soloist performing the same song at three different stages of her life: the eighteen-year-old's wannabe artlessness, the forty-year-old vamp, and the ninety-year-old who knitted while her head wagged.[64] Somehow, it does not seem accidental that this piece about maturation appeared in Gert's first postwar performance in Berlin.

These developments in Gert's work—the formal changes in medium, the softening of a grotesque attitude, and the thematic material—place pressure on the rhetoric of belonging that surrounded Gert's return to Germany. If national identities are constructed by contrast to otherness, these changes raise issues about Gert's performances abroad as well as her return as another form of exile, where she was not allowed to be other, but also was not capable of being not-other.

Coda: On Narrating Otherness

Gert repeatedly claimed that her exile from Germany during World War II caused her to be eradicated from the dance history of her homeland. In her fourth autobiography, she wrote: "People attribute *Ausdruckstanz* to [Mary] Wigman. I was away for too long; people have forgotten what happened in dance back then. *Ausdruckstanz* comes from me, just like the modern contemporary dance pantomime."[65] And the autobiography before that claimed: "At least to the Nazis, I was an enemy; to today's Germans, I am nothing. People know only that Mary Wigman created the new German dance, people know nothing of me."[66] Later she elaborated that "the young people naturally don't know about me because I was hushed up during the Hitler period."[67] To a certain extent, Gert was not incorrect in feeling her position in German dance altered during her absence. By the time she gave a 1949 performance in Berlin, it was reported that she "does not dance (for instance in the traditional sense of classical dance or of *Ausdruckstanz*)."[68] But, perhaps more accurately, she did not dance in the terms by which German dance forms were coming to be understood.[69]

Gert, whose early work had been so based in a certain metaphorical position of exile in terms of pushing artistic boundaries, spent much of her later life trying to invert what she perceived as her own exile from the history of German dance, using gestures toward inclusion to seek a "spiritual compensation"[70] when the government granted only financial ones. She was even once quoted as telling the audience regarding the 1920s: "Pah, [it was] nothing but a passing phase, with the exception of dance art—partially Wigman, but for the most part me."[71] To accept Gert's overstated claim to belong to a central narrative of Weimar dance, rather than the periphery, involves more than a tenuous articulation of belonging. It requires thinking about Gert as carrying that legacy through exile encounters in which she was no longer playing an outsider but instead had to negotiate more explicit experiences of otherness.

When Gert attempted to verbally claim a place in fixed nationalist representations, her repeated performance practices—which had changed at the same time as the nation changed—enacted a certain intervention by being radically Other.[72] By drawing attention to what she perceived as her omission, she not only challenges the construction of Germanness in the postwar codification of *Ausdruckstanz*, but also the Germanness of later twentieth-century *Tanztheater*. Taking Gert at her word and casting her as an *Ausdruckstänzerin*—but one who leaves to carry on, develop, and even change the legacy of Weimar dance through exile encounters—modifies the narrative that constructs a strange lacuna between the Weimar Republic and the generation of choreographers, such as Pina Bausch who emerged in the 1960s as the student of another remigrant, Kurt Jooss.[73] Gert is often cited as a forerunner to such postwar German performance because of her Weimar-era practices. However, comparisons might also be made to the fairy tales and other less overtly grotesque negotiations with political issues that matured through Gert's experiences of exile to appear in her postwar cabaret. These inclusions are possible only by first thinking through the particularities of exclusion, the many modes in which exile can operate.

Notes

1. Valeska Gert, *Ich bin eine Hexe: Kaleidoskop meines Lebens* (München: Franz Schneekluth, 1968), 56.

2. Svetlana Boym, "Estrangement as a Lifestyle: Shklovsky and Brodsky," *Poetics Today* 17.4 (1996), 613.

3. Sergei Eisenstein, "Im Weltmass-stab über Valeska Gert," reprinted in Frank-Manuel Peter, *Valeska Gert: Tänzerin, Schauspielerin, Kabarettistin* (Berlin: Edition Hentrich, 1987), 121.

4. See Laure Guilbert-Deguine, "Tanz," in *Handbuch der deutschsprachigen Emigration*, eds. Krohn et al. (Darmstadt: Wissenschaftliche Buchgesellschaft, 1998).

5. "Must Not See Wife Dance: Nazis' Ban Because She Is Jewess," *News Chronicle*, November 28, 1934, 3.

6. Maria Zampa, "Die verhinderte Haremsdame: Valeska Gert will nicht mehr tanzen—Absurde Leute in der 'Beggar Bar,'" *Telegraf*, March 6, 1949.

7. She appeared in small roles in films by Federico Fellini and by Volker Schlöndorff, who ultimately made a documentary about her, entitled *Nur zum Spaß, Nur zum Spiel* (Biskop Film, 1977).

8. The two major German archival collections of material on Gert, the Deutsches Tanzarchiv in Cologne and the Valeska Gert Archive at the Akademie der Künste in Berlin, are represented by Frank-Manuel Peter's 1987 monograph, which offers an overview of her life and work, and Susanne Foellmer's 2006 *Valeska Gert: Fragmente einer Avantgardistin in Tanz und Schauspiel der 1920er Jahre* (Bielefeld: transcript), which focuses on the artistic side of Gert's Weimar period.

9. Ian Buruma, "The Romance of Exile," *Guardian*, February 12, 2001, 33.

10. For critiques of such politicized narratives, see Christhard Hoffmann, "Zum Begriff der Akkulturation," in *Handbuch der deutschsprachigen Emigration 1933–1945*, 117–126; and Martin Jay, "The German Migration: Is There a Figure in the Carpet?" in *Exiles + Emigrés: The Flight of European Artists from Hitler*, ed. Stephanie Barron (Los Angeles: Los Angeles County Museum of Art, 1997). The "other Germany" was visible in the development of such groups as the German Academy of Arts and Sciences in Exile, and its shorter-lived counterpart in the United States, the American Guild for German Cultural Freedom, which was established, as Thomas Mann explained, to "serve as a protectorate over the threatened German intellectual wealth." Mann, "Seeking to Preserve German Cultural Freedom," *New York Times*, December 12, 1936, 18.

11. Editors' Note: On the experience of remigrant Jean Weidt, see the essay by Marion Kant in this volume. On the experiences of other German dancers in the United States, see the essays by Tresa Randall and Karen Mozingo in this volume.

12. Joseph Lewitan, "Valeska Gert: Schwechtensaal 18 Nov 1930," *Der Tanz* 4.1 (1931), 14.

13. Hans W. Fischer, *Das Tanzbuch* (München: Albert Langen, 1924), 57.

14. Valeska Gert, "Mary Wigman und Valeska Gert," *Der Querschnitt* 6.5 (1926), 361

15. Felix Emmel, "Der zeitgemäße Tanz," *Das Nationaltheater*, 1.3 (1928/1929), 68.

16. Edward Said, "Reflections on Exile," in *Reflections on Exile and Other Literary and Cultural Essays* (1984; reprint, London: Granta Books, 2000), 185–186.

17. Valeska Gert, *Mein Weg* (Leipzig: A. F. Devrient, 1931), 39.

18. Max Hermann [Neiße], "Valesca Gert," *Berliner Tageblatt* (n.d.). The dancer's birth name was Gertrud Valesca Samosch, and on occasion critics used an alternate spelling for her stage name.

19. Leonie Dotzler, "Valeska Gert tanzt: Matinee in der Komödie," *Dresdener Neueste Nachrichten* (1927).

20. Gert, *Hexe*, 38.

21. Valeska Gert, "Valeska Gert," *Berliner Tageblatt*, March 6, 1931.

22. I discuss this relationship in "Petrified? Some Thoughts on Dance Historiography and Practical Research," *Performance Research* 13.1 (2008): 61–69.

23. N [signed], "Schauspielhaus: Tanzabend Valeska Gert," *Düsseldorfer Lokal-Zeitung*, December 11, 1926.

24. Russell Gregory, "Valeska Gert," *Saturday Review*, March 31, 1934, 361.

25. Henry Gilfond, "Valeska Gert," *Dance Observer*, January 1937, 5.

26. See, for example, the formulation in Lub. [signed], "Abend in der Beggar Bar," *Aufbau* 10.44 (November 3, 1944): 10.

27. T.L. [signed], "Valeska Gert's Beggar Bar," *Aufbau*, 9.52 December 24, 1943, 10; Virginia Forbes, "Café Life in New York," *New York Sun*, October 26, 1943, 21.

28. Dorathi Bock Pierre "California," in *American Dancer*, April 1940, 36–37, here 37.

29. Letter dated December 29, 1941, addressed to Gert and signed on behalf of the *Aufbau* editorial staff. The letterhead placed Manfred George as editor, with Kurt Hellmer

and Josef Maier as assistant editors, and listed an advisory board including such famous figures as Lion Feuchtwanger, Leopold Jessner, Thomas Mann, and Albert Einstein. Valeska Gert Archive, Akademie der Künste, Berlin.

30. Sydney Jane Norton, "Dancing out of Bounds: Valeska Gert in Berlin and New York," in *Female Exiles in Twentieth and Twenty-First Century Europe*, eds. Maureen Tobin Stanley and Gesa Zinn (New York: Palgrave Macmillan, 2007), 107–109.

31. Artur Michel, "Valeskas Beggar Bar," *Aufbau* 7.52 (December 26, 1941), 13.

32. "Valeska Gert," *Aufbau* 9.21 (May 21, 1943), 12; and Lub., "Abend in der Beggar Bar."

33. See Marta Savigliano's theorization of exoticism and self-conscious autoexotic performance in *Tango and the Political Economy of Passion* (Boulder: Westview Press, 1995).

34. See Michael Denning, *The Cultural Front: The Laboring of American Culture in the Twentieth Century* (London: Verso, 1997), 325–328.

35. Katrin Sieg, *Exiles, Eccentrics, Activists: Women in Contemporary German Theatre* (Ann Arbor: University of Michigan Press, 1994), 51.

36. This is exemplified by Theodor Adorno's critique in "Service to the Consumer" from *Minima Moralia: Reflections from Damaged Life*, trans. E. F. N. Jephcott (1951; reprint, London: Verso, 1974).

37. *Die Zehnte Muse: Kabarettisten erzählen*, ed. Frauke Deißner-Jenssen (Berlin: Henschelverlag, 1982), 312.

38. See, for example, Gert, *Die Bettlerbar von New York* (Berlin: Arani, 1950), 25, 85.

39. As Anthony Heilbut points out, such projects were particularly tenuous because refugee artists were vulnerable to contradictory criticism from local audiences and from those who had migrated with them. *Exiled in Paradise: German Refugee Artists and Intellectuals in America from the 1930s to the Present* (1983; reprint, Berkeley: University of California Press, 1997), 135.

40. Lub., "Abend."

41. Otto Polemann, "Valeska Gert kehrte wieder: Matinee im Renaissance-Theater," *Die Neue Zeitung*, March 15, 1949.

42. Eva Siewert, "Die Heimkehrerin: Valeska Gert im Renaissance-Theater," *Der Telegraph*, March 15, 1949.

43. Polemann, "Kehrte wieder."

44. Rümpelstilzschen [signed], "Valeska Gerts 'Kohlkopp,'" in *Nu Wenn Schon!* Vol. 12. (April 7, 1932; reprint, Tausend Berlin: Brunnen-Verlag, 1932), 230.

45. On the entangled communities of postwar Germany, see Atina Grossmann, *Jews, Germans, and Allies: Close Encounters in Occupied Germany* (Princeton: Princeton University Press, 2007).

46. rg [signed], "Valeska Gert im Malkasten," *Süddeutsche Zeitung*, November 7, 1957. The writings attributed to the pseudonym Biedermeier came directly after the Romantic period, as both late version and contrast.

47. See Gert, *Hexe*, 206–207. Another later piece in this overtly political vein was *Ilse Koch*, named for the Buchenwald concentration camp commandant whose persona Gert assumed in performance, 212–213.

48. Herbert Pfeiffer, "Valeska Gert: Porträt einer Tänzerin," *Tagesspiegel* 59 (March 11, 1949).

49. Adolph C. Benning, "Valeska Gert: Die Geschichte einer dollen Nummer," *Pardon* (1964).

50. Vogt [signed], "Valeska Gert," *Neues Deutschland* 4.62 (March 15, 1949).

51. A. M. [signed], "Valeska Gerts 'Grotesken,'" *Vossiche Zeitung* (1926); and Valeska Gert, "Tanz," *Deutsche Tonkünstlerzeitung* 23.512 (1929), 728.

52. Walther Kiaulehn, "Tänzerin, Sängerin, Kellerkind, und Dame," [pub. unknown] (1957).

53. Ingevelde Müller, "Mimische Phantasie: Valeska Gert im Renaissance-Theater," *Die Welt*, March 17, 1949.

54. Polemann, "Kehrte wieder."

55. Herbert Pfeiffer, "Valeska Gert im Renaissance Theater," *Tagesspiegel*, March 16, 1949.

56. Vogt, "Valeska Gert."

57. See Gert, *Bettlerbar*, 124–126. I have not found review mentions of *Professor Blitz* prior to Gert's American performances, despite the earlier description of it as a grotesque film in Fred Hildenbrandt, *Die Tänzerin Valeska Gert* (Stuttgart, 1928), 38–48.

58. Ehrhard Bahr, *Weimar on the Pacific: German Exile Culture in Los Angeles and the Crisis of Modernism* (Berkeley: University of California Press, 2007), 21. This combination of fantasy and disaster was used by other exile performance groups for political purposes, such as the Peppermill's 1934 revue "Fairy Tales." See Sieg, *Exiles*, 62.

59. Polemann, "Kehrte wieder"; and C. S. [signed], "Valeska Gert und ihr Künstlercafé 'Valeska,'" *Tagesanzeiger für Stadt und Kanton Zürich* (April 13, 1948).

60. rg, "Valeska Gert im Malkasten."

61. Müller, "Mimische Phantasie."

62. See my "'Berlin ... Your Dance Partner Is Death,'" *TDR: The Drama Review* 53.1 (2009): 73–92.

63. Polemann, "Kehrte wieder."

64. Ibid.; and G. Pliquett, "Renaissance-Theater: Valeska Gert," *Montags Echo* 3.11 (March 14, 1949).

65. Gert, *Katze von Kampen* (Percha am Starnberger See: Verlag R. S. Schulz, 1973), 46.

66. Gert, *Hexe*, 79.

67. Benning, "Geschichte."

68. Bob. [signed], "Valeska Gert," *Neue Zeit*, March 16, 1948.

69. Although the topic of how German dance was reconfigured after World War II is beyond the scope of this essay, I take up this issue in my book, *Watching Weimar Dance* (Oxford University Press, forthcoming).

70. Benning, "Geschichte."

71. H. O. [signed], "Über das Ende hinaus: Zum Tode von Valeska Gert," *Tagesspiegel*, March 21, 1978.

72. See Ehrhard Bahr's propositions on the impossibility of continuity between pre- and postemigration art works in *Weimar on the Pacific*. Because the exiles' creative works had failed them in preventing either the collapse of the Republic or the popular success of the regime that drove them into exile, their artistic forms had to be reconstituted. Bahr's propositions on exile modernism draw attention to the national cultures that structure the exile encounter as themselves always under negotiation resulting both from the forces that brought them into contact and from the contact itself.

73. Editors' Note: On the complex relationship between *Ausdruckstanz* and Pina Bausch's *Tanztheater*, see Sabine Huschka's essay in this volume.

8. *Was bleibt?* The Politics of East German Dance

MARION KANT

Was bleibt? What remains of the culture and the arts of a country that has disappeared from the maps? I take the title of the novella by Christa Wolf, one of the most famous East German novelists, to ask this question. Written in 1979, but rewritten for publication ten years later, after the fall of the Berlin Wall, it became a metaphor for the fate of intellectuals in East Germany and their country's historical legacy. In the book Wolf reflected on her own life, the life of a writer, pursued by the infamous Stasi, the East German secret service. In 1993 evidence surfaced that she had been an unofficial informer for the Stasi. All her previous work was at once dismissed. She worked for a totalitarian state and hence her work must be worthless. In effect, the answer to the question *was bleibt?* was: "nothing."[1]

In his novel *1984*, George Orwell summed up Wolf's dilemma: "'Who controls the past . . . controls the future: who controls the present controls the past.'"[2] Orwell's law of history in *1984* had been drawn from the Nazi and the Communist parties of the 1930s and 1940s, but Orwell added another insight: For the party running the affairs of the totalitarian regime of *1984* "all history was a palimpsest, scraped clean and re-inscribed exactly as often as was necessary."[3] History as palimpsest describes perfectly the deliberate writing and rewriting of German history since 1945.

East Germany has been shredded, assessed, reassessed, and reconstituted. Scholars have descended like carrion crows on the corpse of East Germany and each has ripped off a bit of its flesh in order to partake in that grand banquet of historical production: PhD theses, higher doctorates (a Germanic peculiarity), monographs, and documentary collections. These scraps of past reality have made (or destroyed) careers, secured appointments, and flooded the markets with books. Such a method justified itself as the only possible way to cleanse German history of its totalitarian past, its joint totalitarian Nazi and Communist past. The Stasi files that ruined Christa Wolf have been declared "Documentary Evidence" and "The Incontrovertible and Revealed Truth." The palimpsest has been rubbed until it shines with virtue.

But there are two pasts to rewrite: the Communist and the Nazi. On May 8, 1945, Nazi Germany's last *Reichskanzler*, Hitler's designated successor, Grand Admiral Karl Dönitz, surrendered all German armed forces unconditionally to the Allied armies of Britain, the Soviet Union, and the United States. Although the end of Adolf Hitler's Third Reich did not mark a clean break, the victorious allies tried to create one. They imposed de-nazification as a cleansing process on Germany. The Germans themselves had not asked to be cleansed. Industrialists, bankers, and professors found their internment an outrage and an insult. Somebody else had been to blame, and they Nazis? Never. The more than ten million party cards held in the Berlin Document Center told a different story. The sheer number of membership cards suggested that a very large segment of the adult population had been in the party and more had undoubtedly sympathized. A small number of Germans lost their posts, a few SS men went to jail. The rest survived and rose to high office in the Federal Republic and to public posts in the Democratic Republic, as the Cold War cooled the zeal for purification and revenge.

The two pasts have been, thus, quite differently erased. The erasure of the East German regime has been much more ruthless than de-nazification after 1945. The equation of nearly everything East German with the secret service—as in the case of Christa Wolf—did the job. By another of history's rich ironies, the totalitarian model, invented in the 1950s in the darkest days of the Cold War, became the template to describe and then condemn the East German regime. History—the past—had to be cleansed and rewritten not by those who had lived through it but by those who had not been contaminated. The West Germans expelled roughly two-thirds of all East German intellectuals in universities and research and cultural institutions.[4] More German academics lost their jobs after 1989 than the pathetic handful of professors dismissed as Nazis. East Germans fell silent. West Germans were silent too. When their East German colleagues were dismissed, rightly or wrongly as agents of the regime, they did not protest. Their silence benefited those many second- and third-rate opportunists who took their positions. The expulsion of the Jews had been a similar occasion for German silence and self-advancement. Civil courage has never been a lasting feature of German public life, not in 1933 and not after 1989.

It is thus with mixed feelings that I—brought up in East Berlin—write an essay on dance in East Germany after 1945. I come from a left-wing Jewish refugee family. Most of that family were murdered, the rest driven out and robbed by the Nazis. Like many East German intellectuals, I too lost my job after 1989, my pension, and my professional opportunities; I too have been told to expiate my East German past before I write a word; I too have been accused of Stasi involvement and libeled in German newspapers by sly assertions about my past. This, then, is the first time in two decades that I offer some thoughts on a subject that I can—methodologically speaking—approach as a "participant-observer," as anthropologists define the status.

What Remains of the East German Past at the Moment? Fragments

The assumption that East Germany as a Soviet satellite was an illegitimate state, a dictatorial regime, in German an "*Unrechtsstaat*" that continued Nazi politics under different circumstances, dictates most studies. Scholars have to take sides on the question. The majority accept the unjust state theory; the minority offer a more nuanced judgment. The latter position is tricky because defenders of DEMOCRACY writ large condemn such scholars as apologists for totalitarianism.

The debate begins with 1945 itself. Was there a *Stunde Null* (Zero Hour)—a post-Nazi moment when everything was different and the opportunity for a democracy arose? Did Nazi ideology and Nazi politics simply continue or was there a distinct break? After the fall of the Berlin Wall in 1989 these issues moved to the foreground of public debates. The West Germans turned the category of antifascism into its opposite. Imposed on the (East) German people, it was antifascism by decree, a *"verordneter Antifaschismus."* Antifascism had not really taken hold at all.[5] The "decreed antifascism" became an "abused antifascism," abused by those who defined themselves as antifascist. So the GDR had no legitimacy even on its own terms.

Even if there was no *Stunde Null* in reality, the pretense that there had been one in the dance sphere suited many of the most important dancers who had remained in Germany, such as Gret Palucca and Mary Wigman. By contrast, émigrés like Jean Weidt or Valeska Gert, who came back to Germany, were greeted with apprehension and hostility. Jean Weidt, returning from French exile in 1948, recalled how much he despised the collaborators and opportunists: "I have to tell you that during the first years in Berlin I felt intense hatred for those who had directly or indirectly supported fascism . . ."[6] During a conference, which took place at the Palucca School in Dresden in the early 1990s and concerned itself with the recent history of modern German dance traditions, Hans Richter, dancer and husband of choreographer Emmy Köhler-Richter (ballet director at the Leipzig Opera House from 1958 to 1978), assured me that Weidt never had been an artist to be taken seriously, for he was "a Communist" and never really part of German dance. I asked him whether one excluded the other and he nodded—a Communist could never be a dancer or choreographer and vice versa. Weidt had chosen to incorporate his political beliefs in art and that excluded him from modern dance, or so Richter implied.

This incident demonstrated several aspects of the tradition of modern German dance, above all, its continued cultivation of an "apolitical" art, first defined by Mary Wigman as *absolute dance* in 1921. The purity of such art justified the refusal to revisit the Nazi past, to rethink or even reposition the ideology that fed modern dance in Germany. Thus the integrity of dance depended on its protection from interference by any nonartist and bureaucrat, and particularly by the politically engaged citizen. Richter's answer summed up the myth of modern German dance as something beyond the social, historical, and political circumstances of its time.

From Richter's perspective, serious dancers and choreographers offered heroic and consistent resistance (a form of "inner emigration," i.e., spiritual and intellectual isolation[7]). Thus the long duration of repression could gradually be extended backward as well as forward: taking 1945 and *Stunde Null* as the point of departure, subjugation happened under the Nazis and continued under the Communists. Both governments—or so we have been told—were "totalitarian regimes" and both were intent on destroying modern and avant-garde art. During the years of Communism modern dance could never flourish, for the supposedly apolitical stance of Rudolf Laban, Mary Wigman, and Gret Palucca rendered it impossible to integrate modern dance into the socialist system's opposing value structures. Anyone who attempted to bridge the gap between socialism and dance art was crushed in the middle—Kurt Jooss, Marianne Vogelsang, Jean Weidt. This too followed a previous pattern: in the 1920s, battles for control of the modern dance scene between the antagonists Laban and Wigman led to the exclusion from the master narratives of modern dance of those who had opposed both leaders.

Yet, however uncertain its historiographical status, *Stunde Null* was a lived reality for the survivors of the war in a Germany destroyed physically and under foreign rule. It marks a convenient point to start the stories of the people who choreographed, danced, performed, or wrote about dance before and after May 1945. The biographical perspective and the conceptual framework with which to assess their careers requires us to zoom into the Eastern part of Germany—the Russian- or Soviet-occupied zone, which was established as the German Democratic Republic on October 7, 1949.

Mary Wigman (1886–1973)

In May 1945, Mary Wigman lived in Leipzig and contemplated the collapse of the Third Reich and the loss of all German values. She knew that she was not *"ostisch"*—orientated toward the east—enough to remain in the Russian occupied zone; she was *"abendländisch"*[8]—occidental. But where to go? Were the Americans any better than the Russians in their vulgarity and consumerist approach to art? The Russians and in particular Russian bolshevists, though blessed with a beautiful and noble language, were, in her eyes, barbaric. The political, cultural, and educational measures taken by the Allied occupation seemed to confirm Wigman's reservations about a leveling and creeping proletarianization of everything she loved and held in high esteem. Wigman knew very soon that she would be incapable of partaking in such destructive policies. Even more than the Russian soldiers and army officials, she despised the returning refugees whom, like many Germans, she viewed as traitors. Like Frank Thiess, she was insulted by the concept of de-nazification and considered herself deeply misunderstood. In an open letter Thiess had expressed concern that the distinction between silent sufferer and active Nazi was being overlooked and misunderstood by Allies and German émigrés alike. Not everyone was able to watch the German tragedy "from the comfortable seats of foreign countries."[9] Poor Germany—now governed by Communists and Jews—had to submit to vulgar examinations in the name of antifascism.[10] Wigman suffered Germany's defeat and could barely contain her despair. Germany was lost and Wigman did not know how to cope with such a profound loss. At the core of her being she was German and she needed German values to exist. When the Third Reich vanished, all hope disappeared. Wigman was convinced that Nazi Germany, though not perfect, was preferable to an occupied Germany.

Stunde Null was useful because it provided her with the opportunity to establish her moral integrity and guilt-free past. She was courted by the new powers and initially accepted offers to lend her name to reconstruction efforts led by Russians or newly arrived Communists.[11] But she refused to become a member of any state organization. Her first dance recitals were successful and very well received, but she rejected the offer to head a new state dance school. During her stay in the Russian occupied zone she never adopted or contemplated "realism" as the guiding principle in her own aesthetics. It would have been impossible to change her aesthetic framework and would have meant total surrender, which on political as well as artistic grounds she could not do.

Yet a significant shift occurred in her aesthetic understanding and she turned from smaller and shorter choreographies for her female school groups to large-scale choreography for the theater. She staged Christoph Willibald Gluck's opera *Orpheus* as a deeply tragic composition, without any hope. This work enabled her to contemplate existential loss and total despair. Though Wigman was showered with offers and seductive promises by Russian as well as East German authorities, she left the Russian zone and moved to Berlin-Dahlem in the American sector of Berlin in 1949, where she opened another school, the Mary Wigman Studio. There she taught and inspired the next generation of modern dancers, artists like Pina Bausch, Gerhard Bohner, and Susanne Linke.

With Wigman's departure, Eastern Germany had lost one of its most important artists. She had been prepared to submit to the Nazis; she was not prepared to submit to Communists. *Stunde Null* as the moment of redefinition allowed Wigman to control and obliterate her immediate past and thus control her future as well as that of modern German dance. Her personal history, as that of modern German dance, had been "scraped clean and re-inscribed exactly as" Wigman thought fit. Dance history as palimpsest acquired a new narrative of near destruction through totalitarian systems. Forgotten and uninscribed were Wigman's contributions to a movement ideology that had celebrated the leader, herself as well as Adolf Hitler, the Nazi People's Community (*Volksgemeinschaft*), and a blood-and-soil–based art. Forgotten were her aryanization actions, forgotten were her attacks on Jewish critics, and reinterpreted were the choreographies and performances that had celebrated sacrifice and death for the nation, some of the preferred motives within Nazi aesthetics. On the slate of German dance history were scratched the stories of the heroic grand dame of German dance as the ultimate keeper of modernity.[12]

Gret Palucca (1902–1993)

In May 1945, Palucca had barely survived the Allied bombing of Dresden in February.[13] She was less devastated by the end of Nazism than Wigman, her erstwhile teacher, and more pragmatic. New rulers and new circumstances asked for new attitudes and approaches. She knew how to arrange herself with the Communist regime. Palucca convinced the Russian cultural officers that she needed their help to start over again. She obtained a new identity for her new life, declaring herself a victim of National Socialism. This is one of the most impressive and successful rewritings of history. Nobody disagreed, or if someone did, it was not heard. Palucca opened her school and began teaching in June 1945, within a few months of German capitulation. The Russians gave her the building of the old Wigman school and Palucca gratefully accepted. Russian financial support and, more importantly, Russian political protection secured her a special place in the emerging culture of East Germany. Like Wigman, Palucca immediately offered dance recitals to entertain a depressed and hopeless German public.

If Wigman was "apolitical" because her concept of an *absolute dance* demanded the separation of art from politics, then Palucca was "apolitical" because she was a complete opportunist and willing to give up any kind of ethical principle. While Wigman—a true believer in Germany—waited to be courted and then refused the suitor, Palucca calculated carefully and got what she wanted from the people who were available. Palucca entered into complex arrangements of what one might call "mutual blackmail." This was not blackmail exerted by one individual as a criminal act against a group of people who happened to represent the East German state, but, rather, a mechanism and political device built into the relationship between the East German state and intellectuals in East Germany. The alliance of artists like Palucca with the East German regime was tenuous and doomed to fail, for it never rested on sympathy and conviction but on usefulness in personal or political agendas.

East Germany desperately needed artists, scientists, academics—in short, intellectuals—to legitimize its existence. If intellectuals were willing to support the state by remaining in the country and not defecting to the West, they in exchange received support on every possible level. One such manifestation of mutual endorsement in the early years of the GDR was legalized in the so-called *Einzelverträge*,[14] contracts designed for artists, engineers, medical doctors, etc., that would provide them with materially and financially advantageous living conditions and would, for instance, secure better housing, good schooling, and a university education for their children. The most important aspect of the contracts lay in the recognition that intellectuals were particularly desirable people in the German Democratic Republic.

Palucca, who received such a contract, could thus threaten to leave the country or declare that she would not return from her holidays on the island of Sylt and place pressure on the East German State to force through her preferences in matters of aesthetics and education as well as in personnel questions. Just as the East German state put pressure on Palucca to run her school in compliance with the principles of a socialist education and sanction an art grounded in socialist-realist principles, so she put pressure on the East German system by threatening to leave and, by leaving, to discredit the state.

Unlike Wigman, Palucca never constructed a genuine theory of her own on which her aesthetics rested. Here too she was pragmatic and borrowed from other modern dance systems to establish and govern her school. The evolution of her *Neuer Künstlerischer Tanz* (new artistic dance) was a bowdlerized version of Wigman's *absolute dance*, with elements integrated from various teaching curricula from Laban, Wigman, and eventually even ballet training.

Palucca's relationships to two of the first administrative units set up to regulate and support the arts—the German Academy of Arts, founded on March 24, 1950, and the Staatliche Kommission für Kunstangelegenheiten,[15] a state art commission that preceded the Ministry of Culture, founded on January 7, 1954—illustrate the characteristic relationship between many intellectuals and the East German regime. The demands of artist or intellectual, on the one hand, and those of the administration, on the other, created tension and constant discontent. As a founding member of the German Academy of Arts in East Berlin, Palucca belonged to the ultimate artistic elite. By definition, she was part of the cultural establishment and at the same time its critic. Palucca had secured her membership by eliminating all other rivals from the dance field (including Mary Wigman whose name had also been on one of the first lists for membership in the Academy);[16] as the only dancer and choreographer, she could claim to represent dance per se and cement her monopoly position.

Palucca demanded complete independence and freedom in the way she governed her school in Dresden. Criteria for teaching were to be set solely by herself as artistic director and manager and then institutionalized in all other schools. The Staatliche Kunstkommission disagreed and wished to see active engagement with socialist realism.[17] Yet Palucca's curriculum remained, with very few interventions, exactly the same way as it had been at the beginning of her career as a pedagogue and as it had continued in the early years of the Third Reich; the syllabus was amended by exchanging classes on racial theory with Marxist theory, for instance. Thus she collaborated with the East German regime in the same way that she had collaborated with the Nazi regime.

Her closeness to Otto Grotewohl, minister president of East Germany and lover of the arts, provided vital backing. Next to Russian cultural officers, he was her official protector and she resorted to him as her patron in the endeavor to guard what she considered the authenticity of modern dance. For example, Palucca prevented Kurt Jooss from receiving support in East Germany in the 1950s—in the name of preventing "cosmopolitanism and bourgeois decadence" from entering modern dance.[18] She possessed power and she had significant influence—she applied both and turned herself and her school into a legend as well as an institution that dominated and ruled "modernist" dance in East Germany.

It was at the height of her power in the 1970s that I first met her in the Academy of Arts. I recall the tiny, lean and muscular figure, her boots and trousers, the loose fitting top, short hair, and the voice—soft and supplicating. I recall that voice on the phone, the classic tones of the "suffering servant," but in her case a servant unwilling to serve and equipped with a will made of steel. Nobody questioned Palucca.

Marianne Vogelsang (1912–1973)

In May 1945, Marianne Vogelsang lived near Hannover and waited for the end of the Nazi regime.[19] Only in January had she been released from compulsory labor in military factories.[20] Unlike Mary Wigman or Gret Palucca, she greeted May 8th, 1945, as the day of liberation. She immediately designed programs to entertain American and British army officers in the North of Germany; she "fraternized" as Wigman called it.[21] In 1946 she gladly accepted an offer from the Russian occupied zone to open the department for dance at the Music College of Rostock on the Baltic coast. Two years later she opened her own school in Berlin-Halensee, then part of the British zone. When Mary Wigman left the Russian zone in 1949, Marianne Vogelsang helped her organize and manage her dance studio in Berlin-Dahlem. Wigman had for some time tried to entice Vogelsang to join her. But Vogelsang left the Wigman Studio and once more set up her own place in East Berlin in 1950. We see here the opposite movements and decisions of two dancers, close to each other in aesthetics and distant in existential notions—one leaving the East and the other leaving the West.

On October 24, 1951, Vogelsang's studio in East Berlin was converted into the *Fachschule für künstlerischen Tanz Berlin* (Vocational School for Artistic Dance). Vogelsang's studio thus formed the nucleus for the future State Ballet School in Berlin. She stayed at the school and taught modern dance and choreography until her sudden dismissal in 1958. Her work as a teacher for modern dance and as a choreographer at the Deutsches Theater and for the East German television company ended in 1961 when the Berlin Wall was built and Vogelsang had to decide whether to commit herself to a life in one half of Germany or the other. Marianne Vogelsang left East Berlin and made an insecure living in Cologne, West Germany, until her death in 1973—isolated, lonely, and poor.

Marianne Vogelsang was considered one of the most gifted young German modern dancers. From her first recitals in the 1930s she fascinated fellow artists and critics alike; they recognized an unusual talent for performance and choreography, a sense of intellectual integrity, measure and form, a sensibility for contemporary themes, and the ability to express them in movement. The future of modern German dance seemed secure with her. Vogelsang was a threat to anyone who considered herself the sole keeper of modern dance German style, for which reason both Wigman and Palucca wooed her and tried to keep her under control in their schools. But Vogelsang was an unusually independent person, ambitious only in an artistic sense. Her decency and truthfulness had brought her into conflict with the Nazi regime, driven her to support members of the Communist resistance,[22] and made her question any personal and aesthetic collaboration with her dance colleagues. The first generation of East German dancers and choreographers went through her studio, which later was transformed into the State Ballet School, in Berlin. Thus she established a counterpoint and a counter-concept to the Palucca School in Dresden, as well as to the Wigman Studio in West Berlin.

Vogelsang, unlike other modern dancers, publicly reflected on the recent past, and assessed the strengths and weaknesses of modern dance. She compared it with ballet, which she never simply dismissed, as Wigman and Palucca so easily did. Knowledge of both modern training and ballet technique and contemplation of the philosophies of the modern and ballet body made Vogelsang strive toward a new synthesis of the two conceptions of human movement. Vogelsang examined the aesthetic principles of the two systems and was prepared to adapt them according to the necessities of the time—postwar Germany. In her speeches, lectures, and published articles she demanded that dancers and choreographers create what a new society required. Vogelsang's writings provided the basis for a significant modification of the aesthetics of modern German dance.[23]

In 1954 the newly founded Ministry for Culture of the German Democratic Republic printed her *Gedanken zum Neuen künstlerischen Tanzes* (Thoughts on the New Artistic Dance) as a curricular guideline and textbook for all arts colleges and institutions of higher education. In it Vogelsang laid out the methods and categories of a new dance that integrated practical experiences and theoretical explorations from classical and modern dance; she analyzed the proposals of "realism" and "formalism" and their functional incorporation into her modern dance. She systematized modern German dance and offered a new technical as well as a new pedagogical method on which it could be based.

While Palucca remained within her improvisational teaching parameters of the late 1920s (which were in their own way successful and inspired generations of dancers) and never went beyond the rhetoric of a new methodology, Vogelsang offered feasible procedures to evaluate technique as the source of teaching and creativity. She conceived an original method within which a new socialist dance could be developed. Her discourse aimed at a different type of communication between student and teacher, dancer and choreographer, audience and performer. Not since Rudolf Laban's attempt to standardize and centralize German dance in 1934 had anyone revised the principles of a modern movement system so thoroughly and thoughtfully.

This publication made Vogelsang an eminent cultural force and therefore the most serious threat to Palucca's dominant position in East Germany. Wigman could watch with interest from her safe, apolitical Western haven. Palucca never managed to formulate that new theory and practice for which she received such vigorous backing from the Academy of Arts; she never rethought the pedagogical basis that she applied in her lesson plans over the decades; she never rethought her personal principles and preferences, which she erroneously equated with a method—for she *was* the principle and thus her teaching per se represented a meta-personal system.[24]

Palucca had already in 1950 demanded to lead a Berlin ballet school and she made her further presence in East Germany dependent on the school, together with master classes in dance, which she would teach at the Academy of Arts.[25] In the following years she successfully engaged Walter Felsenstein, intendant of the Komische Oper in Berlin, Bertolt Brecht from the Berlin Ensemble, and other famous artists to defend her case. All questions of dance pedagogy, aesthetics, and performance studies were to be examined by her before any administrative body could release official regulation. She—and through her the Academy of Arts as the political and cultural institution backing her—were to provide the only official interpretation of state guidelines; nothing and nobody else were relevant.[26] Palucca omitted to tell her colleagues at the Academy of the existence of new dance curricula that Vogelsang was already developing and that Palucca's own course syllabi were copied and slightly edited versions of the Laban-oriented teaching methods introduced in 1935 by the Ministry of Propaganda and Popular Enlightenment. Whenever Palucca lost ground, she blackmailed the official political institutions by calling up Felsenstein, Brecht, or anyone else who had a bone to pick with bureaucrats; she threatened, she begged, and she mostly got her way.

On January 30, 1958, Marianne Vogelsang was fired along with four other teachers from the ballet school, following vague accusations of undermining socialist education, alcoholism, and living in one of the Western sectors of Berlin. Not all of the cultural bureaucrats agreed with the treatment and dismissal of the modern dance team and several tried hard to protect the group from attacks coming from their own ranks. These ministerial officials also tried to persuade the ballet mistress of the State Opera Berlin to integrate Vogelsang into the new syllabus and they tried to place the disgraced Berlin pedagogues in the Palucca School. But Palucca, unfortunately, did not have any open spaces. And the ballet mistress had more important things to do than rescue modern dance.[27]

Marianne Vogelsang belonged to those very few people prepared to confront the past and their own involvement in it. She took full responsibility as a German for the evils done in the name of Germany and German culture by the Nazi regime. She revisited the ethical foundation of modern dance and she revised its aesthetic, technical, and pedagogical system. Her revision challenged the Nazi past as well as the socialist society she experienced in East Germany. Her brave confrontation failed, for she had little support and too many enemies.

Jean Weidt (1904–1988)

In May 1945, Jean Weidt was a British soldier fighting in a Pioneer Corps in Italy. In 1946 he returned to Paris, where he had spent most of his years of exile and where he had grown close to Jean Louis Barrault and his circle of existentialist artists and philosophers. In 1947 he won the International Choreography Competition in Copenhagen with his avant-garde and dramatic piece *The Cell*.[28] Weidt arrived in a destroyed Berlin in the autumn of 1948, invited by the dramatist and Communist politician Friedrich Wolf, to become the founder and director of the *Dramatic Ballet* at the Volksbühne in Berlin. Weidt brought with him a rich past of dance and performance practice: he, like

Vogelsang, had significantly changed Laban's and Wigman's modern German dance principles and developed his own version of modern dance.[29]

In French exile Weidt had incorporated existentialist stylistic features and now, in the postwar years, was prepared to explore the concepts of "socialist realism" as proclaimed by Joseph Stalin in 1932 and reissued as a set of fixed rules and guidelines by Andrey Zhdanov in 1945 and 1946. Weidt accepted the new aesthetic credo of a socialist realism, though he would never use such terms, for his terminology was simple and unintellectual. In spite of his loyalty, his particular stylistic approach was too formalist for the bone-headed proponents of "socialist realism." As hard as he tried to convince his comrades that he was working toward the proletarian world revolution and the extinction of capitalism, he was never believed. Like Vogelsang, he was on his own and had little support. He found himself in opposition to the Palucca camp, who had appropriated modern dance; he had nothing in common with the folk dance tradition that considered itself the custodian of "socialist realist dance," and he knew that the ballet people were indifferent. All three parties had cultivated their political and administrative patronage networks.

The same constellation that ended Jean Weidt's career as an independent dancer and choreographer in 1950 later brought down Vogelsang. He had to abandon his artistic plans to build a new socialist modern dance and faced accusations of "immoral" and "unethical" behavior—at the time, code words for homosexuality. He was sent out to the provinces where he was worn down by choreographing light entertainment and operetta for a people who were more interested in escapism than high art. His political loyalties never weakened and he never questioned his comrades or the Communist party. The restrictive and narrow cultural outlook of the official state institutions, backed and utilized by many artists, turned Weidt into a victim, spectacularly sacrificed as a Communist by Communist authorities. Weidt neither wrote nor rewrote the historical chronicles. He was a proletarian and found it difficult to articulate his own narrative. He hoped that one day justice would prevail and the world would turn into the worker's and peasant's paradise that the Russian Communists had predicted and to which he had dedicated his entire life. He was my teacher for many years and I admire to this day his integrity. His kindness, modesty, and honesty, his sharp sense of excellence, as well as his artistic generosity were exemplary.

Fritz Böhme (1881–1952)

Böhme, the last figure to appear in this gallery of biographies, lived in Berlin in May 1945. As veteran dance critic of the conservative *Deutsche Allgemeine Zeitung* in Berlin, Böhme had been one of the most vocal devotees of Rudolf

Laban during the 1920s. He remained loyal to Laban within the official modern dance empire, which the master had erected in Goebbel's Ministry of Propaganda and Popular Enlightenment. Böhme taught race theory as well as dance aesthetics in the Master Workshops (*Meisterwerkstätten*), the central Nazi dance institution in Berlin, from 1936 to 1945 and kept Laban's dance and theory legacy alive. As an active Nazi party member, Fritz Böhme was one of the few representatives of the dance world to be questioned in the de-nazification processes. On June 26, 1947, the Berlin Magistrate refused to declare him "denazified,"[30] yet Böhme never understood why he should not be cleared.[31] He saw nothing wrong with his work and classified himself a victim of Communist propaganda. He suggested to the cultural authorities that the centralized and standardized dance culture that had been institutionalized during Nazism should be continued—under his supervision.

His written requests to the Berlin institutions from 1946 onward demanded the reerection of a national dance academy with an archive and notation bureau. Böhme also supported Palucca's attempts to invigorate modern dance. He advocated the Nazi dance curriculum as the only comprehensible and possible solution for a new dance scene in an emerging socialist state. Böhme, an unreconstructed National Socialist, had learned nothing and forgot nothing. He did not need to repent, alter, admit guilt, or react in any other way to his direct involvement in Nazism. He did not need to rewrite dance history, for he already had devised a powerful narrative of a national German dance culture. Socialism or realism or collective guilt or social justice or de-nazification were irrelevant notions; modern German dance—expressive dance—was eternal and universal and the Communist regime a nuisance that would pass.

* * *

The careers of Wigman, Palucca, Vogelsang, Weidt, and Böhme prove one important thing: there was no *Stunde Null* in dance—there was no successful de-nazification process. Nazified dance concepts—together with their proponents—continued well into the 1950s until a new generation gradually emerged to face the burden of the Nazi past with its ideological baggage; some carry that baggage of their teachers to the present day. The two most thoughtful, reflective, synthetic, and least ruthless artists, Marianne Vogelsang and Jean Weidt, failed. Dance had no intellectual apparatus comparable to literature, music, or theater and remained one of the most impoverished arts in East Germany.

The modern dancers, unlike many other artists in other genres and fields, were profoundly antisocialist because of their ideological history. In theory, the modern dancers should have clashed with the political leadership of the German Democratic Republic. After all, the legitimacy of the East German regime rested on its real or imagined antifascist credentials. It had defined itself as the system that opposed and replaced Nazi ideology, Nazi values, and Nazi policies. The entire first generation of members of the Politburo of the Socialist Unity Party had been interned in concentration camps, imprisoned, or exiled. These people were real antifascists surrounded by the aura of suffering and heroism. As representatives of the state, they thought that a state with an antifascist government had to be antifascist itself. The generation of socialist and Communist revolutionaries who headed East Germany "believed that they were the revolutionary elect, the avant-garde uniquely qualified to govern a socialist Germany . . ."[32] The East German regime played a devious game with these Nazi artists. It needed their names and their prestige. It compromised its antifascist credentials by welcoming Wigman and Palucca with enthusiasm and rejecting figures like the committed leftist Weidt and the humanist Vogelsang.

After 1945 the tradition never changed. Laban lived his lies in Britain. Wigman rewrote her past as a victim of Nazism. Palucca followed her own interests with a shamelessness that allowed her at every political change to invent a new story and abandon her past. The three greatest figures in German modern dance experienced no *Stunde Null*. They never confronted their pasts, never underwent the slightest de-nazification, never confessed a doubt or hesitation. Their art justified everything they had done.

Was bleibt? What remains? Orwell's dictum fits German modern dance. The victors control the past and hence control the future of dance studies. Orwell's totalitarian nightmare has become reality in the history of German modern dance.

Notes

1. For more on the controversy surrounding Christa Wolf, see Stephen Brockmann, *Literature and German Reunification* (Cambridge: Cambridge University Press, 1999) and his article, "The Politics of German Literature," *Monatshefte* 84:1 (Spring 1992): 46–58.
2. George Orwell, *1984*, Centennial Edition (New York: Harcourt Brace, 2003), 35–36.
3. Ibid., 41.
4. Grundsatzentscheidung gegen Intellektuelle. 15.01.2003: Deutschland braucht die ostdeutschen Sozialwissenschaftlerinnen, *Forum Wissenschaft* (January 2003). http://www.bdwi.de/forum/archiv/archiv/441509.html.
5. *Der missbrauchte Antifaschismus. DDR-Staatsdoktrin und Lebenslüge der deutschen Linken.* Konrad-Adenauer-Stiftung e.V. (Sankt Augustin: Herder, 2002).
6. Jean Weidt, *Auf der grossen Strasse*, ed. Marion Reinisch (Berlin: Henschel 1984), 121. Editors' Note: Marion Kant edited this volume under her earlier name Marion Reinisch.
7. "Inner emigration" is a term coined by Frank Thiess, novelist and occasional dance critic and dance theorist, to justify his position in Nazi Germany. "Die Innere Emigration," open letter from Frank Thiess to Thomas Mann, August 19, 1945, reprinted in J. F. Grosser, *Die grosse Kontroverse: ein Briefwechsel um Deutschland* (Hamburg: Nagel, 1963), 24.

8. Diary, June 10, 1945; March 10, 1946; June 21, 1946; July 13, 1947. Wigman Archive, Academy of Arts, Berlin.

9. Thiess, "Die Innere Emigration."

10. Diary, April 6 and May 4, 1945. Wigman Archive, Academy of Arts Berlin.

11. In March 1946, Wigman became a delegate for the Deutscher Zentralausschuss für Volksbildung der Sowjetisch Besetzten Zone and traveled to Berlin to take part in the conference in the German State Opera "Zu neuen Ufern"; she also became a candidate for the Kulturbund, a nonparty cultural organization for the renewal of German Culture and the Arts. In August 1946, Wigman became honorary chair of the Women's Commission in the Russian zone. In November 1946, she received the title of honorary professor for her sixtieth birthday from the Leipzig Lord Mayor. In 1948 Wigman appealed to the Western Allies to support a unified Germany.

12. Editors' Note: For Kant's extended study of dance in the Nazi period, see Lilian Karina and Marion Kant, *Hitler's Dancers: German Modern Dance and the Third Reich* trans. Jonathan Steinberg (New York: Berghahn Books, 2003), originally published in German as *Tanz unterm Hakenkreuz* (Berlin: Henschel, 1999). See also her essays "German Dance and Modernity: Don't Mention the Nazis," in *Rethinking Dance History: A Reader*, ed. Alexandra Carter (London: Routledge, 2004): 107–118; "Joseph Lewitan and the Nazification of Dance in Germany," in *The Art of Being Jewish in Modern Times,* eds. Barbara Kirschenblatt-Gimblett and Jonathan Karp (Philadelphia: University of Pennsylvania Press, 2007): 663–701; "Practical Imperative: German Dance, Dancers, and Nazi Politics," in *Dance, Human Rights, and Social Justice,* eds. Naomi Jackson and Toni Shapiro-Phim (Lanham Md.: Scarecrow Press, 2008): 5–19; "Death and the Maiden: Mary Wigman in the Weimar Republic," in *Dance and Politics,* ed. Alexandra Kolb (Oxford: Peter Lang, 2010): 119–143.

For differently inflected accounts of Wigman's relation to National Socialism, see Hedwig Müller, *Mary Wigman—Leben und Werk der grossen Tänzerin* (Weinheim and Berlin: Quadriga, 1986) and her English-language article drawn from her biography, "Wigman and National Socialism," *Ballet Review* 15:1 (Spring 1987): 65–73; Susan Manning, *Ecstasy and the Demon: The Dances of Mary Wigman*, 2nd ed. (Minneapolis: University of Minnesota Press, 2006); and Laure Guilbert, *Danser avec le IIIe Reich: Les danseurs modernes sous le Nazisme* (Brussels: Editions Complexe, 2000).

13. Editors' Note: On an earlier stage of Palucca's career, see Susan Funkenstein's essay in this volume. For alternative accounts of Palucca's career, see Katja Erdmann-Rajski, *Gret Palucca* (Hildesheim: Geord Olms, 2000); Dianne Howe, *Individuality and Expression: The Aesthetics of the New German Dance, 1908–1936* (New York: Peter Lang, 2001), 137–158; Ralf Stabel, *Tanz, Palucca! Die Verkörperung einer Leidenschaft* (Berlin: Henschel, 2001); and Karl Toepfer, *Empire of Ecstasy: Nudity and Movement in German Body Culture, 1910–1935* (Berkeley: University of California Press, 1997), 186–190.

14. For a definition of *Einzelverträge*, see Birgit Wolf, *Sprache in der DDR. Ein Wörterbuch* (Berlin: De Gruyter, 2000), 51. Also see statistics of university and college faculty in Ralph Jessen, *Akademische Elite und kommunistische Diktatur* (Göttingen: Vandenhoeck und Ruprecht, 1999), 208f, 216, 219.

15. Founded July 12, 1951, dissolved 1954. The Staatlichen Kommission für Kunstangelegenheiten was decreed by the Ministry of the GDR. Its main goal consisted of the regulation of the arts by supporting a realist socialist aesthetic and defying what was seen as the destructive influence of formalism.

16. See the Protocols of the Sektion Darstellende Kunst (Department of Performing Arts) at the Academy of Arts from 1951 on and the discussions on elections of new members. Throughout the 1950s Palucca never nominated another choreographer or dancer to be included in the illustrious circle of Academy elect. She was happy to negotiate with prospective members from other fields but never from her own field.

17. Editors' Note: On the debate around the doctrine of socialist realism, see Franz Anton Cramer's essay in this volume. Jens Richard Giersdorf's essay in this volume then completes the chronological survey of dance in the GDR.

18. Protocol Sektion Darstellende Kunst of the Academy of Arts, November 26, 1951. During the discussion Palucca told her colleagues, among them dramatist Bertolt Brecht and theater critic Herbert Ihering, that choreographer Kurt Jooss was overrated and most of his works, some recently performed at the Titania Palace in West Berlin, were "truly dreadful." Two issues were indirectly connected to the discussion: prospective membership from abroad and suggestions to be made to the government agency responsible for invitations to future performances in East Germany. Palucca had once more disqualified any dance rivals for serious consideration. "Cosmopolitanism and bourgeois decadence" was a catchphrase for anti-Communist behavior.

19. Vogelsang is not a household name, and therefore some biographical data of her early career is helpful: She began her dance career in Palucca's school and later joined her dance group in Dresden in 1929. From 1935 she presented herself as a soloist in dance recitals and gained critical attention. Rudolf Laban employed her at the Deutsche Tanzbühne and the Meisterwerkstätten in Berlin from 1935. In 1938 she taught at the Folkwang School in Essen and worked alongside ballet dancers such as Tamara Rauser and Tatjana Gsovsky. From 1941 to 1943 she was ballet mistress and soloist at the Municipal Theatre in Göttingen and from 1943 until her internment she headed the Chamber Dance Group in Hannover.

20. Vogelsang was detained and sent to work in a salt mine in Volprihausen, near Hannover, in the summer of 1944 and her entire dance group insisted on following her. The group was released after the protest of the Intendant of the Göttingen Theatre, Gustav Rudolf Sellner, where she had been previously engaged. Vogelsang was then sent to work for the war effort in weaving factories near Einbeck until the end of World War II.

21. Müller, *Mary Wigman*, 267.

22. Letter from Fritz Cremer, Berlin December 18, 1942. Private collection.

23. *Gedanken zur Situation des Neuen Künstlerischen Tanzes* (Thoughts on the Situation of the New Artistic Dance); *Gedanken über die Technik des Neuen künstlerischen Tanzes und Vorschläge zu ihrer Fixierung* (Thoughts on the Technique of the New Artistic Dance and Suggestions toward a Methodology); and *Gedanken über die Pädagogik des Neuen künstlerischen Tanzes* (Thoughts on the Pedagogy of the New Artistic Dance)—all written between 1951 and 1953. "Neuer Künstlerischer Tanz" (New Artistic Dance) was a term Palucca had coined, and as her former student, Vogelsang used it to address a new version of Modern German Dance.

24. Palucca even suppressed the works of her own teaching staff. For years she refused to release the manuscript that investigated the evolution of teaching methods at her own Dresden school, authored by Eva Winkler and Peter Jarchow. Winkler had been an assistant of Vogelsang's at the Berlin school before her employment at the Palucca School, while Peter Jarchow was Palucca's pianist and musical advisor. The manuscript lay in

the archives in the Academy of Arts and Palucca strictly prohibited circulation. Only in 1996, two years after Palucca's death, was the manuscript published: Eva Winkler, Peter Jarchow, *Neuer Künstlerischer Tanz. Eine Dokumentation der Unterrichtsarbeit an der Palucca Schule Dresden 1965–1976*, ed. Ralf Stabel (Dresden: Palucca Schule, Tanzwissenschaft e.V. 1996.)

25. Palucca and Central Committee of the Socialist Unity Party (Protokoll Nr. 31 der Sitzung des Sekretariats des ZK am 8.12.1950—Protocol No. 31 of the Meeting of the Secretariat of the Central Committee on December 8, 1950).

26. For instance, the Performance Arts meeting in the Academy of Arts resolved on June 8, 1953, that Palucca's exercises were to form the basis for a new method that would define realistic performance in dance. The meeting of the Performance Arts in the Academy of Arts on June 30, 1953, concluded that in all questions regarding syllabi for universities and colleges the Academy should be informed and asked for its approval first.

The reader has to bear in mind the distinct place occupied by the Academy of Arts in relation to the Ministries of Education and Culture. The Academy of Arts, founded on March 24, 1950 as successor of the Prussian Academy of Arts that the Nazis had closed, acquired a special position because it was responsible directly to the Council of Ministers and could take direct political influence by circumventing arduous bureaucratic procedures to which the various ministries had to adhere. It was thus much more independent and could follow a more dissident course than a regular state organization. Palucca exploited the tension between the Council and the Academy, to her own advantage.

27. Protocol: Ueber die Ueberprüfung der Arbeit der Staatlichen Ballettschule, HA Darstellende Kunst, Ministry of Culture, January 18, 1958. DR1 Ministry of Culture, Bundesarchiv Zwischenarchiv Ruschestrasse.

28. Libretto: Mouloudji; music: Emile Damais.

29. Weidt had come to dance as a member of the working class. He had been born in Hamburg into a dysfunctional family and discovered dance first as a means of individual liberation from a deprived background and later as a means to express the collective will of the workers to emancipate themselves. Weidt swore in the 1920s to devote his life and his talent to the underclass and make its problems seen and heard—in a Germany torn between revolutions, barricades and appeasement, between inflation and depression. Initially he performed as a soloist and later formed his own ensemble. Weidt collaborated in 1931 with director Erwin Piscator in a production of *Tai Yang Erwacht*, a play by Friedrich Wolf, and choreographed several movement scenes. Friedrich Wolf remained an influential force in his life; he convinced Weidt to join the Communist Party and to return to East Germany.

30. Bundesarchiv Berlin. DR 2, 960, Entnazifizierungskommission beim Magistrat der Stadt Berlin für Kunstschaffende, June 26, 1947.

31. Berlin Document Center: Antrag von Fritz Böhme . . . auf Entnazifizierung, eingereicht February 23, 1949.

32. Catherine Epstein, *The Last Revolutionaries: German Communists and Their Century* (Cambridge: Harvard University Press, 2003), 99.

9. Warfare over Realism

Tanztheater *in East Germany,* 1966–1989

FRANZ ANTON CRAMER

In the first half of the 1950s, the *Zentralhaus für Volkskunst* (Central Office for the People's Art) in Leipzig produced a film of about ten minutes in length. Titled *Der Tänzerwettstreit* (*The Dancers' Contest*),[1] it depicts three people in a public park cheerfully dancing to lively accordion music. An introductory voiceover clarifies the film's context:

> The primary function of each and every true work of people's art (*Volkskunstschaffen*) is to provide a reflection of current-day life. The socialist lifestyle, new moral system and relationships among the people ought to determine the content of new dance. There's no need to attempt to resolve contemporary problems by means of dramatic and tumultuous action. We can also demonstrate the spirit of the time through dance works characterized by natural, sympathetic partnerings, by a spirit expressed through the dance itself, and by their style of movement. Let's watch now how this challenge is successfully met here.

Two young men occupy the screen. One, with luxurious blond hair, is in civilian clothing, and the other, with dark hair, wears the uniform of the *Volkspolizei* (People's Police). They are both apparently expecting to meet the same attractive young woman. Once she appears, the two men begin a friendly tussle—a contest, actually—in which each attempts to assert his primacy with gestural dance steps, powerful *soubresauts*, and other forms taken from folk dance. The young woman watches with amusement but does not take part, and at the dance's conclusion, all three walk off arm-in-arm in a swaying step toward a meadow.

This film was made only a few years after the founding of the GDR. It clearly attempts to adhere to the guidelines expressed in the voiceover—that dances be marked "by a spirit expressed through the dance itself, and by their style of movement"—by demonstrating the social and even playful coexistence of various segments of the population. The state (the police officer) and worker are on equal terms; they court the same damsel; they dance to the same accordion music; they dance on the same piece of public parkland; they use the same forms of expression and resolve their individual conflicts in a popular and collective manner. They are, moreover, young and optimistic.

The short film appears to be a direct response to a controversy that had arisen immediately after the founding of the state in 1949 and that reached its first peak by 1953. This controversy, referred to as the *Realismus-Streit* (dispute over realism), was voiced at symposia and on the pages of publications, such as the monthly *Weltbühne*.[2]

In 1953 the *Staatliche Kommission für Kunstangelegenheiten der DDR* (State Commission for the Arts of the German Democratic Republic) brought together a variety of opinion pieces, essays, and responses in a publication dedicated to this heated debate.[3] The aim was to include dance in the integration of art into socialist life, an integration already well established in other disciplines. Martin Sporck, one of the initiators of this debate, writes: "The revitalization of dance will not proceed from form, but from content. Replenish dance with new social content. Then the new forms that are most appropriate for this content will emerge."[4] The concern was to depart from existing styles of art and dance and to develop a form of dance that would be in accordance with the new social ideal: "What we need are new ballets, socialist in content and national in form . . . a new kind of dancer who, embracing life fully, indissolubly binds his thoughts and feelings with the thoughts and feelings of the masses and who serves his people as a singular force."[5]

A popular artistic practice was required, one in which art would draw directly from the social climate and, in turn, work in an educational manner upon this climate. Years later Bernd Köllinger, the artistic and political mind driving the formulation of new East German dance, elucidated the task confronting dance, a task that had already been a central concern for the founders of the GDR: "Both the starting point and the goal of socialist artwork is the new man: the rich, comprehensively cultivated man in socialist society, dedicated to socialism and real social progress."[6] In accordance with this new conception of an active art anchored in society, "the socialist-realist artwork and its intrinsic partiality"[7] are committed to the state, not to individual judgment. This demands a perpetuation of the processes of revolutionary change that marked the early years of the GDR: artists must grasp these processes, represent them, and shape them as they progress. From the perspective of dramaturgy, this is primarily to be accomplished through narration and representation. "One can most certainly abandon story and character in some genres of stage dance. . . .

In every case and as a bare minimum, however, the dance must aim to create a portrayal of the concrete social and psychological circumstances of individuals and collectives in a manner that is almost excessive in its reliance on dance."[8]

This essay will describe the development of East German dance after the proclamation of national independence in 1949. This development was constructed within a larger debate about realism and the role of art-making in a socialist state. As I will delineate, the importance of these questions inspired leading authors to attempt to define the meaning of realism in dance over a period of twenty years. These ideologies evolved along with the broader political and economic situation in the German Democratic Republic. I will focus on the significant 1966 founding of the *Tanztheater* company at East Berlin's Komische Oper and the role played by its artistic director and chief choreographer, Tom Schilling. The unstable legacy of his work reveals that the question of how to create dances that are both politically effective as well as successful works of art has yet to be resolved.

What Does "Realist" Actually Mean?

The revitalization of dance was to draw upon Soviet examples to depict the "new life" of the people under socialist conditions. This project was the beginning of a long-running discussion about the role of art in society that would continue with varying intensity and pitch until the final years of the GDR. Central to this debate was the socialist image of man. Bernd Köllinger thus refers to the declaration of the GDR State Council on November 30, 1967, which proclaimed "the fashioning of the socialist image of man" to be "the century's task."[9] Köllinger continues, "The production of the image of the socialist man and his community is 'at the centre of all great intellectual, ethical and aesthetic debates of our era.'"[10]

This formulation of a core ideological task in the late 1960s continued those attempts that had been introduced with the realism debate of the 1950s and the demand for a socialist realist approach to art. Art conceived in this manner would not exist for its own sake, nor would it be subject primarily to aesthetic considerations. Instead it would, above all, fulfill socialist purposes: "The character . . . of socialist realist art . . . [is] an indispensable medium for the further development of society and for the self-understanding of the millions working towards the realization of a socialist society, *an irreplaceable means of shaping their personality and consciousness.*"[11] Art can only fulfill these demands, however, if it proceeds from the "practical sharing of the socialist proletariat's real-life work." It is only insofar as reality is presumed to be the foundation for truth that an art can develop that "can stand up to the spirit of truth."[12] Such positions reject Western avant-garde conceptions of art: "In this type of 'simple art,' there is no attempt to make a statement. The most extreme individualistic expressive dance has thus reappeared."[13] One observes "the renunciation of the real world and its deep social antagonisms [in] modernist and decadent works of dance or ballet."[14] Only through an analysis of specific social relations and conditions can ballet develop an enlightening and productive social potency. This has nothing to do with bourgeois notions of humanism. On the contrary: "Your work will remain ensnared in the net of imperialist ideology as long as it does not overcome abstract humanism [with generally held 'values']. . . . That is why bourgeois criticism and bourgeois conceptions of humanism remain helpless and powerless: they are unable to escape their bourgeois position."[15]

Socialist revolutionary change in society impacts art not only in an ideological fashion, but also aesthetically: "The move towards socialist realism does not only expand and deepen the aesthetic potential of the arts, including stage dance, but in concert with this, crystallizes the completely unique artistic modes of conception and effect that each specific field of art possesses. The arts come 'into their own' by virtue of their new function in socialist society."[16] Dance's specific aesthetic appearance would result intrinsically from the political and social demands made upon the art and its effects. At the same time, the function of dance is, first and foremost, educational: "Dance has an enviable role to play in the formation and popularization of the new socialist aesthetic and moral ideals. . . . Broad and fruitful prospects are opened for dance by the humanization of life . . . and the creation of the social conditions necessary for all to be able to develop to their own abilities."[17] It is, after all, incumbent upon dance "to work its way into the emotional life of socialist persons and, in developing their repertoire of feelings, to contribute actively to the 'education of sentiments.'"[18] The ability "to capture in a poetic manner those human relationships that are characteristic of socialist society"[19] remains the criterion by which success in this endeavor is to be gauged.

Some ten years later, Karin Feister, who would go on to work in dramaturgy at the Komische Oper, published a dissertation on the new ways of dance theater and its relation to realism as an educational and ideological tool. In it she states:

> If . . . the focus of discussion is on realism in the production of art over the course of history, then the current conceptualization of realism justifies regarding this era as a qualitatively new stage in the history of art, one which exhibits a historically determined relationship to reality. The function of art is positioned in social reality and seeks to address this social reality, and it is itself derived from the process of social development. As such, it obtains its

realistic, historically long-ranging substance from the artistically portrayed humanity of a specific subject.

It is evident that even *Tanztheater* . . . attains its realism from the interaction between theatrical pleasure and the specific point of view based on moral and ethical questioning that seeks to act upon the sensory experience of human life.[20]

The duty of socialist art, and especially realist dance, was to have evolved since the founding of the GDR and the vision Köllinger had formulated earlier: "Thanks to new social conditions, the relationship between the new public and those who produce ballet, *between dance and life in general*, has grown closer over the course of the past twenty years."[21] This closer relationship is due to the historical specificity of the work and the choice of realist material and subject matter. The plot would no longer center on the fates of individuals or a single person's pursuit of happiness, but must instead attest to social contexts and modes of action. This predicates a completely new narratology, which would revolutionize the entire inherited tradition of dance. Köllinger points to the profusion of works in the ballet repertoire that are based on fairytale–like plots or that take the individualistic form of a biographical account of a single person's destiny, and argues, "What's on stage remains stuck in 'human generalities' because of a lack of historical specificity."[22]

Köllinger invokes the lay dance ensemble as a model to counter the professionalism and traditional narrative techniques of established dance and ballet companies. This has less to do with technical or artistic standards and more to do with the composition of these lay ensembles and their ideological qualities, which are necessary components in the production of socialist subject matter. An aesthetic perspective specific to the genre develops, so to speak, directly from these ideological conditions: "The diversity of dance forms springs from the dialectic between object and fashioning subject. . . . It is therefore completely natural that a broad palette of forms results from the process of dance turning its attentions to the socialist present."[23]

Socialist Development of Character

The political-ideological demand for a "socialist development of character" was as prominent in scholarship as it was in the political realm. Sociologist Horst Slomma, a contributor to the collected volume *The Socialist Image of Man*,[24] submitted his postdoctoral thesis at the University of Leipzig in 1968. In it he focused on an "examination of the dialectic between entertainment and the development of character in socialist national culture."[25] The third section of this work attends to the "fundamental developmental tendencies of aesthetic-artistic entertainment culture as a result of interactions between technical and cultural revolution."[26] His primary argument is that the increasing amount of free time "would not be wasted on the decadent products of the profit-motivated, manipulative entertainment industry" but instead "would present new opportunities for active participation in personal development and cultural forms of entertainment that were integral parts of democratic, intellectual and cultural life."[27] From an ideological standpoint, this socialist model of a form of entertainment motivated and driven by society itself "redeems the demands of the Enlightenment, which connect the development of intellect and reason with the most noble forms of entertainment."[28] This is contrasted with capitalism, in which evident contradictions must necessarily "reveal the conflict between culture and entertainment."[29]

Slomma is interested in the establishment of an artistic means of production and, above all, a form of perception that is participatory and deliberate without being able to deny the demands for purity inherent in the production of art. If it is to be socialist, art must entertain but also enlighten; it ought not simply indulge, but rather maintain a distance. It is only in this fashion that a specifically socialist development of character—that is, one created on the level of the community—can follow, one that is not based on effects, but on discourse. Art is suitable only when it works toward changing consciousness, when it impacts social relations and clarifies the perception of society as it exists. To this end, art need not be formalist, decadent, or accusatory, but concrete and, ideally, intelligible to all. The debate over entertainment focuses on this ethically grounded demand for popularity, a demand that guarantees the social effectiveness of art. Style and technique are secondary. They have to serve an overall purpose that is defined by clarity and instruction: "1. The awakening and maintaining of attention . . . by virtue of a generally intelligible, generally accessible, clear and distinctive language. . . . 2. The conveyance of a variety of aesthetic pleasures that provide the people . . . with an enduring vitality and that are based upon both a masterly control of artistic form and humanist insight."[30] Slomma offers another and third basic principle: "The depth of the spiritual-emotional meaning . . . that results from the artistic generalization and aesthetic judgment reveals itself . . . to also be its entertainment value."[31] Realism's three demands on socialist art apply equally to dance. *Tanztheater*, as it evolved in the GDR, is also obliged to strive to meet these demands. Bernd Köllinger accordingly noted in his work:

> Socialist realism is concerned with the person *as a whole*. It refuses to regard the person simply as a biological being, an existence determined completely by its drives, as a one-dimensional, sexually defined phenomenon, as a tool controlled by higher powers, as a being that can only react to, not actively

construct or act upon, its environment, as a fatalist, a moralist or an existentialist. It is concerned instead with the person in the entirety of his social relations and the potential for individual development and fulfillment that results from this for both the single person and for society as a whole.[32]

Tanztheater

As stated earlier, this ideologically motivated demand on the practice of art (the production of art works, art criticism, and research on art) was current until the end of the GDR as a state. The Leipzig-based ballet teacher Werner Gommlich wrote in 1982:[33] "The artistic image (as a portrayal of reality) therefore represents: 1. the dialectic between object and subject; 2. the aesthetic expression of the contradictions in society; 3. the aesthetic expression of subjective contradictions in the artist's character."[34] But even the subject of the portrayal—social reality itself—is constituted "owing to the artistic *malleability* specific to the genre."[35] After all, "*Tanztheater* is not distinguished by any specific thematic aspects, but instead by the distinctiveness of its methods of production, and its productivity is due, not to any small degree, to the variety of forms at its disposal."[36] This variety of forms available to dance plays a role in the construction of the reality that is, at the same time, its object: socialist society. "Tanztheater therefore eminently fulfills the function by which art provides insight, and in this respect, *contemporaneity is revealed to be the premise of dance's aesthetic quality*."[37] Originality or presenting shocking connections between heterogeneous elements, as had become prevalent in West German dance, is not the aim in fashioning dance. The goal instead is to bring into harmony choreographic forms of expression and the ideologically determined course of events as they arise out of socialist reality. The true task of realist, socialist art lies not in artistic experience, but rather in the work's potential for change and its ability to resolve contradictions in the action, an ability that is itself a form of taking action.

The dance ensemble of Berlin's Komische Oper, founded in 1966, became a focal point for these debates. With Tom Schilling[38] as chief choreographer, Bernd Köllinger as artistic director and librettist, and Walter Felsenstein[39] as general director, this company was a model not only in its work toward meeting political-aesthetic demands, but also in effecting a form of self-determination for dance within the framework of those demands.

The GDR experienced increasing prosperity in the early 1970s. For a time the societal and ideological climate shifted thanks to an upturn in the economy, a stabilization in domestic affairs, and increased international recognition of the GDR. (The Transit Agreement and Basic Treaty of 1972 reformed the relationship between the GDR and the Federal Republic of Germany; the GDR became a full member of the United Nations in 1973; and in 1974 the East German team beat the West Germans in the first group round of the FIFA World Cup.)[40] Cultural productions were held in higher esteem than before and aesthetic excellence in particular was promoted. Several of the Komische Oper's *Tanztheater* company's most important productions date from this period, including the adaptations of the classics *Cinderella* (1975), *Schwanensee* (Swan Lake) (1978), and the ballet fairy tale *Undine* (1970).

A New Midsummer Night's Dream

The Komische Oper and those circles most closely connected with it became suffused with an analytical approach to the conceptualization of *Tanztheater*. Numerous meetings, essays in theater programs and articles in the press questioned the rigor of dramatic arts and connected this discussion to the social responsibility of dance. In addition, the issue of dramaturgy increasingly became a subject of academic reflection. In her substantial dissertation submitted in 1983, for example, Karin Feister used a series of discrete examples to examine the form of *Tanztheater*. One such example was the ballet *Ein neuer Sommernachtstraum* (*A New Midsummer Night's Dream*; Figures 9.1, 9.2).[41]

The plot of *A New Midsummer Night's Dream*, only loosely related to Shakespeare's play, is transplanted to government housing on the edge of a city in the present day. Titania and Oberon's flirtatious relationship is increasingly impinged upon by the noisy hustle and bustle of human society. The scene is set in a gray, concrete plaza. Against the backdrop of people hurrying in all directions, one young man, Ludwig, catches the audience's eye as he strolls arm-in-arm with his girlfriend.

Titania sends her retinue back to their fairy woodland and undertakes an exploratory tour of socialist reality on her own. Perched on some scaffolding, she takes note of the numerous conflicts all around her between parents and their children, between unfaithful lovers and newlyweds. Titania falls for the rebellious young man, Ludwig. But the relationship quickly turns humiliating for Titania as Ludwig strikes a macho pose in front of his friends. The scene ends in a general commotion, a brawl even. Only Oberon's appearance brings the unpleasant action to an end.

In the following "forest scenes," Titania and Oberon resolve one conflict after another, bring the bewildered pair of lovers together, and celebrate with a grand bacchanal. In the epilogue, the human characters find themselves back in the place where the quarrel began, and they gradually readopt their old movements. Ludwig is left with only a vague suspicion that the dream scene may actually have been real.

The themes of lost youth, social evils, and the increasingly discourteous norms of social interaction seem incongruous with the image of a society

Figure 9.1. Hannelore Bey (Titania) being shouted at by Ludwig's parents Dorothea (Uta Opitz) and Hermann (Matthias Hösl) in Tom Schilling's *Ein neuer Sommernachtstraum*. Photo: Arwid Lagenpusch.

Figure 9.2. Ludwig, the male protagonist (Thomas Kindt) and his gang in Tom Schilling's *Ein neuer Sommernachtstraum*. Photo: Arwid Lagenpusch.

that measures itself against its foreign enemies, especially capitalist societies, where all evil is supposedly found. In this respect, *A New Midsummer Night's Dream* is quite audacious, even if the conclusion—that it is up to the individual to improve relations—invokes a socially comprehensive responsibility that adheres systematically to the professed values of the GDR. Feister analyzes the work thus: "The apparent loss of ethical-moral values and benchmarks for behavior that mark the portrayal of Ludwig is reversed by the demonstrative exhibition of events in the fictitious second act (dream) and 'converted' into an evident gain in character and personality."[42] What makes *A New Midsummer Night's Dream* a socialist-realist model work is the quality marked by the character's ability to shape himself based on his experiences and to recognize social reality as a space of conflict, one in which he is called upon to act. Thus he demonstrates how individuation can have an effect on society. This holds true in spite of the elements of fairy tales and fantastical aspects of the work. As Feister concludes, "Ludwig is a character under construction."[43]

At the same time that Schilling and Köllinger juxtapose stereotypical and individualized characters, they present symbolically rich descriptions as well as model strategies for transformation or development. This production, then, realizes the demands to reconcile entertainment and intellectual content as well as to connect intellectual comprehension with moral consciousness as expressed, for example, by Horst Slomma. As Feister notes, *A New Midsummer Night's Dream* correspondingly focuses "little on the protagonists' development and hardly at all on individual figures' wrestling with new styles, but rather traces how to possibly correct destructive personal qualities. This take on *Tanztheater* underscores the fact that interpersonal problems can be resolved."[44]

Yet it did not escape commentators' attention that especially the forest scenes and the presence of fairies did not quite fit with this reading. After all, it is the concrete nature of social relations that ought to provide creative benchmarks. To reconcile the demands of this world with the fantastical world of fairies and magic, Feister and Volkmar Draeger postulate romanticism and idealism to be instrumental aspects of reality:

> Romanticism . . . is not a counterpart to socialist realism, but instead a means by which future possible elements of reality can be given form within socialist art. From a Marxist perspective, romanticism is . . . an expression of the breadth and variety of artistic realization. It does not imply an insurmountable cleft between ideal and real based on antagonistic contradictions, but instead uses new dramaturgical structures and forms of composition to grapple more intensely with a reality that, while completely whole and intact, is also marked by contradictions and elements prompting questioning and closer examination.[45]

The notion of individual responsibility thus reconciles the assertion that a true socialist society already exists with a concrete diagnosis of social ills.

The question remains whether dance can concretely influence the shaping of reality, and if so, how. It is a question that underlies Feister's analysis of Tom Schilling's work in *Tanztheater* as well:

> *A New Midsummer Night's Dream*, as choreographed by Tom Schilling, positions itself as a work of transformational theatre modelled on the concept developed by Brecht, a work that seeks to contribute to the transformation of experiential reality through artistic expression. (It would be interesting to compare, for example, the experiential *Tanztheater* of Pina Bausch with the works of dance created at the Komische Oper along the lines outlined above.) . . . In the bacchanal scene, just before the epilogue, humans and elves join together in a dance full of zest for life and love. Then a change of scene and a confused awakening. In the second act's dream, the forces of nature judge and influence the behaviors that were displayed in the first act, but they do not change anything in reality. It is now up to the human characters to bring to fruition their own complete humanization.[46]

This call for participation is precisely the demand made by *Tanztheater* on its public, but no particular radical technique is specified. Whereas West German productions by Johann Kresnik or Pina Bausch, for example, made use of formal breaks with tradition, provocations, and attempts to shock, the *Tanztheater* of the Komische Oper stuck with a reserved, classically oriented and, one could even say, conservative aesthetic.[47]

"Five-Year Plan" 1976–1980

The program of the new five-year plan adopted at the 1975 Socialist Unity Party Congress testifies to social and political confidence, even if it was merely temporary. Following a list of all of the achievements of the preceding years, the document went on to elucidate the resulting new tasks and goals for improving the economic, moral, and political situation in the country. The document's remarks about culture, however, remained general and noncommittal.

At the same time, art and culture were accorded a key mandate in the coming five-year term. The directive's preliminary remarks included the following assertion: "*The growing harmonization between societal and personal interests* has become the decisive drive behind the development of the socialist society of the DDR."[48] It continued: "Considerable progress [could be] achieved in the shaping of the developed socialist society."[49] This charge to work toward the growing harmonization of societal and personal goals also legitimized culture in general. The five-year plan for the period from 1976 to 1980 envisioned succinctly: "Socialist culture and art are charged with developing the people's socialist characters and to support their conscious, creative activity with the goal of contributing to the strengthening of socialist consciousness and the molding of the socialist way of life."[50] While not specifically about dance or *Tanztheater*, the document continues: "Through new works of artistic entertainment, one may *masterfully convey powerfully effective socialist experiences of art* and support a stimulating cultural life."[51] Furthermore: "The appropriation of inherited progressive cultural practices and the nurturing of the best humanist and revolutionary cultural traditions must be carried forth and *supported with masterful artistic interpretations.*"[52]

The heated debates about formalism or realism in dance and other art forms faded away during this period. Artistic displays of splendor and sumptuousness were no longer disreputable. Furthermore, the years between 1975 and 1982 mark the heyday of the *Tanztheater* company at the Komische Oper. In this atmosphere marked by a loosening of the strictures of socialist realism, Tom Schilling and Bernd Köllinger aimed to meet expectations of artistic excellence in their work while simultaneously providing "powerfully effective socialist experiences of art." To these ends, the company proved itself again and again through the quality of its artistic work and its dramaturgical meticulousness. The company earned ample recognition on its extensive tours abroad in the West. Tom Schilling was even invited to West Berlin in 1988 as the guest choreographer for the Deutsche Oper's production of *Orpheus-Stationen*.

However well received was Tom Schilling's and Bernd Köllinger's work in establishing a "popular *Tanztheater*," the project was never completely free of conflict. Political involvement in shaping culture, on the one hand, and aesthetic considerations, on the other, continually provided cause for critical debate. Nevertheless, Bernd Köllinger could write in 1983: "At a relatively early point [Tom Schilling] created an example of choreography that approaches the symphonic in its composition. Abstraction never went so far as to obscure human destinies and individuality. But it was still developed to such a degree that the choreography, as a self-contained, irreplaceable, and untranslatable theatrical art with its own specific set of discursive norms, could stand and endure on its own."[53] It is hardly surprising that this type of approach would not remain unchallenged in the GDR's political climate. Critical essays appeared regularly in the press as well as in the newsletter put out by the Association of Theater Professionals of the GDR in which even Tom Schilling was admonished to never lose sight of the need to fully realize socialist realism.

Conclusion

In her study of the development of *Ausdruckstanz* from the years before World War I to the era following the Second World War,[54] Susan Manning examines the varied connections between the "inheritance" of free dance following its transformation under National Socialist cultural policies and the emergence of a new dance style, namely *Tanztheater*. This form distinguished itself from ballet as well as from the individualistic, free artistic stylizations of the great artists of the 1920s and 1930s. The origin of dance troupes dedicated to "modern" styles that were financed by the state can be traced directly back to the forced integration of such companies in state bodies and agencies under National Socialist cultural policies. Practically, no independent dance scene has existed in Germany since the end of World War II because all dance initiatives are directly or indirectly supported by public funds. As a result, two parallel regimes of *Tanztheater* have arisen in addition to the emergence of a rich ballet scene. On the one hand, the concept of *Tanztheater* has been inherited from an earlier period.[55] Kurt Jooss and Rudolf Laban debated the name itself and the style's artistic and structural content in the 1920s. On the other hand, *Tanztheater* assumed new forms after World War II. The term *Tanztheater*, especially in the GDR, was less a designation of a specific aesthetic and more a particular approach to the styles and forms of choreography and dramaturgy.

Tanztheater, as it developed at the Komische Oper in Berlin, was to act as an example of harmony between demands for a socially responsible and enlightening artistic practice and the aesthetically satisfactory realization and stylization of works for the stage. Choreographers could not avoid fierce debates about the cultural reorientation of a young East German society and the bourgeois-influenced conceptualizations of a closed style that remained conscious of tradition. A select few—Tom Schilling above all—rose to the task of conceiving of the politicization of dance as an artistic challenge and creating aesthetically fulfilling works within the framework of those political demands. What this meant was connecting the complex demands for "realism in art" with the individual demands for "complexity in dance."

In her book on German dance, published shortly after German reunification, Manning justifiably questioned what kind of stance the new united German state would take toward GDR dance culture. Nearly twenty years ago, several possibilities could be entertained: "Now that East and West Germany have reunited, what will be the fate of the two *Tanztheaters*? Will there be a radical change in personnel . . . ? Will choreographers who achieved reputations in what was East Germany now reject Tom Schilling's prescription for *Tanztheater*?"[56]

In 2010 the path that was taken is unambiguously evident: The GDR's traditions, its achievements, have not been continued, indeed have been erased to a great degree. The Komische Oper's *Tanztheater* company was disbanded in 1993.[57] The big ballet companies at the Opera houses in Leipzig and Dresden are today run by choreographers from North America; the Berlin State Opera's Ballet company gained institutional independence in the early 2000s under the joint directorship of Russian ballerino Vladimir Malakhov and West German manager Christiane Theobald. The repertoire in all of the institutions is strictly classical or neoclassical; nothing of realism's legacy remains. Even the Dance Archive in Leipzig, one of the most important collections of documents and artifacts related to the development of dance in the GDR, has been continually downsized and faces the threat of closure. Research on East German dance history is left to a handful of scholars and authors.[58] An exception to this situation could be found in the various projects staged in 2009, the twentieth anniversary of the fall of the Wall, that examined performance art, underground artists, and experimental media art in the GDR.[59]

A real interest in what has been called the "art history of the East," that is, of former socialist countries, has been growing over the past several years.[60] Work on the art history of the GDR profits from this attention, with recent examples including the exhibition "60—40—20"[61] and the project entitled "Grauzone DDR" (Gray zone GDR).[62]

The complicated matter of how one can build an effectual connection between artistic practice and social effectiveness that is both aesthetically and politically satisfactory remains unanswered to this day. It is clear that the control of artistic work and processes by political regulations offered no model. But the experiments in realism in the GDR at least provided some indication of what means might allow dance to develop beyond its confinement to aesthetic criteria.

There is as of yet still no comprehensive, impartial aesthetic and contextual critical examination of choreography in the GDR, especially the work of the *Tanztheater* company of the Komische Oper. Political preconceptions and reservations, the difficulty in accessing archival materials following the liquidation of the Komische Oper's *Tanztheater* company,[63] and the overwhelming focus placed by German dance studies on questions of performativity, the history of ballet, and the genesis of western modern and contemporary dance all contribute to the fact that this subject remains hushed, also and especially in an internationally comparative perspective.

Notes

1. Undated, Tanzarchiv Leipzig (Leipzig Dance Archive).
2. The culmination of this debate was Martin Sporck's article in *Weltbühne* that appeared on December 24, 1952. See, too, the materials collected under the rubric of the exhibition "Between Idealism and Ideology: Dance in the GDR, 1949 to 1956," which was organized by Claudia Jeschke and students in 1996 at the Dance Archive in Leipzig.
3. Staatliche Kommission für Kunstangelegenheiten, Hauptabteilung Künstlerischer Nachwuchs und Lehranstalten, ed., *Zur Diskussion: Realismus im Tanz* (Dresden: Verlag der Kunst, 1953).
4. Martin Sporck, "Realismus im Tanz," in ibid., 7–14. (quotation from 13 f.).
5. Sporck, "Realismus," 13.
6. Bernd Köllinger, "Im Blick—unsere Zeit. Überlegungen zu einigen Entwicklungs-

tendenzen bei der Aneignung der sozialistischen Gegenwart durch den Bühnentanz der DDR," in *Material zur Vorbereitung des 1. zentralen Seminars der Fachgruppe Bühnentanz des Verbandes der Theaterschaffenden in der DDR* (typescript; no place or year of publication, circa 1970), Tanzarchiv Leipzig, Signatur E 2818, 42.

7. Köllinger, "Im Blick," 42.

8. Ibid.

9. "Die Aufgabe der Kultur bei der Entwicklung der sozialistischen Menschengemeinschaft. Beschluss des Staatsrates der DDR vom 30. November 1967," in *Schriftenreihe des Staatsrates der DDR*, vol. 2 (1967). Bernd Köllinger (b. 1944) studied cultural studies and drama at the Fachschule für Bühnentanz (School for Stage Dance) and the Theaterhochschule Hans Otto, both in Leipzig. His dissertation was on "Tanz als Prozeß—der Prozeß im Tanz. Historisch-materialistische Untersuchungen zur ästhetischen Spezifik der Tanzkunst, insbesondere des Bühnentanzes, unter besonderer Berücksichtigung des Widerspiegelungsaspektes" (University of Leipzig, Faculty of Cultural Studies and German, 1972). As a fellow in stage dance in the state Verband der Theaterschaffenden der DDR (Association of Theatre Professionals of the GDR) and then as the chief artistic director and librettist of the dance ensemble of the Komische Oper in Berlin, Köllinger was one of the most influential dance professionals in the GDR.

10. Ibid.

11. Köllinger, "Im Blick," 2, author's italics.

12. Johannes R. Becher, *Auf andere Art so große Hoffnung. Tagebücher.* (Berlin, 1969), 12ff., cited in Köllinger, "Im Blick," 4. Becher had been Secretary of Culture in the early days of the GDR.

13. Köllinger, "Im Blick," 6.

14. Ibid.

15. Ibid., 11.

16. Ibid., 12.

17. Ibid., 13.

18. Ibid.

19. Ibid., 14.

20. Karin Feister, "Beitrag zur Grundlegung einer Berlinischen Dramaturgie des Tanztheaters auf der Basis der Tanztheater-Arbeit an der Komischen Oper Berlin im Zeitraum 1975–1982—vergleichende Betrachtungen zur komplexen Struktur des choreographischen Werkes in der dialektischen Wechselwirkung seiner Elemente Libretto—Musik—Choreographie," Dissertation, Gesellschaftswissenschaftliche Fakultät des wissenschaftlichen Rates der Humboldt-Universität zu Berlin, 1983, 179.

21. Köllinger, "Im Blick," 14, author's italics.

22. Ibid., 16.

23. Ibid., 23.

24. Elmar Faber and Erhard John, eds., *Das sozialistische Menschenbild. Weg und Wirklichkeit* (Leipzig: Karl-Marx-Universität, 1967).

25. Horst Slomma, *Untersuchung zur Dialektik von Unterhaltung und Persönlichkeitsbildung in der sozialistischen Nationalkultur*, Habilitationsschrift (postdoctoral thesis), Karl-Marx-Universität Leipzig 1968.

26. Ibid., 1.

27. Ibid.

28. Slomma is invoking—in this instance and elsewhere—Schiller's *On the Aesthetic Education of Man.*

29. Slomma, *Untersuchung*, 1.

30. Ibid., 291.

31. Ibid., 202.

32. Köllinger, "Im Blick," 44.

33. Werner Gommlich (b. 1927) was the deputy director of the Palucca School in Dresden and subsequently head of the department of choreography and dance pedagogy at the Theaterhochschule Hans Otto in Leipzig. His textbook *Klassischer Tanz: Die Schule des Tänzers* (Classical Dance: The Dancers' School) has remained in print since its first edition in 1974. It was most recently reissued in 2008 by the Henschel-Verlag in Berlin.

34. Werner Gommlich, "Zu einigen Fragen der ballettspezifischen Widerspiegelung/ Aneignung der Wirklichkeit unter dem Aspekt des Schaffens neuer Werke," in *Material zum Theater*, ed. Verband der Theaterschaffenden in der DDR No. 154, vol. 14, (1982), 4–12 (5).

35. Gommlich, "Zu einigen Fragen," 6, author's italics.

36. Ibid., 9.

37. Ibid., 10, author's italics.

38. Tom Schilling (b. 1928) studied with Mary Wigman and Dore Hoyer, among others, and earned his diploma in stage dance in 1944. By 1945 he was a soloist in the ballet company of the State Opera in Dresden; from 1946 until 1952 he was a dancer at the Leipzig Ballet, and from 1953 until 1956 in Weimar. Schilling was the director of ballet in Dresden from 1956 to 1964. In 1965 he was recruited to Berlin. In 1966 he produced Werner Egk's *Abraxas*, his first work choreographed for the newly founded *Tanztheater* of the Komische Oper. He became the chief choreographer and assumed the role of artistic director from 1974 until 1989. Among his defining works are *Phantastische Symphonie* (1967), *La mer* (1969), *Schwanensee* (1978), *Ein neuer Sommernachtstraum* (1981), and *Wahlverwandtschaften* (1983).

39. Walter Felsenstein (1901–1975), of Austrian origin, was an actor and theater director active in Germany since 1923. In 1947 he was called to be director general of the Komische Oper in Berlin's Eastern part. He developed a much-praised style of *Musiktheater* (rather than lyric theater), adapting repertoire operas to contemporary expression.

40. This period of relative freedom was short-lived. Following the forced emigration in 1977 of Wolf Biermann, a singer and musician critical of the regime, the GDR state apparatus reverted to repressive attitudes and policies.

41. *A New Midsummer Night's Dream*, based on the work by William Shakespeare, Libretto: Bernd Köllinger; Choreography: Tom Schilling; Music: Georg Katzer. Premiere: March 22, 1981.

42. Feister, *Beitrag zur Grundlegung*, 215.

43. Ibid., 218.

44. Ibid., 193.

45. Karin Feister and Volkmar Draeger, "Poetisierung von Gegenwartsstoffen im Tanztheater," in *Material zum Theater, Beiträge zur Theorie und Praxis des sozialistischen Theaters*, ed. Verband der Theaterschaffenden der DDR, No. 163, Reihe Bühnentanz, vol. 15, (Berlin, 1982), 6.

46. Feister, *Beitrag zur Grundlegung*, 196.

47. West German critics largely dismissed the works of the Komische Oper. For example, Jochen Schmidt termed the style "fluff aesthetic." See Jochen Schmidt, *Tanztheater in Deutschland* (Frankfurt and Berlin: Propyläen, 1992), 220.

48. *Direktive des IX. Parteitages der SED zum Fünfjahrplan für die Entwicklung der Volkswirtschaft der DDR in den Jahren 1976–1980* (Berlin: Dietz, 1976), 6, author's italics.

49. Ibid., 5.

50. Ibid., 112.

51. Ibid., author's italics.

52. Ibid., 113, author's italics.

53. Bernd Köllinger, *Tanztheater. Tom Schilling und die zeitgenössische Choreographie. Sieben Studien* (Berlin: Henschelverlag, 1983), 33. The choreography discussed here is *Phantastische Symphonie*.

54. Susan Manning, *Ecstasy and the Demon. The Dances of Mary Wigman*, 2nd ed. (Minneapolis: University of Minnesota Press, 2006), specifically: "From *Ausdruckstanz* to *Tanztheater*," 221–254.

55. Editors' Note: On the complex relationship between Mary Wigman's *Ausdruckstanz* and Pina Bausch's *Tanztheater*, see Sabine Huschka's essay in this volume.

56. Manning, *Ecstasy and the Demon*, 252f. For more on the parallel traditions of *Tanztheater*, see the introduction by Susan Manning and Lucia Ruprecht to this volume.

57. Though not without a gala event celebrating Tom Schilling and honoring his work. See Dramaturgische Abteilung der Komischen Oper Berlin, ed., *Tanztheater-Gala für Tom Schilling*, June 11, 1993.

58. The existing literature includes Peter Jarchow and Ralf Stabel, *Palucca: aus ihrem Leben—über ihre Kunst* (Berlin: Henschel, 1997); Angela Rannow, ed., *Die Rechte der Choreographen in Europa: Dokumentation der Konferenz "Die Kollektive Wahrnehmung der Choreographenrechte in Europa."/Les droits des chorégraphes en Europe* (Dresden: Conseil International de la Danse, Nationales Komitee der Bundesrepublik Deutschland, 2002); Angela Rannow, ed., *Mondscheingiraffen: 25 Jahre Winterkurs für Improvisation und 1. Symposium "Improvisation in Kunst und Pädagogik" in Dresden* (Dresden: Tanzwissenschaft e.V., 2004); Angela Rannow, ed., *Strukturprinzip Bewegung: tanzwissenschaftliche Beiträge. Symposium zur Tanzwissenschaftlichen Lehre und Forschung, vom 11.–13. September 1992 in Leipzig* (Leipzig: Arbeitsgruppe Tanzwissenschaft an der Hochschule für Musik und Theater Felix Mendelssohn Bartholdy, 1992); Ralf Stabel, *IM "Tänzer": der Tanz und die Staatssicherheit* (Mainz: Schott, 2008); Ralf Stabel, *Vorwärts, rückwärts, seitwärts mit und ohne Frontveränderung: zur Geschichte der Palucca-Schule Dresden* (Wilhelmshaven: Noetzel, 2001); Ralf Stabel: "Die große Geste—Der sozialistische Realismus im Ballett. Zur Einführung des sozialistischen Realismus der Sowjetunion und zu deren Auswirkungen auf die DDR-Tanzgeschichte," in *Bewegung im Blick, Beiträge zu einer theaterwissenschaftlichen Bewegungsforschung*, eds. Claudia Jeschke, Hans-Peter Bayerdörfer (Berlin: Vorwerk 8, 2000), 213–224. [Editors' Note: In addition to these titles, see the essays by Marion Kant and Jens Richard Giersdorf in this volume.]

59. For example, the exhibit "Without us! An exhibition in 4 locations on art and alternative culture in Dresden before and after '89," September 4, 2009, through April 11, 2011, Dresden, Prager Spitze et al.

60. Compare the noncurated project "East Art Map" (http://www.eastartmap.org) or the 2008/09 collection of events and research projects supported by the German Allianz Kulturstiftung, the Romanian National Center for Dance, the Slovenian project association "maska," and the Tanzquartier Wien entitled "What to affirm, what to perform" (http://www.allianz-kulturstiftung.de/projekte/darstellende_kunst/affirm_perform/index.html). Tellingly, GDR art and performance work was not addressed as part of this project.

61. "60—40—20." Kunst in Leipzig seit 1949. Exhibition at the Leipzig Museum of Fine Arts (Museum der bildenden Künste), October 4, 2009, through January 10, 2010.

62. See Dieter Daniels, Jeannette Stoschek, eds., *GRAUZONE 8 mm—Materialien zum autonomen Künstlerfilm in der DDR*. Accompanying volume for the exhibition "40jahre-videokunst.de: revision.ddr" Museum der bildenden Künste Leipzig, March 25 through May 21, 2006. (Ostfildern: Hatje Canz 2007).

63. A portion of Tom Schilling's archive as well as the administrative records of the Komische Oper's Tanztheater company were transferred in 2010, however, to the archive of the Akademie der Künste in Berlin.

10. Moving against Disappearance

*East German Bodies in
Contemporary Choreography*

JENS RICHARD GIERSDORF

Twenty years ago, with the fall of the Berlin Wall, many socialist countries—including East Germany—that had been prominent players on the world stage began to quickly, and in many cases, literally, vanish from the world map. In the years after the fall of the Wall, some former socialist countries such as Poland were able to recast their experience under Communist rule as part of a national narrative of ongoing resistance, while others, such as the former Yugoslavia, experienced a violent breaking apart into smaller national, ethnic, or religious units, and others, in the case of the former Soviet Union, referenced their national identities back to Czarist colonialism and Bolshevik rule.

However, East German national identification took a completely different trajectory from that of the other socialist states. Nearly a year after the fall of the Wall, the country was subsumed into the West German national structure. Retrospectively, the fall of the Wall simply became a step toward reunification. As a result, the distinct political systems, institutions, and cultures that characterized East Germany have nearly completely vanished. In some instances, this history was actively—and physically—eradicated by the unified Germany, for instance through the destruction of the Palace of the Republic, the seat of the *Volkskammer* (East German Parliament). In other instances, the history of the GDR has disappeared from neglect and disinterest.

The following essay works against the disappearance of East German culture by reconstructing the physicality of the walk across the border on the day of the opening of the Berlin Wall and two choreographic works depicting East German identities on stage. The initial re-creation of the choreography of a pedestrian movement provides a social, political, and methodological context for this essay, a context that relates the two dance productions to the social movement of East German citizens. Both works take stances on the political situation in East Germany during and after the opening of the Berlin Wall in 1989, although one is by a West German artist, Sasha Waltz, and the other by East German choreographer Jo Fabian. Examining the dialectic relationship between bodies' conscious movements during a historical walk across the border, on one hand, and stage choreography as interrogations of such, on the other, exposes shared choreographic and social mechanisms. Yet, most importantly, the comparison reassesses and revives East German identity twenty years after the disappearance of the country and it accomplishes this through a focus on corporeality and physical action.

The Opening of the Berlin Wall: Double Perspective on a Choreographed Response

On November 10, 1989, when we walked toward the Wall dividing East and West Berlin, we already knew how to walk for a cause, how to walk for change, after months of participating in demonstrations throughout East German cities. This walking was never a stroll, nor was it Benjamin's *flaneuring*.[1] It was also not a resolute hike toward a clearly demarcated goal. Rather, the power of the walk accrued through the impact on the space in which it occurred. This walk was a forceful attempt to gain new space. We did not know whether the border guards would put a stop to our walk once we arrived at the checkpoint.[2] This uncertainty about the outcome made us all hyperaware of our spatial choices as well as the choreography of our body postures while walking toward the Wall. This awareness differed from our daily consciousness of surveillance by the East German Intelligence Service.[3] Still, the choreographic tactics that we learned as a result of the surveillance informed our movements.

We looked at each other and realized the collective power created through our walking. Yet, we also sensed the individual choreographic choices in that pattern. As we moved up to the checkpoint, we attempted to conquer rising emotional responses to the unknown situation with more confident body language. We took more ground with our steps and lifted our knees higher. We put more weight on our feet as they hit the ground and we rolled them with more pressure over the pavement. Thus, when the gaze of the border guard who checked our documents hit us, we appeared confident and in control of the situation.

Gradually walking onto the bridge after he gave us the necessary stamps in our papers, we felt swept away by the movement around us.[4] Yet, slowed down by the masses in front, no one was able to rush to the other side of the bridge that connected us with the Western part of Berlin. Deliberately putting one foot in front of the other, I walked in astonishment over that bridge. The actual crossing was unbelievable—outside the realm of any imagined possibility. I started to see myself as though from an outside perspective. How did my body look in this space and moment? I saw myself looking at people and at the machinery that protected the border. I watched myself consciously incorporating my observations of my body's movement and the movement of the surrounding walkers into my own and I became aware of others doing the same. The conscious reflection on the double perspective of that walk on the bridge—the outside view of the body and the sensations inside the body—created the historical moment.

In this essay I employ the pedestrian movement of the walk as a lens through which to view and evaluate how two choreographers—Sasha Waltz, raised in West Germany, and Jo Fabian, raised in the East—staged East German corporeality. Even though both depict East German identity around the fall of the Wall and reunification, their distinct approaches and training produce dramatically different choreography. It is the differing location of agency in their choreography that becomes most essential for a comparison of Waltz's and Fabian's productions, particularly in relation to the historical walk across the Berlin border. This walk amalgamated the double perspective of an internalized awareness of a social referentiality of movements with the outer experience of that movement's historical significance. Jo Fabian understands that integrative double perspective, not only as necessary for the creation of a new social order but also as clearly assigning agency to the body. He is able to communicate his comprehension to the audience by translating it into a compelling choreography that explores in multidimensional tableaux how citizens adjusted their moving bodies to the collapse and subsequent re-creation of societal structures. Even though Sasha Waltz has explored corporeal agency in many of her works, she chose to not fully investigate the connection between movements and their social referent and the role that bodies play in the creation of social systems in her choreography *Allee der Kosmonauten*. In other words, Waltz does not reiterate the double perspective of the walk from East to West.

Sasha Waltz's *Allee der Kosmonauten*: Spectacular Universalization

Sasha Waltz currently inhabits the place of Germany's most sought-after theatrical export. Her invitations to perform abroad have even exceeded Pina Bausch's world-famous Wuppertaler Tanztheater. At the beginning of her career, Sasha Waltz studied dance in Karlsruhe with Waltraud Kornhaas, a pupil of Mary Wigman. Wigman's legacy of a nonnarrative approach to choreography, her abstraction of individuality, and her preference for fixing a work's final form remain influential for Waltz's choreographic style. Following her studies with Kornhaas, Waltz attended the School of New Dance Development in

Amsterdam from 1983 to 1986. The school has an international reputation for its focus on contact improvisation. The technique of contact improvisation has had a big influence on Waltz's creative process by serving as a major tool for the reevaluation of movement vocabulary both for her dancers and her works. Yet, guided by her earlier Wigman-influenced training and its orientation on set choreography, Waltz's dancers rarely improvise on stage. Rather, much of Waltz's movement vocabulary builds on contact's negotiation of weight and encounter as a choreographic component. Three years after her study in Amsterdam, Waltz visited New York for an extended period and exposed herself to yet another approach to dance that relied on collaboration with other arts, such as the fine arts and contemporary music, an approach that became another main influence for her choreographic work.

Returning to Germany, she founded Sasha Waltz & Guests in 1993.[5] Waltz's first piece with this new company, *Twenty to Eight*, the initial part of her *Travelogue* trilogy, earned her the prize for choreography at the International Choreographers Competition in Groningen. In 1996, Waltz opened the Sophiensäle, an influential performance venue in East Berlin with her original choreography *Allee der Kosmonauten*. The piece established Waltz's fame and has been toured worldwide. The following year, the company was invited to showcase *Allee der Kosmonauten* at the annual German theater festival Theatertreffen in Berlin. During the subsequent year, Waltz adapted *Allee der Kosmonauten* into a television film in collaboration with the two government-sponsored TV stations. The original choreography on which the film was based won the prestigious Adolf Grimme Award. In 2011, *Allee der Kosmonauten* was restaged at the Sophiensäle for the piece's fifteenth anniversary.

Waltz has never exclusively focused on choreographing dances, because she is also a remarkable organizer and initiator. For instance, from 1999 to 2004, she was able to broaden her interdisciplinary approach to choreography and her artistic vision of dance in relation to theater by becoming the artistic codirector of the prestigious Schaubühne am Lehniner Platz in Berlin. Together with the dramaturges Jochen Sandig and Jens Hillje, and the playwright and theater director Thomas Ostermeier, she established new leadership. At the Schaubühne she choreographed her signature works, such as *Körper*, *S*, and *noBody*. *Körper*, which opened the Schaubühne under the new leadership, became one of the most widely toured pieces by Waltz. With its focus on the social construction of embodiment through a careful investigation of choreographic possibilities of diverse bodies, it became emblematic of her choreographic approach.

Waltz frequently initiates her investigation of social relations through an exploration of physical encounters between bodies and different environments. *Körper* accomplishes this in one memorable scene in which various nearly naked bodies are crammed into a glass box. Pressed against each other and the translucent surfaces, the dancers shift against and with each other in their struggle for space. Such architectural attention toward simple movement situations defines many of Waltz's key scenes and allows her to juxtapose these scenes with more theatrical stagings of her dancers.

Since 2005, Waltz has managed the interdisciplinary center for training and production—Radialsystem V—which she founded together with Sandig. The center provides one of the stages for her company's many productions, but also serves as a platform for experimental choreographic inventions by young international choreographers. Waltz's own choreographic work has shifted into the world of opera, with her versions of Henry Purcell's *Dido and Aeneas* and Hector Berlioz's *Roméo et Juliette*. Her company performs internationally roughly one hundred times a year and is thus one of the most successful international cultural enterprises.

The title of Sasha Waltz's 1996 choreography *Allee der Kosmonauten* translates as "Avenue of the Cosmonauts," which is one of the major boulevards leading through a suburb of East Berlin that consists solely of large and identical apartment blocks. The East German government built these suburbs to provide affordable housing for its citizens in an expeditious manner. In contrast to North American suburbs—mostly private homes owned by the middle class and upper-middle class—the apartments in the East German suburbs are mostly rented by their inhabitants and do not fulfill the dream of property ownership. These suburbs thus became an icon for anonymous living in the East bloc.

After the reunification, middle-class citizens left the East German suburbs either to live in urban centers or Western-style suburbs outside the city. In the wake of that migration, only working-class families remained in the government housing. These families were hit hardest with unemployment due to the dismantling of East German industries after the reunification. Often, an entire family would become unemployed and even the younger family members who still went to school had no chance to receive a job-oriented education. In their desperation, these disillusioned young men and women sometimes turned toward right-wing, racist, and neo-Nazi organizations. All these developments furthered the reputation of East German suburbs as an undesirable area overrun by lower-class citizens who engage in violent, meaningless behavior.

For the creation of *Allee der Kosmonauten*, Waltz went to the government housing projects in East Berlin and interviewed citizens of the former German Democratic Republic. She crossed the former border from the West to the East after the Wall came down to investigate East Germans' lives in the newly unified Germany. As Waltz repeatedly reports, she went to the East Berlin projects and simply knocked on doors: "The strangers who answered were at first reluctant to talk to me, but soon the ice was broken, and once we established a trust, they began to tell me stories of their lives."[6] Raised in West Germany, Waltz seems surprised about that reluctance. This reluctance is understandable in a former dictatorship, where citizens had to evaluate every step they took and where they had a complicated relationship to any law enforcement member knocking on their doors. East German citizens learned to be cautious toward strangers.

In 1996, while Waltz was creating her piece, German media reported daily on new revelations about the depth of reach of the Stasi, the East German Intelligence Service. The majority of these reports depicted the former socialist citizens as cooperative or at least as affirmative onlookers. East Germans' paranoia and mistrust toward West Germans were furthered by these reports. Not only did the former East German citizens learn over forty years to be careful with strangers as they might be involved with the Stasi, they also might not have wanted to open up to a West German because of a legitimate fear of uninformed and generalizing judgment by one of their Western co-citizens.

Given that Waltz seemed neither fully aware of these fears nor of the reality of East German lives under a dictatorship, it is worth asking how much her representation is able to capture East German identity. Even if the piece set out only to represent a very specific family in the East German projects along the Allee der Kosmonauten, the choreography's extensive international touring inevitably establishes it as a very visible general representation of East German identity. What promises, through its title, to be the depiction of a particular social situation can certainly be read as a universalized interrogation into East German dysfunctional inner-family constellations.

Waltz's methodology for the creation of her piece recalls highly critiqued procedures of early anthropological studies that did not problematize the power structure created by the observer, on one side, and the observed or native informant, on the other. In publicity for the work, Waltz states: "For me the most important thing about the work was to paint a transparent view of the communal life of a family, without judging, sympathetic and ironic, loving and cruel."[7] With this declaration, Waltz evidences that she fully grasps neither the influence of her own subjectivity that informed the choreography of the piece nor her inherent power.

Waltz's restricted awareness of her powerful position as an artist—or at least her decision to not make her authorial position visible in *Allee der Kosmonauten*—informs her choreographic and dramaturgical choices in this piece (Figures 10.1, 10.2). In the opening scenes, a man on a sofa appears reduced to a torso that bumps and rolls around a piece of furniture. Gradually, the rest of the body becomes involved with this acrobatic exercise. As a result, various body parts begin to manipulate each other like props, with no hierarchy provided between the body parts and the sofa. Through movement quality and emphasis, the sofa becomes an equal player in the interaction between body and furniture; the sofa bounces the man back the same way that his own hand

Figure 10.1. Sasha Waltz, *Allee der Kosmonauten*. Photo: Thomas Aurin.

Figure 10.2. Sasha Waltz, *Allee der Kosmonauten*. Photo: Matthias Zölle.

is pulling him up and pushing his torso from side to side. Waltz immediately presents a spectacularized version of daily gestures—in this case the sitting and lying on a sofa. The appeal of her choreography derives from an overdrawing of those gestures and the surrealistic managing of props. It also equalizes bodies and props and, as a result, objectifies bodies.

Waltz often starts with such random collisions of a human body and a prop and then explores all possibilities catalyzed by the initial encounter. Even though she also turns to the more private issue of relations between men and women along with the sociological dimensions of these gender relations, Waltz seems more interested in the spatial and physical constellations that occur when various people inhabit confined rooms. She explores places as well as the way bodies inhabit them. She might begin her investigation with an observation of how one positions a hand while opening a door, or the angle at which someone holds a knee in order to take a step on a stair. Occasionally, an absentminded and vigorous petting of a cheek intensifies into hitting; an unexpected turn of one body toward another one makes the second body shrink back and results in an elaborate choreography of swings and vacillations. Or, in the instance of the beginning of *Allee der Kosmonauten*, Waltz looks at all possible—or even impossible—ways a body inhabits a sofa or a sofa engulfs a body. These variations extend spatially and take over progressively more body parts. Through this type of abstraction, the movements move further and further away from their original circumstances, and with it, from the social situation that caused them.

As an East German, I am thrilled to see my national history reflected in a dance production. But as an East German, I am also disappointed by the level of Waltz's engagement with complexity and her employment of familiar stereotypes. To contextualize my own reaction for a non-German readership, I would like to draw an analogy to the example of blackface minstrelsy or yellowface minstrelsy in early-twentieth-century film. Even though minstrelsy originally allowed nonwhite representation in media, a contemporary employment of the vocabulary would require an extremely careful evaluation of the suitability of the form for today's understanding of African American or Asian American identity. Likewise, Waltz's choreographic representation of an East German family and the depiction's global distribution through the piece's extensive touring has to be critically appraised. In particular, Waltz's choice to represent agency outside the dancers' bodies perpetuates the already existing stereotypes of East Germans as passive recipients of government indoctrination.

Waltz's employment and location of movement vocabulary emphasize the bodies' complete absorption into a highly acrobatic situation without illuminating the social reasons for these situations and without situating the initiation of movement within the bodies themselves. Consequently, Waltz choreographs agency outside the dancers' bodies. Whereas the walkers who crossed the border in Berlin were consciously reflecting on their movement vocabulary, spatiality, and choreographic choices, Waltz's dancers are moved by an unidentified external force. The exclusive focus on movement variations without exploration of cause, motivation, or solution provides an entertaining affirmation of the present moment, but it does so by sacrificing past embodiments and bodies' capacity to choreograph their social environment.

The final scene of *Allee der Kosmonauten* reinforces this analysis. The dancers unite again for the end of the production, where they fight viciously with each other around the sofa that is now surrounded by relatively few props. The fight is continually interrupted as the music abruptly stops and the family members fall into a sudden sleep. After a number of repetitions of this sequence, the characters simultaneously freeze several times. These unexpected moments of stillness do not provide a calming atmosphere on the stage—on the contrary, the dancers' bodies appear to surrender to exhaustion. More importantly, the tableaux depict the bodies in mid-fight or engaged in a situation that depicts boredom and unhappiness. Finally, a blackout ends the piece during one of these tableaux.

As in a cartoon, the dancers' mishandling of each other's bodies never leaves any lasting impact. As a result, Waltz's movement interrogations don't lead to any solutions or even a creation of an opportunity that would empower the involved bodies. Waltz deprives the dancers' bodies of their expressive intelligence by restricting their actions to reactions to collisions and chance encounters without much resistance; there is never an opportunity that would authorize the dancing bodies to initiate change.

Allee der Kosmonauten constructs the audience members as passive consumers of a spectacle. Neither the fragmented structure of the piece nor Waltz's choreographic choices require any involvement on the side of the audience. Rather, the spectacularized movement vocabulary and the repeated interruptions of the depicted family life at the end of the production position the audience as astonished observers. Waltz's one-dimensional imagination of East German identity and the resulting physicalization in the dancers' and spectators' bodies does not grasp the conscious choreography that East Germans were capable of creating.

Jo Fabian's *Pax Germania*: Restaged Political Movements

A comparison of Waltz's production to Jo Fabian's choreographic representation of East German identity in his work *Pax Germania* further illuminates these limitations in her work. Whereas Waltz reduces bodies to animate objects in her display of East German identity, Fabian re-creates the actual transformation process for East German citizens on the bodies of the dancers as well as through the audience members. Trained as an actor in the early eighties, Fabian is a member of the generation that no longer engaged with the socialist system in East Germany. At the end of the seventies and the beginning of the eighties, this new group of artists created a specific form of resistance to that system. Unlike their predecessors, who either supported the socialist regime with more or less critical distance or openly opposed it, these artists "ignored the DDR inside the borders of the DDR."[8] The new generation neither identified with the socialist ideal nor joined underground opposition groups. Fabian's contemporaries refused to function in the state-opposition model. They drew from a lexicon of nonsocialist ways of life in an attempt to create their own reality.

The importance of this subculture derived from artists' individual distancing from the structures of the socialist system. These artists still used state resources, but only to enable their lifestyle, one that stood in contrast to the socialist ideal. A major component of this lifestyle was the artists' unwillingness to function as a part of the socialist collective. The artists of the 1970s and 1980s developed their art by focusing foremost on individuality. Fabian joined the movement by leaving an established career in state theater and by working in the margins of government-sponsored theater from 1984 until 1989. This marginalization enabled him to produce work that departed in style, content, and focus from the official theatrical discourse in East Germany and its dominating traditions of Bertolt Brecht, socialist realism, and Heiner Müller's apocalyptic historicism.

For instance, Fabian's utilization of slow motion in many of his early pieces distanced his choreographic vocabulary from its original source in everyday movement. Observing this temporally extended variation of pedestrian movement, audience members were forced to reevaluate their knowledge of it. This reevaluation removed the dancers' bodies from any immediate reference to the world outside the theater. A North American audience might be familiar with this employment of slow motion in the work of Robert Wilson, or in the traditional Japanese forms of Noh and Butoh. Yet Fabian's use of slow motion was quite distinct in the historical context of the GDR: no other East German choreographer at that time utilized movement as consciously as Fabian to critique predominant socialist theater practices. In Fabian's work, slowly moving bodies created their own reality inside the socialist system—an approach that illustrated the disengagement of Fabian and his generation from the East German socialist system.

At the same time, Fabian destroyed, or at least questioned, the hierarchy of modes of representation in socialist theater at that time by focusing attention on the corporeality rather than the vocality of the socialist realist actor.[9] This is where Fabian refused to collaborate with socialist theater conventions. By nearly eliminating speech or disconnecting it from the actors' and dancers' bodies, Fabian refused to comply with the demanding socialist theatrical tradition. He shared this resistance to narrative with other East German directors, actors, choreographers, and dancers, who worked outside or at the margins of state- and city-sponsored theaters. This new brand of East German theater no longer attempted to reveal the driving forces underneath an ostensibly objective reality. Instead, this theater concurrently emphasized its autonomy and attempted to break down the division between theater and reality. The new generation of artists achieved this goal by emancipating theater from text as well as liberating theater from its function as a political and moral institution. Consequently, the new theater initially received a strong and negative reaction from the government. But growing attention from East German audiences and theater experts enabled its survival and even occasional endorsement by the state officials.

Even though his interests were shared by other East German directors, Fabian found his unique voice and style by focusing on the body and movement in his dance theater pieces.[10] Tableaulike pictures, perpetual repetition, slowed-down movements, and various kinds of projection led to a labeling and even dismissal of Fabian as the "East German Robert Wilson" by West German critics after 1989. However, these same critics hastily turned around to declare him the rising star of the off-theater scene after his invitation to the 1994 Theatertreffen.[11] Fifteen years later Fabian still produces work, yet his company only works on a project-basis due to the Berlin senate's repeated budget cuts of funding for artists and cultural organizations.[12]

Throughout his work, Fabian stages bodies to elucidate their intentional construction as both objects and agents in history.[13] Viewing the body as the main protagonist of historical movement, Fabian returns agency to the body and creates space for resistance. Thus, his dance theater not only explores how a citizen's body undergoes surveillance and is enforced into norms of movement and behavior by a government but also elaborates the body that performs resistance to those norms. His 1997 production, *Pax Germania*, added another element to this exploration by referring to a concrete political situation. Fabian interrogates how the transformation from the socialist Germany to the united capitalist Germany was induced by the construction and collision of collective and individual identities. Fabian's piece symbolizes the history of the forty years of the German Democratic Republic, the fall of the Wall, and the time since the reunification on October 3, 1990.

In the opening of *Pax Germania* an actor walks confidently, but very slowly, onto the stage, shouldering a red flag on a long pole. After he finds his place at the back of the stage facing out toward the audience, he adjusts himself and the flag, which slowly ripples in an artificial wind. Seven actors follow him reluctantly, one by one. They slowly stroll to the back of the stage until they align themselves next to the flag carrier. Eventually, a head's tilt, a gaze, or a twitch develops into an action. Without departing from the almost procrastinating pace of the piece, a dancer is slapped and tries to return the aggressive gesture, but he is too short to reach the offender's head. The offender carries a drum on his waist, but he never plays on it. He only raises the drumsticks high above his head with stretched-out arms and bangs the sticks against each other as if setting the rhythm for the piece. One woman wears a skirt suit reminiscent of the East German party's official dress code. Constantly smiling as if in embarrassment, she attempts to make contact with the flag carrier. Another woman sucks desperately on a cigarette and coughs out the smoke until her body is thrown into her neighbor's arms by the violent spasms. His attempts to ease her coughing with slaps on her back turn increasingly into a violent beating.

Meanwhile, a clock ticks on a projection behind the actors. The digital display counts down the minutes like a time bomb. Only slight variations of the above movements stretch out over the first forty minutes. Constant repetition of the slap, cough, drumstick-raise, smile, and beating in conjunction with the fact that none of the dancers move out of the line at the back of the stage give the appearance of stagnation and perpetual boredom. The audience counts the minutes and starts to get annoyed. Audience members comment loudly on the nonevents on stage. More and more spectators leave, bored and angry, slamming doors on their way out. With their casual behavior, the audience starts to participate in the action on stage.[14]

The interplay between the dancers' bodies on stage and the spectators' bodies reenacts forty years of East German corporeal identity. Fabian does not show a one-dimensional critique of the state-enforced official corporeal identity on stage. Rather, he displays the results of and the resistance to that state control with the dancers' actions and the audience's reactions. The dancers barely move and remain restricted to their position at the back of the stage, a vivid portrayal of East German citizens' literal and discursive immobility under the restrictive socialist regime.

Like the marchers across the border, East German citizens were always hyperaware of their movement due to the constant surveillance by the Stasi. This awareness likely resulted in a more confined movement vocabulary in public, where excessive movements would have attracted the observers' attention. It also accounts for the finely tuned awareness of the inner experience juxtaposed with the outer self-observation of the sort that I described in walking across the border between East and West Berlin. Fabian's use of this idea onstage worked symbolically, revealing with seemingly innocent movements the influence of the socialist state power on its citizens' corporeality. The piece also questions the naturalized claim of the state to hold dominating power over its citizens.

Outside the theater, these kinds of restrictions in East Germany led to individual and collective movements in the late 1980s, in a mass withdrawal of citizens leaving the country via the increasingly permeable border between Hungary and Austria. Resisters also began organizing their life outside the socialist space and demonstrating throughout the socialist country. East German citizens broke out of the dictated movement pattern and started to express their dissatisfaction through individual spontaneous actions or alternatively organized demonstrations. Similar to such off-stage breakouts, the audience members watching *Pax Germania* begin their own resistance: they either leave the general audience body by walking out of the theater and slamming doors, or they begin to get collectively organized as dissatisfied customers in the artistic market economy. Increasingly, the audience comments on the nonaction on stage and even demands an intensification of the minimalist activity.

Finally, the clock runs forward. Confused, the actors seem to break out of their routine and interact with each other and even with the audience. Still in a line at the back of the stage, a man steps forward reluctantly only to return to the lineup with the other dancers, unsure of his own boldness. Soon afterward, the smoking woman moves to the front of the stage and starts to reveal parts of her body in a stripteaselike display. The man, whose comforting touch turned into abuse in the first part of the choreography, endeavors unsuccessfully to convince her to quit her prostitution and return to the line. The woman's refusal later turns into melodramatic regret that shakes her body violently, a movement that seems reminiscent of the coughing from the piece's earlier part (Figures 10.3, 10.4).

Audience members now seems to watch with more satisfaction. They are entertained by the semblance of actions on stage. However, they soon realize that the movements' style is similar to the one performed before the clock turned zero. The action on stage seems to change because the dancers finally leave the line at the back of the stage and move into the up-to-now unexplored stage space in front of them. But still, the dancers perform and repeat abstractions of daily gestures. Fabian's choreography actively transforms the connotation of these movements in different contexts. As soon as the context changes, the meaning changes with it. A familiar movement can become strange and new through its performance at another location, in this case away from the line of dancers at the back of the stage. The staging forces the audience members to participate in this modification of meanings, and in the process of doing so they may realize their position in relation to the events on stage and to the actual historical situation in Germany. At the end of the performance, the following statement flashes at the audience: "We thank the originators of our history,

Figure 10.3. Jo Fabian, *Pax Germania*. Photo: Andreas Stirl.

Figure 10.4. Jo Fabian, *Pax Germania*. Photo: Andreas Stirl.

without whom this evening wouldn't have been necessary." Audience members leave torn between amusement and anger, embarrassment and confusion.

In *Pax Germania*, Fabian combines a collective reminiscence of East German history with more current experiences in the unified Germany. He abstracts stereotypes from both time periods into a series of movements and postures by taking them out of their everyday context. The dancers repeat these movements or stand in their established postures. Audience members are pushed past boredom; unable to watch the monotony any longer, they start to act out their anger. Then, Fabian modifies the movement, spacing, and the pace of the choreography, only to fall back into another display of a corresponding sameness. As a result, he forces the audience members to observe the movement and their own reactions more closely. Fabian employs dance theater as an analysis of societal conditioning by representing the body's agency in history. Most importantly, he illustrates the significance of the dancing body as a site of resistance by relating it back to the moving body in pedestrian practices. In other words, the audience's increasing awareness of a causal relationship between dance and the every-day highlights the physical component of any reaction to social, political, and national formations. Yet, it simultaneously demonstrates the ability of bodies and their movements to produce resistive structures.

Conclusion

Similar to Fabian's staging in *Pax Germania*, Sasha Waltz appropriates pedestrian movement to illuminate social structures in her piece *Allee der Kosmonauten*. Whereas Fabian depicts social immobility through minimal and repetitive movement, Waltz questions family dynamics through a choreographic paroxysm of daily gestures and interaction with household items. Deriving her choreography from a concrete social environment, Waltz does not clarify to whom or to what the bodies surrender their authority and agency. Consequently, social power and agency turn into free-floating concepts that are only temporarily connected to the body in Waltz's work and are not grounded in historical experience and structures. Bodies in Waltz's choreography might react to their surroundings, but they never consciously refuse to participate nor do they create their own social situation.

Fabian, by contrast, choreographs a history lesson that mobilizes the audience. Moving bodies originated the German reunification, which in turn caused very concrete bodily movement in both Germanies. All this movement serves as a model for the abstraction staged by Fabian. His choreographed performance generates a bodily reaction from the audience. This corporeal process mirrors the creation of history by moving bodies and the influence of that history on bodies. Fabian does not provide any historical facts or individual stories.

He turns general movements into a choreography that vividly embodies East German history before, during, and after reunification. The final statement in the piece—"We thank the originators of our history, without whom this evening wouldn't have been necessary"—confirms the cultural construction of history. By choreographing the individual's refusal and neglect to take agency in a historic situation, Fabian not only represents the lack of action, but also evokes the possibility for individuals to claim this agency with their bodies.

As in Fabian's choreography, East German citizens questioned the socialist state's naturalized claim on collective agency. Eventually, an assemblage of interdependent intentional acts of resistance led to the overthrow of the East German government and the subsequent fall of the Berlin Wall. The walk across the bridge that connected East and West Berlin serves as a valuable example for the conscious application of choreographic tactics to an everyday situation. Theatrical recreations and embodied reflections on such movements are part of "a struggle for control over the way that memory will function."[15] Yet, those who choreograph can materialize a major part of their decision-making processes by being aware of the inherent power of their position inside social systems as well as the agency in their movement choices. In turn, this awareness of memory, choreography, and potentiality can illuminate the role of embodiment in the creation of prospective societal structures.

Notes

1. Walter Benjamin, *Das Passagenwerk* (The Arcade Project) (Frankfurt: Suhrkamp, 1982). Benjamin's employment of *flanieren* refers to the German use of the word that connotes more than a simple strolling. It also encompasses a walking along some scenic path, in a park, or along window displays. The action is as much about enjoying the surrounding as being seen while doing so.

2. Armed border patrols guarded checkpoints along the border between West and East Berlin. After the building of the Wall in 1961, the East German government established those checkpoints to allow West Berlin citizens to come to the East and to prevent East German citizens from moving West.

3. This awareness of one's own corporeal identity was captured by Christa Wolf, one of the most famous writers in the GDR, in her novel *Was bleibt*. Christa Wolf, *What Remains and Other Stories*, trans. Heike Schwarzbauer and Rick Takvorian (Chicago: University of Chicago Press, 1993). [Editors' Note: For an account of dance in the early days of the German Democratic Republic that also cites Christa Wolf, see the essay by Marion Kant in this volume.]

4. The bridge is Oberbaumbrücke, which served during this day as one of the first hastily opened makeshift checkpoints.

5. She founded the company in collaboration with Jochen Sandig. For an overview of her impressive choreographic and managerial activities, see www.sashawaltz.de. [Editors' Note: Given her reputation, the critical literature on Waltz is surprisingly sparse. For photographic documentation of her career, see Sasha Waltz & Guests, *Cluster* (Berlin: Henschel,

2007). Also see Yvonne Hardt, *Sasha Waltz: Interviste sulla coreografia contemporena* (Torino, Italy: L'Epos, 2007) and Janine Schulze, "'Komische Geschlechterdifferenz'—Sasha Waltzs Post-Tanztheater," *Jahrbuch Tanzforschung* 9 (1998): 175–194.]

6. As described in a press release, "'I started by simply ringing doorbells,' recalls Sasha Waltz. The search for a new ideal led her into a world she never knew: life in a former East Berlin quarter in a street called 'Allee der Kosmonauten,' where apartments all had the same layout. Despite different furnishings, the focal point of each apartment was always the sofa, which stood in exactly the same part of the living room." Press Release, Advertisement. News release, The Barclay and Cheng Hall, Irvine Barclay Theatre, January 3, 2001.

7. Ibid.

8. "Sie 'ignorierten die DDR in den Schranken der DDR'" was phrased by the painter Moritz Götze, who was born in 1963. Paul Kaiser and Claudia Petzold, *Boheme und Diktatur in der DDR: Gruppen, Konflikte, Quartiere 1970–1989* (Berlin: Deutsches Historisches Museum, 1997), 68.

9. Only through a complex historical and frequent redefinition of realism were the Communist leaders of the GDR able to employ it as the main tool for the development of an East German national identity. Petra Stuber, *Spielräume und Grenzen: Studien zum DDR-Theater* (Berlin: Links, 1998). [Editors' Note: For more on East German definitions of realism, see the essay by Franz Anton Cramer in this volume.]

10. For a discussion of Fabian's work at three distinct stages of his career, see Jens Richard Giersdorf, "The Dance Theatre of Jo Fabian: *Blown Away, Pax Germania,* and *Prometheus,*" *Theatre Forum* 15 (1999): 90–96, and "'Hey, I Won't Let You Destroy My History': East German Dance Theater and the Politics of Restaging," *Maska, Performing Arts Journal* (November 2003).

11. Fabian's work was the only off-theater production invited to this important German theater festival in 1994.

12. See www.nofish-nocheese.de [Jo Fabian's official Web site], last access 06.30.2009.

13. In 2000, three years after *Pax Germania*, Fabian returned with his piece *Steinberg—Born to Be Wild*, a choreographic interrogation of the postreunification process and its implications for the citizens of the unified Germany.

14. I saw *Pax Germania* at the Theater am Halleschen Ufer, which is known for its support of independent dance productions in Berlin. I deliberately unify differing individual spectators into a general audience body in my reading of Fabian's choreography. I am able to do this because Fabian's piece forces the audience into movements and action comparable to the one that moved across the border. In both cases, the growing frustration forced the spectators or citizens into a reaction that changed the space in which it occurred. This change was possible only because the critical mass participated as a unified movement of individual bodies.

15. John Rouse, "Heiner Müller and the Politics of Memory," *Theatre Journal* 45 (1993), 65.

11. Pina Bausch, Mary Wigman, and the Aesthetic of "Being Moved"

SABINE HUSCHKA

Throughout the history of dance performance, the body has been seen as a site of experiences that are being transposed into movement. The *Ausdruckstanz* of the Weimar Republic, for example, appealed under the influence of Mary Wigman to an experiential space of physical movement and the aim of this "language of dance"[1] was to draw the audience into a communicative structure of experience. "Experience" (what Wigman termed *Erlebnis*) became the central aesthetic concept of her dance: from a position of profound skepticism with regard to language, the intention was to show the human being in his or her truest incarnation.

Dance research often draws a genealogy that connects Wigman's approach to that of Pina Bausch, the central representative of German *Tanztheater* as it emerged in the 1970s. The aesthetic appeal of *Tanztheater* stems from shared corporeal and cultural experiences (*Erfahrungen*). It evokes a hunger for lived experience, for sensuous contact with what seems to be real. It caters to the desire to witness what is essential to humanity—from an appropriate distance, and yet with the slight tremor that comes from the feeling of being privy to what really moves people, of seeing real bodies and genuine emotions. Some German authors, among them Norbert Servos, have isolated this theatrical mode of perception as the definitive characteristic of Bausch's work, claiming that it constitutes a "theatre of experience," which follows the topology of immediate and global comprehensibility.[2] Regardless of their cultural background, audience members experience here "theatre as communication of the senses" and an "authenticity of feeling" which is moving.[3] The opinions of Servos and others evince an enthusiasm for the idea of "a meeting with reality" on stage.[4] Illusions of immediacy blur the difference between displaying choreographed figures on stage and viewing them, and fail to acknowledge the models of representation and perception that govern emotional on-stage action.

By analyzing these aesthetic models, however, the differences between Wigman and Bausch become obvious. Bausch took a fundamentally different position compared to the one propagated by her predecessor: turning her attention away from absolute truth and toward the truthfulness of any given physical movement on stage, while retaining the appeal to feeling, she sought to develop emotionally determined forms of movement and to create a shared space of human experience beyond any essentialism. But what about the choreographed body in these theatrical spaces of experience? How do movements and gestures function to reveal a perspective on the human being? Which choreographic or theatrical means are used, at the discretion of the individual body, to produce an impression of unmediated immediacy? The radical difference between Wigman and Bausch can be detected in their aesthetics of representation, in the way in which they choreograph emotion.

Spaces of Emotion: Mary Wigman and Pina Bausch

To begin with, Wigman's style and that of Bausch, their respective physical constructions of emotion, and the politics of the body that they espoused are marked by distinctive social and cultural concerns: Wigman's aesthetic is also a philosophy of life and was developed in the years leading up to National Socialism, whereas that of Bausch was rooted in the revolutionary movement of 1968. Although the two are linked by a more fundamental principle of expression, a shared affective language of the body, historical contextualization of their styles brings to light differences in their respective aesthetics of movement, and in particular the distinction between Bausch's choreographic methods and Wigman's improvisation.[5] Yet this distinction still obscures the two dancers' divergent politics of the body.[6] What evidences their difference more clearly are their acts of staging and choreographing, the physical expression of emotion, and the theatrical figuration of the experience of being moved (*Ergriffen-Sein*): whereas Wigman's system of theatricality constructs an absolutist model of the passively moved subject, Bausch is engaged in a reflexive search for identity in the space of passive emotion (pathos).

The following analyses of choreography, and of the aesthetics and discourse of movement, seek to trace the theatrical concepts behind the range of emotions that motivate the physical movements. My argument thereby reveals the affective potential, the affirmative character, and also the politics of the body implicit in these theatrical concepts. Both choreographers work with the emotional space associated with physical movement and configure their own unique aesthetic of the experience of being moved. With diverging interests and from different historical situations, they aestheticize the human body gripped by and subjected to strong emotions. The tropes that constitute their respective aesthetics of movement, such as the exploratory touching of space and bodies in Bausch's work, and turning and falling in that of Wigman, seek to give rise to discrete moments of experience in order to relate these back to the body as the moving image of the emotional realm. Both choreographers aim to elaborate choreographic and theatrical moments of pathos: the point at which something befalls the body and gives rise to a particular emotion that the sentient being, in keeping with the original Greek derivation of "pathos," experiences passively and with suffering.[7]

With regard to the various choreographic possibilities for the affected and affecting body and the related structure of representation comprising movement, image, and language, the following questions arise: how are the techniques of movement and the technicality of theater used to present the body in the throes of events and emotions to which it must submit? What sort of relations of structure and energy are at work here between body, movement, and space?

Choreographic Figures of Emotion—Feeling One's Way through Space: *Café Müller* (1978)

The stage is in deep darkness. Songs of lamentation, women's arias from Purcell's *The Fairy Queen*, hover over the set. A woman enters almost imperceptibly from the side of the stage, which is crowded with small coffee house tables and wooden chairs strewn wildly about. The dancer (Pina Bausch) feels her way into the room, taking small steps, her eyes closed, her arms stretched out low in front of her. Her palms, directed toward the interior of the stage, lead the way. Gradually the contours of her figure become sharper and our attention is drawn to all the chairs that have been flung down, forlornly populating the stage, which hinder her movement; gently and carefully the dancer steps round each chair. The stage lighting becomes brighter. Turning slightly, the dancer reaches the wall with her left hand and stands still. Her eyes remain closed the whole time, her gaze thus sunk absently into a place beyond this one.

Now we witness somnambulant, almost un–self-conscious movements, which create a physical space that gestures both toward and away from itself and is extended by powerful, rapid, arc-shaped movements of the arm and upper body. Through the choreography, fields of movement unfold from the withdrawn scenery of the body, sinking back as it were into the space that she explores through touch.[8] This female figure has a light, floating air, and she is dressed in a long flowing tunic. Her characteristic touching, searching movements suggest a sense of being lost. Almost stumbling on stage as she does from the wings, this figure remains bound up in another place.

The choreographed body generates a moving image of absence, enveloped in a tenderness that is both uniquely helpless and self-absorbed (Figure 11.1): gentle, personal movements accompany the general movement forward by

Figure 11.1. Pina Bausch in *Cafe Müller*. Photo: Bettina Stöß.

touch, all carried along in a flowing motion. The stage is emotionalized by a sense of touch, which constantly reaches out of kinesthesia into the surrounding space. As more figures enter the stage, one after the other, the piece indicates a drama of hopelessness and perseverance.

Turmoil is never far below the surface, and *Café Müller* maps and frames traces of memory. The desolate setting with its abandoned tables and chairs is taken over by confused figures, who act as if completely lost and whose absentminded movements exhibit the memory of social norms, but one that has long since begun to disintegrate. The signature steps and the intensified moments of time are linked in an arc of repetition that gestures back to the memory of a past and tries in vain to bring that past into the here and now. We gain the impression that the performers act within a space that is located in an Elsewhere; their movements have an external focus that prevents their arrival at *Café Müller*. All four dancers react to one another in seemingly spontaneously arranged sequences of movement, sometimes imitatively but absently, picking up the movements of the others, at other moments, impulsively, with wild gestures, seeking to clear the way for the blind, expanding radius of movement of the others and jerkily throwing to the side all the chairs that block the way. With these continuously interrupted chains of reaction, and with scenes that repeat over and over, the piece choreographs an echo, through which actions and emotionally intense scenes of movement become traces of the memories of forgotten deeds. Their temporality pulsates and flows over the scene in waves, which swell up and ebb away.

    The choreographic design of the piece is, moreover, marked by absurd but serious patterns of reaction. Thus a scene consisting of an embrace, prematurely broken off, between a man and a woman recurs throughout the fifty-minute piece. The embrace is arranged and is built up with determination each time by a third person, another man. The loving embrace stabilizes itself for only a matter of seconds before it collapses again. The male partner in the embrace stands stoically in the middle of the stage, while the arms of the woman, who is being lifted into his arms, circle, wreathlike, around him. The man responds powerlessly to the weight of the woman and allows her to sink. She cannot hold the position by herself, and her body slides down that of the man. With ever-increasing speed the third person intervenes to rebuild the scene.[9]

    The piece, choreographed in 1978, was danced by Pina Bausch herself until her unexpected death on July 30th, 2009, and, together with *Das Frühlingsopfer* (Rite of Spring), was a regular feature on the program of the *Tanztheater* in Wuppertal. In *Café Müller* and other pieces of the 1970s and 1980s, Bausch choreographed the two physical sensations connected with movement: kinesthesia and touch. *Café Müller* realizes itself through choreographing a corporeal loop, which operates kinesthetically, and according to which, the piece seems to comment on Jean-Luc Nancy's notion that "the body is the unity of a being outside itself."[10] By unfolding a space in which it is possible to "be outside oneself," the stage displays choreographic movements as if they were perceptible to the sense of touch. Even the temporal periods during which the dancers move continually come across as spaces of memory recalled in performance. They do not refer back to psychological motivations but reach out to a loss that articulates itself in the body's field of movement: realities remembered and dreamed. Every action and image of movement is in a perpetual and broken state of hovering. Through these actions and images, other spaces of smoldering memory, which oscillate between absentmindedness and searching touch, are opened up in that darkened, long-abandoned room.

The choreography stages the reverberations of pastness. Emotions appear in the structure of repetition, are articulated as external events that affect the body, or find aesthetic form in the gesture of touching, whether this be constant touching of oneself, sliding off of another body or objects, sinking to the floor, or the impact of the body on chairs and tables. Thus Bausch's aesthetics of movement diverge from the theory of expression in dance, a theory that figuratively understands the human body as actively articulating a more fundamental movement, creating speaking gestures. By contrast, the momentum of Bausch's choreographies lies in a passive sensation always kept at a distance, an external event that has been sensed and introduced into the space of performance. Whether it is characterized by suffering, longing, or pleasure, it reveals itself as an aesthetic force, which continually leads the body and its figured movements outside itself. The personal act of searching combined with a sense of one's own history and reality marks out a double figure of movement on the stage, one which, with every position and point of contact between body and space, evokes an Elsewhere, and points to the Elsewhere that is history.

Theatricality, Method, and Materiality

The choreographic work of Pina Bausch is characterized by an aesthetic framing of the experience of being moved. Distinctive for her style is an approach to the body as a refuge of lived, passively experienced occurrences, in order to remember and reflect upon the emotional traces that these have left. Bausch sought to emphasize experiences of life, indeed of suffering, through targeted questions posed to her dancers and transferred their personal and cultural inscriptions through choreography to the stage. The publication of *Tanztheatergeschichten* (Dance Theater Stories)[11] by Raimund Hoghe, the dramaturge with whom Bausch worked for many years, together with a number of TV documentaries, such as *Was tun Pina Bausch und ihre Tänzer in Wuppertal?* (1983) by Klaus Wildenhahn,[12] provide insight into individual phases of work and rehearsal. Catalogues of questions and key words for *Walzer* (Waltzes, 1982) or *Kontakthof* (Space of Contact, 1978) also mark out initial ideas for the range of themes that the pieces would cover. For Bausch, the aim of asking questions was to elicit honest responses from the dancers, which, as reflections emanating from their own, true feelings, could be articulated as phrases of movement or as entire scenes.

This approach to the body, which implied a whole aesthetics of movement, and in particular, engaged the body as the prism of experience and memory marked by the influence of society and gender, created choreographic figures that shocked postwar Germany and the bourgeois culture of dance that was reestablished by the ballet boom. Bausch's theatrical gesture of searching by sensation staged hybrid subjects, through which ran norms of movement and smoldering, sensual desires, always bound to a certain emptiness. Although the pieces dealt with the moods of human beings, with joy and pain, suffering and pleasure, sexual desire, aggression, fear and delight, they did not formalize these states of experience in physical images or expressive codes of movement, nor were they represented as figurative gestures of speech.

Bausch's choreography presented scenes of memory, of lived experience, rooted in the individual, physical recollection of a life marked by society. Its phrases and motifs of movement, its moments of play and narrative, opened up the space of childhood for spectators and brought before them her spine-chilling fairy tales, grimly comic anecdotes, and idiotic, farcical situations. Drawing from the patchwork format of the cabaret or variety show, Bausch elaborated a poetics of choreography, which used montage and alienation to isolate the merciless and threatening aspects of social arrangements and relations between the sexes, so that the physical and emotional field of action would arise from the range of feelings associated with forms of exposure and passive suffering. Moments of affect dominated the early works, with their graphic scenes invested with melancholy but also a hint of comedy.

Pieces such as *Komm, tanz mit mir* (Come, Dance with Me, 1977), *Renate wandert aus* (Renate Emigrates, 1977), *Kontakthof* (1978), and *Keuschheitslegende* (Legend of Chastity, 1979) abduct the body from the realm of "silent" dance, bringing it into the field of oral, linguistic articulation. With speech acts, plotlines, group dances, choreographic formations, and solos at once elegiac and erotic, rapt or powerful, the stage opens into a play area for the figures who enact embodied moods. The choreographed body, in an effort to achieve a fully sensory, more truthful kind of contact, is confronted with elemental things. Thus the choreography requires that the dancer's body works its way through mounds of foliage, wading through water with damp, heavy clothing, or dancing to its limits on heavy peat.[13] The real alienates the theatrical space. The particular aesthetics of movement arises from bodies that move against the resistance of their material surroundings.

Feelings As Scenes—Gestures of Innate Knowledge

In a conversation with Christiane Cibiec, Bausch described her method of working: "I know very precisely what I am looking for; I may be unable to describe it with words, but in fact I don't want to."[14] It is an attitude to work that orients itself entirely toward feeling, a haven shielded from all theoretical or reflexive explication. Bausch always returned to and insisted upon the notion of an innate knowledge implied by her observation and choreographic formation of movement. When asked how she knew when a movement or a scene was right, she replied: " . . . when I feel happy, then I know that it's right. You feel when it's right, and you feel when it's not right. But how you get there, that's another question. That I can't say."[15] Her artistic self-understanding was given over entirely to feeling and to the sense for what is felt. "How can I put it: it's all feeling. . . . Sometimes it breaks your heart. Sometimes you know it, sometimes you find it; sometimes you have to forget everything and try to start from the beginning again. You have to be very alert, very sensitive; there is no system."[16] She placed continual emphasis on the absolute visibility of a person's feeling and state of mind, which for her could be read from the body. For " . . . we are ourselves with and through our bodies first and foremost, and every person is constantly expressing himself, just by being. It's all very plain to see."[17]

Bausch likewise never spoke about techniques. She took a (psycho)analytic view of constellations of gender, which she often presented as bordering on the pathological, and of instances, be they everyday or ritual, of the destabilization of one's emotional state, with the aim of condensing them into often excessive physical scenarios. The patterns of action and relationships, which are inscribed in and perpetually repeated through desiring, rebellious, or anxious bodies, would appear in a staged montage of dance, acting, and silence. The poetics of these performances arose, not from showy poses or clichéd scenes, but from the physical exaltation of being moved emotionally.

Das Frühlingsopfer (1975)—which, in a tradition that established itself on the Wuppertal stage, always followed *Café Müller* in performance—is an apt demonstration of this. Claudia Jeschke has drawn attention to the physical state of fear, which defines the sacrificial role and which radiates energetically from the dancer's kinesthetic space within the choreographed movements of the group that frames her. The choreographic sequence settles around the dancer and gives her the appearance of involvement in a radical and profound experience. Thus she transfers the spell of her sacrificial role to the audience.[18] Bausch's *Das Frühlingsopfer* represents, with considerable aesthetic force, an emotionally orphaned, rejected, and homeless body, a subject necessarily alien to itself and to society. In the process she poses a question central to modernity, namely the pressing and unresolved question of the status of the body in society.[19]

The gesture of abandonment, the gesture, indeed, of the physical abandonment of the dancer, disappeared in the later stages of Bausch's career. The focus on the material conditions of the theatrical space was replaced by a poetic order of composition and a language of stage images. Now, moving images of eroticized, desiring, dreaming, or erupted bodies are displayed within a vision of things and images endowed with an imagined, yielding quality. Airiness and fantasy reign over the settings, carried along by a compositional search for understanding. These artistically woven pieces unfold patterns for a theme of movement already sounded at the beginning of each. The scenes are dominated by the intuition of a distant, aesthetically charged physical potential. Image projections create the illusion of a widening stage and hand over the dancer's space of movement to the realm of the imaginary (as, for example, in *Rough Cut*, 2005). Dancing, remembering and finding oneself in the Elsewhere becomes an illusory event in order to recall the potential presence inherent in dance. In the process, the moments of expression, finely woven nets that they are, entrap highly differentiated qualities of movement. It is as if Bausch wanted to juxtapose a dream world of abandonment, infused with sexual lust, with the social situation of the technological millennium, the endless, overpowering encouragement of wants and desires, and a rampant culture of extreme experience.

Mary Wigman in Search of Transcendence

In clear historical and aesthetic distinction from Pina Bausch, Mary Wigman explored with her early choreographic work in the 1920s the possibility that movement has an emotional foundation. This suggested itself to her via a specific state in which a feeling could be recognized. A specific experience that marked the beginnings of her art abides in her memory: In the film *Mary Wigman (1886–1973): When Fire Dances between Two Poles*,[20] Wigman describes her "discovery" of *dance*, which nominally takes the form of savior: in dance Wigman is able to overcome physical and spiritual pain. Desolate and "desperate," as she puts it, she began to move—alone in the room. The forlorn feeling of loneliness yielded to an ineffable happiness, which gushed through her body. Here, Wigman recounts a memory and historicizes her self-understanding as a dancer. This self-image is evidently bound up with the emotional image of release and of being moved. Wigman later gave it form in *Das Tanzerlebnis* (The Dance Experience).[21] Other texts, including manifestos, school curricula, and pieces of prose, develop the experiential into an aesthetic model and move it into the center of her philosophical and choreographic thinking.

In the opening stages of her solo career after World War I, experience functions as a central aesthetic figure in Wigman's choreographic and pedagogic practice. It acquires an almost mythical weight of significance because it indicates an existential link with life and with liberation.[22] The dance-experience, that is, pain happily overcome in dance, reveals a further dimension of meaning, which is not produced by the emotion felt, but hints, in terms of a theory of expression, at a relationship of images, of original and derivation. The sensation of happiness indicates for Wigman "the original foundation of a still undivided feeling of life"[23]: not an emotional spectrum of experience, or feeling gradated by physical intensity, but rather "wholly fulfilled being," which Wigman conceives of as "a fully charged inner potential."²⁴ In quasi-religious language, Wigman writes: "How the dance-experience reveals itself to the individual may remain his or her secret. The dance act seeks solely to communicate a valid message. The derived image, now given form, is testimony to the original image received in experience."²⁵ For Wigman, this (dance-) experience should hold the spectator in its spell.

Wigman embarks on a choreographic search for this original image, the foundation of movement, in order to create an expressive space for emotional experience that works with phantasmatic notions of a purified body and the religious and political implications of a state of profound emotion. The decisive difference to the aesthetic of Bausch's dance theater consists arguably in the mode of representation of the experience of being moved and its cultural frame of reference. Wigman understands the external event, which impacts the body, as an act of necessary suffering and thereby emphasizes its existential nature as a symbolic act of overcoming adversity. Her early solo pieces—the cycle *Ekstatische Tänze* (Ecstatic Dances) that included *Götzendienst* (Service for False Gods), *Opfer* (Victim), *Der Derwisch* (The Dervish), and *Der Tempeltanz* (Temple Dance), and the cycle *Maskentänze* (Masked Dances) that included *Der Tod* (Death), *Die Qual* (Agony), *Der Wahn* (Delusion), and *Der Schrei* (Scream)—but also the later solo works *Hexentanz* (Witch Dance) and *Drehmonotonie* (Perpetual Spinning) seek to elevate the experience of pain to the level of the transcendental. Here, Wigman integrates ecstatic forms of movement, which are represented, indeed celebrated, as acts of fusion. The aesthetic goal is a celebration of the almost religious act of rendering the body communal.

Choreographic Figures of Emotion II— The Experience of Space: *Drehmonotonie* (1926)

Wigman's choreographic approach to the body develops a pedagogy of movement and seeks to bring about a transcendental experience, through which a charging of the choreographed body with emotion is achieved. Indeed, Wigman practiced and choreographed a religious elevation of the subject in this way: turning in ecstasy around a centered core-self, the subject radiates pure incorporeality. Various of Wigman's prose works provide an insight into this: *Drehmonotonie*, for example, which can be read as the textual, descriptive version of the choreographic piece of the same name from 1926 (Figure 11.2):

> . . . circling and turning in a spiral-sequence of rising and falling, without a beginning and without an end—a tender rocking-movement, the arms reaching out, full of pain and full of joy—rising again in self-destructive desire, swelling and shrinking, flowing back—higher and faster, and faster and faster—the

Figure 11.2. Mary Wigman in *Drehmonotonie*. Photo: Charlotte Rudolph. © VG Bild-Kunst, Bonn 2010. Mary Wigman Archiv, Akademie der Künste, Berlin.

swirling current has me in its grip, the waters are rising. The whirlpool drags me down. Higher still, faster still, hunted, whipped, hounded. . . . A jolt runs right through the body, bringing it from the wildest spin to a standstill, stretched tall, raised onto tiptoe, the arms thrown aloft, clambering for a support which is not there. A breathless pause, an eternity which in reality only lasts a few seconds. And then the sudden release, the limp body falls into the deep. Only one feeling survives: the sensation of being out of body. And one wish: not to have to stand up, ever again, to lie there like this for all eternity.[26]

Thus the sensation of bodilessness is choreographed, arising from a dramatic staging of leitmotivic movements: stepping, dashing, turning, standing still, and falling. The written version of the scene is imbued with a fascination for the bodiless state built up dramatically by the movements. In place of a transformation achieved through the figure of turning, a convention both cultural and spiritual, comes the image of being lifted out of oneself, of falling into another state. The ecstatic moment represents a conception of death, evokes a transcendental movement into another—eternal—state (Figure 11.3).

Figure 11.3. Mary Wigman in *Drehmonotonie*. Photo: Charlotte Rudolph. © VG Bild-Kunst, Bonn 2010. Mary Wigman Archiv, Akademie der Künste, Berlin.

The spectrum of feeling in the opening scene—tenderness, pain, joy—introduces a dramatic aspect with an almost fantastical charge: "faster and faster," "whipped," "hounded"—a state emerges that could not be further from the ritual of the dervish, which is also based on turning, but is calm and transformative.[27] In contrast to this meditative, monkish practice, Wigman choreographs a course of movement that is interrupted by pain. In the manner of a symbol, the gesture of pain rises out of the basic movement and sweeps aside the transformative momentum of the act of turning. In the process an image of the body gripped by emotion arises: "a jolt runs right through the body." In a deathly figure, the body reaches for a last "support which is not there" and falls to the ground.

The Gesture of Death: The Phantasm of the Subject

Wigman incorporated a number of different motifs of turning and circling into her practice and anchored them in a religious image of the body. Their tempo and dynamics varied according to their spatial direction, circling in or around a center. The moment of ecstatic experience—associated in cultural anthropology with a turning movement—creates an inspiring source from which the body fills itself with different impressions of emotional arousal, emerging finally as an expressive image of a state of being passively moved.

The ecstatic moment, which places the body in a state of heightened, religious emotion, as it were an "oceanic" feeling with no perceptible sense of physicality, is visualized in the image of an "unconscious experience of unity."[28] The choreographed body displays an image of pure movement: empty and transcended.

> TURNING
>
> She turns in the middle of the room with small, rapid steps, round and round herself. The steps become faster, she is stretched further over tiptoe, her body becomes tenser. Racing now she turns around her own center. Suddenly, a strange thing happens: she rises above the ground, stands still in the air, hovers calmly.
>
> She knows quite well that she is still turning, but she no longer feels the movement. Elevated and weightless, she hovers in great serenity.[29]

Das Drehen, part of the five-part prose work *Die Tänzerin* (The Dancer) again represents a bodiless state, identifiable through the sweeping aside of all sensation.[30] The body appears in a state that flows freely into the space around it, allowing inner and outer space to collapse into one, and appears to float. But the movement, which suggests a state of Dionysian ecstasy, a merging of spaces, dulls the body's sensations and represents an image of pure emotional dissolution. In its aesthetic form, the dance is, as Alexander Schwan has shown, "soteriologically charged" [suffused with the doctrine of salvation]. "Nothing less than the theological mystery of salvation is the goal of her dance."[31] Yet in it resides a subject which, its frame transcended, now becomes a pure image of movement.

Drehmonotonie, for Wigman, "the progenitor of all the dances which came afterwards,"[32] likewise seeks to represent a state of no sensation as pure and absolute movement: "Rooted hypnotically to the same spot and spinning a web around herself in the monotony of the turning movement, gradually losing herself in it, until the turns seemed to dislocate themselves from the body and the surrounding area began to spin. No longer moving herself, but being moved instead, herself the center, herself the resting point in the whirlpool of rotations."[33] With the practice of ritual dance as a backdrop, Wigman stylizes the act of turning into a dance cult and choreographs overwhelmingly powerful gestures of pain, of death, in order to project a longed-for salvation in images of transcendence. The figure of incorporeality, which also appears for Wigman in the jump, as an "upwards-yearning into bright lightness,"[34] bears the mark of death. Thus, Mary Wigman seeks to represent an emotional space of being moved, which receives its meaning in the soteriological image of incorporeality. The political relevance of this aesthetic ultimately becomes clear in Wigman's self-stylization and her understanding of herself as a teacher. The mystification of death emerges in the figure of the dancer as magician, and reveals here its political gesture. Obsessed with the idea of dance as a sacred religious art, Wigman stylizes herself as a "priestess of dance"[35] and draws with religious pathos an absolutist self-portrait, in which the self prevails as the absolute force. Wigman's aesthetic of representation realizes a theology of dance, whose transcendentally justified formation of the self operates with gestures of powerlessness and submission. The artist-subject becomes its absolute authority. Wigman choreographs gestures of invocation, elegiac steps and positions of the hands, which create a scene of solemn actions and images of a body being guided by a higher power. The stage is ruled by expressive gestures, ordered mass-sculptures, or geometrically arranged groups. The choreographed bodies become, in the flow of being moved, visualizations of pure movement, legible in the prevailing structure of power.

Wigman's aesthetic of dance dramatizes expressions of falling and capitulation, humility and happiness, sacrifice and holy ceremony, calls for death and signs of life. Yet all of these gain shape with reference to the "emotive formulas"[36] of power. As political gestures, a fear-inducing shudder emanates from them, if they follow Wigman's absolutist dictate that they produce "unity of expression and function, a corporeality through which the light shines, a form filled with the spirit."[37] The choreographed body acts as a religious medium and represents the image of its absolutist (dis)empowerment: the language of divine revelation speaks from it. "She [the dancer] is a vessel whose living contents repeatedly make her glow with an intense heat, until the reciprocal process of melting is complete and only the unity of the artistic event now speaks to us."[38] Dance becomes an "absolute art," for it is there that "knowledge of things stops, only experience is law; there begins dance."[39]

In Bausch's *Tanztheater*, a certain type of understanding makes itself felt, which implicitly keeps the choreographic and theatrical space open to questions about the historical horizon of experience of its choreographed bodies. Bausch worked in the knowledge that the subject is fragile and socially conditioned. Mary Wigman, however, conceives of the foundation of movement as pertaining to a theological power relationship that fosters the notion of a unified, absolute subject. Wigman's choreographic space, as aesthetic and theological space, isolates itself from forms of immanent knowledge. The dances and their aesthetics are motivated by an imaginary omnipotence, which appears in the guise of impotence. Its impetus is the experience of being moved.

Wigman's choreographic approach to this experience celebrates an image of the body in the ecstasy of power, a body that is ultimately devoid of empathy. Pina Bausch's works, by contrast, make us aware of the extent to which attention to emotionalized physical states and images of movement enables the choreographic rendering of experience and the creation of a reflective space in the inquisitive search for the subject.

Notes

1. Mary Wigman, *Die Sprache des Tanzes* (Stuttgart: Ernst Battenberg, 1986 [1963]). [Editors' Note: Within a few years, Walter Sorell provided an English translation under the title *The Language of Dance* (Middletown, Conn.: Wesleyan University Press, 1966). The translations in this present volume are new and provide an alternative to Sorell's flowery prose for the reader without a working knowledge of German.]

2. Nobert Servos, *Pina Bausch. Tanztheater* (Munich: K. Kieser, 2003), 22. Susanne Schlicher gives a much more nuanced understanding of the term "theater of experience" in relation to the works of Pina Bausch and juxtaposes a genealogy of her dance theater with Antonin Artaud's theory of theater. Susanne Schlicher, *TanzTheater. Traditionen und Freiheiten Pina Bausch, Gerhard Bohner, Reinhild Hoffmann, Hans Kresnik, Susanne Linke* (Reinbek bei Hamburg: Rowohlt Taschenbuch, 1987), 218 ff.

3. Servos emphasizes that Bausch's language of movement was "understood across all borders," *Pina Bausch Tanztheater*, 23.

4. Ibid., 24. However, this interpretation perpetuates a mythology that surrounds dance performance but fails to recognize that this mythology's central meaning and function originated in the eighteenth century, was socially and politically motivated, and was linked to contemporary debates on education. Contemporary aesthetic perspectives are thus mingled

with notions from the historical discourse on dance: in the mid-eighteenth century, under the reforming influence of the *ballet d'action*, above all of Jean-Georges Noverre, the topos of the immediate effect of authentic emotions became the core of the philosophy and conventions of dance performance. Dance also had sociopolitical significance, for it was one of the agents of the increasing self-confidence of the bourgeoisie. An analysis of the sociocultural functions of dance in the 1930s, as opposed to the 1960s and 1970s, is beyond the scope of this article; see Franz Anton Cramer's analyses of philosophical and cultural models of reflection in Franz Anton Cramer, *In aller Freiheit. Tanzkultur in Frankreich zwischen 1930 und 1950* (Berlin: Parodos, 2008). For eighteenth-century aesthetics, see Sabine Huschka, "Szenisches Wissen im *ballet en action*. Der choreographierte Körper als Ensemble," in *Wissenskultur Tanz. Historische und zeitgenössische Vermittlungsakte zwischen Praktiken und Diskursen*, ed. Sabine Huschka (Bielefeld: transcript, 2009), 35–54; Christina Thurner, *Beredte Körper—bewegte Seelen. Zum Diskurs der doppelten Bewegung in Tanztexten* (Bielefeld: transcript, 2009). [Editors' Note: See also Christina Thurner's essay in this volume.]

5. Cf. Schlicher, *TanzTheater. Traditionen und Freiheiten*, 220 f. Inge Baxmann emphasizes that dance theater forms a language of movement both critical of society and imbued with sensuality, which, in contrast to *Ausdruckstanz*, does not produce a mythologized model of the body, but sketches out a corporeality ruled by the senses (cf. Inge Baxmann, "Tanz und die Materialität des 'Körpers,'" in *Kommunikationsformen als Lebensformen*, eds. Ludwig Pfeiffer and Michael Walter (Munich, W. Fink, 1990) 149–168, here 158. For Jochen Schmidt, the difference lies in the understanding of the relationship between the individual and society: Wigman, he argues, celebrates community uncritically, whereas Bausch seeks critically to "strengthen the power of the individual in relation to society." Jochen Schmidt, *Tanztheater in Deutschland* (Berlin: Propyläen, 1992), 15. Later he notes a paradigm shift in Bausch's work, claiming that she "broke away from all her models": *Tanzgeschichte des 20. Jahrhunderts in einem Band. Mit 101 Choreographenporträts* (Berlin: Henschel, 2002), 301. In spite of the political nature of her approach to Bausch and Wigman, Sabine Sörgel identifies a return of "old, familiar conventions," at least "on the level of expression." Sabine Sörgel, "Tanz-Genealogien: Tanz(Ge)schichte(n) von Kurt Jooss zu Sasha Waltz," in *Theaterhistoriographie. Kontinuitäten und Brüche in Diskurs und Praxis*, ed. Friedemann Kreuder (Tübingen: Francke, 2007), 311–328.

6. Even in the face of the impetus that National Socialism gave to Wigman's work, research in German-speaking countries has struggled to break with the conception, formed in the 1980s, of Wigman as the pioneer of a more modern, "liberating" aesthetics of dance. See Hedwig Müller, *Die Begründung des Ausdruckstanzes durch Mary Wigman* (MA thesis, Cologne, 1986); *Mary Wigman. Leben und Werk der großen Tänzerin* (Weinheim: Quadriga, 1986). It is really American research into dance that has provided a political angle on *Ausdruckstanz*. Most balanced is Susan Manning, "Modern Dance in the Third Reich: Six Positions and a Coda," in *Choreographing History*, ed. Susan Leigh Foster (Bloomington: Indiana University Press, 1995), 165–176.

7. According to its Greek etymology, "pathos" also includes the notion of an event that impacts a being and therefore suggests "all forms of suffering as opposed to positive action," which applies to the whole spectrum of emotions and passions. Kathrin Busch and Iris Därmann, eds., *"Pathos": Konturen eines kulturwissenschaftlichen Grundbegriffs* (Bielefeld: transcript, 2007), 7–31. The authors refer to Rainer Meyer-Kalkus's "pathos" in *Historisches Wörterbuch der Philosophie* (Basel: Schwabe and Co. 1989, 193).

8. Cf. Hartmut Böhme, "Der Tastsinn im Gefüge der Sinne. Anthropologische und historische Ansichten vorsprachlicher Aisthesis," in *Anthropologie*, ed. Gunter Gebauer (Leipzig: Reclam, 1998), 214–225.

9. Ciane Fernandes has shown convincingly in her study that the repetition of key movements, phrases, and actions peels away, as it were, their semantics: "Repetition neither confirms nor denies the social constructions of time registered in the body. As discussed previously [Bausch] works consistently . . . bring emptiness instead of wholeness. The repetitions of a movement sequence cause more and more distortion, provoking multiple and unexpected interpretations and experiences." Ciane Fernandes, *Pina Bausch and the Wuppertal Dance Theater. The Aesthetics of Repetition and Transformation* (New York: Peter Lang Publishing, 2001), 92. Moreover, repetition disrupts the chains of signification in the on-stage action and adds an emptiness and sensuousness into their layers of meaning, which draws attention to the passive emotion of the scene.

10. Jean-Luc Nancy, *Corpus*, trans. Richard A. Rand (New York: Fordham University Press, 2008), 133.

11. Raimund Hoghe, *Pina Bausch. Tanztheatergeschichten* (Frankfurt: Suhrkamp, 1986).

12. *Was tun Pina Bausch und ihre Tänzer in Wuppertal?* documentation by Klaus Wildenhahn for the northern German television (NDR), 1983.

13. The set- and costume-designer Rolf Borzik was responsible for the dressing of the stage: a thick layer of peat (*Das Frühlingsopfer*, 1975), the floor filled with earth (*Ein Trauerspiel*, 1994), covered with foliage (*Blaubart—Beim Anhören einer Tonbandaufnahme von Béla Bartóks "Herzog Blaubarts Burg,"* 1977), flooded with carnations (*Nelken*, 1982), or submerged under water (*Arien*, 1979). *Rolf Borzik und das Tanztheater*, ed. Tanztheater Wuppertal (Wuppertal, 2000).

14. Bausch in conversation with Christine Cibiec in: *Frankfurter Rundschau* (October 17, 1998).

15. Pina Bausch in an interview with Norbert Servos on September 30, 1995, in Servos, *Pina Bausch. Tanztheater*, 230.

16. Ibid., 231.

17. Bausch in conversation with Christine Cibiec.

18. Nicole Haitzinger, Claudia Jeschke, Christiane Karl, "Die Tänze der Opfer. Tänzerische Aktionen, BewegungsTexte und Metatexte," in *Methoden der Tanzwissenschaft. Modellanalysen zu Pina Bauschs "Le Sacre du Printemps,"* eds. Gabriele Brandstetter and Gabriele Klein (Bielefeld: transcript, 2007), 141–157, here 155f.

19. Cf. Gerald Siegmund, "Der Körper als Fragezeichen," in *Methoden der Tanzwissenschaft*, 59–71.

20. *Mary Wigman (1886–1973): When Fire Dances between Two Poles*. A Dance Horizons Video (41 min. black/white), Pennington 1991.

21. Mary Wigman, "Das Tanzerlebnis," in *Mary Wigman—Ein Vermächtnis*, ed. Walter Sorell (Wilhelmshaven: Florian Noetzel/Heinrichshofen, 1986), 154–156. [Editors' Note: In 1975, Sorell had first edited a selection of Wigman's unpublished writings in English translation. See *The Mary Wigman Book* (Middletown, Conn.: Wesleyan University Press, 1975). The 1986 German edition included a different selection of material. As with *The Language of Dance*, the translations in this essay are new and, for the reader without a working knowledge of German, provide an alternative to Sorell's flowery language.]

22. Early research into dance was caught up in this myth for a long time. See Müller, *Die Begründung*.

23. Mary Wigman, "Zum Geleit," in *Die Musik* (XXV/4: Jan. 1933), quoted in Sorell, *Mary Wigman*, 154.

24. Wigman, "Das Tanzerlebnis," in Sorell, 155.

25. Ibid., 156.

26. Wigman, *Die Sprache des Tanzes*, 39.

27. Wigman is referring here to the dances of the dervishes, the Sufi monks who still practice today in the order of Mevlana Rumi. Their dance is based on an even turn on the spot, one arm stretched upward, one toward the ground; neither the speed nor the direction changes, nor do they fall to the floor. In the experience of turning continuously around its own axis, the body is transformed into a medium of spiritual energy.

28. Wigman, "Die Schule," in Sorell, 161.

29. Wigman, "Das Drehen," in Sorell, 280.

30. Editors' Note: Altogether the prose work narrates *Die Füße* (Feet), *Das Drehen* (Turning), *Der Sprung* (Jumping), *Der Kreis* (Circle), and *Der Raum* (Space). The essay was originally in a 1930 issue of *Tanzgemeinschaft*, the house organ for the Wigman School.

31. Alexander Schwan, "Expression, Ekstase, Spiritualität. Paul Tillichs Theologie der Kunst und Mary Wigmans Absoluter Tanz," in *tanz bewegung und spiritualität*, ed. Dagmar E. Fischer, Thomas Hecht (Frankfurt: Henschel, 2009), 214–226, here 218f.

32. Wigman, *Sprache des Tanzes*, 38.

33. Ibid., 39.

34. Wigman, "Der Sprung," in Sorell, 281.

35. Sorell, *Mary Wigman*, 186.

36. "Emotive formula" is a translation of art historian Aby Warburg's term "*Pathosformel*." Warburg coined it in order to describe "postures and gestures from the repertoire of antiquity, which later centuries used to represent specific states of action and psychological arousal." Here it is used in a more general sense. See Kurt W. Forster, "Introduction," in Warburg, *The Renewal of Pagan Antiquity* (Los Angeles: The Getty Research Institute Publications Programs, 1999), 1–75, here 15.

37. Mary Wigman, "Tanz," in *Das Mary Wigman-Werk*, ed. Rudolf Bach (Dresden: Reissner, 1933), 19.

38. Ibid.

39. Wigman, "Das Tanzerlebnis," in Sorell, 157.

12. Negotiating Choreography, Letter, and Law in William Forsythe

GERALD SIEGMUND

Writing the Human

Strange and unusual hammering and thumping sounds fill the air as one enters the performance space. What captures our attention is not what we see, but what we hear. Clang, clang clang: these insistent noises speak of a relentless activity whose nature, however, escapes us. They beckon us to come forward where we are met by a sea of identical tables neatly aligned in three rows that extend to the very back of the hall. The tabletops are covered in white sheets of paper. There were sixty of them in Zurich, Switzerland, where the performance piece premiered in October 2005 in the Schiffbauhalle, a huge hall formerly used for ship building. A year later, in Bockenheimer Depot, in an old tram depot in Frankfurt/Main, Germany, forty of them were enough to fill the room.[1] Cautiously, uncertain of what to expect, we approach. The dancers have taken up residence at the tables and are engaged in strangely contorted movements that seem to absorb them fully. One is lying on his back on the table, arms pressed tightly against his body. In his hands he clutches two carbon pencils with which he marks thick black lines on the paper by wriggling his entire body. He does not use his hands for writing, as is the norm. Here the hands are immobile, while the remaining body is set in motion by rubbing itself against the tabletop. Elsewhere, a female dancer throws a carbon pencil like a dart at her table. The pencil leaves little imprints on the paper before fracturing into little pieces from the impact. When examining the tables more closely, one notices that they are already inscribed. In thin and barely visible lines, words, phrases, and even entire sentences are written on them—in various languages, as one discovers when comparing different tables. The new carbon lines and dots are aimed at these words—a sort of attempt to pin down the words. Yet they also overwrite, miss, or circumscribe them, blurring their contours rather than making them more visible (Figures 12.1, 12.2).

The written phrases derive from the Universal Declaration of Human Rights that the United Nations proclaimed after the catastrophe of the Second World War in Geneva in 1948. They serve the choreographer William Forsythe and Kendall Thomas, Nash Professor of Law and Director of the Center for the Study of Law and Culture at Columbia University, in the truest sense of the term as a basis for *Human Writes*, whose title puns on the homonym "right" for law, and "write" for writing and inscribing. The letters of the law are meant to be written by the performers. Law breaks and mirrors itself in writing, word against flesh, in the writing with the body and its movements. Law is thus ultimately ruptured in the choreography with which it nonetheless enters a close relation.

Curious, we walk along the aisles. Small groups form around the various tables only to disperse after a while when we have become tired of watching the dancers exerting their Sisyphuslike tasks. Whatever they produce, they either seem to undo again with their very next move, or they take what looks like unnecessary detours to perform movements that could be executed in much

Figure 12.1. *Human Writes*, choreographed by William Forsythe and Kendall Thomas. Photo: Dominik Mentzos. Pictured: William Forsythe and Ander Zabala.

Figure 12.2. *Human Writes*, choreographed by William Forsythe and Kendall Thomas. Photo: Dominik Mentzos. Pictured: Jone San Martin.

more direct ways. Standing in the midst of all this activity we have lost sight and track of what other people do at their tables. The space is divided into sixty or forty individual performance spaces, small territories made unique by the tasks their resident dancers have chosen to enact. After we have walked around the tables for a while, stopping here and there to observe and watch, the dynamics of the activities change. The dancers invite the members of the audience to assist them in their activities and to help them make the writing on the tabletops more visible. By working together, the audience and dancers save the thin pencil traces of the Declaration of Human Rights from oblivion and obliteration.

A young dancer, Pipo Tafel, asks me to help him. As I write, he prevents me from writing. Equipped with a charcoal pencil, I begin to overwrite the letters on the table with thick black lines while the dancer grabs my arm and pulls it away. As I write he hits my arm heavily, performing an act of violence on my body. Considering that we are dealing with text from the Declaration of Human Rights this does not seem to be an insignificant act. To redress the balance, we exchange roles later on. At other tables, a performer is tied up in ropes, hands behind his back, holding a stick of charcoal in his mouth as if he were gagged. His head is pressed onto the table where he is trying to write with his mouth. In the context of the performance, the ropes, originally designed to create a certain functional mechanism that makes writing more difficult, take on different meanings that range from bondage to actual images of torture. Read as such the tables become labor camps where human beings are held captive. Each dancer devises his or her own games or tasks. He or she may alter rules at will.

After three or four hours the orderly field of tables has been thoroughly ploughed. Tables have shifted positions, they have been overturned and propped up against each other. The hands and faces of dancers and audience members alike are covered in soot, as if they had just emerged from a coal mine after a hard day's work. Connections between dancers and audience members on the one side and between the isolated islands on the other side have been established. By working and acting together situations have emerged that have helped shape the face of the whole performance. Against all odds, we have worked, group by group, individual by individual, on the Declaration of Human Rights. We have worked on giving it a physical reality.

The aim of *Human Writes*, as Forsythe and Thomas point out in the program leaflet, is "to help think about the role of art in establishing a 'culture of Human Rights.'"[2] What could be the role of art, or more specifically dance, in the field of politics? The social and political context in the first decade of the twenty-first century seems to call for a statement by art and the artists. As a consequence of 9/11, presumed terrorists are held captive at Guantanamo without legal protection and under constant threat of torture. Pictures of U.S. soldiers humiliating and torturing prisoners in Abu Ghraib were published all over the world to outcries of moral indignation for breach of, if nothing else, the Human Rights Convention. On the European side of the Atlantic, thousands of refugees from Africa have lost their lives in desperate attempts to cross the Mediterranean Sea looking for a better life. Yet in response to this, Europe has closed its borders. Those who make it are also held captive in camps or are sent back. The "culture of Human Rights" has by no means been established. Above all *Human Writes* excavates what human rights are based on: the individual body that is protected in its singularity by the Declaration of Human Rights.

The aim of this essay is threefold. First, it will take a closer look at the relation between bodies and the law that regulates our status as citizens and as political bodies. The piece *Human Writes* is emblematic of what choreography does with bodies that engage with the letter of the law, a missed encounter that produces dance. Second, it will take *Human Writes* as exemplary of William Forsythe's methodologies to create impossible choreographies that challenge the dancers and necessitate decisions on their part. This will, third, lead toward a definition of choreography. Choreography appears to be a machinelike structure of relational differences, an inhuman symbolic language that, together with the bodies' manifold possibilities of movement, produces a choreographic text. Choreography is confronted with and simultaneously confronts the body, thereby putting it in a state of dancing. By simultaneously including and excluding the body, choreography creates imaginary bodies, possibilities of bodies that both the dancers and the audiences can then explore.

A Redistribution of Forces and Bodies before the Law

In an essay on William Forsythe's *Human Writes*, Gabriele Brandstetter has emphasized the mediation of the body and the impossibility of simply subsuming it under the law.[3] Forsythe indeed reclaims the body before the law. Since the *Habeas Corpus* act of 1679, ownership of the body—one's own body, has formed a basic element of politics. To have a body is the precondition of personal autonomy as a citizen. To be in possession of a body that can face the law is part and parcel of being a legal person.

Giorgio Agamben has called the *Habeas Corpus* act, which in fact merely pinpointed legal practices that had been current in Britain for hundreds of years, the "birth of modern democracy." The "subject of politics" is the "corpus," the body that must present itself before the law when ordered to do so.[4] The *Habeas Corpus* act, "you will have to have a body to show,"[5] was a concession that the English parliament forced King Charles II to make. It was intended to limit his arbitrary dealings with parliamentary decisions. A subject of the British crown could no longer be imprisoned without trial and without reasons. It is crucial for Agamben's argument that the "act" refers to each body, "by whatsoever name he may be called therein [in the law court]."[6] This means that modern law does not refer to the body independent of the "qualified life of the citizen,"[7] *bios*, i.e., independent of rank, state, or name of the person. Rather it refers to "*zoë*, the bare anonymous life that is as such taken into the sovereign ban."[8] This does not merely imply the protection of individual rights when faced with sovereign willfulness, but also a transfer of the body to the law that now "will have" it. Now there exists a body "before" the law in the double meaning of the term: both before the body becomes a political body, and in spatial terms before the judge who can order it about.

If it is true that the law needs a body to be enforceable, "and if one can speak, in this sense, of 'law's desire to have a body,' democracy responds to this desire by compelling law to assume the care of this body. . . . *Corpus is a two-faced being, the bearer both of subjection to sovereign power and of individual liberties.*"[9] The implicit fiction and ideological closure lie in turning *birth* immediately into *nation*, thereby negating the fact that there are indeed bodies that are *not* recognized by the law. The same applies to the *Habeas Corpus* act, which was primarily designed to safeguard the rights of the upper class against the king. Human rights are attributed to the human (or derive from it) only insofar as the human forms the immediately vanishing (or indeed always obscured) foundation of the citizen who covers it up.[10] The wars and crises of the twentieth century have increasingly exposed the fragility of this fiction. For Agamben, the refugee is the figure that makes the fiction of identity of birth and nation crumble. In the refugee the natural life and status of the citizen appear irreconcilable: "Bringing to light the difference between birth and nation, the refugee causes the secret presupposition of the political domain—bare life—to appear for an instant in that domain."[11] In the figure of the refugee the normal functioning of the legal order is suspended. He happens to exist outside the law, even though his naked existence is the very basis of this law. He is included in his exclusion. The naked existence forms an abject and locked space, a stance within the law, a closet whose walls and borders must continually be redrawn.

The *Universal Declaration of Human Rights* to which William Forsythe and Kendall Thomas refer in *Human Writes* thus stands in a long tradition of this included exclusion. *The Universal Declaration of Human Rights* was passed by the United Nations on December 10, 1948. Although it does not possess binding legal status, it is nonetheless generally regarded as part of the law of the United Nations and as customary law among nations. The universal claims to protect naked existence are tied to the right to citizenship—putting humanitarian institutions in charge of transnational naked existence, while political existence remains detached from it within the sovereignty of the nation.

Agamben's political and legal-philosophical argument does not consider aesthetic phenomena. A transfer of his thinking about the status of the body into the realm of art is therefore not immediately possible. The present essay does not aim at equating the experiences of a refugee in a camp with that of the participants in a performance in a theatrical space. Agamben himself has hinted in his text that the impossibility to subsume the body in the *Habeas Corpus* act mirrors the importance of the body in late-seventeenth-century philosophy.[12] A transfer of his thinking about the body is therefore justified in so far as one views the described concept as a foundational framework within which we can imagine concepts of the body. The structure of included exclusion shapes both our thinking of the body and our relationship with ourselves and the institutions that we are part of. Since the sovereign that once carried the split into *homo sacer* within himself is nowadays the people and thus each and every one of us, modern democracy "shatters [sacred life] and disseminates it into every individual body."[13] These bodies in turn provide the already shaped material of dance and theater whose stakes they also are. The theater is an institution that calls up bodies. In the transfer into dance, whose instrument is the body, one term forms the decisive point of intersection between body and law: *choreography*.

Impossible Choreographies

As director of Ballet Frankfurt, William Forsythe began his work by radically questioning the language and codes of ballet in the 1980s. Since the early 1990s much of his work was concerned with devising choreographic structures that served as "channels for the desire to dance," as he once stated in an interview with Roslyn Sulcas.[14] What exactly are they channeling? How can the relation between the dancing body and choreography be theorized? As this section will argue, Forsythe sets up what can be called impossible choreographies that ask too much of the dancers. Because they contain too much information, the dancers cannot place or posit themselves within the choreographic structure in a direct way. They are, as a result, unable to fulfill the choreography by dancing it correctly or beautifully according to a traditional understanding of dance. Instead, they have to find a way to deal with the constrictions that, in turn, give them a freedom to perform and in performing, a freedom that, as in *Human Writes*, only comes into being against all odds.

One of the earliest and arguably the most complex examples of such an impossible choreography is the piece *Alie/N(a)Ction*. Premiered in 1992, it underwent a radical reworking in the following year. Like *Human Writes*, the piece took its cue from a specific political situation: that of Germany after the reunification of East and West Germany in 1990.[15] In the years that followed, the new Germany saw an outburst of violence against immigrants. In 1993 the house of a Turkish family in the city of Solingen was burned down by neo-Nazis, causing the death of five people. *Alie/N(a)Ction*, however, stages none of these events or conflicts directly. Instead, Forsythe and the company translated what it means to be "alien" or to be in a state of alienation into choreographic and therefore artistic form. The title is a thick description of all these things: "alien action," possibly the dancers moving on stage, "alien nation," as a nation that remains alien to its citizens like the "new" Germany. In the piece the fact of people being alienated from their society is transferred onto the choreographer and the dancers in relation to the choreography. William Forsythe has claimed that the choreography of *Alie/N(a)Ction* is unknown to him. Although the dancers have helped to create it, they, too, cannot claim to have originated the choreography.[16] Dana Caspersen, a dancer with the company since 1987, describes the complex working process that led to the choreography as follows:

We each started by choosing a page from the book, "Impressions of Africa" by Raymond Roussel, picking a word or phrase, freely associating away from it to some other word that struck us and then making a short gestural movement phrase based on that word. We took sheets of transparent paper and drew and cut geometric forms into and onto them. We folded back the cut out forms to create a 3D surface that could reveal surfaces underneath. Then, we placed this paper on top of the book page and photocopied it, took that photocopy, repeated the drawing and cutting and photocopying technique several times, using various surfaces. . . . In the end we had a document rich in layers and information.[17]

This document is thus the result of a long working process. It contains within itself not only material that relates to the topic of alienation but also the traces of dealing and working with strange material. Part of this document is a list of computer-generated times dispersed randomly over a page and another is a flattened version of Rudolf Laban's cube with its twenty-seven directional points spread across a sheet of paper. The document therefore contains information about spatial directions, time brackets for the duration of movements as well as words, letters, and lines that stipulate both floor patterns, spaces, and movement. The document functions as a condensed choreographic notation or score that appeals to potential bodies to be realized and danced.

As "a document rich in layers and information" it serves as the basis for a second working process directly concerned with generating movement. The procedure here is the same as in creating the document. New information is added to the already existing structure to affect the layering of the document, thereby changing its overall outlook. "First, the words that would appear through the cut out shapes on the document were translated into the 27-part movement alphabet that Bill had created. 'Alphabet' refers to a series of gestural movements based on words, for example, 'H' represents a gesture created by thinking about the word 'hat.'"[18]

Using the map, floor patterns were created based on the volumes and lines appearing in the document. The dancers imagined them to be three-dimensional again and directed their movements in space around these imagined shapes. Subsequently, the original movements were altered by feeding more information into the phrases. Caspersen explains it as follows: "I continued expanding on the movement phrases using this iterative algorithm: examining where I was, what I did, redescribing it, and folding the results back into the original material, lengthening the phrases with these inserts and repeating the process several times."[19]

In a third step the results of these operations were placed in a stage environment through which the dancers had to navigate. The environment Forsythe created added further information to the already dense and overcrowded score. On two TV monitors suspended from the ceiling facing upstage and therefore visible only to the dancers, excerpts from the movie *Alien 2* were shown. These film images were used as a further source of information with dancers narrating what they saw or picking out certain forms to set the body in motion. "A cat in the film would be represented by gestures of the letters 'C,' 'A,' and 'T,' which we would perform following the direction of movement taken by the cat."[20] Since each dancer had produced individual maps and operations, sometimes the information was impossible to carry out. Solutions had to be found that were not foreseen in the maps.

Considering this complex procedure for generating movement and organizing its spatial deployment, two points need to be emphasized. First, bodies and their movements here are always linked to, hooked up with, and engendered by specific chains of signifiers. In most cases they are literally letters that trigger movement phrases. In other cases simple lines or shapes serve as graphemes that the body follows, thereby reworking its propositions. I will refer to this procedure below. Second, the maps created provide a surplus of potential information that is impossible to realize in its totality. The bodies of the dancers are constantly confronted by an impossibility that positions them in a specific relation to the document. This positioning that creates placings and spacings on stage and relationships between the individual dancers, however, is by no means experienced as a restriction of freedom. On the contrary, the dancers gain the freedom of choice precisely because they surrender to the document and its impossibilities. The maps "de-create" the dancers in order to put them in a state of dancing that is productive.

For the piece *Decreation* (2003), which provided a series of improvisations with ropes and charcoal that would resurface in *Human Writes* two years later, the company was again working with impossibilities. Based on an opera by the Canadian writer Ann Carson, *Decreation* deals with the decline of a relationship. Access to the loved object is possible only indirectly, by proxy and meditation, an idea that provides the bases for a piece that is based on "junctures of struggle/obstruction." In another text, Dana Caspersen provides insights into the working process: "In rehearsals, we bound ourselves together with ropes and tried to move. We each created what we called a '10 point' sequence, where we tried to connect and observe ten points on our body while adhering to impossibly restrictive rules of behavior. We engaged in various impossible experiments to see how two bodies could be in complete and constant contact with one another."[21] In the text, Caspersen describes her personal struggle with particular tasks that, because of a physical handicap, she was unable to perform. However, once she realized that "struggle/obstruction" was what the piece was intended to bring to light, she surrendered. "I stopped trying to achieve things and let myself be in the state of impossibility."[22]

In *Alie/N(a)Ction* and in *Human Writes* the impossibility of the tasks leads to a choreography that cannot be realized in total. What the audience sees during a performance is always only a version of that spurious abstract totality encoded in signs, letters, and graphemes that can appear nowhere in its totality. What each dancer performs is an individual translation of choreography's potential. As in *Human Writes*, the totality of the text remains extraneous to the actual performance, however foundational it is. Therefore the choreography is owned by no one. No single dancer can realize it; it comes into being in a collaborative effort where what one dancer does escapes and surprises the others. The moving body is confronted with abstract symbols, signs, and signifiers that call on the body, but because of their abstract relational nature, cannot include the body and its physicality. Body and letter depend upon each other but exclude each other at the same time. This tension allows for choices. Dealing with the impossibility of totally realizing the universal, (choreographic) law carves out spaces for subjects on the move and moving, looking for their place in relation to the law, thereby negotiating law and body: *habeas corpus*.

Dancing with Letters

Letters or alphabets appear frequently in Forsythe's pieces. An alphabet of movements was used as early as 1985 in the piece *LDC*. The methodologies involving letters described above were further explored in the pieces *Self Meant to Govern* (1994) and, one year later, in *Eidos:Telos*. As part of the set, huge white letters lined the stage in *Kammer/Kammer* (2000), asking audiences and dancers alike to translate what they saw or heard, just as the entire piece was the translation of a live performance by a camera operating on stage into a film. Smaller letters were used in the installation piece *Heterotopia* in 2006, where a dancer rearranged them on top of a table to build nonsensical words and phrases. As a further step in this methodology, the dancers were asked to imagine what these letters would feel like in their mouths in order to then utter strange sounds creating parts of the acoustic level of the piece.

Historically the connection of body, letter, and choreography has always been a relation between the individual body and the law. The meaning of the term *choreography* as writing (Greek *graphein*) dance or round dances (Greek *choros*) is today usually given as "artistic design and arrangement of movements and steps of a ballet." Yet its earlier meaning, according to the *Oxford English Dictionary*, the "written notation of dancing,"[23] is the one that speaks more clearly. According to its older use, choreography is a means of noting, of writing dance movements. The "written notation" ties the dancing body to the signs of writing that from now on regulate its movements and tell it what it has to do to be a "good" dancer. Choreography is therefore the *law* of the moving, the dancing body.

In this meaning choreography appears for the first time in its Early Modern primal scene in Thoinot Arbeau's *Orchésographie* of 1589.[24] In Arbeau's book, its legitimation happens in a dialogue between a mathematician, a dance instructor, and a priest, Arbeau, and his pupil, the lawyer Capriol, who has returned to Lengres after an absence of several years in order to learn the art of dancing from Arbeau. Here, choreography emerges in the connection of two lawgiving institutions, the priest and the lawyer. In his study, *Exhausting Dance: Performance and the Politics of Movement*, André Lepecki therefore defines choreography "as an answer to a call from and for the law."[25] For Arbeau, the goal of choreography is to learn correct social intercourse. The body becomes entangled in a net of signifiers and thereby, as is implied in Arbeau's animal comparisons, becomes human in the first place.[26] Humanity does not even exist physically without this significant incision of the symbolic law. *Choreography is therefore the common (codified) law that produces and guarantees a civility and a socially respected body.*

The symbols that Arbeau devises for notating his dances are pictorial representations of military men in uniform performing the required steps. Thus picture and dance step are analogous to each other. The small pictures are linked to a short verbal phrase describing the movement and the musical notes to which the step is to be performed. In the strict sense of the term, Arbeau's notation, although devised by a lawyer, is not one of letters. It aims at establishing a civility, while the notation developed in the wake of Louis XIV's founding of the *Academie Royale de la danse* by Beauchamps and later Feuillet, aims at representing the idea of this civility. The notational signs of the floor patterns of circles, lines, and ticks to be traversed by the dancers can be said, as Jean-Noel Laurenti has shown, to be completely arbitrary and relational allowing for this one concept of "French" dance to be universalized around the globe.[27] Already before the development of this specific form of choreography as notation, the court ballets in France and England had developed a practice of linking the dancing body to letter and law. As Mark Franko has shown for the geometrical dances of the Baroque period, they often consisted of figures, letters, or hieroglyphs the dancers had to perform in front of the king or queen. As Franko has argued, the geometrical dances were based on an alternating principle of movement and flux on the one side and immobility and pose on the other. Thus, the readability of the letters and the order they represent is always endangered by the very process of ordering the bodies by movement in the same theatrical space in which their re-presentation takes place. Since by necessity they have to move to form letters, the control over these letters can never be complete.[28] The social order these letters embody can be described as the phantasm of a symbolic order that inscribes itself directly into the social, thereby organizing it around the pivotal point of an undivided subject, the king as representative of God. Thus the appeal of the letter at the very same moment of its inscription onto the body also allows the body to distance itself from the letter by moving away from it. Agency here means giving oneself up to a structure, delivering oneself to it in order to acquire the potential to act through contact and friction with it. Agency most emphatically does not mean abandoning this structure. Instead, there emerges a space inside any fixed choreography in which the relation toward this very choreography is negotiated physically, in dance and movement.

Viewed from this angle, William Forsythe's choreographic negotiations with the letter and the law have a very long history. They explore contemporary possibilities of distancing the body from the power of the letter. But a body that is capable of moving away from the letter is indicative of and produced by a shift in the social fabric. Forsythe's dancing letters are not organized along the dichotomy of order and chaos, of movement and pose, of reconstructing order after a period of misrule. They are articulations of the foundational impossibility to picture our democratic orders because they are no longer embodied in the shape of a king. While the power of the monarch had to be performed (as in the court ballets), contemporary democracy has to be performed even more, because of its constitutional lack of an essentialist foundation in the body of a king. It has to perform its possibilities of access and participation, of representational strategies and institutions in the same theatrical space in which they are also questioned. Therefore both *Human Writes* and *Alie/N(a)Ction* do not abandon the letter and the law. They put it to use by processing it. By working on it, they carve out spaces from which the subject can speak and act.

Toward a Concept of Choreography

Choreography, we recall, prevents Capriol's body from becoming a hybrid monstrous body, half man, half animal. Choreography, which marks exactly the borderline between nature and culture, animal and human being, civilizes. Taken seriously, this throws a different light on the function of choreography as a syntagmatic structure that the dancing body must follow. It must not be understood one-dimensionally as suppressing "the body" or the freedom of movement, but as the very act of making subjectivity possible. It creates and produces exactly because it always involves resistance and friction through the unbridgeable gap between body and law. This enables the subject to escape from its solipsism and to become a social subject by attaching itself to a network of signifiers that *relate*. As such it continues to be important for contemporary choreographers. The political dimension of movement does not emerge when choreography is suspended but when its mission is radically carried out to its logical conclusion. This happens when the body once again enters into a simultaneous *distance* and *relation* to the structure. It means neither the puppetlike dissolution of the body into the choreographic order nor its monstrous individuation outside this order.

Hence to dance means to enter into the absence between body/movement on the one hand and choreography/law on the other in order to bring the two poles into contact. The result of this confrontation is dance and a choreographic text. Choreographic text as it is understood here is a realization of choreography's potential. Thus choreography is here referred to as an abstract sign-based order and choreographic text as its being negotiated by a body. The body with its infinite possibilities of moving, which are always already the result of both cultural and dance techniques, touches the law that in the *act of connecting* also produces this very dancing body. In the absence between the body and its manifold possibilities of moving and choreography, a negotiation of the relation between body and law takes place. This happens in front of an audience that in turn adds the symbolic body of a community-to-be to the equation. Without this gap, this rift, this distance that enables "me" to imagine "myself" with a view toward the Other in order to gain an image of myself, in order to act and fail, there would be no social subject.

Human Writes is a task-based performance. As spontaneous as the movements on and around the tables appear, they still follow specific rules that are described by the production notes as: "The writing down of the declaration of 'Human Writes' follows an overarching rule: the writing must be accompanied by a simultaneous obstruction of writing. No line or letter must emerge directly. The performer is thus forced to employ indirect strategies. Each marking that contributes to the creation of a letter must result from a physical impediment, an imposition or resistance."[29]

On the one hand, this rule of indirect reference to writing tells of the "difficulties of a humanitarian 'conception' in a world of 'ungraspable inhumanity,'" as Forsythe and Thomas themselves declare. On the other hand, it consistently produces references to the law. It creates *communally* acting subjects whose actions become possible through the fact that their individuality meets common linguistic boundaries that push them back but also create them in this moment of *rejection*. The choreographic text that is thereby created in a dancerly fashion no longer necessarily exists in the shape of a detailed catalog of movements, as Arbeau or Feuillet envisaged. Yet even for a choreography that develops and adjusts itself in the moment of the performance, it is crucial that it emerges out of agreements, rules, and limitations that make a communal togetherness possible in the first place. They are ultimately agreements as to how the dancers interact among themselves and with the spectators. The arrangements are made on the basis of a quasi-legal agreement that is universally valid for the duration of the performance and into which everyone, even untrained dancers, can enter—provided they follow the rules of the game. One could therefore also describe *Human Writes* as a basic choreographic and dancerly situation that performatively enacts that which Althusser calls interpellation of the body by the law, by the language that is meant to be written with the body.

In the many small actions that take place on, under, next to, and between the tables, the law is held suspended. All attempts ultimately aim at making the Declaration of Human Rights legible, at giving it a *re-presentation*, an emphasized presence. They aim at giving its idea a *connection* with the body and thus an effect, yet without closing the gap between letter and body. This gap triggers the different options with which the individual participants or groups at the tables can relate to the text and the other human beings *facing* them. Postures are tried out, taken up, and modified. Positions are defined that prove untenable and physically unrealizable, that lead to exhaustion and to yet other strategies. These are indeed *literal* positions taken up by the body: positions infected by the letters of the law that entangle our bodies in the law, that force us to take a stand in relation to these letters by working with and against them.

Tying the body to writing also turns the more or less spontaneous movements of the participants into choreography. It emerges in the interaction with the writing and cares neither for the looks nor perfection of the people involved in it, nor for the success or failure of their strategies. The state of dancing that everyone around the tables enters is created exactly by the choreographic structuring of their bodies through specific movements relating to the letters of the law. The images that are created on top of the tables by dancing are images that carry in themselves the traces of everyone's engagement with and before the law. On the tables their actions with the carbon pens produce palimpsestic overwritings of the words of the law. Sometimes they disappear completely under the traces of completed collective action and become illegible. These effects represent gestural inscriptions into the law, traces of the bodies that stretch out toward the law, yet without becoming one with it. The choreographic writing with the moving body is always also a rewriting, a repositioning of the choreographic model, the common notations that, like the human rights, can only be imagined and effective through collective action. This sharpened profile of choreography becomes clearly visible here. Choreography produces temporary communities in the theatrical space through the structuring confrontation of body and law. At the same time, and this is its political moment, it also puts their efficiency to the test. There can be neither a total or totalitarian enactment nor representation of the law. For the performance of *Human Writes*, only phrases from the declaration were used at the tables, while the integral text of the *Declaration of Human Rights* remained outside the performance space—pinned to a wall as an abstract idea. Each table works on its own realization or version of a virtual law. An infinite number of other versions are possible. Thus the performance creates "a" reality of the law but not "its" reality. The law, in fact does not have a substantial reality because it is structured differentially. It is a structure to which all human beings are subject, but it is not an essence or entity in itself. Only because it is "not all" can it be a universal right.

Today in our postmodern cultures of the West we have been taught to be skeptical about universalizing concepts because they deny cultural, ethnic, or sexual differences. Thus both political and philosophical reasoning about the implementation of the *Declaration of Human Rights* is always caught between the Scylla of cultural relativism that would allow for violations of the law because of cultural traditions and the Charybdis of a totalizing universalism that negates cultural and religious differences. One answer to this dilemma is to think of human rights as having the *potential to be universalized*, implying a performative process of *iteration* that is not identical with the claim that human rights are (always already) universally valid for everybody.[30] To claim therefore that in *Human Writes* Forsythe and Thomas create an environment that speaks only of the failure of the *Declaration of Human Rights* under current political conditions is to ignore precisely this iterative process as the only condition under which the *Declaration of Human Rights* may be implemented. Iteration implies failure, the emergence of differences and individual solutions depending on the situation, the constant working against the odds that is a precondition for human rights to be "universalizable." At each table, Forsythe and Thomas engage us in this process of iteration. Hence writing with movement here does not mean retracing perfectly the shapes of letters or moving as letters in space. Instead it means in a much more general sense to be touched and supported by the Other. It is this Other, absent and impossible at the same time as it is effective and productive, that makes me emerge as a dancing and social body.

In Forsythe's installation pieces the productive bouncing off of the dancers' bodies against the structure becomes visible. Because of the body's precarious exposure, the relation of the dancing bodies and the tables becomes tenuous. The bodies are at risk; they constantly fail at their tasks, falling out of the structure, or hitting the tables hard. Thus the body is articulate precisely at the point of the breakdown of meaningful relations, when it ceases to become an image. Then it becomes an affected body—a body that is affected by the structure and in turn affects us emotionally because it threatens to break down the structure through movement. A dance performance like *Human Writes* stages our foundational and precarious (dis-)integration into the social fabric. As citizens we are always interpellated by the law, creating social choreographies. Choreography restages this interpellation, using the theater and the aesthetic sphere not as havens of beauty and eternal truths, but as a contested site exploring possibilities of access to that which we call our reality.

Notes

1. The first series of performances of *Human Writes* took place October 23–27, 2005, in Zurich at Schiffbauhalle. The Performance-Installation was subsequently shown at the opening for the Festspielhaus in Dresden-Hellerau from September 8–10 and 13–25, 2006. Another series was shown November 14–18, 2006, at Bockenheimer Depot in Frankfurt am Main. After that the performance went to Istanbul in Turkey, where it was shown at The International Istanbul Theatre Festival May 23 and 24, 2008. I have attended one performance in Zurich and one in Frankfurt.

2. William Forsythe and Kendall Thomas, Program Notes for the Performance-Installation *Human Writes*.

3. Gabriele Brandstetter, "Un/Sichtbarkeit: Blindheit und Schrift. Peter Turrinis 'Alpenglühen' und William Forsythes 'Human Writes,'" in *Theater und Medien/Theatre and the Media: Grundlagen—Analysen—Perspektiven. Eine Bestandaufnahme*, eds. Henri Schonemakers, Stefan Bläske, Kay Kirchmann, and Jens Ruchatz (Bielefeld: transcript, 2008), 85–98.

4. Giorgio Agamben, *Homo Sacer. Sovereign Power and Bare Life*, trans. Daniel Heller-Roazen (Stanford: Stanford University Press, 1998), 124.

5. Ibid., 124.
6. Ibid., 124.
7. Ibid., 124.
8. Ibid., 124.
9. Ibid., 124–125.
10. Ibid., 128.
11. Ibid., 130.
12. Ibid., 125.
13. Ibid., 124.

14. Roslyn Sulcas, "William Forsythe: Channels for the Desire to Dance," *Dance Magazine* 69 (Sept. 1995): 2–59.

15. For a description and analysis of other choreographic works created in response to German reunification, see the essay by Jens Richard Giersdorf in this volume.

16. Johannes Odenthal, "Im Gespräch mit William Forsythe," *Ballett International/Tanz Aktuell* 1 (Feb. 1994): 33–37.

17. Dana Caspersen, "The Company at Work. How They Train, Rehearse, and Invent. The Methodologies of William Forsythe," *Bill's Universe, Jahrbuch Ballett Tanz* (Berlin: Friedrich, 2004), 26–32, here 29.

18. Caspersen, "Company at Work," 29.

19. Ibid., 29.

20. Ibid., 30.

21. Dana Caspersen, "Der Körper denkt: Form, Sehen, Disziplin und Tanzen," in *William Forsythe—Denken in Bewegung*, ed. Gerald Siegmund (Berlin: Henschel, 2004), 107–116, here, 113 (original quote in English, yet only the German translation has been published).

22. Ibid., 113.

23. OED, second online edition 1989.

24. Thoinot Arbeau, *Orchésographie*, Réimpression précédée d'une Notice sûr les Danses du XVIe siècle par Laure Fonta, reprint of the edition Paris 1888 (Bologna: Bibliotheca Musica Bononiensis, 1981). [Editors' Note: For another perspective on the relation between Arbeau and contemporary dance, see the essay by Maaike Bleeker in this volume.]

25. André Lepecki, *Exhausting Dance. Performance and the Politics of Movement* (New York: Routledge, 2006), 25–29, here 26.

26. No one should accuse Capriol "que j'aye vn coeur de proc & une teste d'asne" (of having a cowardly pig's heart and the head of an ass). Arbeau, *Orchésographie*, 6, right page.

27. Jean-Noel Laurenti, "Feuillet's Thinking," in *Traces of the Dance*, ed. Laurence Louppe (Paris: Editions Dis Voir, 1994), 81–108.

28. Mark Franko, *Dance As Text. Ideologies of the Baroque Body* (Cambridge: Cambridge University Press, 1993), chapter 1.

29. Forsythe and Thomas, Program Notes to *Human Writes*.

30. For this debate, see Christoph Menke and Arnd Pollmann, *Philosophie der Menschenrechte zur Einführung* (Hamburg: Junius, 2007), 79–85.

13. Engagements with the Past in Contemporary Dance

YVONNE HARDT

Dance is usually considered the most ephemeral form of art in Western society. This transitory character of dance dominates both historical and contemporary discourse. Nonetheless, historical investigations trace not only the history of dance, but also demonstrate how dance embodies historic and cultural corporealities. Only in more recent years, however, has a focus on history and memory appeared in research on contemporary European concert dance. As Aleida Assmann states, "Today it is most prominently art, which discovers the crisis of memory as its topic and finds new modes in which the dynamic process of cultural memory and forgetting configures."[1] For a long time, what has been considered "avant-garde" embodied the "new" and was perceived as different from those dance forms considered traditional, historical, or marked by ethnic inheritance.[2] This essay traces how contemporary dance performances and dance historical writing have challenged these demarcations as one detects a remarkable trend toward evoking the past in contemporary dance. Numerous artists and festivals increasingly feature works that address the past, having discovered the potential for a self-reflexivity of dance in conversation with its history. From this larger group of artists, I have selected four contemporary European choreographers: Jérôme Bel, Xavier Le Roy, Eszter Salamon, and Martin Nachbar to discuss what working with the past in contemporary performance can entail.

These artists have already received considerable attention in German dance scholarship. One could even say that no other form of dance development has inspired and helped recent dance scholarship in Germany grow so intensively as has the engagement with this group of artists.[3] So far this conceptually driven dance form has been predominantly analyzed in terms of deconstruction, refiguration, critical potentiality, and discussions of presence and absence (to name just a few key words).[4] An increasing interest in historical reenactments encourages a shift in focus. In this line my essay will demonstrate how artists have discovered the past as a playground for the present and at the same time allow for conceptualizing a performative notion of "doing history."

The aforementioned choreographers expose different modes of taking up the past; however, they all engage a concept of history understood as a construction based on the needs of the present.[5] While they work with quotations, historical references, and re/construction,[6] these devices are simultaneously reflected in their citational use and re-contextualization. The past becomes a playground for the present, but a present that is highly reflective of the inescapability of the past. As such, this artistic practice can be placed within a wider academic discourse that has similarly introduced an understanding of memory and history. What I would like to suggest then is that the performances I will explore dissolve the gap between present and past and complicate the distinction between the artistic and academic fields. They make us rethink notions of quoting, re/constructing, and archiving, which I propose as central choreographic strategies to evoke historicity. While I have chosen to discuss these categories separately, focusing in the first part of the essay more explicitly on practices of quoting and in the second part on re/constructing and archiving, the overall aim is to demonstrate that these practices are intertwined with each other and all contribute to a performative understanding of history and the archive. As such, my use of the verbs "quoting," "re/constructing," and "archiving" is deliberate as I conceive of them as actions. Furthermore, by placing a detailed analysis of selected choreographies in dialogue with scholarship on cultural memory, the archive, and historiography, I argue for a performative understanding of history and aim to provoke a critical reading of the theories that encourage such a viewpoint. By investigating the wider possibilities of what a performative aesthetic of memory can mean, I would like to demonstrate how these choreographers have taken up the challenge of storing the past "*in* and *as* a critical performance."[7]

Quoting

Quoting[8] (the German verb "*zitieren*") has become an omnipresent term with regard to describing choreographic strategies of contemporary dance. However, one still needs to ask more precisely how such a linguistic term can be and is transferred onto a physical practice.[9] Conventionally, quoting refers to the literal repetition of text or visual elements that make reference to a distinct author. How, though, do dancers quote? How do they literally repeat what seems impossible to repeat? How do we distinguish between evoking a resemblance, showing a historically influenced fragment, or drawing on a certain style of dancing referencing historicity or literally quoting? These are all dimensions in which the term *quoting* has been utilized in recent German texts on contemporary dance.

Nelson Goodman has been influential in establishing a notion of quoting as a central cultural practice beyond the realm of language in anthropology and cultural studies. Saying that making is remaking, he asks how such a remaking takes place.[10] Broadening the definition of quoting from the literal repetition of the same words to realms of the symbolic and asking to what extent a gesture can be quoted, Goodman's thoughts help to delineate a more focused understanding of quoting in contemporary dance.[11] Not every reference is a quotation; simple mimetic copying needs to be distinguished from a deliberate way of taking up the world. Performing bodily images and movement sequences as a mimetic reproduction without making any apparent reference or context is not yet quoting. The performance would also need to expose the citational character through the "framing." In the dances that I consider in this essay, the framing of a scene acts as a substitute for the quotation marks that characterize verbal citations. Such a focus on framing can help to transpose the notion of quoting to movement, a challenge that Goodman left unanswered as he asked his readers to ponder it on their own.[12] It helps to conceptualize the reflective and strategic act of "taking up" of movements, while framing and displacing them.

The two examples I would like to describe offer very different possibilities of quoting and framing. One takes the body as an image, focusing on the medial aspect of storing, while the other literally frames the quotation through a story. The first example is *Giszelle* (2001) by Xavier Le Roy and Eszter Salamon, the second *Véronique Doisneau* (2005) by Jérôme Bel in cooperation with Doisneau, a Paris Opera ballet dancer. Both include quotations of the classic romantic ballet *Giselle*, yet they do not have a classical format and play with the expectations of the audience.

Xavier Le Roy, who is known for such pieces as *Product of Circumstances* (1999), is one of the central figures of conceptually driven dance in Europe. Together with Eszter Salamon he created *Giszelle* as a piece that works solely on the basis of quoting and transforming the movements of others.[13] Movement sequences from *Giselle* are only a small component within a repertoire of movement quotations. As such, this piece—out of my selection of works—is the one that works most indirectly with reflecting dance's historicity, but it allows me to investigate the relationship between movement and its medium of storage, which is crucial for working with dance history both on and off stage.

In *Giszelle*, steps from classical ballet are presented next to movement sequences from Michael Jackson's *Moonwalk*, disco dancing, and the movement of an ape. Salamon performs all of these movement sequences as a solo in jeans, a pink T-shirt, and sneakers. Over the course of the piece, Salamon breaks up the movement sequences into smaller parts. She inverts them, puts them into slow motion, or even enacts the flickering of an image as if it were put on hold when a video is stopped. The medium in which these movements were stored, the film footage that was likely the basis for such movement appropriations, is thus not only exposed, but the choreographic principles that embody medial effects become transparent. It is through this referentiality that the framing in the sense of quotation is made visible. Through these choreographic principles of inversion and changes in tempo and phrasing, the quotations not only reflect the similarities between the media of film and choreography, but the movements are re-contextualized.

The result is a very specific, eclectic movement assemblage that quickly changes the body parts, orientations, qualities, and tempo of movement. The details, which were so striking in the first appearance of the movement quote, remain vivid while the transitions between them become increasingly blurred as the piece progresses. As such, the process of choreographic work, the question of how to appropriate and make one's own material out of that of others is made visible. Meanwhile, the original quotes remain present and function as a backdrop for comparison. The audience is vividly engaged in deciphering and naming the "originals." Thus, the piece opens into a realm of imagination and associations that eventually become deconstructed, drawing attention to the context of movement as a crucial aspect of contributing meaning to motion. *Giszelle* illustrates how a shifting context alters the reading. In an act of accumulation and layering, several possible meanings of movement are made visible. The piece also reveals the importance of the audience in the process of recognizing historical references: When and how can "preexisting" movement material or that which evokes dance's historicity be recognized by the audience? *Giszelle* evidences that the past is present only through the observer's perception of it—a point that reveals the link between choreography and broader considerations of how history is performed.

Salamon's performance also illustrates the physical challenges and preciseness necessary to execute movement quotations. What is striking in her performance is the attention given to detail; how the shoulder is placed when performing an ape and how the feet are set in Michael Jackson's *Moonwalk*. Such physical preciseness is usually not the first thing we associate with conceptually driven dance, which has become known for the notion of arresting movement, movement repetition, and simplicity of movements.[14] Therefore, it is often depicted as avoiding obvious virtuosity or lacking in physical skill. But even a more sympathetic interpretation also relegates the physical work of quoting to the background. For instance, Ramsay Burt proposes a comparison to the avant-garde Duchampian *readymade* when reflecting on historical quotations. Although this interpretation underlines the importance of the act of quotation for contemporary dance, it also disregards the physical difference it takes to quote a movement. Such a comparison implicitly conceives of the medium of memory as a fixed, static object to be found.[15] Quoting with the body, however, requires a very specific bodily precision. It is the clarity and distinctness that stays vivid even as Salamon progresses into ever-quicker combinations, dissolving the quotations into a new choreographic mixture that arrests one's attention. Quoting movement is a process and not a found product; it marks the performative aspect in evoking the past of dance.

Quoting the Repertoire

My second example more explicitly links to an exploration of the dancer's own physically incorporated and experienced past. The focus does not lie on the reworking or transformation of movements but is geared toward a reflection of the power structures involved in working with the repertoire in dance. In *The Archive and the Repertoire*, Diana Taylor has suggested that repertoire challenges conventional means of storing the past. For her, the repertoire "enacts embodied memory: performances, gestures, orality, movement, dance, singing—in short, all those acts usually thought of as ephemeral, nonreproducible knowledge."[16] These physical cultures have been left out of standard historical investigation and can be understood as challenging more established notions of the archive. Interestingly enough, the term *repertoire* has a different connotation in the dance world. Here, it signifies that which has made it into the canon, that which is institutionalized and has been granted the possibility to continue living on stage or to be perpetuated in dance classes.

Not surprisingly, contemporary performances have been more interested in questioning the repertoire than enforcing it. This is evident in Jérôme Bel's *Véronique Doisneau* in which the classical repertoire is both quoted and commented upon. The strategy of quotation in this piece, however, is not only different from Salamon and Roy's *Giszelle* in regard to the physical implications and embeddedness of the dancer within the tradition she is performing, but also by the framing that is accomplished through storytelling.

The main structure of *Véronique Doisneau* consists of Doisneau recounting her story as a dancer at the Paris Opera to her audience. She informs us that she is forty-two years old and that she will soon retire from the Opera. Doisneau reveals herself to the audience in terms of choreographers that she likes, including Balanchine and Robbins; those whom she dislikes, including Bejart; and those from whom she's learned a lot, including Cunningham. While Doisneau begins the piece standing alone on the huge stage and talking into a mobile microphone attached to her body, she eventually progresses into an alternation between speaking and demonstrating, or sometimes simultaneously doing both. In this way an audience that might have been otherwise unable to recognize steps from Petipa's *La Bayadère* or Cunningham's *Points in Space* is able to obtain an impression of these dances. Doisneau tells us of her preferences for certain roles like Giselle that she was not permitted to perform because she only had the status of a "*sujet.*" "*Sujet*," she explains, means to be situated in the hierarchy of the ballet between "*étoile*," the star or prima ballerina, and the "*corps du ballet*," the mass of dancers. Her position allowed her to dance small solo parts but also confined her in many sequences to the "corps."

The performance is a ballet that informs the audience about its history and working structures. At the same time, the piece is clearly aligned with contemporary dance practice through the use of speech and the omission of the most significant dance passages that are referred to only verbally.

The most striking and emotionally evocative scene in this regard is when Doisneau performs the role of a swan in the corps in *Swan Lake*. Before demonstrating, Doisneau explains that she sometimes feels compelled to scream when she dances the famous second act. Despite its beauty, the passage is "torture" for the performer of the corps, she explains. This becomes emphatically clear for the audience in the performance that follows. While Doisneau stands mostly still, Tschaikovsky's emotionally charged music mounts to a climax. Conventionally, the attention in this scene would be directed toward the "étoile" who would be dancing center stage framed by thirty-two little swans in the corps. Doisneau's stillness, turned with her back to the audience, one leg crossed behind the other, plays with the memory of the audience, because it is very likely that they imagine how the spectacle of *Swan Lake* would usually appear. Similar to Salamon's and le Roy's *Giszelle*, the past is evoked as an imaginary, a backdrop that is not present but informs the perception of the present. Even if one has not seen *Swan Lake* in a more conventional production, the audience probably has an image of ballet, which is not characterized by the immobility that Doisneau exhibits. This scene exposes not only how much "not dancing" is part of classical dance but also the hierarchies involved in that structure, aligning mobility both literally and symbolically with those who are on the higher level of the hierarchy. In quoting and de-contextualizing repertoire, the audience is led to reflect on the traditional hierarchical nature of ballet. This is an effect that Goodman describes as the reorganization, or in this case, even as a double organization because the re-contextualized quotation reflects back onto the original, which cannot be seen with the same eyes again.

The quoting process is embedded in a double strategy in which narration is crucial both in order to establish the framing of the quoted scene and also to evoke sympathy and understanding for Doisneau. This rather classical form of story line draws the audience into gaining revelations through empathic involvement. This is crucial, for if an audience member does not identify with Doisneau, she or he might just be annoyed or could find the performance boring. Intellectual revelation is here tightly linked to the emotional, not as something that is expressed but as something produced through the dramaturgical setup that strives to make us intimately drawn to Doisneau.

The specific use of narration in *Véronique Doisneau* tackles issues of representation in theater: it questions the dichotomy between fiction and reality. The emotional strategy in narration does not only make us identify with and reflect on Doisneau, but is also embedded within fictional traditions of theater and thus evokes questions: To what extent is Doisneau's story true? Who has chosen these examples and how have they been knit together? These are questions we do not necessarily anticipate when we go to see classical theater or when listening to a lecture. As such, the project reflects on narration and the border between fiction and reality, which has been pivotal in the rethinking of memory and culture. For instance, Mieke Bal has captured the dissolving boundaries between fiction and reality as an essential project of cultural analysis.[17] In the same way, Hayden White has reshaped the understanding of historical writing and the relevance of narration for it.

In his seminal *The Content of the Form*, White exposed how narration is part of a political foundation of history that not only allows for historicity to appear, making historical writing different from chronicles or other forms of historical documentation, but that it is also the compositional device that links the single event to a structure. For White the plot is more than a means to transmit information; it has the function of presenting the notion of historicity. This narrational structure and its embedded symbolic meaning would not be possible without a subject as a point of reference, which is always grounded in a social law.[18] As White demonstrates the importance of narration for the construction of history, the artists I investigate do not only exemplify White's concepts as a performative practice but simultaneously take up the challenge to rethink narrationality on stage. This becomes even more apparent where quotational practices are used by those working with re/construction.

Re/constructing and Archiving

In contrast to the notion of quoting, re/constructing and archiving do not so readily evoke an association with contemporary dance. Until quite recently, these activities had been relegated to the realm of specialists. Their image is still haunted by a focus on historical detail, often not perceived as an aesthetic endeavor. However, re/constructing and archiving suggest an ideal realm of linking theoretical inquiry and dance practice. As such, it is no surprise that one can detect a growing interest in re/construction within the conceptually driven European dance scene. Contemporary art's integration of re/construction challenges older notions of reconstructing and archiving, which had been included in theoretical discourses since the 1980s.

Archiving is usually thought of as taking place prior to reconstructing. I have deliberately changed this order to view the process of re/constructing as one that embeds the act of archiving. Archiving is no longer seen as independent or a priori to the act of commemorating the past. Such a reading is inspired by a changing conceptualization of what both reconstruction and archive have meant in regard to historiography and dance. On the one hand, the aforementioned focus on how re/construction always includes construction has dissolved a belief in the possibility of exact restagings. On the other hand, the archive was repoliticized, most prominently by Jacques Derrida in his seminal essay "Mal d'archive" (*Archive Fever*).[19] Reminding us that "*arkhe*" originally signifies not only "beginning," but also the place where jurisdiction was produced and stored, Derrida links the archival within a political realm. Investigations that followed Derrida's exploration question the structures of ordering archives, the admittance and rejection of certain material into them and policies of access and transparency.[20] More so, the archive was discovered as a site where academia and other institutions safeguard knowledge through establishing and arresting canons.

However, the archive has become a site of movement and constant transformation of archival material. Where collections once sought to acquire completeness and stored material was static in nature, the archive is now a place for dynamic reorganizations. It becomes increasingly apparent that the lifespan of media is limited through the loss of access to analog image- and sound-storing devices as well as the deterioration of paper. In order to ensure the durability of images, words, sounds, and movements, documents are constantly transferred to new storing devices. This process means a loss of the original media and favors content over form.[21] It also allows for conceptualizing an archive that is no longer bound to place and time, but that is a dynamic process.[22] Dance necessarily provokes a reflection of the change of media as it is stored and reenacted. The body of the dancer archives and transmits as it re/constructs.

Martin Nachbar's *Urheben Aufheben*[23] (2000–2009) works along these lines of probing dimensions of re/constructing and archiving. It also helps to demonstrate that working with re/constructions provides a potential to create the new, to investigate structures, hierarchies, and choreographic principles. Analyzing this piece elucidates that even if re/construction does not allow fulfillment of the frequently fostered wish to maintain and or restage the past ("as it originally was"), it can illustrate the importance of the history of dance for today's dance practice.

Nachbar, a Berlin-based contemporary choreographer, has been working on Dore Hoyer's 1962 dance cycle *Affectos Humanos* (Human Affects) since 2000. Hoyer (1911–1967) belonged to the second generation of expressionist dancers. Hoyer's interest in the precise, formal structure of dances inspired Nachbar to work with her material, professionally filmed for public TV in 1967. This footage has secured a continual interest and several re/constructions of *Affectos Humanos*, most prominently in the version by Susanne Linke (1987).

From the onset, Nachbar was interested in the difference that surfaces when working with movements created by someone of a different tradition and gender. As he proclaimed in a lecture: "Such a type of reenactment is, according to Elisabeth Grosz, never a reproduction of the same thing, but a driving force for something new."[24] More so, he perceived himself as creating the copy of a copy working from a video. To be granted permission to use and perform the dances, however, Nachbar had to get in touch with the heirs of the rights to the dances, the German Dance Archive and Waltraud Luley, the former assistant of Hoyer who currently supervises the continuity of Hoyer's work.

This encounter led to further investigation that resulted first in a solo lecture performance by Nachbar, which continually changed as it toured internationally. This lecture performance, called *Urheben Aufheben*, included Nachbar talking about the project and his interests. It featured a video of Hoyer's dance *Hass* (Hate) as it was filmed in a studio setting and film footage of Nachbar's first encounter with Waltraud Luley as he presented to her his version of *Hass*, which he had learned from the video. Furthermore, it showed physical demonstrations of how his movements have changed through working with Luley, culminating in Nachbar dancing three of the pieces (Figure 13.1).

Like other choreographers of his generation, the question of authorship and origin led Nachbar to appropriate movements and dances of a different period. Nachbar embarked first on studying three of the dances (*Eitelkeit, Hass, Angst*—Vanity, Hatred, Fear) with Waltraud Luley. The working process between the woman in her nineties and the young choreographer, which Nachbar has made public in the lecture performance as well as in interviews and publications, shows the significance of transmission, explanation, and feedback in the appropriation of a movement material so distant from his training. Trained in release technique, he found Hoyer's tension-filled movements at odds with his body.

However, the failure to perfectly reproduce the physical challenges posed by the highly tensed, complex, and dense movements of *Affectos Humanos* is productive for a reflection on the act of re/construction. In fact, this "failure" is a source for insights for both performer and audience. The setup and the framing with the video and text allow the observer to trace the differences.

Figure 13.1. Martin Nachbar in *Urheben Aufheben* performing and explaining the use of tension down to the little finger in Dore Hoyer's *Hass*. Photo: Gerhard Ludwig.

Indeed, the detection of difference is only possible because Nachbar tries to stay as close as possible to the movements shown by Hoyer.

More so, the contemporary performance quality and structure allow *Affectos Humanos* to be accessible to a contemporary dance audience. The shift in the performative quality of the dances when performed by Nachbar dissolves prejudices that a contemporary audience might have with regard to *Ausdruckstanz*. The notion that Nachbar's performance is a re/construction disappears as one keeps watching. Increasingly, the pieces look like they are based in a type of movement research that has become characteristic of contemporary dance. *Hass* appears in Nachbar's version as a postmodern investigation of movement, especially as it is performed without the costumes and music that are so reminiscent of their historical context. This is strikingly evident in the movement sequences on the floor and in many movements that seem awkwardly out of flow and are not what dancers call "organically" connected to each other. Rather, they recall the early works of Merce Cunningham and early postmodern dance.

Thus, *Urheben Aufheben* provokes a rethinking of the demarcating lines between modern and contemporary dance that are often vehemently upheld. This difference allows the audience to engage with a relation to the present that is often subdued when presenting re/constructed dance, since it attempts to be like the "original." As controversial as Nachbar's approach might be, especially to those still engaged with their physical and artistic training rooted in *Ausdruckstanz*, he is successful not only at attracting a contemporary audience but also at keeping the relevance of Hoyer's performance alive by bringing attention to the audience's expectations about dance. Mark Franko calls such an approach a construction rather than re/construction, which "opens a dialogue between forms and periods on the basis of style, vocabulary, and theory rather than history alone."[25] Franko has convincingly argued that when the context of a piece and the audience's perception of it are ignored, re/construction becomes mere replication. It even loses the "predetermined effect" that the piece once evoked.[26] Appropriating dance in re/construction is not only about re/discovering and learning the movement, but is also about understanding in what contextual relationship the artistic endeavor was placed. Dance modernity has been crucially interested in finding new dance languages and often aimed to disturb the viewer's expectations of dance. Audience response is, as Cynthia Novack has remarked, a part of constituting "a culturally significant utterance."[27] Hoyer definitely challenged her viewers who were either struck by her physical ability and the formalistic structure of her dances or troubled by her performances, because her dances, being neither openly narrative nor emotional, did not resonate with them. The challenge she posed to the viewer in her *Affectos Humanos* is part of its representational code and needs to be evoked by the re/construction. Keeping this representational context in mind ensures that the re/construction does not become what Ramsay Burt has called an "illustrated corps."[28]

In choosing to dance pieces that seemed at odds with his own physicality and his inability and unwillingness to make it appear like any "original," Nachbar reproduces Hoyer's aesthetic endeavor that, itself, was marked by an analytical interest in movement and that challenged conventional codes of presenting dance. This provocation opens a dialog between past and present. Nachbar's acceptance of his failure, casualness, calmness, reduction of movement, and irony while performing clearly situates him in the context and artistic strategies of the previously mentioned artists who tackle representational codes of dance.

One other aspect of Nachbar's constant reworking of *Urheben Aufheben* is his reflection on narration for the act of presenting and doing history on stage. In 2007, he received public support to revisit the piece and to learn and integrate the two missing dances, *Begierde* and *Liebe* (Desire and Love). This resulted in an evening-long production that kept the title of the lecture performance but now dissolved the strict demarcations between lecture and dance, exposing how these divisions might have never been fully operative. More specifically, Nachbar uses storytelling to tackle the border between fiction and reality in order to focus the audience's attention on the performative aspect of telling (his)story. In the new version, he writes names and dates on a blackboard (Figure 13.2). More so, drawing wild charts and terms on the blackboard presents a cartographic aspect of reconstruction. As one continues to watch, the "what" of the writing (the content) becomes increasingly a backdrop for its staging, a tool for drafting choreography. Drawing lines and patterns refers to how choreography has always been a medium of storing dance that is bound to its past. The piece chronicles how the choreographic process and its graphing are intertwined. This challenges readings that see the graph as capturing what otherwise will be lost or those readings that place the act of graphing movement in contrast to its practical performance.[29] Michel de Certeau laments this loss when critiquing the notion of trajectory in *The Practice of Everyday Life*. Originally, de Certeau had used the term "trajectory" as a way of thinking about temporal movements through space. It demonstrated "the unity of a diachronic succession of points through which it passes, and not the figure that these points form on a space that is supposed to be synchronic or anachronic."[30] However, he finally concludes that even this mapping is insufficient to capture the practice of walking and the tactics bound to it, which he perceives as an act taking place in time that is based on opportunity and not on securing a fixed space, or what he calls a "proper" place from which power emanates. De Certeau laments that the "graph takes the place of an operation. . . . It is thus a mark in place of acts, a relic in place of performances: it is a remainder, the sign of their erasure."[31] This notion has been widely taken up in German dance studies. However the negative evaluation arrests the performative quality of writing that one encounters in Nachbar's piece. He encourages an understanding of reconstructing as an act where writing and notation are included in the dance performance.

A perspective that relegates the sketching, drawing, and notation as the other of dance, as a loss of the performative event of dance, neglects to see that those practices are a part of and inform how choreography is developed.

Figure 13.2. Martin Nachbar sketching his research thoughts and movements on a blackboard in *Urheben Aufheben*. Photo: Susanne Beyer.

They structure choreographic work in a reciprocal process: ideas arise when a text is written or a system is made transparent to a dancer by the choreographer through a chart. To identify the writing and the drawing as essentially different from the performance hides how much they interact and shape each other even in the process of production.

The interrelatedness of learning and creating movement is also highly pertinent to memory in dance. The more there is an interaction between all of the dimensions of dance—its teaching of technique and movement, language, charts, video—the more it secures the continuity of a certain practice, or the livelihood of a piece. What first looks like Nachbar's inability to easily and mimetically acquire the movement material is also the starting point for a deeply analytical approach to the dances in order to develop tools to make the movements accessible and danceable for someone trained in a different technique. It encouraged Nachbar to find exercises to communicate these dances to other dancers of his generation. He believes that analytical understanding is an archival tool for dance. This links to yet another string of theories of memory, mostly those engaged in cognitive sciences, which propose that things that are appropriated through different levels of learning will remain more stable in long-term memory.[32]

Working with the past in contemporary dance—as these examples demonstrate—challenges demarcations between performance and theory, between performing and doing history. Moreover they provoke us to conceive of archiving as a process and might also encourage dance historians to reflect on their own performative strategies in doing history.

Notes

1. Aleida Assmann, *Erinnerungsräume. Formen und Wandlungen des kulturellen Gedächtnisses*, 3rd ed. (Munich: Beck, 2003), 22.

2. The focus on memory appeared mostly when writing about non–Western Dance. See Theresa Jill Buckland, ed., *Dancing from Past to Present: Nation, Culture, Identities* (Madison: University of Wisconsin Press, 2006). For publications on contemporary dance, see Ramsay Burt, "Memory, Repetition and Critical Intervention: The Politics of Historical References in Recent European Dance Performances," *Performance Research* 8:2 (2003): 34–41.

3. See Gerald Siegmund, *Abwesenheit. Eine performative Ästhetik des Tanzes*, William Forsythe, Jérôme Bel, Xavier Le Roy, Meg Stuart (Bielefeld: transcript, 2006); Pirrko Husemann, *Choreographie als kritische Praxis*. Arbeitsweisen bei Xavier Le Roy und Thomas Lehmen (Bielefeld: transcript, 2009); *Susanne Foellmer: Am Rande der Körper. Inventuren des Unabgeschlossenen im zeitgenössischen Tanz* (Bielefeld: transcript, 2009); André Lepecki, *Exhausting Dance: Performance and the Politics of Movement* (New York: Routledge, 2006).

4. See Siegmund, *Abwesenheit*.

5. See Jan Assmann, *Das kulturelle Gedächtnis. Schrift, Erinnerung und politische Identität in frühen Hochkulturen* (Munich: C. H. Beck, 1992).

6. My use of the slash in re/construction is deliberate because my choreographic examples draw attention to the element of construction in their restaging of past works.

7. Mark Franko and Anette Richards, eds., "Actualizing Absence: The Past of Performance," in *Acting on the Past. Historical Performance across the Disciplines* (Hanover: Wesleyan University Press, 2000), 2.

8. Although English has two words—*quoting* and *citing*—German knows only one: *zitieren*. Etymologically this sounds closer to "cite"; however, the German *zitieren* is more restricted in its original meaning as a literal quotation. For this reason, I chose to use the word quoting here, although in English scholarship both citing and quoting have become omnipresent terms for describing the phenomenon in dance. For the understanding of the following argument it is necessary to work from the narrower notion of quoting, which is immediately evoked in the German use of the word *zitieren*. When German scholars use the word *zitieren*, they could, in a conventional understanding of quoting, only distinguish between a closer and more open meaning of quoting by speaking either of a direct or an indirect quote. However, this practice rarely happens in regard to dance.

9. An exception is Christel Weiler, "'Nijinsky'?—'Marceau'? Zitieren in Ballett und Pantomime," *Zeitschrift für Semiotik* 14:13 (1992): 225–233.

10. Nelson Goodman, *Ways of Worldmaking* (Indianapolis: Hackett Publishing Company, 1978).

11. For a detailed discussion of applying Nelson Goodman to the realm of movement quotation see Martin Stern, *Stil-Kulturen. Performative Konstellationen von Technik, Spiel und Risiko in neuen Sportpraktiken* (Bielefeld: transcript, 2010), 178, 182–189.

12. Goodman, *Ways of Worldmaking*, 56.

13. This appropriation and personal transformation process is already suggested in the title, Giszelle, with a "z" (making reference to the particular spelling of Eszter).

14. See Lepecki, *Exhausting Dance*.

15. See Burt, "Memory, Repetition, and Critical Intervention," 39.

16. Diana Taylor, *The Archive and the Repertoire. Performing Cultural Memory in the Americas* (Durham, N.C.: Duke University Press, 2003), 20.

17. Mieke Bal, ed., *The Practice of Cultural Analysis. Exposing Interdisciplinary Interpretation* (Stanford: Stanford University Press, 1999), 1.

18. Hayden White, *The Content of the Form. Narrative Discourse and Historical Representation* (Baltimore: Johns Hopkins University Press, 1990).

19. Jacques Derrida, *Archive Fever*, trans. Eric Prenowitz (Chicago: University of Chicago Press, 1995).

20. See A. Assmann, *Erinnerungsräume*, 344f.

21. Ibid., 355f.

22. See Derrida, *Archive Fever*.

23. Editors' Note: The title *Urheben Aufheben* is difficult to translate. The German "Urheben" comes from "Urheber," which means author or creator; it is not usually used as a verb. "Aufheben" means both to keep something and to abolish something. When used in a philosophical sense, "aufheben" is translated as to sublate. On *Urheben Aufheben*, see also Maaike Bleeker's essay in this volume.

24. Martin Nachbar, "ReKonstrukt," in *Moving Thoughts. Tanzen ist Denken, Dokumenta Choreologica*, eds. Janine Schulze and Susanne Traub (Berlin: Vorwerk 8, 2003), 89–95.

25. Mark Franko, "Epilogue. Repeatability, Reconstruction, and Beyond," in *Dance as Text: Ideologies of the Baroque Body* (Cambridge: Cambridge University Press, 1993), 133–153, here 135.

26. Franko, "Epilogue," 136.

27. Cynthia Novack, *Sharing the Dance: Contact Improvisation and American Culture* (Madison: University of Wisconsin Press, 1990), 223.

28. Ramsay Burt, "Reconstructing the Disturbing New Spaces of Modernity: The Ballet Skating Rink," in *Preservations Politics: Dance Revived Reconstructed Remade*, ed. Stephanie Jordan (London: Dance Books, 2000), 21–30.

29. See Gabriele Brandstetter, "Choreography as a Cenotaph. The Memory of Movement," in *ReMembering the Body. Körper-Bilder in Bewegung*, eds. Gabriele Brandstetter and Hortensia Völckers (Ostfildern-Ruit: Hatje Cantz Publishers, 2000), 102–134, here 104.

30. Michel de Certeau, *The Practice of Everyday Life*, trans. Steven Rendall (Berkeley: University of California Press, 1984), 35.

31. Ibid.

32. See Harald Welzer, *Das kommunikative Gedächtnis* (Munich: Beck, 2005).

14. Lecture Performance as Contemporary Dance

MAAIKE BLEEKER

"This must be one of these projects where science meets the arts," observes Bill Aitchison in Ivana Müller's *How Heavy Are My Thoughts* (2004).[1] This performance reports on Müller's attempts to find an answer to the question: "If my thoughts are heavier than usual, is my head heavier than usual too?" We see Müller (on video) talking to a scientist, a psychologist, a psychiatrist, and a philosopher, and we witness documentation of a series of specially designed experiments. Following Descartes, Müller sets out to doubt everything; yet instead of solid knowledge, her quest only brings more questions that lead to more doubt. She gets stuck, literally, in one of her experiments and therefore cannot be present at her own performance. On stage, the audience does not get to see her; instead, someone else—Aitchison—reports on her quest. Aitchison introduces himself by his own name and refers to Müller's absence as unforeseen. He is well aware that we were expecting to see not him but Ivana Müller (Figure 14.1). He tells us that he was asked only at a very late moment to step in. Sitting behind a desk, he sets out to explain Müller's experiments starting from the moment her question occurred. He takes us step by step through the chronology of the events leading to her current absence and illustrates his account of her research with documents found in her computer. The descriptions are functional, performed in a nonemotional matter-of-fact manner, and are accompanied by a PowerPoint presentation, as if he is lecturing.

How Heavy Are My Thoughts is an example of a genre that has come to be known as lecture performance. Prominently present in the early-twenty-first-century scene of experimental dance, this genre is not limited to dance only, nor is it exclusively German. This being so, writing an essay on lecture performance for a book titled *New German Dance Studies* may seem to be an odd choice. However, I hope to demonstrate that, understood as the "product

Figure 14.1. Ivana Müller in *How Heavy Are My Thoughts*. Photo: Nils de Coster.

of circumstances" (Xavier Le Roy), interest in lecture performances among avant-garde dancers at the beginning of the twenty-first century exemplifies the situation within which avant-garde dance finds itself at this particular time in Germany. In this context, lecture performances emerge as a genre that gives expression to an understanding of dance as a form of knowledge production—knowledge not (or not only) about dance but also dance as a specific form of knowledge that raises questions about the nature of knowledge and about practices of doing research.

The specificity of this knowledge and the place of dance knowledge within our knowledge society was also the subject of the 2006 conference *Knowledge in Motion: Perspectives of Artistic and Scientific Research in Dance*, which drew over 1,700 participants to Berlin. The conference organizers reminded us of the three legendary German dance congresses held in Magdeburg (1927), Essen (1928), and Munich (1930), a tradition that they aimed to bring to life again. These historical conferences, in addition to uniting dancers and other dance-minded individuals within a professional organization, also reflected the issues at stake at that moment in dance: the ways in which dance bears the hallmark of its era and the inconsistencies of its era, as well as the questions each respective society puts to dance. The dance conferences marked the establishment of *Ausdruckstanz* as dominating German avant-garde dance and as a specifically German contribution to modern dance. The rise of this new dance form paralleled the emergence of a more general interest in physical culture. German culture between 1910 and 1930 cultivated an attitude toward the body that, as Karl Toepfer observes, was unprecedented in its modernity, intensity, and complexity. This body culture encompassed a wide range of activities, including the performing arts, literature, the fine arts, sports, athletics, medicine, sex, sexology, fashion, advertising, labor, ergonomics, architecture, leisure activities, music, physiognomic study, and military discipline. The construction of the modern body, Toepfer suggests, involved two large categories of performance: nudity and physical movement, particularly ideas about movement introduced by the most turbulent dance culture in history.[2] This dance culture itself developed in interaction with, and brought forth, extensive theoretical reflection on the power of movement as a means to physical and psychological health. Emile Jaques-Dalcroze developed his method of teaching musical concepts through movement (now known as *eurhythmics*). Rudolf Laban saw the movement choir as a means for promoting a sense of community among members of a fragmented society and established the formal basis for *Ausdruckstanz* with his concept of "free dance."[3]

At the time of the early-twentieth-century dance conferences, "the focus was on dance as a means of liberation from straight-laced conventions, of comprehending a chaotic world through a new, danced order and asserting the autonomy of dance as an art form."[4] In 2006, the focus had shifted to knowledge production in and about dance. This idea of dance as a form of knowledge and as a practice of doing research is, of course, not new. Many contributors to the conference noted the many precedents for contemporary questions and practices: attempts by the historical avant-garde to uncover the body as a source of knowledge, (among others, Rudolf Laban, Mary Wigman, Gret Palucca, Matthias Alexander, and Moshe Feldenkrais); the work of Mabel Todd on the thinking body; and conceptualizations of artistic creation as a kind of research practice (among others, Brecht, Cage, Cunningham, Conceptual Art, Minimalism, the Surrealist's Bureau de Recherche, Peter Brook's Centre International de Recherche Théâtrale, James Lee Byars's World Question Center). There also exists a long tradition of lively artistic research by artists who have not necessarily conceived their work in these terms, as Marijke Hoogenboom observes in her contribution to the proceedings. As Sarat Maharaj remarked, "Many of us must feel we have been doing 'artistic research' for years without quite calling it that."[5] These practices have gained a new urgency in the context of transformations in the scientific understanding of what knowledge is and how understanding is achieved. In this context, Alva Noë demonstrates in his contribution to *Knowledge in Motion* that a practical technology for modeling dance may make a theoretical contribution to our understanding of perceptual consciousness.[6] More than that, Gabriele Brandstetter suggests, dance may shift the boundaries of what we consider to be knowledge, theory, and research. "For, however important it may be that dance achieves a wide basis in educational and formative institutions, not only as an appendage to sports but rather as 'theory' of dance and choreographic art forms of movement, it is even more important to make the potential of dance stand out as a challenge to our established concepts of knowledge and science."[7] This situation invites a reconsideration, not only of what dance is and what it can do, but also of the position of dance within the interdisciplinary field of artistic and other practices of knowledge production. Lecture performances are both an expression—and expressive—of such reconsiderations taking place from within avant-garde dance and in dialogue with the interdisciplinary field.

A self-reflexive attitude with respect to one's own doing and the conditions of production and reception is a prominent characteristic of many lecture performances. In many cases, as Husemann observes, this self-reflexivity is motivated by a critique of commercially oriented production and presentation forms. This critique inspires a search for other modes of working and presenting, often aiming to use these alternative modes as a critical practice. With their work, artists aim to question or resist taken-for-granted practices, expectations, opinions, and institutions "in order to bring to light the potential of one's own field of work and influence, a potential yet unknown or forgotten."[8] Often, this also involves resistance to the understanding of the artist as a genius whose creations are disconnected from "work" in the more profane sense of "labor" and a revaluation of the work undertaken in the process of creation, a process that is shared with an audience and in which the audience participates. "Past moments and states of work as well as their professional and private circumstances become part of the present performance by means of evidence like image and sound documents."[9] Together with the artist, the audience traces circumstances, implications, ideas, and is invited to adopt a self-reflexive attitude as well. "Just as the directors and choreographers question their own doings, the audience questions its own perception. In an ideal case, this results in a shared meta-reflection on the common thought movements evoked by the events on stage. This two-sided self-reflexivity locks production and reception together as accomplices into one relationship, in that both sides take part simultaneously and sometimes of equal measure in the production of sense and knowledge."[10]

In *Urheben Aufheben*[11] (2008), for example, Martin Nachbar takes the audience along in a series of reflections on his own attempts at restaging Dore Hoyer's cycle *Affectos Humanos* (Human Affects). Hoyer is a representative of what might be called the second generation of German expressionist dance.

She studied at Dalcroze's school at Hellerau and later with Gret Palucca, worked with Mary Wigman, and created and performed a great number of solo performances from 1930 until her death in 1967. Since 2000, Nachbar has been working on a redoing of a cycle of these solos (Figure 14.2). In 2008, he created the lecture performance *Urheben Aufheben*, in which he traces the circumstances of his attempts at redoing Hoyer's work in front of an audience. This has resulted in a highly self-reflexive working through of his own ideas as they inspired and emerged from these attempts at redoing Hoyer's dances, and the conclusions that may be drawn from his experiences in so doing.

The circumstances of which lecture performances may be considered the product are also quite literally the subject of Xavier Le Roy's *Product of Cir-*

Figure 14.2. Martin Nachbar in *Urheben Aufheben*.
Photo: Renata Chueire.

cumstances, the performance that marks the beginning of the "boom of lecture performances" observed by Husemann.[12] In *Product of Circumstances*, Le Roy reflects on the circumstances that brought him to dance and were formative for how his dance practice took shape. Originally trained as a molecular biologist, Le Roy became dissatisfied with science and more and more attracted by dance. First he tried to connect to the then very much Cunningham-inspired dance scene in France, which was not entirely satisfactory for him. After his move to Berlin, he set out on a journey of explorations, investigating basic definitions of dance as well as the circumstances of dance's creation and reception. *Product of Circumstances* reflects on this journey and the ways in which both dance and his own involvement in it can be considered products of circumstances. It does so in the format of a lecture staged as a performance.

Product of Circumstances also illustrates what might be the "Germanness" of dance in Germany in the early twenty-first century. Lecture performances as they emerge from within the avant-garde dance scene in Germany at the beginning of the twenty-first century are exemplary of a situation in which German dance has become a highly international undertaking and in which the "Germanness" of dance in Germany is not a matter of the nationality of the artists involved (that is, holding German citizenship), nor necessarily of the place where a particular work was first performed, but rather of Germany being the geographical location of the circumstances of which (to echo Le Roy again) something that might be considered German dance is the product.[13] In the early twenty-first century, Germany is a location where performances created elsewhere pass through or are being coproduced with international partners, where festivals draw international audiences, education draws international students as well as teachers, and dance conferences and symposia bring together international experts with international audiences. *How Heavy Are My Thoughts* is a typical example of such internationalism. Ivana Müller, notwithstanding her German-sounding name, is a Croatian artist living and working in Paris and Amsterdam. The show was coproduced by Mousonturm in Frankfurt and Gasthuis Theater in Amsterdam, created partly in Germany and partly in the Netherlands, and in collaboration with artists and academics from Germany, the Netherlands, Great Britain, France, and Slovenia. The show has toured and, at the time of writing, is still touring internationally. In the case of *Product of Circumstances*, Berlin as the place for international collaboration and experimental dance production is explicitly and intensely part of the circumstances of which the French Xavier Le Roy's radical reconsideration of dance is the product.

Finally, both *Product of Circumstances* and *How Heavy Are My Thoughts* may be called exemplary of the situation within which avant-garde dance finds itself at the beginning of the twenty-first century for yet another reason, namely for how these performances confront their audiences with a prominent absence of dance understood as continuous movements of a body on stage. Lecture performances may be considered artistic projects that, following André Lepecki, exhaust what is often considered to be the ontological ground of dance, namely movement. The assumption that dance's essence and nature is to be found in movement, Lepecki observes, is actually a fairly recent invention. It was only in the 1930s, with the emergence of Modern dance, that the strict ontological identification between uninterrupted movement and dance's being is articulated as an inescapable demand for any choreographic project. Lepecki refers to John Martin's remark that the beginning of dance's true ontology was "the discovery of the actual substance of dance, which is to be found to be movement."[14] The movement of the body is the medium of dance and the great achievement of modern dance is the way in which it abstracts its material to this essence. Martin, although acknowledging the importance of German artists like Wigman and Laban in the development of this new dance form, nevertheless proposes to understand this abstraction as "eminently in accord with the simplicity of the characteristic American background, the great puritan tradition with its functional philosophy, its devotion to essentials and its abhorrence of waste and indulgence."[15] I will come back to this presumed American character later.

This ontological bind between dance and movement, Lepecki observes, might in fact itself be considered the product of the circumstances of the development of dance as an autonomous art form in the West, a development that emerges from the formation of choreography as a peculiar invention of early modernity: "as a technology that creates a body disciplined to move according to the commands of writing."[16] Lepecki traces this formation to one of the most famous dance manuals of that period: *Orchesographie* by Thoinot Arbeau. "Compressed into one word, morphed into one another, dance and writing produced qualitatively unsuspected and charged relationalities between the subject who moves and the subject who writes. With Arbeau, these two subjects became one and the same. And through this not too obvious assimilation, the modern body revealed itself fully as a linguistic entity."[17]

The body becoming a linguistic entity coincides with the unfolding and consolidation of the project of modernity. In this process, dance increasingly turns toward movement to look for its essence during a historical period in which modernity unfolds, in the words of Peter Sloterdijk (quoted in Lepecki), as "a being-toward-movement."[18] Against this historical development, Lepecki argues, we have to understand late-twentieth-century and early-twenty-first-century dance makers' "betrayal of dance's very essence": "If choreography emerges in early modernity to remachine the body so it can 'represent itself' as a total 'being-toward-movement,' perhaps the recent exhaustion of the notion of dance as pure display of uninterrupted movement participates in a general critique of this mode of disciplining subjectivity, of constitute being [sic]."[19]

Dance's increased focus on movement as its essence is thus conceived as symptomatic of an ideology that demands an unstoppable motility. Symptomatic as well is one's disciplining of how movement is controlled, how it is made productive, efficient, and effective. This supposed essence of dance and the modes of thinking from which it emerges, are questioned in the projects of contemporary choreographers such as La Ribot, Jérôme Bel, Xavier Le Roy, Boris Charmatz, Meg Stuart, Vera Mantero, Thomas Lehmen, Jonathan Burrows, and Juan Dominguez. In dialogue with poststructuralist thinkers and building on the work of a previous generation of critical avant-garde artists, their projects exhaust the implications of what constitutes the rule of the game of Western theatrical dance through questioning Western theatrical dance's most important characteristics: "the inextricable alliance between writing and dancing (where writing serves the purposes of the archive in its triple function of historical memory, of ideal model and of structure of command)" and "dance's relentless dissatisfaction with the structural impermanence of the body."[20] Their projects invite a reconsideration of what dance is and allow for new subjectivities to emerge. They also invite an expansion of dance studies' object of analysis, asking dance studies to "step into other artistic fields and to create new possibilities for thinking relationships between bodies, subjectivities, politics, and movement."[21]

This expansion is fundamental to what the phenomenon of lecture performance is about, while at the same time many lecture performances also suggest something else. Often, lecture performances not only invite a reconsideration of what dance is or what dance studies could be about, but also conceptualize dance itself as a mode of thinking, investigating, and understanding. In *Product of Circumstances*, Le Roy reflects on his dissatisfaction with academic research (asking him to produce, not to search) and his move toward dance as an alternative practice of doing research. The "artist twin" Kattrin Deuffert and Thomas Plischke[22] regularly use the format of the lecture for artistic proposals that demonstrate how poststructuralist thinking not only inspires performances that question the ontology of dance but also, and more than that, how the performative turn invites a reconsideration of the relationships and differences between artistic and academic methods of doing research. Deuffert and Plischke deploy the poetics of dance and performance to engage with the implications of performativity as a general condition of how we perceive, think, and make sense. Dance, their work suggests, may be understood as a set of practices of embodied engagement through which meaning is generated. Although the work of Deuffert and Plischke does not look like dance as we (think we) know it, their modes of conduct are deeply informed by contemporary dance practice.

Plischke studied at Anne Teresa de Keersmaeker's program P.A.R.T.S. in Brussels.[23] Deufert was a member of the graduate college Körper-Inszenierungen at the Free University in Berlin.[24] Dance, it might be argued, is part of Plischke and Deufert's mode of conduct. It is a perspective that informs modes of doing, thinking and engaging. As such, dance in their practice functions as a *dispositif* understood in the Deleuzian sense as a formation that opens up possibilities of contact, participation, and play.

Dispositif, I will argue, allows for an approach to the development described by Lepecki as "exhausting dance," explaining this development not from a historical connection between choreography and writing, but rather allowing for an understanding of dance itself as a set of discourses and practices that may inform modes of conduct constitutive of subjectivities and their realities. Dispositif as a perspective on the relationship between dance and modernity shifts attention from Western modern dance as a practice of disciplining bodies according to the demands of writing/choreography toward dance as a practice from which subjectivities emerge (in Deleuzian terms) as the "eject" of modes of conduct. These modes of conduct and the ways in which subjectivities and their realities emerge from them are, as Lepecki also observes, intimately intertwined with the cultural historical moment of their emergence. Yet, how subjectivities emerge is not necessarily a matter of yielding to commanding voices of masters or submitting to disciplinary regimes (nor emerging from resistance to these). Understood as dispositif, dance itself emerges as a practice of exploration and experiment, a practice of thinking through cultural formations, not only to exhaust or to being exhausted, but also to relate, transform, and produce.

Dispositif, usually (mis)translated in English as "apparatus," was first introduced by Foucault to describe the network of connections between heterogeneous elements from the perspective of how their interplay results in a historical formation that produces power structures and knowledge.[25] An analysis of a given phenomenon, say dance, in terms of the Foucaultian dispositif exposes how the way in which this phenomenon manifests itself at a given time and place is the product of the interplay between discourses, propositions, laws, and scientific statements through which this phenomenon is understood. This grid of intelligibility, more than explaining the phenomenon, is itself constitutive of it. The dispositif thus understood is, following Lepecki, the rule of the game defining what can appear as dance and what not.

The notion of dispositif was later taken up by Deleuze, who, as Frank Kessler observes, "shifts the focus from the idea that dispositif establishes relations and connections between the heterogeneous elements that constitute it, to the disjoint and rather precarious character of such a formation."[26] Kessler quotes Deleuze, who writes:

But what is a *dispositif*? In the first instance, it is a tangle, a multilinear ensemble. It is composed of lines, each having a different nature. And the lines in the apparatus do not outline or surround systems which are homogeneous in their own right, object, subject, language, and so on, but follow directions, trace balances that are always off balance, now drawing together and then distancing themselves from one another. Each line is broken and subject to *changes in direction*, bifurcating and forked, and subject to *drifting*. Visible objects, affirmations that can be formulated, forces exercised and subjects in position are like vectors and tensors. Thus the three major aspects which Foucault successively distinguishes, Knowledge, Power and Subjectivity, are by no means contours given once and for all, but series of variables which supplant one another.[27]

Deleuze's account radicalizes the dynamics and the transformations involved in the reality-producing potential of the dispositif. This possibility was taken up and elaborated in a body of texts collected in a 1999 issue of *Hermès* (no. 25, 1999), exploring the dispositif as a type of formation that not only produces control and constraints but also opens up possibilities of contact, participation, and play. Building upon Michel de Certeau's critique of Foucault's "panoptic" conception of the dispositif, these studies work toward a concept of the dispositif as the "in-between."[28] Opening up possibilities of contact, participation, and play, as well as bodily and sensual experiences, dispositif, thus conceived, describes the relationship between modes of conduct and the realities that emerge from them.

Deuffert and Plischke demonstrate the potential of an understanding of artistic practices like dance as a dispositif. Dance is part of how they engage and confront the world, how they investigate and make sense of experience. Their work does not engage with the rules of the game for differentiating dance from nondance, but rather with the rules of the game of dance as a set of discourses and practices that may inform modes of conduct constitutive of subjectivities and their realities. Work like theirs invites reflection on the relationship between modes of conduct of dance (among others), and the realities that emerge from these modes, as well as on the differences between these modes of conduct and other modes of research and making sense. Adopting the lecture as format for a performance, their performances also invite a reconsideration of the performativity of philosophical and scientific practice through the lens of performance and choreography and, by extension, question the relationships and differences between the two. Similar questions informed the series of lecture performances organized by *Unfriendly Takeover* in Frankfurt (featuring Deuffert and Plischke, as well as among others, Xavier Le Roy, Jérôme Bel, Stefan Kaegi, Marten Spangberg, Felix Kubin, and Tim Etchell).

Such an understanding of the potential of dance is actually remarkably close to the accounts of early modern dance in Germany by Toepfer and Brandstetter. Toepfer begins his observation on early-twentieth-century body culture by pointing, like Martin does, to a certain abstraction of the body in movement in German dance photographs of the period, showing dancers in different costumes (or nude) assuming different poses against a white background. Often the names of the dancers or any other information on the dancers' identity, or the circumstances of the photographs, is absent. Their bodies seem to have no "context": "suspended in a white void, the body demands that the viewer look at nothing but itself as an autonomous force, free of definition by anything external to it."[29] Unlike Martin, Toepfer does not present this abstraction as in accord with an American background but as part and parcel of an analysis of the Germanic construction of the modern body. This construction, as Toepfer argues, "involves two large categories of performance: nudity and physical movement, particularly ideas about movement introduced by the most turbulent dance culture in history." In this context, Toepfer argues, nudism and dance emerge as answers to questions circulating, often unconsciously, within the social reality that created the culture.[30] Dance and nudism may be considered "answers" to questions circulating within the social reality in the sense that they provide a response to such questions by means of a working through, which turns them into both a product of their times and a reflection on issues defining their times. Quite similarly Brandstetter demonstrates how the development of early-twentieth-century modern dance reads as an exploration of new body images and spatial configurations in and through dance. Dance is used to "think through" body images and spatial configurations, to experiment with them, and in doing so, to allow new subjectivities to emerge.[31]

Toepfer and Brandstetter's accounts of early modern dance suggest that late-twentieth-century experimental practices in dance may be understood as a continuation of early modern practices in which dance appears as a means of engaging with questions emerging from social and cultural transformations. What has changed is the nature of the questions that dance engages. Müller's *How Heavy Are My Thoughts* illustrates and comments on this change.

How Heavy Are My Thoughts reads as a lecture performance about lecture performances, a meta-theatrical reflection on the phenomenon of lecture performances. The performance reports on the research conducted by the artist Ivana Müller. However, here it is not the artist herself lecturing on her own research but someone else. Or, better to say, it is Ivana Müller staging Bill Aitchison to report on the research conducted by an artist named Ivana Müller, who, within the performance, is referred to as I.M. This I.M. sets out to investigate the material weight of her thoughts and does so by means of a mixed approach. She conducts scientific experiments like having her head scanned in an MRI scanner as well as experiments that seem to be inspired by a scientific mode of thinking, such as weighing the heads of fifty friends involved in respectively heavy and light thinking. She talks to a scientist, a psychologist, a psychiatrist, and a philosopher, and their answers to her questions are also included in the performance. Scientific modes of doing and thinking are placed next to experiments that seem to be closer to artistic modes of conduct. We witness I.M. experiment with intuitive visualizations, intoxication, and physical expression. She conducts experiments in which she attempts to separate heavy and light thoughts by means of a trampoline, to sense traces of objects that are no longer there, and to stop thinking altogether. Aitchison reports on all these experiments and modes of conduct in an equally serious way. His lecturelike performance invites us, spectators, to look at these rather diverse research activities as equal. All of them are presented as equally serious, or equally nonserious. The contrast between Aitchison's deadpan seriousness and the unconventional character of I.M.'s approach is at points hilarious. Framed by Aitchison's extremely serious account, even aspects of her research that in themselves are much closer to conventional academic behavior begin to look less self-evident. Both the instances of serious scientific research and the alternatives placed next to it begin to look like theater in the sense of being staged in order to meet with expectations and assumptions concerning the nature of research and how to report on it.

Müller's *How Heavy Are My Thoughts* is not a confrontation between arts and science. It is a performance about such confrontations and what such confrontations might be about. In this performance, I.M.'s research is literally framed by Aitchison as "one of these projects where science meets the arts." Aitchison then takes us, the audience, along in an attempt to understand what it was all about. Müller's staging of Aitchison's "reconstruction" of I.M.'s experiments invites us, the audience, to go along with I.M.'s train of thought. This staging highlights the address presented to the audience, which causes what Husemann (quoted above) describes as "a shared meta-reflection on the common thought movements evoked by the events on stage." Seen this way, the absence of bodily movement from *How Heavy Are My Thoughts* is not a matter of exhausting what is considered to be the ontological ground of dance, namely movement, but rather of a transformation of the kind of movement dance is about, or can be about. Here the reflection evoked is on the movement of thought itself and the relationship between the thought-movements presented on stage and the Cartesian subject. That is, the reflection evoked is not about the relationship between modern subjectivity and the rule of the game of dance. Instead, the performance draws attention to how I.M. as the subject of the thoughts represented on stage emerges from the movements of thought reconstructed by Aitchison. In this movement of thought, I.M. functions as what Deleuze and Guattari have termed a conceptual persona.[32] The conceptual persona is the "I" that speaks through the philosophical speech act. This philosophical speech act is in some ways comparable to the speech act as theorized by Austin and Searle in what has become known as speech act theory. The important difference is that: "In philosophical enunciations, we do not do something by saying it but produce movement by thinking it, through the intermediary of a conceptual persona."[33] This conceptual persona is the "I" that says "I think therefore I am" and in this way founds the Cartesian cogito.

I.M.'s question "If my thoughts are heavier than usual, is my head heavier than usual too?" touches the core of Cartesian mind/body dualism and questions the distinction between the material body (*res extensa*) as part of the natural world and governed by physical laws and the mind as a thinking entity (*res cogitans*) supposedly outside or distinct from the natural and material world. This kind of questioning is central to the current reconsiderations of the position of dance within the interdisciplinary field of artistic as well as scientific practices of knowledge production. The critical attitude and the modes of thinking informing this attitude, it might be argued, are part of the dispositif through which I.M. engages with the subject of her research and informs her modes of thinking as well as her modes of conducting research. In *How Heavy Are My Thoughts* Ivana Müller stages these modes of thinking and researching, i.e., she puts them literally on stage and in such a way that highlights how they are structured. With this staging, she demonstrates that not only may the history of modern subjectivity provide a perspective on contemporary dance as a practice of exhausting the rule of the dance-game, but also, conversely, the practice of dance and performance may provide a perspective on the subject of modernity and the modes of thinking from which this subject emerges.

How Heavy Are My Thoughts presents an image of thinking as a performative act that sets the stage for the appearance of conceptual personae as vectors of the movement of thinking. In such thinking, we never coincide with the "I" that is the subject of our thoughts. Thinking, Deleuze and Guattari observe, is a self-positing, and it is from this positing that we as subjects emerge. However, the "I" that emerges as the subject of our thoughts is not the self that does the positing. We are being thought rather than thinking. This is nicely illustrated in *How Heavy Are My Thoughts* where I.M. emerges from Aitchison's attempt at thinking through Ivana Müller's thoughts. Aitchison thinks and "therefore I.M." With his reconstruction of I.M.'s thinking, he sets the stage for I.M. to appear as a position for us to take up from where to imaginarily enter I.M.'s field of consciousness. "I think therefore I am," "I think therefore I.M.": like Derrida's *différance*, this difference touches the core of what is at stake here.[34]

Notes

1. *How Heavy Are My Thoughts*, a performance by Ivana Müller in collaboration with Bill Aitchison and Nils de Coster and with the participation of Prof. F. Siemsen (physicist—Germany), Prof. Bojana Kunst (philosopher—Slovenia), Prof. W. A. Wagenaar (psychologist—Netherlands), Dr. Christian Röder (psychiatrist—Germany), Alexandra Thiel (trampoline instructor—Germany) and I.M.'s fifty friends. Produced by Gasthuis Theater (Amsterdam) and Mousonturm (Frankfurt).

2. Karl Toepfer, *Empire of Ecstasy: Nudity and Movement in German Body Culture 1910–1935* (Berkeley: University of California Press, 1997), 6ff.

3. See Susan Manning and Melissa Benson, "Interrupted Continuities: Modern Dance in Germany," *The Drama Review* 30:2 (1986): 18–21.

4. Hortensia Völckers, "Preface," in *Knowledge in Motion. Perspectives of Artistic and Scientific Research in Dance*, eds. Sabine Gehm, Pirkko Husemann, Katharina von Wilcke (Bielefeld: transcript, 2007), 9–14, here 10.

5. Marijke Hoogenboom, "Artistic Research as an Expanded Kind of Choreography Using the Example of Emio Greco|PC," in *Knowledge in Motion*, 81–90, here 84.

6. Alva Noë, "Making Worlds Available," in *Knowledge in Motion*, 121–128.

7. Gabriele Brandstetter, "Dance as a Culture of Knowledge: Body Memory and the Challenge of Theoretical Knowledge," in *Knowledge in Motion*, 37–48, here 45. See also Pirkko Husemann, *Choreographie als kritische Praxis. Arbeitsweisen bei Xavier Le Roy und Thomas Lehmen* (Bielefeld: transcript, 2009).

8. Pirkko Husemann, "The Absent Presence of Artistic Working Processes: The Lecture as Performance," Lecture Performance presented in Frankfurt May 8th, 2004. Text (English version, update March 2005) available on the Web site of Unfriendly Takeover (http://www.unfriendly-takeover.de/f14_b_eng.htm). Last accessed on September 6, 2009.

9. Ibid.

10. Ibid.

11. Editors' Note: The title *Urheben Aufheben* is difficult to translate. The German "Urheben" comes from "Urheber," which means author or creator; it is not usually used as a verb. "Aufheben" means both to keep something and to abolish something. When used in a philosophical sense, "aufheben" is translated as to sublate. See also Yvonne Hardt's essay in this volume.

12. *Product of Circumstances*, a performance by and with Xavier Le Roy. Produced by In Situ Productions and Le Kwatt in collaboration with Podewil/TanzWerkstatt, Berlin and Senatsverwaltung für Wissenschaft, Forschung und Kultur, Berlin. Premiere: April 2, 1999, Berlin.

13. Interestingly, Toepfer observes that many people who contributed significantly to the early-twentieth-century body culture in Germany did not originally come from Germany either. "The body culture was 'German' insofar as distinct personalities regarded Germany as somehow decisive in shaping their ideas and careers, but it did not exist only and entirely in Germany." Toepfer, *Empire of Ecstasy*, 8.

14. Martin quoted in André Lepecki, *Exhausting Dance: Performance and the Politics of Movement* (New York: Routledge, 2006), 4.

15. John Martin, *Introduction to the Dance* (New York: W. W. Norton and Co, 1939), 241.

16. Lepecki, *Exhausting Dance*, 6.
17. Ibid., 7.
18. Sloterdijk in Lepecki, 12.
19. Lepecki, *Exhausting Dance*, 7.
20. Ibid., 123.
21. Ibid., 5.
22. "Artist twin" is the term chosen by Deuffert and Plischke to describe their artistic identity. Sharing, as they put it "work in life and life in work" they call themselves artist twin. See http://www.artistwin.de.
23. Founded in 1995, P.A.R.T.S (Performing Arts Research and Training Studios) has quickly become one of the most prominent training programs in contemporary dance in Europe. The school is a joint initiative of Anne Teresa de Keersmaeker's dance company Rosas and the Belgian National Opera De Munt/La Monnaie. The aim of the school is to help students develop into "thinking performers." Research and reflection play an important part in the training curriculum. See http://www.parts.be.
24. Körper-Inszenierungen (Staging the Body) is the name of an interdisciplinary graduate school started in 1997 by Erika Fischer-Lichte at the Free University in Berlin. The graduate school explores embodiment as a cultural practice in different cultures and historical periods. See http://www.geisteswissenschaften.fu-berlin.de/we03/forschung/forschungsprojekte/koerper-inszenierungen/index.html.
25. Michel Foucault, *The History of Sexuality Volume 1: An Introduction*, trans. Robert Hurley (New York: Vintage Books, 1990), especially the chapter "The deployment of sexuality," 75–132. See also his *Power/Knowledge. Selected Interviews and Other Writings 1972–1977*, ed. Colin Gordon (New York: Pantheon Books, 1980), 194–195.
26. Frank Kessler, "Notes on Dispositif," unpublished seminar paper (2006), accessible through http://www.let.uu.nl/~Frank.Kessler/personal/notes%20on%20dispositif.PDF.
27. Gilles Deleuze "What Is a Dispositif?" in *Michel Foucault Philosopher*, ed. Timothy J. Armstrong (New York: Routledge, 1992), 159.
28. Michel de Certeau, *The Practice of Everyday Life* (Berkeley: University of California Press, 1984).
29. Toepfer, *Empire of Ecstasy*, 1.
30. Ibid., 7.
31. Gabriele Brandstetter, *Tanz-Lektüren. Körperbilder und Raumfiguren der Avant-Garde* (Frankfurt: Fischer Taschenbuch, 1995).
32. Gilles Deleuze and Félix Guattari, *What Is Philosophy?* (New York: Columbia University Press, 1994).
33. Ibid., 65.
34. For a more extensive reading of *How Heavy Are My Thoughts* in terms of Deleuzian thinking, see Bleeker, "Thinking through Theatre," in *Deleuze and Performance*, ed. Laura Cull (Edinburgh: Edinburgh University Press, 2009), 147–160.

15. Toward a Theory of Cultural Translation in Dance

GABRIELE KLEIN

Looking at the history of dance in the modern West, and especially in Europe, where aesthetic modernism began around 1900, there are two characteristics of dance. Whether it is so-called popular dance or a more artistic form, from a sociological perspective, the history of dance is the history of globalization and transnationalism. It is also the record of how urban experiences have been expressed physically. The artistic avant-garde of the twentieth century thrived in large cities, and even folk dances rarely originated in the countryside.

Whether tango from Buenos Aires, samba from Rio de Janiero, punk from London, techno from Detroit, house from Chicago, or hip-hop from New York: Popular dance culture, as it arose in European cities in the course of the twentieth century, was always subject to ethnic and social influences such as the urban middle and lower classes, cultural traditions outside Europe, or trends in popular culture. Assimilating these, dance spread globally, representing experiences of urban living that stretch from the white middle class, with their particular ethical code, to the active rebelliousness of black adolescents. Dance and the city are connected by a secret link: Dances represent urban ways of life; they capture the spirit of a city, which, in performance, is turned into a sensual experience. Cities, with their dynamic energy, their social density, and cultural diversity, are in turn fertile ground for new dances. In the modern era, dances always reveal the changeable history of urban places, caught between restoration and revolution, mainstream and opposition, social in- and exclusion, globalization and locality. Popular dances tell this story as a physical exercise, as a sensual history of controlling and releasing body movements. It considers the traditional hierarchy of gender and its reorganization, as well as social difference and cultural heterogeneity. It takes into account resistance to one's basic instincts and surrender to the drive, the longing for affiliation and solitude, the affirmation of and resistance against Western consumer culture.

The following will address tango as a specific example of urban transnationalism in dance. In particular, it will explore the relevance of a theory of cultural translation for the analysis and historiography of dance and show how such a theory can arise from the embodied practice of tango.

Global Dances, Local Practices: Ethnographic Reports on Tango

Buenos Aires is mythical place of origin and a mecca for global tango tourism. It offers multiple tango-locations, *milongas* and *practicás* as diverse as the cultural hybridity of tango itself. Male and, more often, female tourists frequent places like the Niño Bien, a renovated turn-of-the-century ballroom with bright lights and elegant tables; or the Club Espanol and the Confitería Ideal, art nouveau halls decorated in gold, complete with chandeliers, tarnished mirrors, and old-fashioned bistro tables and chairs. So called "taxi dancers" will find plenty of customers here. This profession witnessed a short-lived boom during the Roaring Twenties in Germany due to the First World War's many male casualties; in today's Buenos Aires, it is an important source of income for mostly older, good-looking Argentinean men who embody the type of the authentic *milonguero*. Taxi dancers can be hired by women. Doubts about the decency or political correctness of such deals are swept away by the desire for authentic experience that can be found in the retained passion and sustained tension of the *milonguero*'s embrace. Cheek to cheek with "her" man, the woman-turned-into-goddess glides across the dance floor. In her film *The Tango Lesson*, which once more fueled tango's mythical attractiveness for tourists, Sally Potter tells precisely this tale: a white middle-class woman discovers the power of tango. Next to the taxi dancers, prominent local dance teachers take on female tourists for marketing reasons; after the dance, they distribute their flyers and take reservations for private lessons.

The situation is different in places less frequently visited by tourists. Here, the global and allegedly "authentic" sign system of tango is lacking. No red velvet, roses, black chairs, or dimmed lights. A different kind of production of authenticity is provided, for instance, by El Arranque, an afternoon *milonga* at La Argentina: a room without windows in a 1970s building with a tiled floor, neon light, walls covered in a faded brown color, tables in green and red, plastic plants. El Arranque plays traditional tango music. The dancing is close and restrained, without any jumps or complicated figures. Male tourists appreciate this event because they can practice their steps with older Argentinean women. But similar to any other *milonga* in the suburbs of Buenos Aires, there are mostly regulars. Consider for example the Sunderland-Club: an old sports facility with abandoned basketball baskets and advertisements on the walls. On Saturdays, it houses "La Milonga del Mundo." Small tables with photocopied menus and plastic chairs are draped around the dance floor. In contrast to tango habits outside of Argentina, the guests here usually indulge in lavish dinners. Couples predominate; single women are placed immediately next to the dance floor so that they can be seen. The visibility of those who are dancing as well as those who are sitting and eating is important. Yet there is a clear hierarchy between a "good" and a "bad" side; the "good" side is reserved for the well-known dancers.

The wide variety of tango locations in Buenos Aires finds its complement globally. For many dancers, these venues offer much more than an opportunity for dancing. They are places where visitors familiarize themselves with the rhythms of a city, where social networks are formed—places that represent a home. Take, for instance, Le Chantier, a tango venue in the Parisian district Montreuil. It consists of a living room with imitation leather sofas, IKEA shelves with private photographs and toys, a table with chandelier, and a makeshift kitchen opening up into a dance hall decorated in red velvet and containing a variety of old wooden chairs. The *milonga* takes place on Saturdays only; it is a local secret. People know each other; they meet after midnight for a barbecue in the midst of the courtyard's discarded cars, bikes, and bathtubs and dance until breakfast. The Egyptian doorman spends his weekends here, dancing, watching football, and fixing old cars. Like other tango locations, Le Chantier embodies a kind of heterotopia: a collaborative space for people of different cultures, ethnic origins, and religions.

Transnationalism and Transcultural Translation in the Age of Globalization

"What is tango good for?"[1] Pina Bausch asked in 1980 during rehearsals for her piece *Bandoneon*. At the time, tango had been around for roughly one hundred years in Europe and in Japan, and it was experiencing one of its periodic revivals. It is not easy to answer Bausch's question because tango is a global myth carrying many often contradictory connotations. Tango is at once metaphor, ideology, and symbol; dance, music, and text. It is history, culture, and business; poetry, kitsch, and politics; global, national, and local; demimonde, bourgeois, and cosmopolitan. It symbolizes style, attitude, and feeling; passion, eroticism, and jealousy; convention, avant-garde, and masquerade. Tango is an experience of noncommittal commitment; it is authentic, theatrical, and exceptional; masculine, feminine, and queer; it is promise, hope, and consolation; a leisure activity, movement therapy, and alternative culture, practiced by the young, the eternally young, and the old.

Above all, tango is an example of the globalization of popular dance cultures. But popular dance is not only a representation of a globalized popular culture. It also helps to create a cultural memory, which depends upon a principle of in- and exclusion, subjecting it to relations of power. Therefore, dance historiography is a political area, which produces a special kind of meaning. The cultural history and the cultural translation of dance forms are an element of power relations, which manifest themselves as "body politics."

This principle of in- and exclusion between high and popular cultures of dance is characteristic for the European culture of dance. Popular dances in particular epitomized a modern, hybrid urban culture, strongly influenced by immigrants. At the beginning of the twentieth century, waves of emigration from Latin America transformed European dance culture fundamentally: Black dances, accompanied by jazz, took the dance clubs by storm, which were the entertainment venues of the city's new residents. These dances deconstructed the traditional concept of the body in European dance in a very subtle, unconscious manner. They enabled dancers to experience alternative gender-specific figures. Also, they introduced principles of polycentrism and polyrhythm into European dance, making the hips the center of movement. From the Charleston to hip-hop, popular dances are an eruptive expression of social and urban feeling. These forms of movement and dance have already had a lasting influence on the contemporary art of dancing. They are important seismographs of a physically perceivable, socially fragmented, multi- and transcultural adherence. A myriad of popular dances of the twentieth century are hybrid forms of dance, which developed from the tensions of regionalization, globalization, and renationalization.

It is no coincidence that the concept of hybridism, which became a key term in the postcolonial debate on migration, globalization, and diaspora culture, was brought to fame by an urban sociologist from Chicago, Robert Ezra Park.[2] He first used it in his 1928 essay on the role of immigrants in American culture. Park refers to the immigrant as "the marginal man," and as "a cultural hybrid," since he regarded him as marginal in his new world as well as in his original culture. In doing so, Park established the concept of the hybrid as a sociological term, not only as a biological one. He also assigned it a positive connotation: The hybrid "marginal man," for Park, is the cosmopolitan individual of the future. Later, Mikhail Bakhtin and Homi Bhabha were to take up this concept as well.

How can we describe transnationalization and globalization of popular dances? How can we refer this to the socially and culturally relevant forms and methods of cultural translation? In the course of globalization, dances become subject to a permanent global, reciprocal translation process, by means of de- and re-contextualization. Globalization in this sense means migration of culture, which is spread globally by the media. In spite of, or perhaps just because of these cultural crossovers, popular dances reinvent dance as a universal language.

Transregional dance cultures address cultural distinction, hybridization, or creolization per se. This raises the question as to the mode of cultural translation. Dance cultures tell the story of cultural translations, revealing the impossibility of both cultural boundaries and global amalgamation. It is a story of tensions, of the movement, or the mediation that occur in a performance. The success of cultural translation always contains an element of failure, which becomes apparent in the insecurity and intangibility of the translation process. Therefore, failing is not the opposite of the success of the translation process but a genuine component of the process itself.

A concept of cultural translation is necessary in order to understand the structure behind these translation processes: one that analyzes their transformatory potential, rather than viewing translation as a rhetorical figure or metaphor, as often happens in debates within Cultural Studies. An analytical approach to translation allows one to formulate concepts of cultural theory more precisely, which concern interculturalism, hybridism, creolization, locality of dance, or diaspora. It also does justice to the transcultural migrations of dance.

Cultural Translation and Postcolonial Theory

The concept of cultural translation, which I elaborated in my empirical research project "Transnational Identity and Physical-Sensual Experience," supported by the German Research Foundation, arose theoretically from the "cultural turn" in translation studies,[3] as a subdivision of social sciences, and from postcolonial studies.[4]

There are two main links to the debate on cultural theory. One is the discourse on multiculturalism and interculturality, which regards every cultural form as unique and original.[5] According to this view, there is not one universal culture, but a multitude of different cultures, which define themselves in an essentialist manner. Either they acknowledge one another, or repel the other, possibly with violence. This intercultural concept argues that every culture is essentially linked to an ethnic, gender-based, and sexual origin: Muslim and Christian cultures, male and female, white and black cultures have identities that may perhaps be communicated interculturally, but which cannot be bridged. This intercultural concept is firmly connected with the idea of the national state. It provides the conceptual basis for a state policy that "creates culture" in the majority's sense. This would protect what is assumed to be the "original" culture, as outlined in the canon of cultural knowledge. In addition, this intercultural notion provides the foundation for a liberal, middle-class policy, which seeks to enable peaceful, intercultural exchange by establishing a stable social order.

Another concept of cultural translation originates from the idea of deconstruction. This line of argument, supported by postcolonial studies, does not examine the particular relationship between cultures. Instead, it tries to undermine the notion of an original cultural identity as such. According to this theory, culture is not a given original but rather a system of signs, which relate to one another, leave traces, and draw from their origins independently. Therefore, being German, black, or gay is only the result of a certain cultural activity, which is part of the process of translation itself. As semiotician Peeter Torop asserts, "In the discipline of semiotics of culture, it comes naturally to say that culture is translation, and also that translation is culture."[6]

Homi Bhabha refers to the space of translation as a hybrid space, a "third space"[7] in which transformation or transgression is possible. There, binary cultural codes can change and create something new. It would be wrong, however, to consider this hybrid space as a singular cultural sphere. Culture is translation, and as such is continually in transition. "What is called trans-culture," says Gayatri Chakravorty Spivak, "is culture in progress. Trans-culturation is nothing special or different, it is an aspect in the normal taxonomy of what we call culture."[8] Regarding transculture as something specific means to place culture in a certain political (mostly national) context. Here, we see the necessity of placing cultural translation in a political context, since it always occurs within political and symbolic spheres.

According to this interpretation, cultural translation does not point to one beginning or ending point, nor to an original. By means of retrospection, translation creates the idea of culture as a unity, based on originality and a linear sense of time, as Barbara Johnson explains in her book *Mother Tongues*. Her argument is based on Walter Benjamin's essay "The Translator's Task," in which he claims that translation reveals supposedly natural integrity as facade, proving that translation contains a potential of strategic power.[9] Following this interpretation, Tomislaw Longinovic terms cultural translation "the practice of everyday life."[10] This is a kind of performance, and because of this, a pattern of subjectivity.

This is precisely what cultural translators experience. Cultural translators in globalized societies are, for example, immigrant workers, war victims, refugees, or traveling intellectuals, and (dance) artists. In "Liquid Modernity"[11] (Bauman), the travelers create subject-based structures and cultures, which Richard Sennett[12] calls the flexible beings of neocapitalism.[13] These people present new patterns of transcultural identity, as well as hybrid artistic and intellectual practices. At the same time, their life reveals the disadvantage of transcultural translation: It can be considered a positive "intermediary zone," but also a pattern for social in- and exclusion. This, in turn, is characteristic of a postcolonial or national strategy for globalized societies.

Cultural translation is always linked to a concept of power. Since the "cultural turn," culture has not replaced the concept of society on the political stage,[14] as is so often assumed. By turning political conflicts into cultural ones, and by raising the cultural dialogue to a topic of international political relations, culture has become a political stage itself. Nancy Fraser and Gayatri Chakravorty Spivak have addressed this culturization of politics.[15] They point to the difference between the political use of exclusive cultural concepts on the one side and the constructive character of these concepts on the other. Thus, cultural translation is always also a political category, which can have a subversive as well as an affirmative effect.

From this perspective, cultural translation does not mean cultural understanding or bridging cultural divides. Neither does it focus on a (supposed) original culture. Instead, translation seeks to explore the "in-between spaces," disregarding the perspective of binary structure. It examines these spaces of negotiation for the processes of cultural translation. An analytical concept of cultural translation looks at how the complex cultural processes of exchange and negotiation take place beyond the transfer between original and translation. It focuses on the sense of multidimensional transformation in the spaces in between.

Dance as Cultural Translation

Dance is one of these spaces of negotiation. Dancing illustrates cultural translation, since dance is "travel," migration, and continuous movement. This makes it a genuine "translation term," a bodily method of translation. The notion of originality, taken from the intercultural discourse, can then be applied to dance only if it happens to be a purely local dance, such as some traditional folk dances. Most modern dances, especially the urban ones, are hybrid cultural techniques.[16] They are subject to the multifaceted dynamics of transcultural exchange. This, in turn, finds expression in diverse media and in different means of communication, which can be dance, writing, speech, song, film, or photography.

The German-speaking world uses the term "transference" for describing dance-specific languagelike qualities. This is used metaphorically, drawing upon the terminology of information technology or psychoanalysis. However, to examine its particular mechanisms, we require an analytical, empirically usable concept of transference. It would also help to explore how this transfer, with its transitory potential, can sustain the continuous reassertion of meaning in the context of local lifestyles.

From the social and political viewpoint, transference is an analytical and empirically adaptable concept with three main areas:

- the transformation of forms of dance, which take place in a cultural context defined by space and time, by means of dancing bodies,
- the complex, overlapping, and reciprocal movements of transmission, which occur between techniques of dancing, images, texts, and music,
- the performance that influences this transmission—here, the special features and the poetic potential of transmission in different cultures of dance can be brought to bear.

Transferences in dance find their "material" in and between dancing bodies, which perform and perceive these movements. The "third body" in dancing is the intercorporeal space. However, the globally circulating narrative of a certain dance is as important as the bodies' movements in dancing: for example, tango as passion, salsa as party and fun, hip-hop as a subversive practice. Transference in dance is therefore not only movement between different bodies, dance styles, and cultures, but also a permanent translation between the complicated levels of meaning in the dance itself, fed by images, music, and texts from different media.

Dance as a Cultural Narrative

The narrative of dances creates imaginary social worlds. These are translated into various cultural contexts and locally anchored in the process of global translation. Peter Berger and Thomas Luckmann[17] describe dance genres and locations as sensual worlds, which create social rules, symbolic codes, social interactions, ritualized actions, dance techniques, and subjective emotions, and incorporate them.[18] Examples are genre-specific theatrical performances, such as *milongas*, *salsatecas*, battles, or jams. Individual action, feeling, and thinking form the framework for the narrative, whereby this "creation of locality" does not necessarily have to be a mere imitation.[19] The performance of social, ritual, and dancing techniques has the transformatory potential of translation. For one, this leads to local differences in globalized cultures of dance. For another, it turns the experience of dancing into a process that transforms the global narrative, since it is performed by people who are subject to cultural and social influences.

Globalized dance cultures rely on a more or less structured, but not necessarily hierarchical, system of narratives. These stories create meaning; they constitute the identity of the dancers but also the collective identity of the local dance scene. The term *narrative* does not refer to the story itself, but to the act of relating it. This story contains the imagined social world of the dance. It includes the narrative process into a linear chronology and thus ensures the narrative's permanent continuation.[20] Meaning is derived from the performative strategies of narration. For one, there is the continuous "creation of locality," connected with re-contextualization, e.g., the tango scene in Buenos Aires, New York salsa, or L.A. hip-hop. These create patterns of social in- and exclusion, which in turn construct social and local identity. For another, performing dance is in itself a story, which helps to form identity. The continuous relating of stories in images, texts, and the social practices of dance is a complex, contradictory, brittle, translocal translation process, which alternates between global and local spheres. It can constitute physical experience as well as an individual or collective identity. In this process of identification, the narrative is adapted to the local, cultural, and biographical surroundings and shared with the world as a newly transformed dance—whether by travel or by representations of dance in the media (internet, flyer, picture book, film, or video clip).

Cultural Translation and Transcultural Identities

The personal identity of the dancer and the collective identity of local dance scenes stem from "fictional" stories and their reception.[21] This can be the notion of tango as the dance of a disreputable milieu or hip-hop as ghetto culture. Equally, there are "factual" stories, e.g., the "unification" of two bodies in tango or violence in hip-hop, which are presented as real experience. In these cases, fiction and fact are inextricably connected. These narratives give rise to identities and lifestyles, which find expression in the self-image of *tangueras* and *tangueros*, of B-boys or B-girls. They integrate their experiences, such as dance itself, into dance history, thereby linking this to the story of their own lives. Narrative identity becomes the guarantee for the truth, originality, and authenticity of an imagined story.[22] The mimetic circle at work in such identities, described by Paul Ricoeur, encompasses, first, being intertwined with various stories (e.g., in dancing); second, recounting them explicitly;[23] and third, adapting them by means of interpretation. Using this template, Ricoeur deals with the wide-reaching definition of the term "narrative." It includes spoken and textual, as well as non–language-based media, e.g., events, experiences, parties, physical activities. These are legitimized by narratives, which provide their framework. By reference to a global narrative, they are taken as authentic experiences, establishing a form of identity through their interpretation.

The movements of translation illustrate the connections between the macro-level of globally circulating images and symbolic codes, which affect each individual dance scene, and the micro-level of local adaptation techniques and identities. Additionally, they constitute a central argument for research into dance theory: Dancing as movement is not something untranslatable because of its physical focus. Instead, relating what is indescribable in dance, or failing to do so, is a key part of the narrative. This is where the retrospective element comes in. In translation, narrative strategies emphasize the idea of "the original," but only in retrospect. The Argentine tango danced in Buenos Aires for example, becomes in this intercultural production of authenticity an authentic experience through this binary positioning of dancing and speaking, original and fake.

Narratives in global dance cultures adapt via the media through writing, images, music, and oral transmission. This narrative is a feature of dance cultures, especially couples' dances: They belong to those social practices in which abstract narratives become physically and emotionally perceptible as an intersubjective experience. With these translation processes between bodies, dance experience becomes an event beyond everyday life. These translations are sometimes accepted as transcendental occurrences, which can provide them with a religious dimension. In other words, dancing adapts narratives just as the essence of dancing itself is only perceived through these narratives as "real," "authentic," or "natural." Global narratives homogenize the cultural disparity of dances in different national cultures, (e.g., "Finnish tango" as opposed to "Japanese tango"), in local dance scenes (East Coast and West Coast hip-hop), or in gender traditions in dance (e.g., homosexual club cultures or Queer-tango). This gives rise to the assumption of a homogenous sphere of any respective dance culture. Symbolic codes of dance scenes worldwide reflect this, as well as color, clothing, accessories, and those rituals, ritualized actions, and rules of interaction that have been adapted by nearly all local dance scenes. This notion also manifests itself in a linear sense of time, in a dance history that creates tradition and offers cultural and social orientation. At the same time, it contributes toward building a mythology of dance. Events such as *milongas*, battles, or *salsatecas* turn the narrative of each dance performance into a myth, thus raising dance cultures to scenes beyond everyday existence. Dancing also provides orientation in a theatrical environment, not only of the dancing area (e.g., the hall, club, disco), but also in a global, spectacle-based society. Above all, dancing is believed to be and discussed as an essential, authentic experience. Yet it is also this micro-story of bodies, or in Spivak's words, this "strategic essentialism," which makes dancing a physical experience of contingency. For Niklas Luhmann, contingency is a category of cultural translation: "Something is contingent insofar as it is neither necessary nor impossible; it is just what it is (or was or will be), though it could also be otherwise."[24]

Just here, in the possibilities of translation, lies the poetic potential of dance as a non–language-based cultural practice. This potential arises from the unpredictability of transmissions in cultural narratives. In dancing, as this essay has attempted to show, these occur not only in the perception of professional performance or through theatrical representation. The complicated interconnection of narrative strategies in social, everyday performance practices is equally significant, as well as their oral and written, physical and image-based record.

When the dancers of the Wuppertal company tried to simply imitate the steps that they had seen and learned on tour in Argentina in response to the question "What is tango good for?" Pina Bausch said, "If this is all you can come up with, you have missed the point of tango."

Notes

1. Raimund Hoghe and Ulli Weiss, *Bandoneon—Für was kann Tango alles gut sein? Texte und Fotos zu einem Stück von Pina Bausch* (Darmstadt and Neuwied: Luchterhand, 1981), 1.

2. Robert Ezra Park: "Human Migration and the Marginal Man," *American Journal of Sociology* 33 (1928): 881–893.

3. See Karl-Heinz Stoll, "Translation als Kreolisierung," in *Kultur, Übersetzung, Lebenswelten. Beiträge zu aktuellen Paradigmen der Kulturwissenschaften*, eds. Andreas Gipper and Susanne Klengel (Würzburg: Königshausen und Neumann, 2008), 177–201.

4. See Doris Bachmann-Medick, "Übersetzung in der Weltgesellschaft. Impulse eines 'translational turn,'" in *Kultur, Übersetzung, Lebenswelten. Beiträge zu aktuellen Paradigmen der Kulturwissenschaften*, eds. Andreas Gipper and Susanne Klengel, 141–159.

5. See Boris Buden, "Cultural Translation: Why It Is Important and Where to Start with It," *Beyond Culture: The Politics of Translation*. Multiyear research project, ed. European Institute for Progressive Cultural Policies. http://translate.eipcp.net/transversal/0606/buden/en.

6. Peeter Torop, "Translation as Translating as Culture," *Sign Systems Studies* 30: 2 (2002): 594–605, here 603.

7. Jonathan Rutherford, "The Third Space. Interview with Homi K. Bhabha," in Rutherford, ed., *Identity: Community, Culture, Difference* (London: Lawrence and Wishart, 1990), 207–211; Homi K. Bhabha, *The Location of Culture* (London: Routledge, 1994).

8. Gayatri Chakravorty Spivak, "More Thoughts on Cultural Translation," *Beyond Culture: The Politics of Translation*. Multiyear research project, ed. European Institute for Progressive Cultural Policies. http://translate.eipcp.net/transversal/0608/spivak/en.

9. Barbara Johnson, *Mother Tongues. Sexuality, Trials, Motherhood, Translation* (Cambridge: Harvard University Press, 2003), 40–64.

10. Tomislaw Longinovic, "Fearful Asymmetries. A Manifesto of Cultural Translation," *Journal of the Midwest Modern Language Association* 35:2 (2002): 5–12; Longinovic and Boris Buden, "The Answer Is in Translation," *Beyond Culture: The Politics of Translation*. Multiyear research project, ed. European Institute for Progressive Cultural Policies. http://eipcp.net/transversal/0908/longinovic-buden/en.

11. Zygmunt Bauman, *Liquid Modernity* (Cambridge: Polity, 2000); Bauman, *Liquid Times: Living in an Age of Uncertainty* (Cambridge: Polity, 2006).

12. See Richard Sennett, *The Corrosion of Character: The Personal Consequences of Work in the New Capitalism* (London: W. W. Norton and Co., 1998).

13. For more detail on dance as a social metaphor in "liquid modernity," see Gabriele Klein, "Das Flüchtige. Politische Aspekte einer tanztheoretischen Figur," in *Wissenskultur Tanz. Historische und zeitgenössische Vermittlungsakte zwischen Praktiken und Diskursen*, ed. Sabine Huschka (Bielefeld: transcript 2009), 199–208.

14. See Adrienne Goehler, *Verflüssigungen. Wege und Umwege vom Sozialstaat zur Kulturgesellschaft* (Frankfurt: Campus, 2006).

15. See Nancy Fraser, *Justice Interruptus. Critical Reflections on the "Postsocialist" Condition* (New York: Routledge 1997) and see Gayatri Chakravorty Spivak, "Can the Subaltern Speak?" in *Marxism and the Interpretation of Culture*, eds. Cary Nelson and Lawrence Grossberg (Urbana: University of Illinois Press, 1988), 271–316.

16. Editors' Note: On dance as a hybrid cultural technique in the nineteenth century, see Claudia Jeschke's essay in this volume.

17. See Peter L. Berger and Thomas Luckmann, *Die gesellschaftliche Konstruktion der Wirklichkeit* (Frankfurt: Fischer, 1987).

18. See Gabriele Klein and Melanie Haller, "*Café Buenos Aires* und *Galeria del Latino*. Zur Trans-lokalität und Hybridität städtischer Tanzkulturen," in *Bewegungsraum und Stadtkultur. Sozial- und kulturwissenschaftliche Perspektiven*, eds. Jürgen Funke-Viennaeke and Gabriele Klein (Bielefeld: transcript, 2008), 51–74.

19. See Arjun Appadurai, "Globale ethnische Räume. Bemerkungen und Fragen zur Entwicklung einer transnationalen Anthropologie," in *Perspektiven der Weltgesellschaft*, ed. Ulrich Beck (Frankfurt: Suhrkamp 1998), 11–40; Appadurai, "The Production of Locality," in *Counterworks. Managing the Diversity of Knowledge*, ed. Richard Fardon (London: Routledge, 1995), 192–211.

20. See Wolfgang Müller-Funk, *Die Kultur und ihre Narrative* (Vienna: Springer, 2008), 29.

21. Paul Ricoeur's concept of narrative identity is helpful here; see his *Time and Narrative I*, trans. Kathleen McLaughlin and David Pellauer (Chicago: University of Chicago Press, 1990); and his *Time and Narrative III* (Chicago: University of Chicago Press, 1990).

22. See Benedict Anderson, *Imagined Communities: Reflections on the Origin and Spread of Nationalism* (London: Verso, 1991), 20.

23. See Gabriele Klein and Melanie Haller, "Präsenzeffekte. Zum Verhältnis von Bewegung und Sprache am Beispiel lateinamerikanischer Tänze," in *Body turn, Perspektiven der Soziologie des Körpers und des Sports*, ed. Robert Gugutzer (Bielefeld: transcript, 2006), 233–247.

24. Niklas Luhmann, *Social Systems* (Stanford: Stanford University Press, 1995), 106.

Contributors

SUSAN MANNING is professor of English, theater, and performance studies at Northwestern University. She is the author of *Ecstasy and the Demon: The Dances of Mary Wigman* (1993, 2nd ed. 2006); *Modern Dance, Negro Dance: Race in Motion* (2004); and *Danses noires/blanche Amérique* (2008). She is past president of the Society of Dance History Scholars and director of "Dance Studies in/and the Humanities," a Mellon-funded program designed to develop and disseminate strategies for interdisciplinary research and teaching.

LUCIA RUPRECHT is an affiliated lecturer in the Department of German and Dutch at the University of Cambridge and a Fellow of Emmanuel College. Her book, *Dances of the Self in Heinrich von Kleist, E.T.A. Hoffmann and Heinrich Heine* (2006), received a special citation for the de la Torre Bueno Prize. She coedited *Performance and Performativity in German Cultural Studies* (2003) as well as a special issue of *German Life and Letters* on cultural pleasure (2009). Her current project, carried out from 2005 to 2010 in collaboration with the research center Kulturen des Performativen at the Free University Berlin, deals with charisma and virtuosity as key terms of an aesthetic of performance around 1900.

MAAIKE BLEEKER is professor and chair of theater studies at Utrecht University. In addition to her academic career, she works as a dramaturge for various theater directors, choreographers, and visual artists. She is the author of *Visuality in the Theatre: The Locus of Looking* (2008), editor of *Anatomy Live: Performance and the Operating Theatre* (2008), and coeditor of *Parallax 46: Installing the Body* (2008) and *Body Check: Relocating the Body in Contemporary Performing Art* (2002).

FRANZ ANTON CRAMER is a Fellow at the Collège international de philosophie in Paris and teaches at the University of the Arts in Berlin. He contributes regularly to the dance press and holds workshops on the history of contemporary dance, dance criticism, and related issues. He was managing director of the Dance Archive in Leipzig, and researcher in residence at the Centre national de la danse near Paris. Since 2007 he has been project coordinator for the national dance heritage program launched by Tanzplan Deutschland. Recent publications include the study *In aller Freiheit: Tanzkultur in Frankreich zwischen 1930 und 1950* (2008), and the internet platform on dance, www.digitaler-atlas-tanz.de (2011).

KATE ELSWIT became a fellow in the Andrew W. Mellon Fellowship of Scholars in the Humanities at Stanford University after finishing her PhD in 2009 at the University of Cambridge. Her past and present teaching includes Stanford, CalArts, Laban, and Cambridge. Her 2008 *Modern Drama* essay won the Sally Banes Publication Prize from the American Society for Theatre Research, and her 2009 *TDR: The Drama Review* essay won the Gertrude Lippincott Award from the Society of Dance History Scholars. Her essays have also appeared in *Performance Research* and *Art Journal*. She is currently finishing a book entitled *Watching Weimar Dance*, forthcoming from Oxford University Press.

SUSANNE FRANCO is assistant professor at the University of Salerno and teaches dance history at the University IUAV of Venice. She is the author of *Martha Graham* (2003, 2nd ed. 2006) and the editor of *Ausdruckstanz: il corpo, la danza e la critica*, a special issue of Biblioteca Teatrale (2006). In collaboration with the Centre national de la danse she coedited, with Marina Nordera, *Dance Discourses. Keywords in Dance Research* (2007; originally published as *I discorsi della danza. parole chiave per una metodologia della ricerca*, 2005). With Marina Nordera she also coedited *Ricordanze. Memoria in movimento e coreografie della storia* (2010). She is the editor of the book series "Dance for Word/Dance Forward: Interviste sulla coreografia contemporanea," in which appeared her own book on *Frédéric Flamand* (2004).

SUSAN FUNKENSTEIN researches depictions of dance in Weimar visual culture. Her essays have appeared in *Modernism/Modernity*, *German Studies Review*, *Gender and History*, *Woman's Art Journal*, and *Women in German Yearbook*. At work on her book *Visualizing Weimar Dance: Gender, Body, Modernity*, she has taught at Carnegie Mellon University, the University of Pittsburgh, the University of Wisconsin-Madison, and the University of Wisconsin-Parkside.

JENS RICHARD GIERSDORF is associate professor of dance at Marymount Manhattan College in New York City. He received his PhD in dance history and theory from the University of California-Riverside and a Magister in dance, theater, and music theater theory from the University of Leipzig. His research focuses on training and disciplining of bodies in dance and other movement practices and choreographies of resistance to normative identity constructs in national and global contexts. His book titled *The Body of the People: East German Dance from 1945 to the Present* is forthcoming from the University of Wisconsin Press.

YVONNE HARDT is professor of applied dance studies and choreography at the University of Music and Dance in Cologne. Previously, she helped create the first master program in dance studies at the Free University in Berlin and taught in the Department of Theatre, Dance, and Performance Studies at the University of California-Berkeley. In addition to her academic career, Hardt has pursued a career as a dancer and choreographer with her company BodyAttacksWord. She is the author of *Politische Körper: Ausdruckstanz, Choreographien des Protest und die Arbeiterkulturbewegung in der Weimarer Republik* (2004) and *Sasha Waltz* (2007) as well as the coeditor of *Tanz—Metropole—Provinz* (2007).

SABINE HUSCHKA is a guest professor at the Free University in Berlin, where she teaches in the master program of dance studies and in theatre studies. She studied German literature at the University of Hamburg, graduating in cultural studies at the Humboldt University in Berlin. The recipient of grants from the German Research Foundation, she is the editor of *Wissenskultur Tanz* (2009) and the author of *Moderner Tanz: Konzepte-Stile-Utopien* (2002) and *Merce Cunningham und der Moderne Tanz* (2000). She has also been active as a dance critic and dance dramaturge.

CLAUDIA JESCHKE is professor of dance studies at the University of Salzburg and director of the Derra de Moroda Dances Archives. Her body of publications focuses on dance history and theory as well as on movement research and notation. She is the author of *Tanz als BewegungsText: Analysen zum Verhältnis von Tanztheater und Gesellschaftstanz 1900–1960* (2000) and coauthor of the recent publication *Interaktion und Rhythmus: Zur Modellierung von Fremdheit im Tanztheater des 19. Jahrhundert* (2010). She has restaged dances from the eighteenth through the twentieth centuries and has collaborated with Ann Hutchinson Guest to reconstruct Nijinsky's *L'Apres midi d'un faune* from the artist's original notation system.

MARION KANT earned her PhD in musicology at Humboldt University in Berlin, and she currently teaches at the University of Cambridge. She is the author of *Giselle* (2001) and *Hitler's Dancers: German Modern Dance and the Third Reich* (2003) and editor of the *Cambridge Companion to Ballet* (2007). Together with musicians Marshall Taylor and Samuel Hsu she has organized and presented a series of concerts commemorating *Entartete Musik*, music forbidden by the Nazis.

GABRIELE KLEIN is professor for movement and dance studies and director of performance studies at the University of Hamburg. Her research interests include movement and the body, sociology of culture and arts, dance studies, gender studies, and urban sociology. She is the author of *Der Choreographische Baukasten* (2011), *Electronic Vibration: Pop Kultur Theorie* (1999), and *FrauenKörperTanz: Eine Zivilisationsgeschichte des Tanzes* (1992); coauthor of *Is This Real? Die Kultur des HipHop* (2003); editor of *Tango in Translation* (2009); and coeditor of *Bewegungsraum und Stadtkultur* (2008), *Methoden der Tanzwissenschaft* (2007), *Performance* (2005), and *Tanz-Theorie-Text* (2002).

KAREN MOZINGO is a lecturer at The Ohio State University, where she also held a Presidential Fellowship to complete her dissertation on the choreography of exiled dancers Valeska Gert, Lotte Goslar, and Pola Nirenska. She received her MFA in dance from the University of North Carolina at Greensboro and her MA from Case Western Reserve University.

TRESA RANDALL is assistant professor of dance at Ohio University. Her writing has appeared in *Dance Research Journal*, *Theatre Journal*, and *Tanz-Metropole-Provinz*, edited by Yvonne Hardt and Kirsten Maar. She served on the Congress on Research in Dance Editorial Board as proceedings editor from 2007 to 2010 and served on the Ohio Arts Council Panel for Arts Criticism in 2009.

GERALD SIEGMUND is currently professor for dance studies and head of the MA program "Choreography and Performance" at the Justus-Liebig University in Giessen. He studied theatre, English, and French literature at the Goethe University in Frankfurt/Main and previously taught at the University of Berne. Author of numerous articles on contemporary dance and theater performance, he is the editor of *William Forsythe—Denken in Bewegung* (2004) and the author of *Theatre als Gedächtnis* (1999) and *Abwesenheit: Eine performative Ästhetik des Tanzes* (2006).

CHRISTINA THURNER is professor at the Institute of Theater Studies at the University of Berne. She studied in Zurich and Berlin and previously taught at Basle University. The recipient of grants from the Swiss National Foundation, she is the author of *Der andere Ort des Erzählens* (2003) and *Beredte Körperbewegte Seelen: Zum Diskurs der doppelten Bewegung in Tanztexten* (2009) and coeditor of *Original and Revival: Geschichts-schreibung im Tanz* (2010). Since 1996 she has been a dance journalist working mainly for *Neue Zürcher Zeitung*.

Index

absolute dance, Wigman's, 81, 133, 135
Abstraktion und Einfühlung (Abstraction and Empathy) [Worringer], 69
Académie Royale de la danse, 210
Academy of Arts (East Berlin), 136, 139, 140, 145n16, 146n26
"aesthetic gymnastics" (*Tanzgymnastik*), 6. *See also* gymnastics
affective correspondence between stage and audience, dance as, 17–30; ballet reform and, 2, 20–25, 26, 28n13; universal effect of language of dance, notion of, 19–20, 23, 25–27
Affectos Humanos (Human Affects) [Hoyer], 225, 226, 227, 235–36
Agamben, Giorgio, 204, 205
agency: corporeal, 167; in dancing with letters, 211; outside dancers' bodies, Waltz's representation of, 172–73, 179; returned to body by Fabian, 175, 179–80
Aitchison, Bill, 232, 242, 243, 244, 245n1
Albers, Josef, 46
Alexander, Matthias, 234
Alf, Fé, 85, 86–87
Alie/N(a)Ction (Forsythe), 206–8, 209, 211; stage environment for, 207–8; working process leading to choreography of, 206–7
alienation, Gert's techniques of artistic, 114
Allard, Marie, 22
Allee Der Kosmonauten (Waltz), 167–73; audience as passive consumers of spectacle in, 173; bodies and props equalized in, 170–72; comparison to Fabian's *Pax Germania*, 173–74; limitations of, 172–74; methodology for creating, 169–70, 181n6; spatial and physical constellations in, 172; stereotypes employed in, 172
Allgemeine Theorie der Schönen Künste (General Theory of the Fine Arts) [Sulzer], 17
alterity: construction of, 32; Hahn's definition of, 31; Lola Montez's marketing of public and private, 40–42; in mid-nineteenth century dance world, criteria for defining, 41; as mode of emancipation, 31, 42; Montez's staging of different levels of, 38; Montez's strategies of consuming and producing, 32–33
Althusser, Louis, 213
amateur dance culture: dance as life reform and, 81–83; Holm's assessment of American students and, 87; school as community and, 83–85
American Guild for German Cultural Freedom, 127n10
American modern dance. *See* modern dance
American *Tanzgemeinschaft*, Holm and, 79–98; American migration, 92–94; assessing American rhythms, 85–88; dance as life reform, 81–83; political tensions, 89–92; school as community, 83–85
Amerikanismus, Weimar-era German discourse on, 86–87
Andersen, Hans Christian, 104

Angiolini, Gasparo, 25
anthropology, dance expressing new directions taken in German, 21
antifascism, 132, 134, 142–43
Arbeau, Thoinot, 210, 212, 238
Arbeitsgemeinschaft (working community), ideal of, 83, 84–85
Archive and the Repertoire, The (Taylor), 221
Archive Fever ("Mal d'archive") [Derrida], 224
archiving, 223–30; analytical understanding as archival tool for dance, 229; as dynamic process, 224; embedded in process of re/constructing, 224; repoliticized, 224
art, socialist realist approach to, 149–50, 152–53, 158; in *A New Midsummer Night's Dream*, 154–57
art history of the East, interest in, 160, 164n60–62
artistic research, 234. *See also* knowledge, dance and; *Konzepttanz* (conceptual dance); lecture performance(s)
artist twin (Deuffert and Plischke), 239, 246n22
arts and science, lecture performance about confrontations between, 243
Assmann, Aleida, 217
Association of Theater Professionals of the GDR, 158
Ateliers D'Ora of Paris, 70
audience: dance as affective correspondence between stage and, 17–30; empathic involvement in *Véronique Doisneau*, 222–23; expectations about dance, bringing attention to, 227; importance in process of recognizing historical references, 220; interaction in Southern European dances, 33; participation in Fabian's *Pax Germania*, 176, 177–79, 181n14; participation in *Human Writes*, 202; self-reflexive attitude of, in lecture performances, 235, 236
Aufbau (German-Jewish newspaper), 118, 119, 127n29
Ausdruckstanz (dance of expression), 4–8, 63, 66, 101, 102, 105, 197n6, 227; development of, 158–59; dominance in German avant-garde dance, 233–34; exhibition (1993) staged at Academy of Arts in Berlin on history of, 5; Gert on, 125; Goslar's critique of, 103; Goslar's departure from tragic moods and narratives of, 100; Nazi ideals supported by expressionist modernism of, 5, 105; paradox of, Goslar's *Valse Very Triste* exposing, 105; pioneer dancers' downfall after 1936 mythologized, 104, 105. *See also* Hoyer, Dore; Laban, Rudolf; Palucca, Gret; Wigman, Mary
Austin, John L., 244
avant-garde, 53, 217; attempts to uncover body as source of knowledge, 234–35; Bauhaus women's notions of themselves as both within and outside of, 57; in cities, 247; Josephine Baker and, 71; lecture performance and, 233–35, 237–38, 239; Palucca as, 45, 49, 52, 57; Weidt and, 140, 143; Western conceptions of art, socialist rejection of, 150
"Avenue of Cosmonauts" (*Allee der Kosmonauten*) [Waltz], 167–73

Bach, Rudolf, 103
Bahr, Ehrhard, 129n72
Baker, Josephine, 71
Bakhtin, Mikhail, 250
Bal, Mieke, 223
ballet: *ballet de cour* vs. *ballet d'action*, 22, 197n4; court, 17, 20, 22, 23, 210, 211; in East Germany, 148, 150, 151, 154–57, 159; eighteenth-century redefinition of, 18; Forsythe's questioning of language and codes of, in 1980s, 206; post-war ballet boom, 4, 5, 187; quoting, 219, 222; representations of women, fairy godmothers as modernist critique of, 107–9; representative form of French, 20; traditional hierarchical nature of, 222; Vogelsang's comparison of modern dance and, 138–39. *See also* discourse of dance, eighteenth-century
ballet reform, 2, 20–25, 26, 27, 28n13
ballroom dance in 19th century, 35
Bandoneon (Bausch), 249
Barchan, Pawel, 48
Barrault, Jean Louis, 140
Barzun, Lucretia, 91, 98n57
Bauhaus: contradictory attitudes and policies about women, 46, 49; Goslar's exposure to, 102; gymnastics classes at, 57–59; ideal of unity vs. fractured reality of, 46; metal workshop, 52; modernism, 55–57; Palucca and, 45–62; Palucca's family connections with, 48, 49; Palucca's 1925 dance concert at, 46, 48–49, 55; photo-

Index

graphic experimentation, 57; Schlemmer at, 6, 47; typography, 51–52, 59
Bauman, Zygmunt, 252
Bausch, Pina, 4, 126, 129n73, 134, 157, 167, 183, 184–90, 196, 249, 257; aesthetics of movement, 184–87, 188; *Bandoneon*, 249; in *Café Müller*, 184–87, 189; feelings as scenes for, 188–90; *Das Frühlingsopfer* (Rite of Spring), 186, 189; gestures of innate knowledge, 188–90; *Rough Cut*, 190; Schmidt on, 197n5; theatre of experience and, 182, 196n2; theatricality, method, and materiality of, 187–88; Wigman and, 8; Wigman and, comparison between, 182, 183
Baxmann, Inge, 82, 197n5
Bayadère, La (Petipa), 222
Bayer, Herbert, 52
Beauchamps, Pierre, 210
beauty: Lola Montez's writing on, 39–40, 44n29, 44n32; marketing of beauty products, 44n32
Beggar Bar, 114, 118, 119, 120
"being moved" (*Ergriffen-Sein*), aesthetic of experience of, 182–99; Bausch and, 183, 184–90, 196; spaces of emotion, 183–84; Wigman and, 183, 184, 190–96
Beiswanger, George W., 94
Bel, Jérôme, 217, 239, 241; *Véronique Doisneau*, 219, 221–23
Benjamin, Walter, 166, 180n1, 252
Bereska, Dussia, 68, 73
Berger, Peter, 254
Berlin, Gert's return to (1949), 120–25; death pieces, 124–25; reviews of postwar appearances, 121, 122–24; shift in performance methods, 122, 123, 125
Berlin State Opera's Ballet company, 159
Berlin Wall, fall of (1989), 132; double perspective on choreographed response to, 166–67; impact on socialist countries, 165; reconstructing physicality of walk across border, 165–66. *See also* East German corporeality in contemporary choreography
Berlin Wall checkpoints, 166, 180n2
Bhabha, Homi, 250, 252
Biedermeier, 121, 128n46
Bienert, Friedrich "Fritz," 48, 49
Bienert, Ida, 48
Bienert, Ise, 48
Biermann, Wolf, 162n40
Blecher, Miriam, 91

Bleeker, Maaike, 9, 232–46
Boas, Franziska, 91
bodilessness, choreographing sensation of, 191–93, 194; turning movement and, 194, 195
body(ies): centrality of, in discourses on modernism, 59; dancing body as site of resistance, 175, 176, 179; Habeas Corpus and ownership of one's, 204; as linguistic entity, 238; melancholic awareness of impermanence of dancing, 3; pre-discursive status, assumption of, 3; redistribution of forces and bodies before the law, 204–6. *See also* East German corporeality in contemporary choreography
body and soul, discourse on relationship between, 20, 21; reciprocal relationships, 21–22, 25, 26
body culture, 234, 245n13; movements, 82
body images, dance used to "think through," 242
body language, 22–24, 166
body politics, 250
Böhme, Fritz, 141–42
Bohner, Gerhard, 4, 134
Borzik, Rolf, 198n13
bourgeoisie: bourgeois life reform, 82; dance as agent of increasing self-confidence of, 197n4; Gert and, 113, 114, 116, 121; Montez as both Spanish and bourgeois, 38–42
Boym, Svetlana, 113
Brandstetter, Gabriele, 2, 3, 10, 204, 235, 242
Brandt, Marianne, 50, 59; photomontage of Palucca, 52–54, 59
Brecht, Bertolt, 157, 174, 234; Gert and, 113, 114, 115; Palucca and, 139, 140, 145n18
Breuer, Marcel, 102
Brook, Peter, 234
Bücher, Karl, 82
Buenos Aires, tango locations in, 248
Bühne Im Bauhaus, Die (The Theater of the Bauhaus), 47
Burrows, Jonathan, 239
Burt, Ramsay, 220–21, 227
Buruma, Ian, 114
Byars, James Lee, 234

Café Müller (Bausch), 184–87, 189; touching, searching movements in, 184–85, 187; traces of memory mapped and framed in, 185–87

Cage, John, 234
Canaille (Riffraff) [Gert], 116
Carner, Mosco, 103
Carson, Ann, 208
Cartesian mind/body dualism, 244
Caspar, Golli, 68
Caspersen, Dana, 206–7, 208
Cell, The (Weidt), 140
censorship, social, 3
Centre International de Recherche Théâtrale, 234
Cerito, Fanny, 34
Chantier, Le (tango venue), 249
character, political-ideological demand for socialist development of, 151–53
Charles II, King, 204
Charmatz, Boris, 239
Choreographic Institute, 74
choreographic strategies to evoke historicity, 218–30; quoting, 218–23, 230n8; re/constructing and archiving, 9, 223–30
choreographic text, 212
choreography: choreographed response to opening of Berlin Wall, 166–67; choreographic figures of emotion, 184–87, 191–94; dancing with letters, 209–11; Forsythe's impossible choreographies, 203–4, 206–9; as law of moving, dancing body, 210; *Oxford English Dictionary* meaning of, 209–10; as peculiar invention of early modernity, 238; sketching, drawing, and notation as part of development of, 228–29; structuring confrontation of body and law, temporary communities produced through, 213; toward concept of, 203, 211–15; toward definition of, 203–4. *See also* East German corporeality in contemporary choreography
Choreosophie (Choreosophy), 67
Cibiec, Christiane, 188
ciné-dance genre, 74
cinema. *See* film projects, Laban's dance
citing. *See* quoting, evoking the past through
citizenship: body as precondition of personal autonomy as citizen, 204; human rights and, 205
city, dance and the, 247. *See also* cultural translation in dance, toward a theory of
classical dance: hierarchies involved in, 222; quoting, 219–21, 222. *See also* ballet
Classical Dance: The Dancer School (Klassischer Tanz: Die Schule des Tänzers) [Gommlich], 162n33

clowns, Goslar's, 7, 99–112; clown sketch series in autobiography, 99–100; comedy as alternative path for resistance, 105–7; in *The Disgruntled*, 102–3, 105; fairy godmother characters, 107–10; resistant history of female fools in German fairy tales and, 101, 111n10
clowns in modernist theater and dance, examples of, 111n12
Cold War, 131
Columbia University, "4 star" series at, 100
comedy as alternative path for resistance, 105–7
Comeriner, Erich, 51–52, 53, 54, 59
Communism, modern dance during years of, 132–33
community: developing, through group dance, 84–85, 88; school as, 83–85
Conceptual Art, 234
conceptual dance. *See Konzepttanz* (conceptual dance)
conceptual persona, 244
conferences, historic dance, 233–34
contemporary dance, engagements with the past in, 217–31; quoting and, 218–21, 230n8; quoting the repertoire and, 221–23; re/constructing and archiving, 223–30, 230n6, 243, 244. *See also Konzepttanz* (conceptual dance)
contemporary dance, lecture performance as. *See* lecture performance(s)
Content of Form, The (White), 223
contracts for intellectuals, East German, 136, 144n14
Coolemans, Fred, 89
Corbett, Mary Jean, 38, 44n37
corporeal agency, 167
corporeal identity, awareness of one's own, 166, 180n3
corporeality of Southern European dances, 33
court ballet, 17, 20, 22, 23, 210, 211
Cramer, Franz Anton, 7, 8, 147–64
Crary, Jonathan, 76
crystalline structure of icosahedron in Laban's dance theory, 69–70, 71
cultural community (*Gemeinschaft*), 76, 82, 84
cultural conventions/differences, 26, 30n46; political tensions of 1930s and, 91
cultural films (*Kulturfilme*), 65, 67, 70, 75
cultural memory, 9, 217, 218, 250
cultural relativism, 214
cultural studies, German, 2–4, 9

cultural translation in dance, toward a theory of, 247–58; dance as a cultural narrative, 254–55; dance as cultural translation, 253–54; global dances, local practices, 248–49; postcolonial theory and, 251–53; transcultural identities and, 255–57; transnationalism and transcultural translation in age of globalization, 249–51
culture: globalization as migration of, 251; of Human Rights, as aim of *Human Writes*, 203; as political stage, 253; as a unity, 252
Cunningham, Merce, 227, 234, 237; *Points in Space*, 222

Dalcroze, Emile Jaques, 102, 236
Dalcroze Rhythmic Gymnastics, 85, 234
dance: as cultural narrative, 254–55; as cultural translation, 253–54; development as autonomous art form in the West, 238; integration of art into socialist life and, 148, 150–51; as practice from which subjectivities emerge as "eject" of modes of conduct, 240; reform between two world wars, 5; role in pervasive myth of *Gemeinschaft*, 82, 84; transitory character of, 217
Dance Archive in Leipzig, 160
"dance community" (*Tanzgemeinschaft*), 5
Dance Community-Quarterly of Dance Culture (*Die Tanzgemeinschaft-Vierteljahresschrift für tänzerische Kultur*), 81–82
Dance Curves ("Tanzkurven") [Kandinsky], 49–50, 57, 59, 61n18
dance-drama (*Tanzdrama*), 76
dance history (*Tanzgeschichte*), 10. See also history
Dance Observer (periodical), 91
Dancers' Contest, The (*Tänzerwettstreit, Der*) [film], 147–48
Dancer World, The (*Welt des Tänzers, Die*) [Laban], 67
"dance science" or "dance studies" (*Tanzwissenschaft*), 10; expansion of object of analysis, 239; infrastructure for dance studies, changing, 10
Dance Theater Stories (*Tanztheatergeschichten*) [Hoghe], 187
dance writing, 3–4
Dauberval, Jean, 22
death: Gert's death pieces, 124–25; Wigman's gesture of, 194–96

Death (*Der Tod*) [Gert], 124
de Certeau, Michel, 228, 241
deconstruction, cultural translation and, 252
Decreation (Forsythe), 208–9
Deleuze, Gilles, 240–41, 244
democracy: compelling law to assume care of the body, 204–5; performance of, 211
de-nazification of Germany, 131, 134, 142
Derrida, Jacques, 224, 244
dervishes, dances of, 194, 199n27
Descartes, René, 21, 232
Deuffert, Katrin, 8, 239–40, 241
Deutsche Allgemeine Zeitung, 141
Deutsche Oper, 158
Deutscher Gymnastik Bund (German Gymnastic League), 68
Deutscher Tanz (German Dance), 5. See also *Ausdruckstanz* (dance of expression)
Dewey, John, 85
discourse analysis, 3. See also discourse of dance, eighteenth-century; Spanish dance in 19th century
discourse of dance, eighteenth-century, 17–30; ballet reform and, 2, 20–25, 26, 27, 28n13; books on gesture, 24; dance as universal emotional force in, 19–20, 23, 25–27; limitations on reception of dance, 25–26; metaphors of performer-spectator relationship, 25; sensualist aesthetics of effect, 18, 20, 21, 23, 26; stage performer stylized into human of self-conscious emotions through, 24
Disgruntled, The (Goslar), 102–3, 105
dispositif: dance functioning as, 240–41, 244; reality-producing potential of, 241
Doisneau, Véronique, 219, 221–23
Dominguez, Juan, 239
Dönitz, Karl, 131
Donna Della Dondolo, La (Goslar), 107–9
"double past," Germany's preoccupation with, 6
Drachentöterei (Dragon Slaying) [Laban], 68, 69
Draeger, Volkmar, 156
Drehmonotonie (Wigman), 191–94, 195
Dudley, Jane, 90, 91
Dujarier, Alexandre Henri, 43n20
Duncan, Isadora, 102, 104

East German corporeality in contemporary choreography, 7–8, 165–81; double perspective on choreographed response to opening of Berlin Wall, 166–67; Fabian's

Pax Germania and, 173–80; Waltz's *Allee der Kosmonauten* and, 167–73, 179

East German dance, politics of, 7, 130–46; "Between Idealism and Ideology: Dance in the GDR, 1949 to 1956" (exhibition), 160n2; Böhme and, 141–42; five-year plan (1976–1980) and, 157–58; fragments remaining, 132–33; harmonization of societal and personal goals, five-year plan (1976–1980) and, 157–58; Palucca and, 135–37, 143, 145n16, 145n18, 145n24, 146n26; *Stunde Null* as moment of redefinition, 132–33, 134, 135, 142, 143; Vogelsang and, 137–40, 142, 143; Weidt and, 132, 140–41, 142, 143, 146n29; Wigman and, 133–35, 143, 144n11

East Germany, 132, 149–64; antifascist credentials, legitimacy based on, 142–43; erasure of regime, 131–32; founding of, dispute over realism after, 148, 149–51; government-built suburbs in, 169; increasing prosperity in early 1970s, 153–54, 162n40; individual and collective movements in late 1980s in, 177, 180; national identification after fall of Berlin Wall, 165; need for intellectuals, 136; new brand of theater in, 175; publications on Palucca from, 60n9; research on history of dance in, 160, 163n58; Stasi in, 130, 131, 132, 166, 170, 176; subculture of 1970s and 1980s distanced from structures of socialist system, 174–75; *Tanztheater* in (1966–1989), 7, 152, 153–64; unjust state theory of, 132

Egk, Werner, 105, 162n38

Eidos:Telos (Forsythe), 209

eighteenth-century aesthetic discourse on dance. *See* discourse of dance, eighteenth-century

Einzelverträge (East German contracts for intellectuals), 136, 144n14

Eisenstein, Sergei, 113

Eisner, Lotte, 66

El Arranque, 248–49

El Oleano (Spanish dance), 33, 34–35, 43n15

Elsaesser, Thomas, 66

Elssler, Fanny, 33, 34, 37, 41

Elswit, Kate, 7, 8, 113–129

emancipation. *See* freedom

Emmel, Felix, 82

emotion(s): choreographic figures of, 184–87, 191–94; communication between performers and audience founded on knowledge of, 24–25, 29n33; language of, 17; privileging of, in eighteenth century, 23; as soul set in motion, 21; spaces of, 183–84

"emotive formulas" (*Pathosformeln*) of power, 195–96, 199n36

Engel, Johann Jakob, 23

Enters, Agna, 100

entertainment, dialectic between development of character in socialist national culture and, 151–53

Erdmann, Paul, 38

Erfahrungen (shared corporeal and cultural experiences), 182

Ergriffen-Sein. *See* "being moved" (*Ergriffen-Sein*), aesthetic of experience of

escuela bolera, 33

estrangement as performance technique, Gert's theories of, 7, 115–25; outside of Germany, 118–20; played in Weimar Republic, 115–17; upon return to Germany (1949), 120–25

Etchell, Tim, 241

eurhythmics, 234

European culture of dance: characteristics attributed to Southern European dances, 33–34; transformed by immigrants, 250

Evan, Blanche, 91

Exhausting Dance: Performance and the Politics of Movement (Lepecki), 210, 240

exile, fashionable idea of, 114

exile modernism: Bahr's propositions on, 129n72; fundamental political component of, 124

exile research, on women, 99; autobiographical practices and, 101. *See also* Gert, Valeska; Goslar, Lotte

experience, theatre of, 182, 196n2. *See also* "being moved" (*Ergriffen-Sein*), aesthetic of experience of

expression, dance of. *See Ausdruckstanz* (dance of expression)

expression in dance, theory of, 187

expressionism, 46, 54; second generation of expressionist dancers, 225, 235; Weimar cinema and, 66; Worringer's Abstraction and Empathy treatise and, 69. *See also* Hoyer, Dore; Laban, Rudolf; Palucca, Gret; Wigman, Mary

Fabian, Jo, 7, 166, 173–80; agency returned to body by, 175, 179–80; comparison of

Waltz and, 167, 173–74; disengagement from socialist system, 174–75; double perspective of walk from East to West, 167; labeled as "East German Robert Wilson," 175; *Pax Germania* production, 173–80; utilization of slow motion, 174

Fachschule für künstlerischen Tanz Berlin (Vocational School for Artistic Dance), 138

fairy tales: Goslar's fairy godmother characters, 107–10; Goslar's parody of, 103–4, 107–9; resistant history of female fools in German, 101, 111n10

Farfan, Penny, 105, 106

Feininger, Andreas, 55–57, 61n29

Feininger, Lyonel, 48, 55

Feininger, T. Lux, 55, 56, 57, 58, 61n29

Feister, Karin, 150–51, 154; analysis of *A New Midsummer's Night Dream*, 156–57

Feldenkrais, Moshe, 234

Fellini, Federico, 126n7

Felsenstein, Walter, 139, 140, 153, 162n39

femininity: Goslar's challenge to ballet's representation of, 103; Montez's self-fashioning through stylized, 31, 32, 36, 38–39, 40, 42; Palucca as model of New Woman, 47, 48–49, 52–54, 57, 59, 101; of Palucca in 1925 Bauhaus performance, 55; Wigman's expression of feminine "witchness" as otherness, 103. *See also* gender; New Woman

Fernandes, Ciane, 198n9

Festkultur (festive culture), Laban's idea of, 72

Feuillet, Raoul Auger, 75, 210, 212

fiction and reality, border between, 223, 228

Fighting League for German Culture, 89

film projects, Laban's dance, 63–78; awareness of vision/knowledge/power relationship, 66; classification of, 65; golden age of world cinema and, 66; materials related to, 64–65; merging of interests in, 66; ways of showing and seeing dance, 67–73; written images and notated movements for visual pleasures, 73–76

Fischer-Lichte, Erika, 29n33, 246n24

"folk community" (*Volksgemeinschaft*), 5

fools, female, 101, 111n10

foreignness of Gert. *See* estrangement as performance technique, Gert's theories of

Forsythe, William, 9–10, 200–216; *Alie/N(a)Ction*, 206–8, 209, 211; dancing with letters, 209–11; *Decreation*, 208–9; *Eidos:Telos*, 209; *Heterotopia*, 209; *Human Writes*, 200–204, 205, 206, 208, 209, 211, 212–14, 215; impossible choreographies of, 203–4, 206–9; *Kammer/Kammer*, 209; *LDC*, 209; redistribution of forces and bodies before the law, 204–6; *Self Meant to Govern*, 209; toward a concept of choreography, 203, 211–15; writing the human, 200–204

Foucault, Michel, 240, 241

Fraktur typeface, 51, 52

framing of scene, as substitute for quotation marks, 219; in *Giszelle*, 220; in *Urheben Aufheben*, 225–26; in *Véronique Doisneau*, 221–22

Franco, Susanne, 6, 8, 63–78

Franko, Mark, 210, 227

Fraser, Nancy, 253

free dance, 82, 158, 234

freedom: alterity as mode of emancipation, 31, 42; Forsythe's impossible choreographies and, 206, 208; kinesthetic, 102, 104; Palucca's representation of female liberation, 49

Free University in Berlin, 10; Körper-Inszenierungen (Staging the Body) at, 240, 246n24

Freikörperkultur (movement for free body culture), 67

Frühlingsopfer, Das (Rite of Spring) [Bausch], 186, 189

Funkenstein, Susan, 6, 8, 45–62

Gallo, Regine, 68

Gautier, Théophile, 36, 43n20

Gay, Peter, 114

GDR. *See* East Germany

Gedanken zum Neuen Künstlerischen Tanzes (Thoughts on the New Artistic Dance) [Vogelsang], 139

Geiger, Willi, 70

Geistige Emigration, Die (The Intellectual Emigration) [Kaufmann], 99, 110n2

Gemeinschaft (cultural community): role of dance in myth of, 82, 84; transition to mass culture from trope of, 76

gender: actress as prototype of unconventional woman, 38; complexity of Palucca's performance of, 46–47, 49; female spectatorship in 1920s, modes of, 54; modern Weimar woman, 52; Palucca as model of New Woman, 47, 48–49, 52–54,

57, 59, 101; tragic woman artist, myth of, 104. See also femininity; New Woman
General Theory of the Fine Arts (*Allgemeine Theorie der Schönen Künste*) [Sulzer], 17
Georgi, Yvonne, 112n25
German Academy of Arts and Sciences in Exile, 127n10
German anthropology, dance stylized as aesthetic expression of new directions taken in, 21
German cultural studies (*Kulturwissenschaft*), 2–4, 9
German Dance Archive, 225
German dance congresses, historical, 233–34
German Dance School (*Meisterwerkstätten*), 142
German Democratic Republic. See East Germany
German émigré experience in United States, 6–7. See also Gert, Valeska; Goslar, Lotte; Holm, Hanya
German Gymnastic League (Deutscher Gymnastik Bund), 68
"Germanness" of dance in Germany, 237
German reunification: changing infrastructure for dance studies after, 10; eradication of East German history with, 165; fall of Berlin Wall as step toward, 165; migration from East German suburbs after, 169; *Tanztheater* and, 159–60; unemployment after, 169; violence against immigrants after, 206. See also East German corporeality in contemporary choreography
German Society for Dance Notation, 74
German studies (*Germanistik*), 2–4
Germany, de-nazification of, 131, 134, 142
Gert, Valeska, 7, 101, 102, 113–29, 132; artist as outsider pushing aesthetic and social boundaries, 114, 115–17; audience in Weimar Republic of, 115, 116–17; audience reception in New York, 118–19; on *Ausdruckstanz*, 125; *Canaille* (Riffraff), 116; chronological overview of, 113–14; Death (*Der Tod*), 124; death pieces, 124–25; emigration to U.S. (1939), 114; forced migration, 114, 118–20; German archival collections of material on, 127n8; narrating otherness, 125–26; *Der Remigrant* (The Remigrant), 121–22; remigration to Germany, 114–15, 120–25; *The Strange Journey of Professor Blitz*, 124, 129n57; thematic engagement with low culture, 115
gesture: books on, 24; language of, 18, 22, 23, 24, 29n23
Giersdorf, Jens Richard, 3, 7–8, 165–81
Gilbert, Eliza. See Montez, Lola
Giszelle (Le Roy and Salamon), 219–21, 222, 231n13
Gitelman, Claudia, 92
global dances, local practices of, 248–49
globalization: as migration of culture, 251; transnationalism and transcultural translation in age of, 249–51
Gluck, Christoph Willibald, 134
Goebbels, Joseph, 142
Goethe, J. W. von, 3
Gommlich, Werner, 153, 162n33
Goodman, Nelson, 219
Goslar, Lotte, 7, 99–112; alternative discourse within exile studies, 107; artistic strategies in exile, 100–101; comedy as alternative path for resistance for, 105–6; critique of *Ausdruckstanz*, 103; *The Disgruntled*, 102–3, 105; *La Donna Della Dondolo*, 107–9; double parody with *Waltzmania*, 102, 103–4; emerging style, 102; emigration/exile to U.S., 100, 110n6; fairy godmother characters challenging closed narratives of history and women's representation, 107–10; first clown character, 102–3; *Grandma Always Danced*, 109–10; studying dance, 100, 102; Thornton's categories of dances of, 110n6; *Valse Very Triste* (Very Sad Waltz), 105–6
Graff, Ellen, 92
Graham, Martha, 79, 90, 93, 100; Goslar compared to, 105; Holm's description of work of, 88
Grandma Always Danced (Goslar), 109–10
Grimm, Brothers, 103, 104
Gronberg, Tag, 53
Gropius, Ise, 50
Gropius, Walter, 50, 52, 58, 102
Grosch, Karla, 57–58, 62n32
Grosz, Elisabeth, 225
Grotewohl, Otto, 137
group dance, developing community through, 84–85, 88
Gruppenform-Lehrfilm (educational film about group forms), 77n10
Gsovsky, Tatjana, 145n19
Guattari, Félix, 244

gymnastics: aesthetic, 6; Dalcroze Rhythmic Gymnastics, 85; Laban and, 68, 71; Palucca's dance style and, 48, 49, 57–59; Wigman's system of dance-gymnastics, 81, 82–83, 86, 87, 94
Gymnastics for Children (*Kindes Gymnastik, Des*) [Laban], 68
Gymnastik und Tanz (Gymnastics and Dance) [Laban], 68

Habeas Corpus act of 1679, 204, 205
Habermas, Jürgen, 6
Haeckel, Ernst, 69
Hahn, Alois, 31, 32
Hamburg Dramaturgy (Lessing), 21
Hanya Holm and Group of New York Wigman School of Dance, 93
Hanya Holm Company, 93
Hanya Holm Studio, 92
Hardt, Yvonne, 9, 217–31
Hasting, Hanns, 85
Haunted Screen, The (Eisner), 66
Heilbut, Anthony, 128n39
Heterotopia (Forsythe), 209
Hexentanz (Wigman), 102–3, 105
Hillje, Jens, 168
historicity, choreographic strategies to evoke, 218–30; quoting, 218–23, 230n8; re/constructing and archiving, 9, 223–30
history: of German Democratic Republic, Fabian's *Pax Germania* on, 175–80; narration for construction of, importance of, 223; as palimpsest, 130, 131, 135; performative notion of "doing history," 218; understood as construction based on needs of the present, 218. See also dance history; past in contemporary dance, engagements with the
Hitler, Adolf, 105, 131, 135. See also National Socialists (Nazis)
Hochschulübergreifendes Zentrum Tanz Berlin (Inter-University Center for Dance), 10
Hoerisch, Werner, 89
Hofmannsthal, Hugo von, 3
Hoghe, Raimund, 187
Hollaender, Friedrich, 120
Holm, Hanya, 6–7, 45, 79–98; accommodations to American modern dance, 90–92, 94; Americanization narrative about, 79–80, 94; assessing American rhythms, 85–88; break with Wigman School, 92; comparison of American and German modern dance, 88, 97n46; concept of dance, mandate of, 80, 81, 94; dance as life reform to, 81–83; dance company debut in Denver, Colorado (1936), 92–94; Demonstration Program, 91; as missionary for Wigman, 79, 82–83, 84; New York Wigman School, 79, 83–85, 89, 92; outreach to progressive education advocates, 85; political tensions and, 89–92; on 'primitive' dance, 83; recognition of, in America, 90; reoriented mission of, 93–94; in *Sarabande*, 80; true migration from Germany to U.S. (1936), 92–94
Holm, Klaus, 90
Hoogenboom, Marijke, 234
Horst, Louis, 90, 91
How Heavy Are My Thoughts (Müller), 232, 233, 237–38, 242–44, 245n1
Hoyer, Dore, 4; *Affectos Humanos* (Human Affects), 225, 226, 227, 235–36
Human Affects (*Affectos Humanos*) [Hoyer], 225, 226, 227, 235–36
human being, eighteenth-century German anthropological understanding of, 21
human rights: potential to be universalized, 214; refugees and, 203, 205; Universal Declaration of Human Rights, 201, 202, 203, 205, 213, 214
Human Writes (Forsythe and Thomas), 200–204, 205, 206, 208, 209, 211; aim of, 203; audience participation in, 202; interpellation of body by the law, 213, 215; performative process of iteration, 214; series of performances of, 215n1; as task-based performance, 212–14
Humphrey, Doris, 79, 90, 93, 100; Holm's description of work of, 88
Hurok, Sol, 79
Huschka, Sabine, 8, 182–99
Husemann, Pirkko, 235, 237, 243
hybridism, 250
hybrid space, space of translation as, 252

icosahedron, Laban's dance theory and crystalline structure of, 69–70, 71
idealism, as instrumental aspect of reality, 156
Ideas on Mime (*Ideen zu einer Mimik*) [Engel], 23
identity(ies): corporeal, awareness of one's own, 166, 180n3; cultural translation and transcultural, 255–57; narrative, 255, 258n21

Idol, Das (The Living Idol) [Laban], 68
Ihering, Herbert, 145n18
immigrants: as "cultural hybrid," 250; transformation of European dance culture by, 250; violence against, after German reunification, 206
impossible choreographies, 203–4, 206–9; *Alie/N(a)Ction*, 206–8, 209, 211; bodies and movements linked to specific chains of signifiers in, 208, 209; *Decreation*, 208–9; surplus of information created by maps in, 208
improvisation, contact, 168
"in-between": cultural translation exploring in-between spaces, 253; dispositif as, 241
incorporeality: soteriological image of, 195; Wigman's choreographing the sensation of, 191–93, 194, 195
inner emigration, 143n7
Institute for Applied Theater Studies (Giessen), 10
Institute for Theater Studies (Berne), 10
Intellectual Emigration, The (*Geistige Emigration, Die*) [Kaufmann], 99, 110n2
intellectuals, relationship between East German regime and, 136–37
intercorporeal space, 254
interculturality, 251
International Dance Day, 26–27
internationalism, 237
Inter-University Center for Dance (Hochschulübergreifendes Zentrum Tanz Berlin), 10
Italian Tarantella, 35
Itten, Johannes, 46

Jackson, Michael, 219
Jaques-Dalcroze, Emile, 234
Janik, Vicki, 111n10
Jarchow, Peter, 145n24
Jardin Mabille, 35
Jeschke, Claudia, 2–3, 11, 31–44, 189
Jewish Cultural Union (*Jüdischer Kulturbund*), 113
Jewish emigré artists, social place reserved for returning Weimar, 115, 121. See also Gert, Valeska
Jewish teachers and pupils, Wigman's treatment of, 89–90, 97n57
Johnson, Barbara, 252
Jooss, Kurt, 4, 68, 126, 133, 137, 145n18, 159
Jüdischer Kulturbund (Jewish Cultural Union), 113

Kaegi, Stefan, 241
Kammer/Kammer (Forsythe), 209
Kammertanzbühne Laban, 68
Kandinsky, Wassily, 45, 46, 48, 54, 102; "Tanzkurven" essay for *Palucca Tanz*, 49–50, 57, 58–59
Kant, Marion, 7, 8, 104, 130–46
Karsavina, Tamara, 71
Kaufmann, Arthur, 99
Kaufmann, Nicholas, 67
Keersmaeker, Anne Teresa de, 240, 246n23
Kessler, Frank, 240–41
Kindes Gymnastik, Des (Gymnastics for Children) [Laban], 68
kinesthetic freedom, 102, 104
Kinetographie or *Schrifttanz* (written dance), 74–76
Kirchner, Ernst Ludwig, 48
Klamt, Gustav, 72
Klamt, Jutta, 72
Klassischer Tanz: Die Schule des Tänzers (Classical Dance: The Dancer School) [Gommlich], 162n33
Klee, Felix, 50, 59
Klee, Paul, 45, 46, 48, 49, 50, 54, 57, 102
Klein, Gabriele, 11, 247–58
Kloepper, Louise, 90
knowledge, dance and, 9–10; dance as form of knowledge production, 233, 234–35, 244; innate knowledge, Bausch's gestures of, 188–90
Knowledge in Motion: Perspectives of Artistic and Scientific Research in Dance (2006 conference), 233, 234
Köhler-Richter, Emmy, 132
Köllinger, Bernd, 148, 149, 151, 152–53, 156, 158, 161n9
Komische Oper (Berlin): *Tanztheater* archives, 164n63; *Tanztheater* of, 153–57, 158, 159, 160; West German critics on, 163n47
Konzepttanz (conceptual dance), 4, 8–10; theoretical attitude, 8–9. See also artistic research; Deuffert, Katrin; historicity; knowledge, dance and; language; lecture performance(s); Le Roy, Xavier; Nachbar, Martin; past in contemporary dance, engagements with the; Plischke, Thomas; Salamon, Eszter
Kornhaas, Waltraud, 167
Körper (Waltz), 168–69
Körper-Inszenierungen (Staging the Body) at Free University in Berlin, 240, 246n24

Körperkulturbewegung, 68
Koser, 116, 117
Kresnik, Johann, 4, 157
Kreutzberg, Harald, 105, 112n25
Kubin, Felix, 241
Kulturfilme (cultural films), 65, 67, 70, 75
Kulturwissenschaft (German cultural studies), 2–4, 9
Kundera, Milan, 81
Kunstblatt, Das (journal), 49
Kuntze, Reinhold Martin, 82

Laban, film projects: *Befreiung des Körpers: Filmreportage über den Tanz, Die* (The Liberation of the Body: Dance Reportage), 72; Dance and Society (*Tanz und Gesellschaft*), 71; Dance Is Life (*Tanz Ist Leben*), 70–71, 74, 75; Dance of Humanity (*Tanz der Menschheit*), 72; *Drachentöterei* (Dragon Slaying), 68, 69; Film about the Harmonious Movement of Human Body (*Film über die Harmonische Bewegung des Menschlichen Körpers*), 73–74; "Filmpantomime," 63–64, 76n3; A Game of Cards (*Ein Spiel Karten*), 68; Ghost in the Casino (*Spuk im Spielklub*) [alternate title for Game of Cards/*Spiel Karten*], 68; *Das Lebende Bild* (The Living Picture), 75, 78n42
Laban, Rudolf, 5, 6, 63–78, 102, 104, 105, 133, 145n19, 159; Böhme's loyalty to, 141–42; career in public institutions, 64; cube, 207; dance theory, 68–71; dance works, *Das Idol* (The Living Idol), 68; dance works, *Orchidée* (Orchid), 68, 72, 73; dance works, *Schwingende Gewalten* (Swinging Powers), 68; departure from Germany, 64; disciples and audience of, cultural contexts of, 72; free dance concept, 234; interest in cinema, 63–65; movement choir, 72, 75, 77n10, 234; students of, 112n25; ways of showing and seeing dance, 67–73; written images and notated movements for visual pleasures, 73–76
Labanschule (Laban School), 63–64
Lang, Fritz, 72
language: body, 22–24, 166; body's prediscursive status, challenge to, 3; of emotions, 17; of gesture, 18, 22, 23, 24, 29n23; *Konzepttanz* and, 8–9; moving corporeal, ballet reform and, 2, 20–25, 26, 27, 28n13; thought movement and, 4. See also affective correspondence between stage and audience, dance as; "being moved" (*Ergriffen-Sein*), aesthetic of experience of; discourse of dance, eighteenth-century; lecture performance(s); writing, dance and
La Ribot, 239
Laurenti, Jean-Noel, 210
law, the, 200–216; interpellation of body by, 213, 215; of moving, dancing body, choreography as, 210; redistribution of forces and bodies before, 204–6; resistance and friction through unbridgeable gap between body and, choreography involving, 211–12; ruptured in choreography, *Human Writes* and, 201; spaces for subjects on the move and moving carved out in, 209; Universal Declaration of Human Rights, 201, 202, 203, 205, 213, 214
lay dance ensemble, 151
lay movement choirs, Laban's work with, 72, 75, 77n10, 234
LDC (Forsythe), 209
Lebensreformbewegung (life reform movement), 67–68
Le Breton, H. M., 22
lecture performance(s), 9, 232–46; dance as form of knowledge production in, 233, 234–35, 244; dance functioning as dispositif and, 240–41, 244; of Deuffert and Plischke, 8, 239–40, 241; *How Heavy Are My Thoughts* (Müller), 232, 233, 237–38, 242–44, 245n1; inviting expansion of dance studies' object of analysis, 239–40; Le Roy's *Product of Circumstances*, 236–38, 239, 245n12; self-reflexive attitude and, 235, 236; *Unfriendly Takeover* (Frankfurt), 241; *Urheben Aufheben* (Nachbar), 224, 225–28, 229, 235–36
leftist dance, 91–92
Lehmen, Thomas, 8, 239
Lepecki, André, 210, 238, 240
Le Roy, Xavier, 8, 217, 219–21, 222, 233, 239, 241; *Giszelle*, 219–21, 222, 231n13; *Product of Circumstances*, 236–38, 239, 245n12
Lessing, Gotthold Ephraim, 21, 29n33
letters, dancing with, 209–11
Letters on Dancing and Ballets (Noverre), 17–18
Liberated Theatre (Prague), 100
life reform, dance as, 81–83
life reform movement (*Lebensreformbewegung*), 67–68

linguistic entity, body as, 238
Linke, Susanne, 4, 134, 225
Liquid Modernity (Bauman), 252, 257n11
Living Idol, The (*Das Idol*) [Laban], 68
Longinovic, Tomislaw, 252
Louis XIV, 210
Lucian of Samosata, 25, 29n38
Luckmann, Thomas, 254
Ludwig I of Bavaria, 32, 34, 35, 38, 40, 42n6
Luhmann, Niklas, 256
Luley, Waltraud, 225
Lumley, Benjamin, 35, 40

Mabille, Charles, 35, 36, 43n16
Madách, Imre, 72
Maharaj, Sarat, 234
Malakhov, Vladimir, 159
"Mal d'archive" (*Archive Fever*) [Derrida], 224
Malerei Fotografie Film (Painting Photography Film) [Moholy-Nagy], 52
Mann, Erika, 100, 111n6, 120
Mann, Thomas, 127n10
Manning, Susan, 1–16, 79, 92, 104, 158–59; *Ecstasy and the Demon*, 103
Mantero, Vera, 239
Marey, Étienne, 74
marketing: by Montez, 36, 38–42, 44n37; professionalism and, 44n37
Martin, John, 79, 85, 90, 238, 242
Mary Wigman (1886–1973): When Fire Dances between Two Poles (film), 190
Mary Wigman Dancers, 91
Mary Wigman Studio, 134–35, 138
mass culture: Holm's critique of American mass consumption/production, 86, 87–88; mass literature of nineteenth century, 39; transition from cultural-historical trope of *Gemeinschaft* (community) to, 76
Master Workshops (Meisterwerkstätten), 142
materiality, Bausch's aesthetics of movement and, 188
Mauss, Marcel, 82
Maywood, Augusta, 43n16
McKnight, Nancy, 91
McManus, Donald, 101
Medea and Jason (Noverre), 18–20
Meisterwerkstätten (Master Workshops), 142
memory: appropriation through different levels of learning and, 229; cultural, 9,
217, 218, 250; repertoire enacting embodied, 221. *See also* past in contemporary dance, engagements with the
Mendelssohn, Moses, 21
Metropolis (film), 72–73
metropolis, Holm's critiques of, 88, 93
Michel, Artur, 119
milongas, 248–49
milonguero, 248
mimesis, 18, 19, 20, 22
mind/body dualism, Cartesian, 244
Minimalism, 234
modern dance, 71, 72; American, Goslar at juncture of dialectics within community, 100–101; American, Holm as one of pioneers of, 79; American, Holm's accommodations to, 90–92, 94; American, "humanist" wing of, 92; dance's essence and nature found in movement, assumption of, 238; German and American, similarity of, 105–6; as life reform, 81–83; reception of, Laban on, 76; rethinking of demarcating lines between contemporary dance and, 227; Vogelsang's revision of principles of modern movement system, 139, 140. See also *Ausdruckstanz* (dance of expression)
modernism: Bauhaus, 55–57; centrality of body in discourses on, 59; "fairy tale" entrapment of modernist dance narratives for women, 101; feminist critical discourse as defining feature of, 106; tensions and contradictions of (dance), 74
modernity: America as epitome of, 86, 87–88; choreography as invention of early, 238; dispositif as perspective on relationship between dance and, 240; doubled mystique of, 71; question of status of body in society, 189; Wigman's dance-gymnastics as solution to ailments of, 82–83, 86, 87
Moholy-Nagy, László, 45, 46, 48, 49, 52, 55, 56, 61n29, 102
Montez, Lola, 2, 31–44; as author of autobiography, 38–40, 44n27; on beauty, 39–40, 44n29, 44n32; brief biography of, 32, 42n7; caricature of, 37–38; as critic of critics, 40–42; critics' reactions to, 36–38, 40, 43n15; debut of, 33, 34–35, 40; dilettantism of, 31, 36; liaison with Ludwig I, 32, 34, 35, 38, 40, 42n6; marketing by, 36, 38–42, 44n37; performative elements of shows, 36, 43n21; repertoire

of, 35–36; self-fashioning of, 2, 31, 38–42; as Spanish dancer, 33–38; staging of different levels of alterity, 38; strategies of consuming and producing alterity, 32–33; successful writings, 31; use of the press, 32, 40–42
Moonwalk (Jackson), 219
Mother Tongues (Johnson), 252
movement: ontological bind between dance and, 238–39; of thought, 4, 243–44
movement for free body culture (*Freikörperkultur*), 67
movement notation, Laban's, 74–76
movement quotations, 218–23; in *Giszelle*, 219–21, 222, 231n13; physical challenges and preciseness necessary in, 220–21; in *Véronique Doisneau*, 219, 221–23
Mozingo, Karen, 7, 8, 99–112
Müller, Hedwig, 5, 8, 79, 82
Müller, Heiner, 174
Müller, Ivana, 232, 233, 237, 242–44, 245n1; *How Heavy Are My Thoughts*, 232, 233, 237–38, 242–44, 245n11
multiculturalism, 251

Nachbar, Martin, 8, 217, 224–29, 235–36; *Urheben Aufheben*, 224, 225–28, 229, 231n23, 235–36, 245n11
Nancy, Jean-Luc, 186
narration: importance for construction of history, 223; questions evoked by, 223; in *Urheben Aufheben*, 228; in *Véronique Doisneau*, use of, 221–22, 223
narrative: dance as cultural, 254–55; emphasizing idea of "the original," in retrospect, 256; in global dance cultures, 256; wide-reaching definition of, 255
narrative identity, 255, 258n21
national dances, emancipation from stage, 35–36
nationalist agenda, service of dance to, 105–6
National Socialists (Nazis): *Ausdruckstanz*'s support of ideals of, 5, 105; cultural agenda, 103, 104; Goslar's critique of, 102, 103; ideology, 76; ideology, German dance and body culture used as tool for diffusion of, 64; Laban's involvement with, 64; Laban's movement choirs under, 77n10; leftist dance protesting, 91–92; Master Workshops (Berlin), central dance institution under, 142; Nazi language, 96n29; place of Wigman schools in bureaucracy, 89–90, 97n57; surrender of (1945), 131; *völkisch* tradition and, 68; Wigman's collaboration with, 5, 80, 89–90, 92, 98n68, 197n6. *See also* Gert, Valeska; Goslar, Lotte
National Socialist Teachers League, 89
national state, idea of, 251–52
"natural" bodily expression, 22, 24; indirect nature of representation, contradiction between, 26
Naturphilosophie, German tradition of romantic, 69
neocapitalism, 252
Neuer Künstlerischer Tanz (new artistic dance): Palucca's, 136, 145n23; Vogelsang's, 139
New Historicism, 3
New Midsummer Night's Dream, A (Neuer Sommernachtstraum, Ein) [Schilling], 154–57; plot of, 154; as socialist-realist model work, 156; themes of, 154–56
New Objectivity, 52
New Theatre (leftist journal), 91
New Woman, Palucca as model of, 47, 48–49, 57, 101; Brandt's identification with, photomontage portraying, 52–54, 59; geometric abstraction fused with personal expression of, 59; typeface used to express, 52, 59. *See also* femininity; gender
New York, Wigman's legal battle with Sabbath Laws of, 96n35
New York Wigman School, 79, 83–85; curriculum of, 84–85; expectations of Holm at, 84; leftist dancers at, 92; obstacles felt by Holm at, 89; promotional literature on, 83; school as community, 83–85
Nicolai, Friedrich, 21
1984 (Orwell), 130
nineteenth century: alterity in mid-nineteenth century dance world, crtieria for defining, 41; ballroom dance in, 35; mass literature in, 39; Spanish dance in, 31–44; stage dance in, 35
Noë, Alva, 234–35
No Kidding (McManus), 101
nonverbal communication, 22–24
Norton, Sydney Jane, 119
notation system of Laban, 74–76
"Notes on the American Spirit" (Holm), 85
Novack, Cynthia, 227
Noverre, Jean-Georges, 17–20, 197n4; ballet reform and, 20, 28n13; on cultural dif-

ferences, 26; effective artist, conception of, 26; on language of words vs. gestures, 17–18, 23; on performer-spectator relationship, 25
nudism and dance, 242

Olympic Games 1936, 105
Orchésographie (Arbeau), 210, 238
Orchidée (Orchid) [Laban], 68, 72, 73
Orpheus (Gluck), 134
Orpheus-Stationen (Schilling), 158
Orwell, George, 130, 143
Ostermeier, Thomas, 168
"other Germany," exiles as keepers of, 115, 127n10
otherness: Spanish dancer as figure of, 2; two dimensions of being "other," 31. See also Gert, Valeska
Outsider as Insider, The (Gay), 114

pain, elevation to level of the transcendental through dance, 190–91, 194
Painting Photography Film (Malerei Fotografie Film) [Moholy-Nagy], 52
palimpsest, history as, 130, 131, 135
Palucca, Gret, 4, 7, 45–62, 132, 133, 145n23–24, 234; Bauhaus students and junior faculty, relationships with, 47, 50–59; career success, 54; critics' reactions to, 48; dance style, 45, 46–47, 53–54; decision to remain in East Germany after World War II, 47, 60n7; family connections of, 48; as former Wigman student, 45, 47, 81; images of, 49, 51–57; meta-personal system of teaching, 139; as model of New Woman, 47, 48–49, 52–54, 57, 59; new artistic dance, 136, 145n23; nickname, 50; 1925 performance for Bauhaus, 46, 48–49, 55; opportunism in postwar East Germany, 135–37, 143, 145n16, 145n18, 145n24, 146n26; publications from East Germany on, 60n9; school in Dresden, 135, 136, 137; students of, 100, 102, 236; success at Bauhaus, reasons for, 46–47; training of, 45; Vogelsang and, 138, 139–40; women's magazines promoting, 48
Pantomime Circus, 100
Park, Robert Ezra, 250
P.A.R.T.S. (Performing Arts Research and Training Studios), 240, 246n23
past in contemporary dance, engagements with the, 9, 217–31; quoting and, 218–21, 230n8; quoting the repertoire and, 221–23; re/constructing and archiving, 9, 223–30
pathos, choreographic and theatrical moments of, 184, 197n7
Paths to Strength and Beauty (Wege zu Kraft und Schönheit), 67–68, 70, 71, 73
Pavlova, Anna, 71
Pax Germania (Fabian), 173–80; audience participation in, 176, 177–79, 181n14; comparison of Waltz's Allee der Kosmonauten to, 173–74; influence of socialist state power on citizens' corporeality, 176–77; transformation from socialist to united capitalist Germany depicted in, 175–79
pedestrian movement: double perspective on walk from East to West of Berlin, 166–67; in Fabian's Pax Germania, 175–77, 179; Fabian's use of slow motion as variation of, 174; Waltz's appropriation of, in Allee der Kosmonauten, 170–73, 179
Peppermill Theater (Die Pfeffermühle), 100, 111n6, 120, 129n58
perception, suspension of, 76
performer-spectator relationship, metaphors for, 25
Performing Arts Research and Training Studios (P.A.R.T.S.), 240, 246n23
Peter, Franz-Manuel, 8
Petipa, 222
Pfeffermühle, Die (The Pepper Mill), 100, 111n6, 120, 129n58
Pfeiffer, Herbert, 122
phantasm of subject, Wigman's, 194–96
physical culture, 6, 101; activities, 234; emergence of interest in, 234
Picasso, Pablo, 48
Piscator, Erwin, 146n29
Plischke, Thomas, 8, 239–40, 241
Poege, Gabi, 90
poetics of dance and performance, 239–40, 256–57
Points in Space (Cunningham), 222
Polaczek, 105
Polemann, Otto, 121
politics: body, 250; culturization of, 253. See also East German dance, politics of; National Socialists (Nazis)
polycentrism and polyrhythm, principles of, 250
popular dance culture: ethnic and social influences on, 247–48; in- and exclusion between high dance culture and, prin-

ciple of, 250; tango as example of globalization of, 250
postcolonial theory, cultural translation and, 251–53
Posthofen, Renate, 107
poststructuralist thinking, contemporary dance and, 239–40
Potter, Sally, 248
power: cultural translation and, 253; "emotive formulas" of, 195–96, 199n36
Practice of Everyday Life, The (de Certeau), 228
Prager, Wilhelm, 67, 68, 70, 71, 73; Dance Is Life (*Tanz Ist Leben*), 70–71, 74, 75
Praise of Folly, The (Erasmus), 111n10
Preston-Dunlop, Valerie, 5
primitive dance, Holm on, 83
Product of Circumstances (Le Roy), 236–38, 239, 245n12
Punkt und Linie Zu Fläche (Point and Line to Plane) [Kandinsky], 49
Puritanism, influence on American culture of, 86–87, 97n35

quoting, evoking the past through, 218–23, 230n8; in *Giszelle*, 219–21, 222, 231n13; quoting the repertoire, 221–23; in *Véronique Doisneau*, 219, 221–23

Radialsystem V, 169
Randall, Tresa, 6–7, 8, 79–98
Rauser, Tamara, 145n19
readymade, avant-garde Duchampian, 220
realism, warfare in East Germany over, 147–64; emergence of, 148; "five-year plan" 1976–80 and, 157–58; meaning of realism, debate over, 149–51, 181n9; *New Midsummer Night Dream, A*, 154–57; reunification of Germany and, 159–60; socialist development of character, political-ideological demand for, 151–53; *Tanztheater* and, 153–54; three demands on socialist art, 152
Realismus-Streit (dispute over realism). See realism, warfare in East Germany over
reciprocal relationships: between body and soul, 21–22; of stage and audience, 25, 26
reciprocity (double movement), focus on, 21–22, 26
re/constructing and archiving, 9, 223–30; cartographic aspect of reconstruction, 228–29; *How Heavy Are My Thoughts* (Müller), 232, 233, 237–38, 242–44,
245n1; Nachbar's *Urheben Aufheben*, 224, 225–28, 229, 231n23, 235–36, 245n11; significance of transmission, explanation, and feedback in, 225; use of slash in re/construction, 230n6
re-contextualization, 255
Red Shoes, The (Andersen), 104
refugees, human rights and, 203, 205
Remigrant, Der (The Remigrant) [Gert], 121–22
repertoire, quoting, 221–23
repetition: Bausch's use of, 185–86; Fabian's use of, 175, 176; Fernandes on, 198n9; quoting as, 218, 219; Waltz's use of, 173
representational context, 227–28
research culture, 11
research practice, conceptualizations of artistic creation as kind of, 234
resistance: comedy as alternative path for, 105–7; dancing body as site of, 175, 176, 179; to East German government, 177, 180
reunification. *See* German reunification
rhythm: Holm's assessment of American, 85–88; Laban on, 67; in Laban's *Tanz ist Leben*, 71; of Southern European dances, 33
Rhythmus und Tanz [Klamt and Prager], 72
Richter, Hans, 74, 132–33
Ricoeur, Paul, 255
Riffraff (*Canaille*) [Gert], 116
Rite of Spring (*Das Frühlingsopfer*) [Bausch], 186, 189
Robst, Robert, 68
Roehn, Charles, 38
Roller, Jochen, 8
romanticism: Goslar's feminist disruption of, 100, 103–4; as instrumental aspect of reality, 156
Rough Cut (Bausch), 190
Rudolph, Charlotte, 49, 52, 53–54
Rudolph, Johann Joseph, 18
Ruprecht, Lucia, 1–16

Sabbath Laws in New York, Wigman's legal battle with, 96n35
Said, Edward, 116
Salamon, Eszter, 8, 217; *Giszelle*, 219–21, 222, 231n13
Sallé, Marie, 20
Sandig, Jochen, 168, 169, 180n5
Sarabande (Holm), 80

Sasha Waltz & Guests, 168, 180n5
Schaubühne am Lehniner Platz (Berlin), 168
Schiller, Friedrich, 17, 21; discourse on relationship between body and soul in, 20
Schilling, Tom, 4, 7, 149, 153, 159, 162n38, 164n63; choreography of, 157, 158; *A New Midsummer Night's Dream*, 155, 156–57; *Orpheus-Stationen*, 158
Schlemmer, Oskar, 6, 47, 48, 57, 62n32, 71
Schlicher, Susanne, 196n2
Schlöndorff, Volker, 126n7
Schmeichel-Falkenberg, Beate, 110n6
Schmidt, Jochen, 163n47, 197n5
school as community, 83–85
School of New Dance Development (Amsterdam), 167–68
Schoop, Trudi, 100
Schroeder, Drucilla, 98n57
Schwan, Alexander, 195
Schwingende Gewalten (Swinging Powers) [Laban], 68
Searle, John, 244
self-fashioning, Montez and, 2, 31, 38–42
Self Meant to Govern (Forsythe), 209
self-reflexive attitude, 235, 236
Sellner, Gustav Rudolf, 145n20
Sennett, Richard, 252
sensualist aesthetics of effect, 18, 20, 21, 23, 26
serialized novel of nineteenth century, 39
Servos, Norbert, 182, 196n3
Sieg, Katrin, 120
Siegert, Arila, 4
Siegmund, Gerald, 9–10, 200–216
Skoronel, Vera, 45
Slomma, Horst, 151–52, 156
Sloterdijk, Peter, 238
slow motion, Fabian's utilization of, 174
Smith, Sidonie, 101
social censorship, 3
social intercourse, goal of choreography to learn correct, 210
socialist artwork, starting point and goal of, 148
socialist development of character, political-ideological demand for, 151–53
socialist image of man, 148, 149, 151
socialist realism, Weidt and, 141
socialist realist approach to art, 149–50, 152–53, 158; in *New Midsummer Night's Dream*, 154–57

Socialist Unity Party Congress (1975), five-year plan adopted at, 157–58
societal conditioning, dance theater as analysis of, 179
Sophiensäle, 168
Sorell, Walter, 79, 196n1
Sörgel, Sabine, 197n5
soteriological image of incorporeality, 195
Southern European dances, characteristics attributed to, 33–34
space(s): dance used to "think through" spatial configurations, 242; of emotion, 183–84; feeling one's way through, in *Café Müller*, 184–87; intercorporeal, 254; of translation as hybrid space, 252
Spangberg, Marten, 241
Spanish dance in 19th century, 31–44; critics of, 36–38; hispanomania in theatrical and ballroom dance, 33; Montez as Spanish dancer, 33–38; Montez's marketing of Spanish identity in her autobiography, 38–40; Western notions of Spanishness, 36, 38
speech act theory, 244
Spivak, Gayatri Chakravorty, 252, 253, 256
Sporck, Martin, 148, 160n2
Staatliche Kommission für Kunstangelegenheiten der DDR (State Commission for the Arts of the German Democratic Republic), 136, 137, 144n15, 148
stage dance in 19th century, 35
Stalin, Joseph, 141
Stasi (East German Intelligence Service), 130, 131, 132, 170; surveillance of, movement and, 166, 176
State Ballet School (Berlin), 138
Steinberg-Born to Be Wild (Fabian), 181n13
Stöckemann, Patricia, 8
Strange Journey of Professor Blitz, The (Gert), 124, 129n57
Stuart, Meg, 8, 239
Stunde Null (Zero Hour) in dance, 132–33, 134, 135, 142, 143. *See also* East German dance, politics of
subjectivity, 21; emergence as "eject" of modes of conduct, 240
Sulcas, Roslyn, 206
Sulzer, Johann Georg, 17, 29n23
Sunderland-Club, 249
Surrealist's Bureau de Recherche, 234
surveillance by Stasi, influence on movement, 166, 176

suspension of perception, 76
Swan Lake, 222
Swinging Powers (*Schwingende Gewalten*) [Laban], 68
Sylvie (ballet), 22
symbiosis in movement, notion of, 21

Tafel, Pipo, 202
Taglioni, Marie, 33, 34, 37, 41
Tai Yang Erwacht (Wolf), 146
tango, 11, 248–50; ethnographic reports on, 248–49; as example of globalization of popular dance cultures, 250; global myth carrying contradictory connotations, 249–50
Tango Lesson, The (film), 248
Tanzdrama (dance-drama), 76
Tänzerwettstreit, Der (*The Dancers' Contest*) [film], 147–48
Tanzgemeinschaft ("dance community"), 5. *See also* American *Tanzgemeinschaft*, Holm and
Tanzgemeinschaft-Vierteljahresschrift für tänzerische Kultur, Die (Dance Community-Quarterly of Dance Culture), 81–82
Tanzgeschichte (dance history), 10
Tanzgymnastik ("aesthetic gymnastics"), 6. *See also* gymnastics
Tanz Ist Leben (Dance Is Life), 70–71, 74; Laban's notation system spread by, 75
"Tanzkurven" (Dance Curves) [Kandinsky], 49–50, 57, 59, 61n18
Tanztheater, 4, 5, 101; aesthetic appeal stemming from shared corporeal and cultural experiences (*Erfahrungen*), 182; demand made on its public, 157; in East Germany (1966–89), 7, 152, 153–64; "five-year plan" 1976–80 and, 157–58; after German reunification, 159–60; *New Midsummer Night Dream, A*, 154–57; of 1970s, Gert as stylistic progenitor of, 114; realism's three demands on, 152–53; two parallel regimes of, 159, 163n56
Tanztheatergeschichten (Dance Theater Stories) [Hoghe], 187
Tanzwissenschaft ("dance science" or "dance studies"), 10, 239
tarantella, 35
Tatar, Maria, 104
Taubert, Gottfried, 30n46
taxi dancers, 248
Taylor, Diana, 221

Theatertreffen, 175, 181n11
Theaterwissenschaft ("theater science" or "theater studies"), 10
theatricality of Bausch, 187–88
Theobald, Christiane, 159
Thiess, Frank, 134, 143n7
thinking body, ideas of, 4
"third body" in dancing, 254
Third Reich. *See* National Socialists (Nazis)
Thomas, Kendall, 201, 202, 205, 212; *Human Writes*, 200–204, 205, 206, 208, 209, 211, 212–14, 215
Thornton, Annette, 110n6
thought-movements, 4, 243–44
Thoughts on the New Artistic Dance (*Gedanken zum Neuen Künstlerischen Tanzes*) [Vogelsang], 139
Thurner, Christina, 2–3, 4, 17–30
Tod, Der (Death) [Gert], 124
Todd, Mabel, 234
Toepfer, Karl, 234, 242, 245n13
Torop, Peeter, 252
totalizing universalism, 214
touch, feeling one's way through space in *Café Müller*, 184–87
tragedy: Goslar's resistance to, 100, 105–6; role in curbing women's resistance, 105
Tragedy of Man (*Die Tragödie des Menschen*) [Madách], 72
trajectory, de Certeau on notion of, 228
transcendence, Wigman's search for, 190–91; in *Drehmonotonie*, 191–94, 195; gesture of death, 194–96; theological mystery of salvation as goal of dance, 195
transcultural identities, cultural translation and, 255–57
transcultural translation in age of globalization, 249–51
trans-culturation, 252
transdisciplinary approach, 10
transference in dance, 253–54
Transit Agreement and Basic Treaty of 1972, 153
translation, cultural. *See* cultural translation in dance, toward a theory of
"Translator's Task, The" (Benjamin), 252
transnationalism in age of globalization, 249–51
transregional dance cultures, 251
Trial, A., 22
Trümpy, Berthe, 81

Twenty to Eight (Waltz), 168
typography, Bauhaus, 51–52, 59

UFA-Kulturabteilung, 65
United States, German émigré experience in, 6–7. *See also* Gert, Valeska; Goslar, Lotte; Holm, Hanya
Universal Declaration of Human Rights, 201, 202, 203, 205, 213, 214
universal emotional force, dance as, 19–20, 23, 25–27; persistence of idea of, 26–27
universalism, totalizing, 214
Universum-Film Aktiengesellschaft (UFA), 65, 67, 70, 71
Urheben Aufheben (Nachbar), 224, 225–28, 229; as lecture performance, 224, 225–28, 229, 235–36; Nachbar's constant reworking of, 225–28; narration in, 228; translating, 231n23, 245n11

Valse Very Triste (Very Sad Waltz) [Goslar], 105–6
Van der Lubbe, Marinus, 91
Van Der Lubbe's Head (Blecher), 91
Véronique Doisneau (Bel), 219, 221–23
Vestris, Gaetano, 19
Vocational School for Artistic Dance (*Fachschule für künstlerischen Tanz Berlin*), 138
Vogelsang, Marianne, 7, 133, 142, 143; assessment of modern dance and ballet, 138–39, 140; departure from East Germany, 138; detention and work for war effort, 137, 145n20; dismissal from ballet school, 140; early career, 145n19; independence and integrity of, 138; postwar experience, 137–40, 142, 143; similarity of Weidt to, 141; studio in East Berlin, 138; willingness to confront Nazi past, 140
Vogt, Marianne, 111n6
Volkish tradition: Holm's connection to, 86; Nazis and, 68
Volksgemeinschaft ("folk community"), 5, 77n10, 135
von Hilverding, Franz Anton Christoph, 20
von Kobell, Luise, 44n22

Waltz, Sasha, 7, 27, 166, 167–73, 179, 180n5; "Avenue of Cosmonauts" (*Allee der Kosmonauten*), 167–73, 181n6; brief biography of, 167–69; comparison to Fabian, 167, 173–74; influences on, 167–68; interdisciplinary approach of, 168; methodology of, 169–70, 181n6; representation of agency outside dancers' bodies, 172–73, 179; restricted awareness of her powerful position as artist, 170; *Twenty to Eight*, 168
Waltzmania (Goslar), 102, 103–4
Warburg, Aby, 199n36
Warner, Marina, 109
Was bleibt? (Wolf), 130, 180n3
Was tun Pina Bausch und ihre Tänzer in Wuppertal (documentary), 187
Weaver, John, 20
Wedekind, Kadidja, 119
Wege zu Kraft und Schönheit (Paths to Strength and Beauty), 67–68, 70, 71, 73
Weidman, Charles, 90
Weidt, Jean, 7, 140–41, 142, 143, 146n29; *The Cell*, 140; return from exile, 132, 140–41; Richter on, 132–33
Weimar cinema, 65, 66. *See also* film projects, Laban's dance
Weimar dance, 4–8; Gert's metaphorical exile in Weimar Republic, 115–17; Palucca's 1925 dance concert, 46, 48–49, 55; postwar scholarship on, 47
Weimar-era *Amerikanismus* discourse, 86–87
Weimar Jewish artist, social place reserved for returning, 115, 121
Weimar on the Pacific (Bahr), 129n72
Weimar woman, modern, 52
Welt des Tänzers, Die (The Dancer World) [Laban], 67
Werther (Goethe), 3
What's So Funny? Sketches from My Life (Goslar), 99; clown sketch series in, 99–100
White, Hayden, 223
Whitney, Allison, 72
Wiesenthal, Grete, 103
Wigman, Mary, 7, 71, 102, 105, 132, 137, 143, 144n11, 184, 190–96, 197n6, 234, 236; absolute dance, apolitical art defined as, 81, 133, 135; Bausch and, 8; Bausch and, comparison between, 182, 183; collaboration with Nazis, 5, 80, 89–90, 92, 98n68; dance as sacred religious art to, 195; The Dance Experience (*Tanzerlebnis, Das*), 190; dance-gymnastics, system of, 81, 82–83, 86, 87, 94; The Dancer (*Tänzerin, Die*), 194; *Das Drehen*, 194; *Ekstatische Tänze* (Ecstatic Dances), 191; experience as central aesthetic concept of her dance, 182, 190–91; experience of

space in *Drehmonotonie*, 191–94, 195; Gert on, 125; gesture of death, 194–96; *Hexentanz*, 102–3, 105; Holm as missionary for, 79, 82–83, 84; international renown and influence, 81–82; Jewish teachers and pupils, treatment of, 89–90, 97n57; legacy of, 167; methods associated with, 5–6; mystical aura, 82; New York Wigman School, 79, 83–85, 89, 92; postwar departure from East Germany, 133–35, 138; Schmidt on, 197n5; school as community for, 83–85; in search of transcendence, 190–91; self-understanding as a dancer, 190; students of, 4, 45, 47, 81, 100, 112n25; *Die Tänzerin* (The Dancer), 194; *Das Tanzerlebnis* (The Dance Experience), 190; turning in ecstasy around centered core-self, practice of, 191–96; U.S. tour (1930–1931), 79; vision of dance, 81–83; Vogelsang and, 138, 139

Wigman Schools in Germany, 81, 84; Central Institute (Dresden), 79, 84; Central Institute (Dresden), Holm's reports to, 86, 89; modeled on religious community, 87; number of students in, 95n8; place in Nazi bureaucracy, 89–90, 97n57

Wildenhahn, Klaus, 187
Wilson, Robert, 174, 175
Winkler, Eva, 145n24
Witch Dance (Wigman), 102–3, 105
Woitas, Monika, 18
Wolf, Christa, 130, 131, 180n3
Wolf, Friedrich, 140, 146n29
Women, Modernism, and Performance (Farfan), 105
working community (*Arbeitsgemeinschaft*), ideal of, 83, 84–85
World Question Center, 234
Worn-out Dancing Shoes, The (Brothers Grimm), 103, 104
Worringer, Wilhelm, 69
writing, dance and, 3–4, 238–39, 240; dancing with letters, 209–11; indirect reference to writing, rule of, 212. *See also* lecture performance(s)
writing women, Lola Montez and, 38–40
written dance (*Kinetographie* or *Schrifttanz*), Laban's, 74–76
Wundt, Wilhelm, 82
Wuppertaler Tanztheater, 167, 186, 189, 257

Zero Hour (*Stunde Null*) in dance, 132–33, 134, 135, 142, 143
Zhdanov, Andrey, 141
zitieren (quoting), 218–23, 230n8
Zwingenberger, Marianne, 60n7

The University of Illinois Press
is a founding member of the
Association of American University Presses.

_____

Composed in 9.75/13 Fairfield
with Scala Sans display
by Jim Proefrock
at the University of Illinois Press
Manufactured by Thomson-Shore, Inc.

University of Illinois Press
1325 South Oak Street
Champaign, IL 61820-6903
www.press.uillinois.edu